CW00725028

Working in Human Service Organisations

Working in Human Service Organisations

A Critical Introduction

Andrew Jones and John May

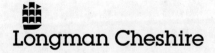
Longman Cheshire

Longman Cheshire Pty Limited
Longman House
Kings Gardens
95 Coventry Street
Melbourne 3205 Australia

Offices in Sydney, Brisbane, Adelaide and Perth. Associated companies, branches and representatives throughout the world.

Copyright © Longman Cheshire 1992
First published 1992

All rights reserved. Except under the conditions described in the Copyright Act 1968 of Australia and subsequent amendments, no part of this publication may be reproduced, stored in a retrieval system or transmitted in any form or by any means, electronic, mechanical, photocopying, recording or otherwise, without the prior permission of the copyright owner.

Edited by Maja Ingrassia
Set in 10/12 Palatino
Produced by Longman Cheshire Pty Ltd
Printed in Malaysia – PA

National Library of Australia
Cataloguing-in-Publication data

Jones, Andrew, 1950—   .
    Working in human service organisations.

    Bibliography.
    Includes index.
    ISBN 0 582 71271 8.

    1. Human services. 2. Social work administration. 3. Public welfare administration.
    4. Social service. 5. Public welfare. I. May, John, 1947—   . II. Title.

361

Foreword

Possessing an understanding of and the ability to work effectively in human service organisations was never easy, but it is now of greater importance than ever. Societal resources for social welfare are declining at the very time that demand for services is increasing because of economic decline, social turmoil, rapidly changing demographic profiles, and the growing gaps between those with and without resources, both within countries and between countries. Many social workers experience serious stress and frustration because they have not been prepared to face this new environment with its radically different challenges. Perhaps the only analogous period was that at the end of the nineteenth and the beginning of the twentieth centuries when social work was a developing profession in many countries that were experiencing the impact and trauma of industrialisation, war and major movements of peoples from one country to another.

Jones and May present a cogent conceptual framework for social and welfare work in human service organisations today. They offer us a practice theory which views organisations as structures that shape and are shaped by human actions. Social workers as actors hold multiple and shifting subject positions which are enacted, resisted, reproduced and changed over time in response to internal and external forces. A theory of practice also demands attention to the structures and relations of power that constrain and enable action in the world. Such a theory should incorporate and not contradict the philosophical, value and epistemological bases for welfare policies and programmes.

Working in a human service organisation today needs to be considered in the larger historical context of where the field of social welfare and the profession of social work have come from. Historical events within this country as well as those in the international arena have shaped the contemporary welfare state. Part of the disenchantment with the welfare state perspective in recent years is the result of the past ineffectiveness of organisations and professionals to achieve the mandates prescribed by society. Moreover, while vaguely espousing social justice and moral values as the basis for the welfare state, there has been a lack of professional responsibility in articulating clearly to the various publics what is required if we are to achieve social justice, equity and full citizenship for all the people. Dissatisfaction extends to the private and the public sectors as well as to the various fields of social welfare. Remaking of the welfare state will require the alleviation of this dissatisfaction.

Meeting the challenge of preparing social and welfare workers to be more effective workers is the task that Jones and May have established for themselves in this book, and they have succeeded in meeting that challenge to a substantial degree. Although this book is primarily written to new social workers and experienced practitioners, supervisors and administrators will also find it extremely helpful because of its excellent review of the relevant literature, the analytic questions that are posed and the case studies which illustrate the issues addressed in each of the chapters. Gender and cross-cultural perspectives as critical elements in practice are also incorporated. The book is primarily directed toward the Australian audience, but others in Asia, Europe and the Americas will also find it extremely useful and applicable.

Social work educators have often stated their task as one that involved preparing students to apply very specific limited and individually oriented technologies within the confines of bureaucratic organisations. Moreover, these technologies assumed that individual deviance or pathology was the critical problem to be corrected. Emphasis on the individual as the focus of change constrained the development of organisational and community strategies that could have complemented and often fundamentally shifted the emphasis in the preparation of social and welfare workers. Lack of attention to training for organisational work meant also that there was little attention to the ways in which these organisations operated inadvertently to subvert the very programmes and goals that they were established to maintain.

Jones and May provide social work educators with a book that is of great significance because they challenge the social pathology model as well as the view that social work is a free-standing professional activity, when in reality the roles and positions are defined and controlled by organisational structures and processes. The type of clientele an organisation serves, the nature of the services provided and how they are delivered are only determined in a minor way by the actions of individual workers. Thus, it is critical that a professional understand fully the realities of organisational life and not just view it as a passive context within which to practise.

Change and its importance is a recurrent theme throughout the book. The authors stress the need for social workers to be able to initiate and implement change, but also to be able to respond to changes that they confront rather than resist dealing with them. Viewing social change from a political perspective provides a framework for incorporating both rational and non-rational approaches.

Their concluding chapter in which they analyse corporate management ideologies and practices is perhaps one of the most salient for social workers in the 1990s. They refer to corporate management as 'managerialism' and assert that it is a political ideology advocated by those who wish to reduce social welfare expenditures overall and who believe that state functions can be better performed by the private sectors. The emphasis on managerialism coincides with contemporary fiscal crisis in many countries and adds to the crisis of legitimacy of the welfare state. Those who support this perspective argue that the role of the state should be very limited and that social goals and individual needs can better be met in other (albeit, unspecified) ways. In response, Jones and May present us with an alternate practice theory for addressing social welfare issues and problems, one that incorporates social justice and citizenship values. Moreover, because of their change orientation, their approach is one which envisages the ability of the organisation and the workers to adapt successfully to new challenges and opportunities as these emerge in the future. Whether or not one agrees fully with Jones and May's perspectives and conclusions, one will be challenged by the quality and insight of their analysis. For social workers, it provides an excellent introduction for effective work within human service organisations that will increase accountability to disenfranchised populations as the profession's social ethic demands.

Rosemary Sarri
University of Michigan

Contents

List of figures

List of tables

Preface

The aim of this book is to assist social and welfare workers to understand organisations and thereby become more effective workers. Most social and welfare work takes place in an organisational context and almost all workers are employed or sponsored by organisations. Organisations provide the mandate and resources for social and welfare work. The activities of workers are extensively defined and shaped by organisations. Organisations are usually the means through which workers achieve social goals and respond to the needs of consumers. They are also often the targets of workers seeking to address issues of individual or social injustice. In this book, the implications of the centrality of organisations for social work and welfare work are explored, and theories and concepts to guide workers are developed, explained and applied to practice situations.

The concepts and materials in this book are presented with social workers and welfare workers in mind. However, the need to understand organisations is common to all workers in the human services including youth workers, community development workers, nurses, psychologists, therapists, counsellors, legal workers, teachers and doctors. We hope that the book will be used by students and practitioners in many of these occupations. It may also be used as a text by those teaching about organisations in courses of professional education in the human services.

A fundamental difficulty in writing such a book is to find the appropriate terminology to describe those workers for whom the book is written. The term 'social workers and community welfare workers' is clumsy and it excludes some of the closely related occupational groups listed above. The term 'human service workers', while increasingly popular, is arguably too general for a book that is primarily directed at those engaged in 'welfare practice' (O'Connor, Wilson and Thomas 1991). With some misgivings, as a matter of convenience, we have decided to use the terms 'social workers' and 'social and welfare workers', abbreviated wherever possible to 'workers', as the main, generic terms throughout the book. This does not signify lack of awareness of the complex issues concerning boundaries among occupations in the human services. Rather, it reflects a view that the organisational issues that we address are similar for all workers.

The book has a number of distinctive features. Firstly, it focuses on workers in human service organisations, rather than on the managers of those organisations. While there is much in the book of relevance to managers, it is not written from a managerial viewpoint. It is concerned with how workers can deal with organisations, including those who manage them, rather than with how managers can deal with workers. In this sense, it has a 'bottom-up' rather than a 'top-down' perspective. Secondly, it aims to develop concepts and frameworks relevant to all kinds of human service organisations. It is concerned with organisations whether large or small, government or non-government, mainstream or alternative. Certainly, each organisation has its own distinctive characteristics which must be understood. But the theory developed in the book is applicable to the range of organisations employing social and welfare workers including hospitals, prisons, schools, mental health clinics, counselling agencies, community centres, government departments, crisis accommodation services, community health centres, legal aid agencies, probation services, family support agencies, and so on. It is intended that the book be relevant to a diversity of situations and settings.

The other distinctive feature of the book is that it provides a critical introduction to organisations. This is discussed in the opening chapters. We believe that workers should adopt a questioning and challenging approach to the dominant view of the organisations in which they work and with which they interact. The book is written from a political economy perspective which emphasises the importance of viewing organisations as comprising individuals and groups with competing and often conflicting interests, existing within the broader political and economic structure. It is also written from a value perspective which views the central organisational agenda items for social and welfare workers to be the pursuit of social justice and responsiveness to the needs of consumers.

The book is divided into three parts. Part I examines the relations between workers and organisations, the nature of organisations, the characteristics of human service organisations, and the location of these organisations in the broader society. Part II develops a theoretical framework for understanding organisations based on the concepts of organisational environment, organisational goals, organisational structure and organisational culture. It shows how an understanding of these concepts assists workers to make sense of, and act purposively in, organisations. Part III focuses on practice in organisations. It analyses the nature of 'front-line' work in organisations, ways of making organisations more responsive to consumers, processes of organisational resistance and change, and the challenges posed for workers by managerialism.

Each chapter is followed by a case study based on a practice situation. These case studies provide opportunities to apply the concepts presented to practice situations. Accompanying each case is a key question and a series of discussion points. Teachers and readers can use these cases to further their understanding of the materials in each chapter.

The book draws on the authors' diverse experiences of human service organisations as employees, managers, consultants, advisers, critics, members and consumers. It also draws on ideas and materials from many academic sources, particularly organisation theory, public administration, social policy and social work. The study of organisations is a meeting place for many academic disciplines.

No textbook alone can teach workers to be effective participants in organisations. Organisational skills are also acquired by on-the-job experience and training. Personal qualities also influence organisational effectiveness. We outline in useable and accessible form the theoretical materials that we have found most relevant to understanding human service organisations, and we show how these materials can be applied to practice situations and issues. We hope that better understanding will lead to workers being more effective in their efforts to achieve sensitive, responsive and accountable human service organisations.

We wish to give special acknowledgement to the assistance of Rosemary Sarri, who provided extensive, critical comments on the manuscript during her stay at the University of Queensland in 1991. Our colleagues, Catherine McDonald, Allan Halladay and Ian O'Connor also provided helpful comments, advice and critique of the manuscript. Sue Tasker provided secretarial assistance. Ron Harper of Longman Cheshire was unfailingly patient, supportive and encouraging. Our families and friends provided much support throughout the research and writing process. Finally, we thank the final-year social work students at University of Queensland on whom these ideas were 'tried out' during 1987–1991, and who encouraged us by their interest in and, in some cases, enthusiasm for our endeavours.

Andrew Jones and John May
Brisbane

PART I

The organisational context

Part I provides an introduction to organisation theory and its relevance to social and welfare workers.

Chapter 1 re-examines the relationship between social and welfare work and organisations. Firstly, a number of conventional themes concerning organisations that have been influential in social and welfare work are challenged and elaborated upon. The significance of an understanding of organisations for workers is then considered under three main headings: the location of social and welfare workers; the nature of social and welfare work as an occupation; and the purposes and roles of social and welfare work. It is then argued that an understanding of organisational context provides the basis for connecting policy and practice. The chapter concludes with an overview of the organisational knowledge and skills required by workers.

Chapter 2 provides an overview of the study of organisations as it has evolved during the twentieth century. It is argued that it is important for workers to be aware of the many sources of ideas and theories of organisations. The major perspectives on the study of organisations are critically reviewed and their implications for practice are considered and discussed.

Chapter 3 examines the nature of the organisations that employ social and welfare workers, and through which workers achieve their purposes. The chapter addresses the question 'What (if anything) is distinctive about human service organisations?' It discusses three types of characteristics commonly used to distinguish human service organisations from other kinds of organisations: purpose, technology and public auspice. It argues that an awareness of the implications of these characteristics helps workers to understand the distinctive issues and problems facing human service organisations, those that work in them, and those who use and depend on their services.

1

Social and welfare workers in organisations: a re-appraisal

If social workers must be bureaucrats—and they must—they might as well be good ones (Pruger 1973, p. 32).

Social and welfare work, as practised in Australia, is an organisational as well as a professional activity. Social and welfare workers in this country, almost without exception, are dependent on organisations for employment, resources, legitimacy and consumers. Their relations with consumers are shaped by their membership to organisations, as are their efforts to affect social, political and community change. If workers are to provide an effective service to their consumers and to the broader community, it is essential for them to be aware of the organisational character of their work, and to develop skills in organisational analysis and practice.

Organisations in the literature on social and welfare work

Emphasis on the importance of organisational context in social and welfare work is not novel. Many writers have pointed to the ways that organisational factors shape practice (e.g. Warham 1977, p. vii; Smith 1979 p. ix; Weissman, Epstein and Savage 1983). There is a long tradition of concern with the importance of the setting of practice and the influence of 'agency context' (Perlman 1957, pp. 40-52; Briar and Miller 1971, pp. 91-92 and pp. 99-102). Many social work and welfare texts

Table 1.1 Critique of conventional themes concerning organisations in social and welfare work writings

Conventional themes	*Critique*
1 Organisations are a secondary sphere of knowledge and practice for workers	Workers are primarily engaged in organisational as well as professional activities
2 Organisational understanding is relevant only to limited areas of practice e.g. policy and administration	Organisational understanding is central to all areas of practice, including case work, group work and community work
3 Organisations are 'social work agencies' i.e. provision of social and welfare work is a central goal	Provision of social and welfare work is rarely a central organisational goal
4 Organisations are presented as bureaucracies in the pejorative sense	The term 'bureaucracy' should be used analytically to inform practice
5 Workers are assumed to be central players in organisations	Workers often have a position of limited power, influence and authority in organisations
6 Workers' professional value orientation tends to be corrupted by organisations	Workers have to make complex judgements about professional and organisational orientations
7 Conformity to organisational expectations indicates professional maturity	Workers need to adopt a critical approach to both organisational and professional authority
8 Social and welfare work is a freestanding professional activity	The nature and purposes of social and welfare work are determined in organisational contexts

devote some space to relations between workers and organisations (e.g. Compton and Galaway 1989, pp. 228-269). Why, then, the need for a book that re-examines the importance of organisational analysis? Our argument for such a re-appraisal is contained in Table 1.1.

Firstly, there is often a tendency for organisational context to be treated as a secondary sphere of knowledge and practice. This is illustrated by the widely used textbook by Compton and Galaway, *Social Work Processes* (1989). In the introduction, these authors identify the key tasks for workers as the linking of people with systems that provide them with resources, services and opportunities; and the development of effective service systems (pp. 6-7). However, in the main body of their text, Compton and Galaway give limited attention to organisational issues. Social work is discussed primarily as a freestanding professional activity, and organisational issues are dealt with in detail only in one chapter entitled 'Sanctions for social work practice'.

Many writers give the impression that social and welfare work can and should be understood primarily as a professional activity, and that an understanding of organisations is needed only in so far as organisational factors impinge on professional tasks and purposes. This emphasis can be questioned. It can be argued that social and welfare work needs to be conceptualised as both an organisational activity and a professional activity, rather than as a professional activity that just happens to be lodged in organisations.

Another tendency is for organisational knowledge and skills to be marginalised, that is, to be seen as relevant to only limited areas of practice. This is illustrated by Zastrow's *The Practice of Social Work*. Zastrow provides an important and detailed review of the range of knowledge and skills required by practitioners, but his discussion of 'knowledge of organisations' is confined to two parts of his text. Firstly, he sees a knowledge of organisational functioning as necessary for what he terms community organisation and macro practice (pp. 202-203). Secondly, under the heading 'surviving and enjoying social work', he discusses the need for skills in 'surviving in a bureaucracy' (pp. 288-292). The need for organisational knowledge and skills in respect to these two areas is not in dispute. However, it can be argued that these are not the only areas in which an understanding of organisations is central. Workers undertaking casework, group work, counselling and therapeutic activities are members of organisations as well as professional practitioners, and need skills in understanding and negotiating the organisational context of their work.

The literature can be questioned for using terms that do not adequately portray the complex realities of organisational life. One such term is 'social work agency', an expression which has long been used in social and welfare work. While this term has some value as a shorthand for 'the organisations in which social and welfare workers are employed', it can be argued that its use encourages students and practitioners to view their organisational context from a somewhat narrow perspective. It suggests that the organisational purposes can be defined and understood in primarily professional terms, and that the organisation's purposes are subordinate to the provision of a social work service. But is this the case? Social and welfare workers participate in organisations that have many different purposes and functions, some stated and many unstated. Often workers play subordinate roles in these organisations. As Warham argues, 'If social workers perceive themselves as members of "social work agencies" and not of . . . "organisations" they will see and understand much less of the full picture than is available to them.' (1977, p. 4).

Another term frequently used to describe the organisational context is 'bureaucracy'. Bureaucracy tends to be used synonymously with the term 'organisation' (e.g. Compton and Galaway 1989, pp. 228-269). This is unhelpful. Firstly, the term 'bureaucracy' has pejorative connotations that may impede reasoned discussion. Secondly, while it has been given many meanings, it usually refers to a particular form of organisational structure, as will be discussed in chapter 2. Whether or not, and in what ways, any particular organisation is a bureaucracy is a matter for analysis and debate. The use of both terms—'social work agency' and 'bureaucracy'—arguably encourages workers to make unexamined assumptions about the nature of their organisational contexts.

Another tendency in some writings is to exaggerate the power and influence of social and welfare workers within organisations. Workers often have subordinate and peripheral roles within organisations. Often they are front-line workers in organisations dominated by other professionals. In these circumstances, workers need to carefully negotiate their position and role. The role of professionals in organisations can be tenuous. This circumstance is not always fully acknowledged in some of the professional literature which sometimes presents workers in a somewhat heroic light. For example, it is not uncommon for social workers to be portrayed as 'change agents' that is, persons 'specifically employed for the purpose of creating planned change' (Pincus and Minahan 1973, p. 54). This perspective sometimes suggests that organisations can be viewed as the clients of social workers, and that organisations are analogous to individuals and families in this respect. For example, the Australian Association of Social Work (AASW) Code of Ethics states that 'the social work profession takes as its clients individuals, families, groups, organisations, communities or societies'.

The importance of worker involvement in organisational and social change should be strongly affirmed. But it can be argued that it is necessary to base discussion of the change agent's role on a careful analysis of a worker's location within a particular organisation. In particular, the sources and extent of power, authority and influence of workers need to be critically analysed. It should also be recognised that social and welfare workers, as well as being initiators of change, can be, and often are, the targets of other organisational participants' change strategies. Their activities in organisations may involve resistance and may be defensive and adaptive, as well as proactive. Change activities usually involve negotiation and accommodation of a range of organisational and other interests.

The themes of corruption and conformity, sometimes found in the literature on which social and welfare work is based, can also be questioned. The corruption theme is based on a dichotomy between professional goals and values and bureaucratic goals and values (e.g. Green 1966; Finch 1976), and an assumption that many of the practice issues confronting workers can be usefully understood in these terms. It is suggested that workers are often corrupted by losing their professional orientation and increasingly identifying with the organisation (George 1982; Billingsley 1964). Two questions arise.

Firstly, is the dichotomy itself useful? There are many similarities and overlapping elements between bureaucratic and professional orientations; these two modes are to some degree complementary as well as having conflicting elements. Secondly, is an organisational orientation necessarily a bad thing? Not all organisational goals and values are to be resisted; not all professional goals and values should be uncritically embraced. These are matters requiring workers to make judgements, often complex and difficult, as individuals, professionals and members of organisations.

The theme of conformity can also be questioned. This is the notion that acceptance of organisational authority, rather than being evidence of corruption of professional values, is a sign of professional maturity. Scott's study of social workers in an American public welfare department found that this view was commonly used by supervisors as a form of organisational control (Scott 1969, p. 117). Quite a different view can be presented. It can be argued that workers should adopt a critical and sceptical approach to both organisational and professional authority. Recognition of legitimate authority has a place, but this is quite different from uncritical acceptance of authority, especially in the name of professional maturity. There are more creative ways of conceptualising the relations between workers and organisations.

Finally, social and welfare work is sometimes portrayed as an activity that stands alone or outside of its organisational contexts. Many textbooks attempt to codify social and welfare work to clarify the nature of professional practice. Such exercises have their place, but this ought not be done at the expense of portraying such work in isolation from the social structures, social policies, and organisational arrangements in which it is embedded. Social and welfare work is not just practised in organisations, it is created in organisations. These organisations are themselves located in broader social and economic processes and structures. Whatever the textbooks say social and welfare work is, and whatever the content of the curriculum, the actual nature of practice is largely shaped by the organisational context.

The significance of organisational context

We have argued that social and welfare work needs to be re-appraised in relation to organisations. Our starting point for this process is the question, 'Why do workers need skills in organisational analysis and practice?' The answers to this question are to do with the location of workers, the nature of social and welfare work as an occupation, workers' roles and purposes, the needs of consumers, and the personal needs of workers. These are summarised in Table 1.2.

Table 1.2 The significance of organisations for social and welfare work

Propositions	Implications
A LOCATION Almost all workers are located in organisational settings	1 Workers and organisations are mutually dependent
	2 The nature of social and welfare work is shaped in significant ways by organisations
	3 Social and welfare workers have a capacity to shape and influence organisations
	4 Workers are perceived as organisational members by others in the organisation, including consumers
	5 Organisations are a strategic location for participation in reform and change processes
B NATURE OF THE OCCUPATION Social and welfare work is an organisational as well as a professional occupation	1 Claims to professional standing are negotiated in organisational settings
C PURPOSES Social and welfare work aims to enhance the problem-solving and coping capacity of individuals, families and communities, and to link people with resources, services and opportunities	1 The nature of direct practice is shaped by the organisational context
	2 Direct consumer work involves extensive dealings with organisations
	3 The complexities of care and control roles have to be negotiated in organisational settings
Social and welfare work aims to promote the effective operation of human service systems, to develop and improve social policy, and to contribute to social change and development	1 Organisational understanding is needed for workers' roles in policy, planning, administration and social action
	2 Front-line workers need skills to participate in political processes in organisations
D CONSUMERS Organisations shape the lives of all citizens, and are particularly powerful in the lives of dis-advantaged people	1 A key task for workers is to promote the responsiveness of organisations to consumers' needs

Propositions	Implications
	2 Workers should view it as their role to work towards organisations based on the social justice principles of access, equity, rights and participation
E PERSONAL NEEDS OF WORKERS Workers need to be able to cope with the stresses of organisational life	1 Workers need to develop specific coping skills and they need to understand the nature of organisations and their own organisational roles

The location of social and welfare workers

Australian human services are highly fragmented involving three levels of government, a variety of government departments, and an extensive non-government sector comprising some large, established, state-wide organisations and numerous local community-based organisations. Consequently, employment in the welfare field is diverse. Workers are spread through the public sector and the not-for-profit, non-government sector and a small, but increasing, number are located in the private sector. The non-government sector employs the highest number of workers, followed closely by the state governments. Significant numbers of workers are also employed by the Commonwealth government and local government. Most social and welfare workers are employed in the welfare and health industries, with significant numbers also employed in fields such as education and corrections (Healy and Martin 1989, p. 9).

This diversity means that workers are located in many different kinds of organisational contexts. Social and welfare workers may be part of a nation-wide organisation with thousands of other workers, or they may be the sole employee in a local community organisation. They may work in a small group of social and welfare workers in an organisation predominantly comprised of people from other occupations, or they may be the predominant occupational group. They are likely to be employed in a specialised field of service (for example rehabilitation, child welfare, aged care), although some may have more general responsibilities. Many are involved directly with consumers and are located on the front-line of the organisation; others have managerial and planning responsibilities. Many work in jobs advertised and designated as social work or welfare work positions, but a large number have positions designated in some other way (for example, child protection worker, project officer) which are open to people with a variety of qualifications and attributes.

Several key practice implications flow from this discussion of organisational location. Firstly, workers and the organisations that employ them are mutually dependent. Individual workers depend on the organisations for employment, resources (facilities, equipment, money), legitimacy and authority, and consumers. Conversely, organisations, to varying degrees, need qualified workers. They need the skills that workers offer, the legitimacy and standing that comes with the employment of a trained and qualified worker, and the resources or consumers that workers may attract to the organisation.

Secondly, the nature and content of practice is shaped by organisational location, and specifically by the organisational goals, culture, structure and environment. Depending on their organisational location, workers perform many different tasks: assessment, case management, individual and family counselling, community liaison, policy formulation and administration, and so on. Workers need the ability to negotiate the nature of their practice, in the light of the diversity of demands generated by the organisational context, and their individual and professional values.

The organisational location of workers also means that they are perceived by others as organisational members, as well as professionals. This has considerable implications. Other groups and individuals in the organisation, such as other professionals, administrators, workers and members of boards of management, have expectations about the contributions that social and welfare workers will make to organisational goals and processes. Workers need to be cognisant of these expectations, and be able to negotiate their organisational roles with this awareness. In addition, workers are perceived as organisational members by consumers, and their organisational role shapes worker–consumer relations.

Finally, their organisational location means that workers may have an important strategic location from which to pursue social change and social reform goals. While workers have opportunities to engage at a general level in social action and political activity as citizens and through professional associations, their daily work in human service organisations also involves them directly in the making and implementation of social policy, and the provision of human services. Workers need a full understanding and awareness of the implications of their organisational location. Social and welfare work does not just happen to be lodged in complex organisations, rather, it is an occupation, that is in nature, both organisational and professional. Workers must fully recognise this structural feature of their work, and develop the capabilities required to work effectively from an organisational as well as a professional stance.

The nature of social and welfare work as an occupation

The approach of workers to the organisations in which they work is shaped in part by their aspirations for professional status. For example, the emergence of social work as a distinct occupation in Australia is conventionally portrayed as the development of a new profession (Lawrence 1976). In these accounts, social work is viewed as a professional activity which, though strongly embedded in social service organisations, is mainly characterised by its common knowledge, skills and values acquired through processes of professional socialisation and reinforced and extended through membership of a professional community (Lawrence 1976, p. 1).

This view is predicated on a particular view of professionalism and the role of the professions in society. According to this view, an occupation is granted professional status when it has acquired certain defining traits or characteristics (Wilding 1982, pp. 2-3). The characteristics of an established profession are commonly listed as systematic theory, community sanction, authority, an ethical code and a professional culture (Greenwood, 1957; see also Toren 1972, p. 37). Much education and practice in Australia is couched in terms of this professional ideal. Dominant themes in the literature are the importance of the development and communication of a body of professional knowledge, the centrality of professional ethics and values, the principle of client service, and the distinctiveness of social work and welfare work vis-a-vis other human service occupations.

Claims to full professional status have, however, been challenged. Some writers have urged social and welfare workers to accept semi-professional status, alongside teaching and nursing. Etzioni suggests that the characteristics of the semi-professions are that 'their training is shorter, their status is less legitimated, their right to privileged communication less established, there is less of a specialised body of knowledge, and they have less autonomy from supervision or social control than (the established) professions' (1969, p. v). In the Australian context, it has been argued that the difference between social work and community welfare work is that of profession and semi-profession. This distinction is increasingly difficult to sustain. Both share a similar body of knowledge, the differences in length of training are narrowing, and educational institutions and employers are tending to view them as overlapping rather than discrete occupations. From our perspective, the key issue is not whether one or the other, or both, are professions. The more important question is whether or nor the label 'profession' is an adequate way of describing the nature of both occupational groups given their organisational location.

The conception of social and welfare work as a profession needs critical appraisal. Warham argues that the key question is not whether social work is a profession or not, 'but rather in what respects this concept, which has so far been central to both theory and practice, is of use in helping them to understand the nature of their particular occupation' (1977, p. 8). There are a number of ways in which the concept of 'professional' may be unhelpful and misleading, in and of itself, as a way of understanding the nature of social and welfare work.

At a general level, the assumption that there is something called professional work, that is different to other work, needs critical examination. Professions are not totally dissimilar to other occupations, but rather share some characteristics with them. Some writers suggest that the term profession is merely an honorific title that some groups have managed to secure, and that professions be viewed 'simply as occupational groups which have secured a dominant position in the division of labour' (Wilding 1982, pp. 6-7). All claims to professionalism should be viewed critically, whether made by social workers, community welfare workers, lawyers, doctors, or anyone else.

An emphasis on professionalism can also lead to lack of attention to the political nature of social and welfare work. Decisions to employ workers are based on a wide range of considerations, and are the outcome of complex political processes. The level of professionalism that such workers are perceived to possess is only one of the factors at work in these processes. There is a danger that if social and welfare work is viewed simply as a profession, the social and political factors that have led to its current place in Australian society will be obscured.

These social and political processes are, in the main, played out in organisations, and reflect these organisations' interactions with the broader society. This brings us back to our main theme, namely that it is necessary to conceptualise social and welfare work in organisational terms.

There have been attempts in the literature to develop concepts to encapsulate the organisational nature of occupations such as social and welfare work. Scott (1965) and Toren (1972), borrowing a term from Max Weber, have characterised social work as a 'heteronomous profession'. Heteronomous means subject to or involving different laws, and is the opposite of the more familiar word 'autonomous', meaning subject to its own laws only. Applied to social work,

Heteronomy . . . means that members of the profession are guided and controlled not only from 'within'—that is, by internalised professional norms, expert knowledge and the professional community—but also by administrative rules and by superiors in the organisational hierarchy (Toren 1972, pp. 52-53).

This concept is compatible with the approach of this book as it emphasises that social and welfare work is an occupation which by its location and nature must negotiate organisational and professional norms and authority. However, the term 'heteronomous' is neither well-established nor especially communicative. Similar problems are faced by the term 'bureau-professionalism', coined by Parry and Parry to describe the hybrid mode of organisation (part professional, part bureaucratic) and used to provide social services in local authorities in England and Wales (1979, p. 47). We will avoid these terms and refer to social and welfare work simply as an occupation that claims professional status, and that has to negotiate these claims in organisational, social and political contexts.

The purposes and roles of social and welfare work

The purposes of social and welfare work are notoriously difficult to define in ways that are meaningful and that command a high level of consensus (Gilbert 1980, pp. 457-458; O'Connor, Wilson and Thomas 1991, p. 11). Statements of purpose tend to be couched in broad terms such as 'meeting human needs', 'developing human potential', 'achieving social justice', 'fostering maximum self-determination' and 'enhancing opportunities for those most vulnerable in the community' (these examples are taken from the Australian Association of Social Worker's Code of Ethics). Such terms may well signify social and welfare work's broad social purpose, but they do not distinguish social and welfare work from many other occupations. Nor do they necessarily provide a clear guide to what workers do in practice; the stated goals of an occupation need to be clearly distinguished from its operational goals, that is what it is actually aiming to do.

Historically, the purposes and roles of social and welfare work have often been couched in terms that emphasise the duality of the occupation's concerns. While these have been described in many different ways, they are mainly variations on the theme that workers are concerned with social intervention on the one hand and individual helping on the other (Schwartz 1974, p. 348). This dualism has been expressed in terms of the social and the psychological aspects of social and welfare work, in terms of cause and function, in terms of a concern with both public issues and private troubles, and in terms of practice and policy.

A persistent theme has been a desire to integrate these elements (Schwartz 1974) and there have been many attempts to bring them together in definitions or models of social work. For example, in the North American context, Pincus and Minahan have described the purposes of social work thus:

> Social work is concerned with the interactions between people and their social environment which affect the ability of people to accomplish their life tasks, alleviate distress, and realize their aspirations and values. The purpose of social work therefore is to (1) enhance the problem-solving and coping capacity of people, (2) link people with systems that provide them

with resources, services, and opportunities, (3) promote the effective and humane operation of these systems, and (4) contribute to the development and improvement of social policy (1973, p. 9).

Similarly, in the British context, attempts to define social work have re-emphasised that it is concerned both with work with individuals and with the prevention of social problems, and a model of practice that combines the two is being sought to be developed (National Institute for Social Work 1982, p. x). An understanding of organisations is relevant to workers' concerns with both individual helping and social intervention, and is essential to workers who conceptualise their work as combining these two elements.

Organisations and direct practice
So-called 'direct practice' activities include therapy, counselling, education, advocacy, information gathering and referral, and are often viewed collectively as the methods of casework and group work (Gilbert and Specht 1976, p. 319). These activities encompass the specific purposes of 'enhancing the problem-solving and coping capacities of people' and 'linking people with systems that provide them with resources, services and opportunities'.

Skills in organisational analysis and practice are central to these purposes and roles. Direct practice is shaped by its organisational context. In their text on social casework, Briar and Millar write:

> The need for consistency in bureaucratic organisations, for adherence to a common set of policies and procedures, creates a pressure toward uniformity in therapeutic ideology, diagnostic classification, and treatment methodology. Thus, in some agencies diagnostic categories and treatment classifications are formalized, and workers are expected to adhere to these categories in their practice . . . The worker, for example, who attempts family group treatment in an agency where the norms are that definitive treatment can be conducted only in individual interviews runs the risk of being regarded unfavourably by his supervisors and his peers (1971, p. 101).

Direct service workers need to be able to understand the factors that lead organisations to adopt certain practice methods, and they need the organisational skills to negotiate the nature of their own practice in the light of these organisational practices and values.

Direct service workers also need to develop organisational skills because their work with consumers involves extensive interaction with organisations. A key aspect of direct practice is 'system linkage', that is connecting consumers with resources. These resources are found in many places, including informal helping networks. However, key resources are often held by human service organisations. The direct practice roles of advocate, arbitrator, broker, case manager, mediator, negotiator and referrer constantly involve relations with organisations (Lister 1987, p. 385). Often the organisation concerned is the one employing the worker. For example, a hospital social worker may feel that patients and their families are not being given adequate support by other hospital staff, and considers it her responsibility as a worker to intervene to improve relationships. Or, a youth worker employed in housing project may feel that the problems experienced by young people stem from administrative procedures or staff attitudes within the organisation. To be effective in advancing consumers' interests in these circumstances, workers need considerable organisational knowledge and skill.

Those workers engaged in direct practice also need skills in organisational work in order to understand and deal with the complexities of their role. It is a truism that social and welfare work in many organisational settings involves elements of both social care and social control. In Jordan's terminology, workers are both helpers and officials (1984, pp. 13-17). Social and welfare work does not only comprise helping, caring and therapeutic activities. It must also be understood in terms of the 'official, bureaucratic, legal and even potentially coercive powers and responsibilities it entails . . . The truth is that—unless they are working in some very protected or specialised corner of the field—social workers neglect either side of the job to their peril' (Jordan 1984, p. 13).

The issue of care versus control is sometimes portrayed as essentially a moral choice for workers, that is will they be carers or controllers? (Bailey 1980). The issue, however, is far more complex. Gilbert writes:

> . . . social workers often regard social control as a reprehensible objective that should be purged from the profession's repertoire. However, separating activities relating to caring and change objectives from activities marked by elements of social control is often impossible. It is difficult to deny that many professional efforts involved in the provision of care and the implementation of change are aimed at getting people to behave in socially acceptable and productive ways. Objectives of social control, therefore, cannot be written off without rejecting a substantial portion of professional activities conducted in the areas of child welfare, probation, mental health, and public assistance (1980, p. 463).

Gilbert goes on to distinguish between oppression and social control, arguing that the latter is a legitimate objective of social work (1980, pp. 462-463). In a similar vein, Green, writing about work in public welfare settings, argues that there is a legitimate role for social work in social protection and social control programmes, but that there needs to be careful, ongoing appraisal of the elements of social control and oppression (Green 1976).

For workers involved in direct service these are complex practice issues. Their complexity stems in large part from the necessity to negotiate these issues within an organisational context. Direct service workers, especially those employed in areas such as child welfare, corrections, income security and mental health, do not deal with their dual roles as helpers and officials in a vacuum. The approach they take in arbitrating or mediating the requirements of the organisation, law and policy on the one hand and the needs, wishes and circumstances of the consumer on the other must, of necessity, take into account the organisational context (Healy 1988). Direct service workers must be skilled in understanding their level and degree of discretion within the organisation, in relating to and negotiating with other organisational participants and other organisations, and in being able to understand the organisational consequences of their actions. Workers are not simply individuals helping other individuals. Rather, their helping activities are enmeshed in complex relations with organisations that often have multiple and conflicting purposes.

Organisations and social intervention

Aspirations to social intervention have been an important part of the history and development of social and welfare work. However, the conversion of these aspirations into practice has been problematic. One writer has described the social worker's role in social intervention as often amounting to little more than that of 'ineffectual consciences-in-residence' (Specht 1976, p. 485). Workers are able to involve themselves in political activity as individuals and through professional associations and trade unions. But social and welfare workers have also sought to incorporate social intervention into practice roles and methods. Social work views itself as an occupation that intervenes in larger systems, and in the lives of individuals (Rein 1976).

This has been attempted mainly in two ways. The first has been through the development of practice methods for promoting the effective and humane operation of service systems and the development and improvement of social policy (Pincus and Minahan 1973, p. 9). The roles and activities associated with these purposes include planning, policy analysis, community organisation, social action, programme development, administration, research, and programme evaluation. These activities are conceptualised in different ways by different writers. Some refer to them collectively as 'macro-practice' (Meenaghan 1987), others as 'community organisation practice' (Kramer and Specht 1983). These are now widely accepted as part of the generic, practice repertoire of social and welfare work.

The need for workers undertaking macro-practice roles to acquire organisational understanding and skills is readily apparent and well accepted (Meenaghan 1987, p. 86). Roles such as planning, policy development and administration are inherently concerned with the operation and functioning of organisations. It is important not to underestimate the importance of these roles. Many workers take on macro-practice roles within their early years of practice, as their career takes them from direct practice and into administration and related areas. Many others, particularly those working in small non-government organisations and decentralised offices of government departments, are required or have opportunities to undertake policy, planning and administrative tasks as part of their work.

The second approach to social intervention has focused explicitly on the direct practice or front-line work. The main concern has been to examine the ways that front-line workers can work in and through their daily activities to bring about desired social change. There are two main sets of writings relevant to this concern. The first arises from the attempts to develop radical and Marxist approaches to practice. An example is Corrigan and Leonard's book, *Social Work Practice Under Capitalism: A Marxist Approach* (1978). These writers are concerned with questions such as, 'Can social workers . . . make alliances with others in order to oppose welfare cuts, defend local communities and struggle for change within their own organisations? . . . How can "progressive" work be undertaken within a generally oppressive state apparatus?' (Corrigan and Leonard 1978, p. ix). Their book examines the strategic and tactical considerations for workers seeking answers to these questions (see also the readings in Brake and Bailey 1980; Galper 1975, pp. 195-207). The second set of writings focuses on workers as lower level participants in organisations seeking to extend their influence to bring about desired changes in the organisations that employ them. 'Such change, though ordinarily modest, is important nonetheless. Even modest change can have significant consequences in the lives of large numbers of people who are touched by the human services' (Brager and Holloway 1983, p. 199).

These two sets of writings are particularly relevant to considerations of social intervention. For many workers, their main opportunities to be involved in change activities occur within and in relation to their own and allied organisations. Social intervention in practice often means organisational intervention, that is attempting to influence the goals, rules, policies, programmes, practices and resources of organisations. This being the case, skills in organisational analysis and practice assume central importance.

Organisations and consumers

We have seen that social and welfare workers require skills in organisational analysis and practice because of their location, the nature of their work, and their roles and purposes. However, the underlying reason for workers to acquire organisational understanding and competency is the impact that organisations have on consumers. The lives of all citizens in modern societies are shaped by organisations. The nature and quality of service provided by organisations impacts on the well-being of us all. Organisations shape the pattern of life chances and opportunities in the society, distribute resources of many kinds, and influence the quality of life for individuals and groups.

The relations of individuals and groups that are socially disadvantaged with organisations are particularly important and problematic. For these people, organisations are often the instruments of oppression, exclusion and marginalisation. Paradoxically, disadvantaged people are likely to be highly dependent on organisations, particularly state organisations, to meet their needs for health care, housing, income, personal security, transport and so forth. Moreover, the capacity of disadvantaged groups to assert effective claims as consumers is limited by their relatively powerless position in the overall society.

It follows that a central task for social and welfare workers is to promote the responsiveness of organisations, particularly the organisations in which they are located, to consumers. Our argument is that workers should conceptualise their practice in these terms. Underpinning this task are the key social justice concepts of access, equity, rights and participation. Working to achieve organisations that are accessible and equitable, that establish, promote and respect consumers' rights, and that promote participation of consumers in organisational activities and decision-making should be central concerns of workers. This conceptualisation of social and welfare work is developed throughout the book, and is given particular attention in chapters 9 and 11.

The personal needs of workers

The final set of reasons for social and welfare workers to develop skills in organisational analysis and practice concern their personal needs as workers. If workers are to be effective in organisations, they need to understand and be able to deal with the personal stress frequently experienced in organisational life.

There is considerable evidence that many workers, particularly new graduates, feel lacking in the skills and understanding required to cope at a personal level with organisational settings (Herrick et al. 1983; Wasserman 1970; Smith and Sanford 1980). The study by O'Connor and Dalgleish (1986) of the experiences and perceptions of graduates from an Australian school of social work during their first year of practice is of particular relevance. They found that most new workers experienced considerable difficulty coping with organisational life. They felt unprepared for the difficulties of working in settings where others did not share their interests, perspectives or goals. This was the case in both small voluntary agencies and large public sector organisations. Many viewed themselves as 'lone professionals cast adrift in an alien and unfriendly environment' (p. 442). Many encountered difficulties in defining their work role (p. 441). Many also felt a strong sense of professional isolation and lack of support, and felt lacking in the organisational skills to deal with their circumstances (see also Hugman 1987).

It is important for workers to develop specific skills in dealing with the personal stresses of organisational life. We address these issues specifically in chapter 8. However, in our view, workers' capacity to deal with the pressures that organisational life bring is related to their understanding of the nature of organisations, and their own organisational roles. Understanding the factors that shape organisational processes, and developing ways of working effectively through those processes, is central to achieving a sense of personal satisfaction and fulfilment as a social and welfare worker.

Connecting policy and practice

A capacity to analyse and work within organisations cannot only make workers more effective, but also provide the basis for linking their concerns with social intervention and individual helping. To put this another way, an understanding of how organisations work enables the connection between policy and practice to be made.

One of the main difficulties of conceptualising social and welfare work as an essentially professional activity is that it tends to present workers as separate from and independent of their social and political context. For example, as discussed earlier in this chapter, workers are sometimes portrayed as change agents who intervene at the community, organisational or societal level. This portrayal ignores the reality that social and welfare work is itself embedded in a particular political, social and institutional context. Workers are not 'free agents'. The shape, nature and, indeed, existence of their roles is subject to ongoing negotiation in a wide variety of organisational and policy contexts. Workers must struggle to achieve their purposes primarily as participants in societal arrangements, rather than as agents located outside of and separate from these arrangements.

All social and welfare workers operate within a public policy context. By public policy we mean 'the actions and positions taken by the state as the overriding authoritative collective entity in society' (Hill and Bramley 1986, p. 2). Many of these policies are conventionally termed 'social policies', although it is difficult to reach agreement about what distinguishes social policies from other kinds of policies (Hill and Bramley 1986, pp. 3-18). Policy is an integral feature of the daily work of most workers. For example, workers in the child protection field operate within a framework of legislation and organisational rules and procedures that shape the choices and options available to them in their relations with consumers. Similarly, the role of social workers in the Department of Social Security is shaped by the provisions of the social security legislation, and the regulations, procedures and instructions that are part of the income security policies of the department. Policy is not only a feature of the work situation of workers doing so-called 'statutory work'. All workers employed in public agencies, including organisations dependent on public funds, have their work shaped, in direct and indirect ways, by state policies.

It is useful to think of public (or social) policies as involving 'a set of interrelated decisions taken by a political actor or group of actors concerning the selection of goals and the means of achieving them within a specified situation . . . ' (Jenkins, quoted in Hill and Bramley 1986, p. 3). One important subset of decisions in any policy field concerns the nature of the organisation or organisations that will be the vehicle for policy implementation and service delivery. The nature of the organisations through which human services are provided is determined through such policy processes. For example, in the late 1980s it was the established policy of the Commonwealth government that income security payments be made through a large, nation-wide, bureaucratically structured, public organisation. It was also Commonwealth policy that accommodation and support services for homeless young people be provided in the main by non-government organisations, funded and regulated by a Commonwealth department. Many state governments provide family support services via non-government organisations that are required to be community-based.

Public policies, therefore, shape both the institutional arrangements (organisations) within which social and welfare work takes place and the nature of this work. This must be borne in mind when considering the ways in which workers participate in and influence policy.

When workers contemplate participating in policy processes, this is often conceptualised in terms of influencing decisions made at central government level be it Commonwealth or state. Policy is viewed as the decisions made by Cabinet, by ministers and senior public servants, and by people in the upper echelons of political parties and pressure groups, particularly those representing capital and organised labour. In this sense, policy is often viewed as something remote, rather inaccessible, and divorced from the world of practice.

Clearly, the policy-making processes that occur at central government level are of great importance, and workers should attempt to influence them via the pressure groups and political parties that represent their interests and beliefs, and via processes within the organisations in which they are employed. However, there are other opportunities for participation in policy processes closer to hand. In particular, the policy implementation process provides workers with significant opportunities to influence policy (Ham and Hill 1984, pp. 95-

112). Lipsky refers to workers such as social and welfare workers who are located in the front-line of organisations as 'street-level bureaucrats' and argued that their role in the policy process is a crucial one:

> ... the decisions of street-level bureaucrats, the routines they establish, and the devices they invent to cope with uncertainties and work pressures, effectively *become* the public policies they carry out ... public policy is not best understood as made in legislatures or top-floor suites of high-ranking administrators, because in important ways it is actually made in the crowded offices and daily encounters of street-level workers (Lipsky 1980, p. xii).

The implications of this analysis (which will be discussed in detail in chapter 8) for workers are considerable. They suggest that the distinction often made between policy (something occurring mainly in and around central government) and practice (what workers do with consumers in their daily work) needs re-consideration. In a very real sense, practice is policy, and policy is, in considerable part, what practitioners do and fail to do. In rationing access to services, deciding how to spend their time, applying rules and exercising discretion, developing programmes and determining the nature of professional practice, workers are engaging in policy processes (Schorr 1985).

This view of the nature of social and welfare work, and its relations with policy and organisations, underlies the analysis in this book, and is developed in later chapters. This perspective stresses that workers are part of and not detached from the organisational and policy processes and structures that they seek to influence. They are one group of participants in policy and organisational processes, not detached professionals or change agents. From this perspective, a central task of workers is the attempt to shape the organisational and policy processes in which they are inextricably involved. Shaping organisational and policy processes is integral to the achievement of desired outcomes for consumers.

What is organisational understanding?

It has been established that workers need a sophisticated understanding of the organisations in and through which they work. But what exactly is organisational understanding? Specifically, what knowledge and skills do workers need to acquire to function effectively in organisations?

In Table 1.3 we have outlined in summary form the main elements of organisational understanding and skills. The table also indicates where this material is covered in the book, so it provides an overview of the contents. Essentially, we conceptualise the organisational knowledge and skills needed by workers under three headings. Firstly,

Table 1.3   Organisations: knowledge and skills required by social and welfare workers

Knowledge	Skills	Chapter
Critical understanding of the major perspectives in organisation theory, and their implications for social and welfare work	The ability to study an organisation from a variety of analytical perspectives, and gauge the implications for practice	2
Understanding of the distinctive characteristics of human service organisations, stemming from their purpose, technology and auspice	The ability to identify the distinctive and potentially problematic features of a human service organisation	3
Understanding of the concept of organisational environment and its significance for human service organisations	The ability to analyse the environment of a human service organisation, assess the opportunities and constraints offered, and act strategically	4
Understanding of the concept of organisational goals, and its significance for human service organisations	The ability to critically assess the goals and objectives of an organisation, and participate in goal analysis processes	5
Understanding of the concept of organisational structure, and its significance for human service organisations	The ability to assess the implication of various structural arrangements, and to use structure strategically	6
Understanding of the concept of organisational culture, and its significance for human service organisations	The ability to identify organisational cultures, and develop cultural competency	7
Understanding of the concept of 'front-line worker', and the opportunities and constraints of front-line work	The ability to survive and work strategically within the opportunities and constraints posed in the front line of organisations	8
Understanding relations between organisations and consumers	The ability to analyse the circumstances of consumers in an organisation, and develop strategies to make organisations more responsive to consumer needs	9

Knowledge	Skills	Chapter
Understanding of the nature of power, influence and authority in organisations, and processes of organisational change and resistance	The ability to participate in processes of organisational change and resistance	10
Critically understand the concepts of efficiency, effectiveness, equity and excellence as applied to human service organisations	The ability to work strategically towards efficiency, effectiveness, equity and excellence in human service organisations	11
Understanding of the concept of social justice and its applicability to human service organisations	The ability to work strategically in advancing social justice in and through human service organisations	11

workers need a broad understanding of the nature of organisations, including the various theoretical perspectives on organisations and the distinctive characteristics of so-called 'human service organisations'. In practice terms, they need the skills to analyse their own organisation (or any other human service organisation) in terms of this theoretical material. Chapters 2 and 3 focus on these issues. Secondly, workers need a framework of concepts and theories through which to analyse and interpret organisational process and issues. In part II of the book we provide such a framework, focusing on the concepts of organisational environment, organisational goals, organisational structures and organisational culture. These concepts are approached as tools to aid understanding of organisational processes, and as concepts around which needed practice skills can be identified and taught. Each chapter in this section includes discussion of practice skills and techniques.

In part III the focus shifts to workers' roles in organisations. We analyse the organisational issues and practice tasks associated with front-line work in organisations, and with organisational change and resistance. We also examine the vital roles of workers in making organisations more responsive to consumers, and in participating in processes designed to make organisations more efficient, equitable and effective.

Chapter review questions

1   Identify and critique some of the main themes in the literature on the organisational context of social and welfare work.

2 What implications stem from the fact that most social and welfare workers in Australia are located in organisations?
3 What are the limitations of viewing social and welfare work primarily as a 'professional' occupation? How would you characterise the nature of this occupation?
4 What do you understand the purposes and roles of social and welfare work to be? How is an understanding of organisations relevant to these purposes and roles?
5 How do organisations shape the lives of disadvantaged people, and what are the implications for social and welfare workers?
6 How does an understanding of organisations assist workers to cope with the stresses of organisational life?
7 How do you conceptualise the relations between organisations, policy and practice?
8 What organisational knowledge and skills are needed by workers?

Further reading

A useful introduction to the issues raised in this chapter is Warham 1977, pp. 1-6. For examples of some of the traditional approaches to the relations between social work and organisations see Compton and Galaway 1989, pp. 228–269 and Finch 1976. The difficulties often faced by workers, especially new graduates, in coming to grips with the organisational context are considered in George 1982 and O'Connor and Dalgleish 1986. Some difficulties with the notion of professionalism as applied to social and welfare work are usefully covered in Gilbert 1980 and Rein 1976. The need for workers to negotiate conflicting expectations in organisations are discussed from a variety of perspectives in Green 1976, Jordan 1984, pp. 13-17, and Bailey 1980. An introduction to the nature of the policy process, focusing on the role of 'street-level bureaucrats' and professionals can be found in Ham and Hill 1984, pp. 136-147.

Case study

THE CLASS OF '88'

'It seemed like a good idea at the time', thought Jane Henderson, as she walked down the corridor towards the seminar room in the School of Social and Welfare Work at the University of Northern Australia. Jane held the position of field work co-ordinator in the school, and thus had responsibility for organising the 'on-the-job' practice experience of the undergraduate social work students. The 'good idea' had been put to her by a small group of former students who had graduated some nine months earlier. According to Kay Mitter, the student who contacted Jane, a number of students were finding difficulty in relating what they had learnt in their undergraduate course to their work situations. 'What we want to do', Kay had said, 'is just spend some time talking together and with you about our experiences of working in organisations, relating this to what we expected social and welfare work to be like, and seeing if we can find better ways of dealing with the problems we are facing'. In a weak moment Jane agreed to take part. Now entering the seminar room, she resigned herself to another afternoon in which 'keeping in contact with the field' would take priority over her languishing research projects.

There were four former students waiting in the seminar room, and all were known to Jane. Kay Mitter was working in a suburban child guidance clinic that was part of the Health Department of the state government. Peter Simpson had been employed since graduation in the psychiatric unit of a large public hospital. Alison Delaney had found difficulty obtaining employment immediately after graduation, largely because she was clear that she wanted to work in a community work setting. Eventually, after about two months, she had obtained a job as the only paid worker in a community centre in an inner city suburb. Katherine Smith was employed by the state welfare department, where she had case responsibility for juvenile offenders in a secure residential facility.

'Perhaps the best way to get started', suggested Jane 'would be for each person to briefly recount their experiences of working in an organisation. When everyone has done that, we could look together at what these experiences suggest about the organisational knowledge and skills that workers require. Kay, you are largely responsible for us all being here this afternoon, so why don't you start?'

'I am happy to', said Kay, 'although I should begin by saying that I am not nearly as dissatisfied with my work situation as I was two months ago, when I initiated this meeting. I have been working in a suburban child guidance clinic run by the State Health Department. My first four or five months in the job were terrible, and at that stage I was applying for other jobs. It was not that the people I was working with were difficult, or anything like that; on the contrary, everyone was very nice. My main problem was that I didn't know what to do. In fact, during the first few months of the job I had very little work at all. I expected when I went to work at the clinic that there would be a clear work role to fit into, and I certainly had some ideas, which I now think of as rather naive, about what a worker should be doing. I expected to be very busy. But what happened was that I was referred hardly any cases. The operations of the clinic are very much dominated by the medical director. It is he who decides who will be allocated what cases and so forth. I think that he just didn't trust me to do good work, new graduate and all that. The clinic has a very clear approach to child guidance. Basically, we take the view that the problems manifested by children have their origins in the early childhood experiences of their parents. This means that our main focus is to work through the parents' problems. When I arrived at the agency, fresh from my studies, I found this approach hard to accept. It didn't seem to be consistent with the things I had learned at uni like consumer self-determination, dealing with the presenting problem, accepting the consumer's definition of problems and all that stuff. Every time I met with a family, I felt I was taking on the 'expert' role and I felt very uncomfortable with it. I did try to do things the agency way, but it just didn't work out. I remember being very pleased with myself in one interview with a woman, because I got her to talk a lot about her own childhood. At the end of the interview she said, "Boy, didn't we get diverted today!" Somehow, the whole thing didn't seem to make sense.

Over the last few months, though, things have changed. For those first months I just "stewed in my own juice". But then I decided, especially after talking to colleagues in other clinics, that I had to confront the problem. I became much more assertive, and consciously tried to negotiate a role for myself. Much to my surprise, this turned out to be easier than I thought. I guess by now my views about the clinic and the way things are done have changed. Now I can largely accept that we have to explore the root causes of the parents' feelings about their children, and that my role is to assist them to explore these feelings. I now get plenty of referrals. I suppose at the moment I have two anxieties about the job. Firstly, I wonder if I am sufficiently competent as a therapist. Secondly, I'm not sure if I am really doing what I am supposed to be doing. A lot of the stuff I learnt in my undergraduate studies just doesn't seem to enter into practice here. Should I be worried?'

'I think you should be worried,' said Alison Delaney, who had been increasingly and noticeably irritated as Kay told her story. 'It seems to me that you have simply caved in to the organisation. If your view of social and welfare work amounts to nothing more than accepting whatever therapy happens to be popular wherever you go to work, I wonder if we actually did the same course? But before you answer that, let me tell you about the joys of life in the community centre. When I was a student I developed a strong interest and involvement in community work and community development. When I graduated, I was determined to find a job as a community worker. When I was offered the job at the community centre I was ecstatic and I accepted it straightaway. I saw it as an opportunity to put my community development principles into practice. I envisaged the centre as a base for bringing people together and developing the local community. I saw my role as a facilitator of local people getting together to build community. That sounds very idealistic now.

The first day in the centre was a bit of a rude awakening. The previous community worker stayed on for a few days, and in the first couple of days she introduced me to all her "clients". That's right, clients in a community work agency. They all had complex problems of one kind or another, and there seemed to be an expectation that I do something about them. This sort of "welfarism" was not what I had in mind at all, but the volunteers and most of the committee seemed to think that was what I should do. My initial efforts to link some of these clients (how I hate that word) with other local community members who could give them support didn't really work very well. I think this was partly because a strong expectation had built up over the years that the centre would provide help or at least refer people on to others who would.

Anyway, for a few months I resisted getting involved too much in casework. I tried to spend a lot of time making contacts in the local community, and getting people together. The trouble was that I started to feel guilty that I was not actually getting anything done. Here I was being paid a full-time salary, and all I seemed to be doing was having endless chats and cups of coffee. I could have taken more of a leadership role on local issues, but I felt that this would mean that I was becoming too central. After a while I found myself doing more and more of the dreaded casework, to keep me busy, give me a challenge, and stop me from feeling guilty. Casework now takes up about two-thirds of my time. I am still a bit worried about not working in a true community development fashion, and the job has certainly turned out differently from what I expected. But I think that as time goes on I have been able to develop more community development work using the centre as a base. I think I can come to some sort of accommodation between what I want to do and what the people at the centre expect of me'.

'Do you realise, Alison,' interjected Kay, 'that what you just described is exactly the same process that happened to me and that you took such strong exception to? You have caved in as well!' 'Not at all', said Alison, 'What you must realise is . . . ' But at that point, Joan intervened. 'Before we get into discussion, I think we should hear from Katherine and Peter, then we may be better placed to see the complexities of the relations we are concerned with.' 'In that case, I think I should go next', said Peter.

'My experiences of work have been quite different in many respects from those that Alison and Kay have described. As I explained earlier, I have been working in the psychiatric unit of the general hospital. When I fronted up for work on day one, I thought I had a pretty good idea of what to expect. Before doing my undergraduate course I had worked extensively in psychiatric hospitals overseas. I had thought a lot about mental health issues, and had some clear ideas about what I wanted to do. When I arrived that Monday morning I expected that the day would consist of getting to know my way around, getting a feel of the place, and so on. No way. I was grabbed by one of the staff on the team at 8.35 a.m., after arriving at 8.30 a.m., and was carted up to one of the wards, introduced to everybody and plonked into a "community meeting" of all the staff and patients on the ward. I would have been wise, in retrospect, to resist that, but at the time I didn't realise what was happening. A little later I discovered that this process occurred to thwart one of the consultants who was about two minutes behind, who also wanted to grab me . . . It became apparent that I had landed myself in a war zone. There were two warring factions in the unit, and they were both trying to formulate their alliances with the new worker, before the other, to get me on side.

That's pretty much the way things have been ever since. There is almost no agreement among staff about the way the unit should be run, and a massive amount of time is spent on infighting among the staff. The easiest part of my job is relating to the consumers. If that was all I had to do it would be a very comfortable place to be. I have had to work things out for myself. I have had to take stock of the situation, sift it all out and determine my position. I've had to carefully realign myself to the position I wanted to be in, rather than what other people wanted me to be. If I had not had previous experience I think I would have been lost. Basically, I have found that my expectations of what I can do have been lowered. I still hold to a strong personal belief in a community orientation to psychiatric services as an ideal, and to practice principles like seeking to counteract the power imbalance between worker and consumer. But in practice, I have lowered my expectations about what can be achieved in a hospital context like this. I have to say that I am quite envious of Kay and Alison. You both seem to have been able to work something out. At our place there has been so much conflict that I just feel I have been treading water for the whole year.'

'Well before you get too envious, Peter, have a listen to my tale of woe,' said Katherine, joining in the discussion for the first time. 'But before I begin, I want your agreement that anything I say be treated in confidence. I'm probably being paranoid, but that's how I feel. I did my final placement in the youth legal service, and while I was there I became very interested in the juvenile justice system, and found that I actually liked working with juvenile offenders. More fool me. When the department offered me a position to work in a secure residence for young offenders it seemed like a good opportunity, and I jumped at it. I was excited and optimistic and looked forward to putting some of my ideas into practice. It seemed to me that coming to the attention of the juvenile justice system tended to have really bad consequences for kids and their families, and I saw my role as trying to avoid or lessen these destructive consequences.

I was a bit worried at first about my lack of experience and about how easily I seem to be intimidated by authority. I am such a "nice" person with a "nice" background. But I felt confident I could do the job. Three months later, I was a wreck—anxious, upset, and very unhappy about my work. When I look back, I was so naive. In my first weeks in the organisation, on quite a number of occasions, I complained to my boss and to other workers about things that were going on in the institution that affected the young people. I was not saying anything radical, just raising issues of general care. All that happened was that I was reprimanded and, in my view, scapegoated by other staff when things went wrong. In those first few weeks I felt like a naughty child. I got into trouble almost every day. It was all very confusing. I tried to be open with people, but I didn't realise quickly enough that there was very little support for my ideas in the organisation. I had assumed that people involved in welfare would share my general philosophy and orientation. Big mistake.

After the first few weeks, I realised that I had to change my approach. I started to keep my thoughts to myself more, and to try to "professionalise" my work. By that, I mean that I tried to delineate more precisely what was expected of me, and to relate to other people on that basis, rather than allowing my personal feelings to come through. I felt, and still do feel, very constrained by the organisation—I feel they want me to become a robot. My main concern over the last few months has simply been survival. I feel daunted by the structure of the institution and basically powerless. Initially I was angry, but I could only keep that up for a short while. Now I mainly feel apathetic. I do what I can for the kids, but I don't really feel able to do much about the basic problems of the structure of the institution and the effects it is having on the children.

I just wish that I had been better prepared to work in organisations, particularly in situations where there are a majority of people who don't share my view of the world. At the moment, I suppose I feel a bit directionless and unsure about how to improve things.'

No one spoke up straightaway when Katherine finished speaking. Then Kay turned to Jane. 'It seems to me,' she said, 'that working in an organisation is a rather bloody business. Wouldn't you agree?' Jane sighed. It was clearly going to be a long afternoon and the research projects would have to wait.

*This case is adapted from accounts by social workers of the first nine months of practice as reported in O'Connor 1984, pp. 241-287 and pp. 539-646. We are grateful to Dr O'Connor for permission to use this material in this case study.

Key questions

What does this case suggest about the nature of the relations between social and welfare work and organisations? What organisational knowledge and skills would assist the workers to deal effectively with their circumstances?

Case discussion points

1 What does the case suggest are the practice implications of the organisational location of social and welfare work?
2 What does the case suggest is the nature of social and welfare work as an occupation?
3 How would an understanding of organisations assist the workers in the case to pursue their individual and professional goals?
4 What are the relations between organisations, policy and practice in each of the situations described in the case?

2

Approaching organisational analysis: towards a critical perspective

No matter what you have to do with an organization—whether you are going to study it, work in it, consult for it, subvert it, or use it in the interests of another organisation—you must have some view of the nature of the beast with which you are dealing. This constitutes a perspective on organizations (Perrow 1970, p. 1).

Although the study of organisations is sometimes viewed as a secondary concern in social and welfare work, this is not the case in the social sciences as a whole. Organisations are a major focus of inquiry in the social sciences, and organisation theory is a primary concern of sociologists, psychologists, political scientists and economists, as well as specialists in applied fields such as management and public administration. The study of organisations has a long history and, particularly in the last two decades, has become central to many areas of social inquiry. It has been claimed that 'the study of organisations must be at the core of all social science' (Perrow 1986, p. vii). Our argument for the centrality of organisational knowledge and skills in social and welfare work runs parallel to this emphasis in the social sciences as a whole.

The attention paid to organisation theory in the social sciences is both helpful and difficult for social and welfare workers. On the positive side, there is no shortage of materials from which workers can build and develop their understanding of organisations. However, finding a way through the morass of competing perspectives, frameworks and theories can be daunting. This chapter provides assistance in this task. Firstly, it overviews the development of organisation theory and some of the main perspectives on organisational analysis. The purpose of this overview is to enable workers to recognise the main sources of ideas about organisations, and to be able to critically appraise the assumptions, strengths and weaknesses of the various perspectives. There have been many previous summaries of the development of organisation theory (e.g. Clegg and Dunkerley 1980; Hasenfeld 1983, pp. 12-49; Mouzelis 1975; Perrow 1986). Our approach is distinctive in that we directly address the question: what bearing do the various perspectives on organisation theory have for social and welfare work?

Secondly, the chapter lays the groundwork for workers to develop their own critical perspective on organisations. By this we mean an ability to analyse organisations in terms that go beyond 'received' beliefs and opinions or official statements. We consider this to be a fundamental part of becoming an effective worker in organisations.

Perspectives on organisational analysis

The influence of organisations on individuals and social relations in late-twentieth century industrialised, urbanised societies is profound. It is through organisations that goods and services are produced and distributed, that political interests are aggregated and expressed, that cultural and recreational pursuits are conducted, and that societal functions such as socialisation and social control are exercised. This has led some writers to describe contemporary societies as 'organisational societies' (e.g. Presthus 1978; Sosin 1980). Etzioni conveys the pervasiveness of organisations in our social life thus:

> We are born in organizations, educated by organisations, and most of us spend our lives working for organizations. We spend much of our leisure time paying, playing and praying in organisations. Most of us will die in an organization, and when the time comes for burial, the largest organization of all—the state—must grant official permission (1964, p. 1).

The centrality of organisations in our social life has led to a large body of literature aiming to understand their role, how they function, and how their operation can be improved. However, this has not resulted in the emergence of one uniform, commonly accepted body of theory. Rather, the study of organisations is characterised by many, competing orientations and perspectives, which sometimes complement and sometimes contradict one another. In the material which follows, we examine ten of the most important of these perspectives:

1 the theory of bureaucracy;
2 scientific management;
3 human relations;
4 systems and ecological perspectives;
5 decision perspectives;

6 market perspectives;
7 neo-Marxian perspectives;
8 political economy perspectives;
9 feminist perspectives;
10 Aboriginal perspectives.

The theory of bureaucracy

Social and welfare workers often use the terms 'bureaucracy' and 'organisation' interchangeably, and conceive their work as taking place in 'welfare bureaucracies' (e.g. Howe 1986). What must be recognised is that this formulation is based on a particular view of the nature of organisations. Use of the term 'bureaucracy' can be traced back to the mid-eighteenth century (Albrow 1970, pp. 16-18). However, its systematic use in organisation theory stems from the writings of Max Weber (1864–1920). Weber's writings are broad-ranging, being concerned with explanations of the overall changes that took place in European societies in the eighteenth and nineteenth centuries, in particular industrialisation and the rise of the capitalist economy (Clegg and Dunkerley 1980, pp. 33-41, 75-82). These historical circumstances, Weber observed, saw the emergence of bureaucracy as the dominant form of organisation in modern societies. Weber's concept of bureaucracy was based on his ideas about the nature of power, domination and authority. He was particularly concerned with the nature of authority, that is the belief in the legitimacy of commands and orders, and consequently the likelihood of obedience.

According to Weber, three types of authority can be distinguished: traditional authority, charismatic authority and legal–rational authority (Etzioni-Halevy 1985, p. 27). Traditional authority is that which is legitimated by its existence over time, the sanctity of tradition. Charismatic authority is based on the outstanding characteristic of an individual: people obey because of the exceptional sanctity, heroism, character or other personal qualities of the person issuing commands. Legal–rational authority is legitimated and exercised by virtue of being in accordance with rules and procedures that are accepted by those concerned. People obey because they accept that those who have attained certain positions according to laid down rules and procedures have a legitimate right to issues commands and expect compliance.

Weber argued that the predominance of legal–rational authority as the basis of the power relationship between rulers and the ruled is a central feature of modern societies. These relations are manifested in organisational structures that have certain typical characteristics. Bureaucracy is the term he used to describe the form of organisation corresponding to and based on legal–rational authority. The main characteristics of the legal–rational, bureaucratic type of organisation, as listed by Mouzelis, are:

- a high degree of specialisation;
- a hierarchical authority structure with limited areas of command and responsibility;
- impersonality of relations between organisational members;
- recruitment of officials on the basis of ability and technical knowledge;
- differentiation of private and official income and fortune.

Mouzelis argues that these characteristics are linked by a common element: 'the existence of a system of control based on rational rules, rules which try to regulate the whole organisational structure and process on the basis of technical knowledge and with the aim of maximum efficiency' (1975, p. 39).

Bureaucracy, in this sense, is not a wholly modern or Western phenomenon. For example, many of the features of legal–rational bureaucracy were present at various stages in ancient Egyptian, Roman and Chinese state administrations, and in the Roman Catholic Church from the late thirteenth century (Etzioni-Halevy 1985, p. 29). Moreover, few, if any, modern organisations are wholly bureaucratic, in the sense of exhibiting the characteristics of bureaucracy in pure form. However, it was Weber's argument that bureaucratic forms of organisation proliferated and extended into many spheres of social life as a consequence of the circumstances of modern societies. These circumstances included the creation of a money economy, the emergence of capitalist economies, the trend towards rationality in Western society, the development of democratic political institutions, rapid population growth, modern forms of communication and the emergence of especially complex administrative problems in the modern state (Etzioni-Halevy 1985, pp. 30-31). Bureaucracy developed, in short, because it was an efficient tool to deal with the tasks and circumstances of complex, modern society:

> The decisive reason for the advance of bureaucratic organisation has always been its purely technical superiority . . . The fully developed bureaucratic mechanism compares with other organisations exactly, as does the machine with the non-mechanical modes of production (Weber, quoted in Clegg and Dunkerley 1980, p. 80).

Although Weber argued that bureaucratic forms of organisation were the most efficient in dealing with the tasks facing modern societies and the modern state, he by no means espoused an uncritical view of bureaucracy. He was concerned about the impact of bureaucracy on the individual, seeing it as inherently dehumanising and producing 'specialists without spirit' (Weber, quoted in Etzioni-Halevy 1985, p. 32). He was also concerned about the political implications of the growth of bureaucracy. The qualities that made bureaucracy so essential to modern society also resulted in the possibility of immense power being concentrated in the hands of bureaucratic organisations, and difficulties in holding bureaucracies, and particularly their managerial elites, to account.

Weber's elaboration of the concept of bureaucracy holds a central place in organisation theory. Most introductions to twentieth century analysis of organisations begin, as we have done, by reviewing Weber's ideas. The strength of Weber's analysis stems in large part from its breadth: he provides explanation, description and critique of modern organisations and their place in society. His ideas have, however, been subject to extensive criticism.

The first main line of criticism concerns the idea that bureaucracy is the most efficient form of organisation. The critics suggest that, far from being the most efficient means of getting the work of society done, bureaucracy is inherently inefficient. The emphasis in the bureaucratic mode on precision and reliability in administration has self-defeating consequences. Officials become excessively prudent, rules become ends in themselves, hierarchies slow decision-making, change is resisted and relations are conducted in an excessively impersonal fashion. Collectively, such behaviour has been referred to as 'bureaupathology' (Smith 1979, p. 27). It is further argued that while bureaucratic organisational forms may be suitable for certain routine tasks, they are entirely inappropriate for creative or non-routine activities. For example, it is argued that much of the work in human services is non-routine, requiring complex judgements and sensitivity to consumer needs. In these circumstances hierarchy and rigid rules inhibit, rather than advance, the effectiveness of the organisation.

A related view is that Weber focused almost exclusively on the formal elements of organisational structure, ignoring the pervasive influence of informal relations within organisations. The behaviour of officials is influenced by many factors additional to the administrative code, including his or her individual interests, prejudices, fears and friendships (Albrow 1970, pp. 55-56). 'Bureaucracy's other face' includes informal relations, informal norms and values, an informal power hierarchy and informal power struggles (Etzioni-Halevy 1985, p. 35).

Workers seeking to understand the organisations in which they are located need to come to grips with Weber's theory of bureaucracy. Arguments that attribute the ills of society wholly or partially to bureaucratic features of organisations such as hierarchy, prescribed rules, specialisation, and impersonality of relations have wide currency. These characteristics of bureaucratic organisations are certainly problematic, and require critical analysis. However, dealing with the question of bureaucracy involves far more than criticising hierarchy, rules and so forth.

Firstly, Weber's arguments about bureaucratic efficiency need to be given full consideration. Undoubtedly, many examples of bureaupathology can be found, but whether this represents a decisive argument against bureaucratic organisation must be questioned. For example, consider the administration of the social security system. The tasks of assessing the eligibility of individuals for pensions and benefits, ensuring that payments are made on time, and monitoring and controlling the whole process is currently undertaken by an organisation that has many of the characteristics of a bureaucracy—the Department of Social Security. Many criticisms can be levelled at this organisation, and the policies it implements. However, given the task of processing claims for many millions of dollars every week, on behalf of several million people, in a large country, is there a viable alternative to an extensive body of rules and regulations, a hierarchical structure to maintain control, and an impersonal (in the sense of not favouring or discriminating against individuals on the basis of racial, gender, regional or ethnic characteristics) approach?

Similar issues can be raised about many other human service tasks, although the extent to which a service is relatively routine (such as processing social security payments) or relatively non-routine (such as marriage counselling) is an important variable. The key point to consider is whether human services can be provided effectively, efficiently, equitably, and in an accountable manner, other than through organisations that have some bureaucratic features.

Workers also need to understand the significance of Weber's emphasis on the importance of legal–rational authority in modern societies and organisations. Legal–rational authority is a basic and characteristic feature of almost all organisations in which workers are likely to be employed: in this sense, almost all workers are located in bureaucracies. Understanding the nature and bases of authority is important for social and welfare workers who are themselves both subject to and part of the authority systems of organisations.

Finally, Weber's concerns about the concentration of power in bureaucracies and the difficulties of holding bureaucracies to account are highly relevant to those in the human services who are concerned with the power that bureaucratic organisations exercise over consumers and the society as a whole. It may be that developing means of controlling the power of bureaucratic organisations is a more relevant and pressing concern than bureaucratisation as such. As Perrow suggests:

> When we attribute the ills of organizations and those of our society to the bureaucratization of large-scale organizations, as we are so wont to do, we may be only fooling ourselves . . . The presence of hierarchy, rules, division of labor, tenure provisions, and so on can hardly be blamed for maladministration or abuses of social power . . . Critics, then, of our organisational society . . . had best turn to the key issue of who controls the varied forms of power generated by organizations, rather than flail away at the windmills of bureaucracy (1986, pp. 46-47).

Scientific management

Weber wrote about the causes and consequences of the dominance of bureaucratic organisation in the early twentieth century, although it was not until mid-century that his work was translated into English and gained currency in the English speaking world. Meanwhile, an extensive and influential body of writing about organisations had developed, particularly in the United States. The first dominant perspective to emerge was scientific management, the principles of which were enunciated by Frederic W. Taylor in 1911. Scientific management was a response to the needs of the managers and owners of industrial enterprises in the United States to increase productivity and profits, and exercise control over labour (Clegg and Dunkerley 1980, pp. 82-86). While Weber's perspective was broad-ranging and concerned with social explanation and analysis, scientific management was narrowly focused on the needs and concerns of the managers of industry. Taylor, whose background was in mechanical engineering, essentially approached organisations as machines requiring careful design and fine-tuning. He argued that there was always one best way to perform any task or industrial process, and that this could be discovered by scientific observation and experiment. His view was that through time and motion studies, and careful study of job techniques and work processes, industrial production could become more efficient and management could become a truly scientific activity (Mouzelis 1975, pp. 79-83).

Underlying Taylorism were a number of important assumptions about the nature of organisations and the purposes of organisation theory. His model of organisation as machine assumed that there were no inherent conflicts between management and workers, or among any other groups in the organisation. Taylor saw trade unions as unnecessary because workers and management shared common interests. He also assumed that workers were motivated essentially by financial rewards and that their attitude to work was essentially instrumental; psychological and sociological aspects of the worker were largely ignored in Taylor's organisation theory. Taylor sharply distinguished between management, who had responsibility for planning, organising, supervising and making decisions, and workers, who were viewed essentially as adjuncts to the industrial machinery and as being without knowledge of organisational goals and processes. The role of management theory, as Taylor presented it, was to assist the former to organise and control the latter, in order to maximise productivity.

Closely related to the theories of scientific management are the writings often collectively referred to as the 'formal theories of administration' or 'classical management theory'. While Taylor was concerned primarily with the organisation of work on the factory floor,

Fayol, Gulick and Urwick and other formal theorists directed their attentions to the overall structure of organisations. Writing mainly in the inter-war period, they developed principles that, they argued, should guide organisational design. These included precepts such as the importance of the division of labour (the assumption that the more people specialise, the more efficient they will be), unity of command (each employee should receive direction for a particular operation from only one person), clear lines of authority, span of control (limits on the number of people to be supervised by one person) and the division of work according to established principles (that is by purpose, place, person or consumer or process) (Mouzelis 1975, pp. 87-96; Stoner, Collins and Yetton 1985, pp. 44-51).

Why should social and welfare workers concern themselves with these theories of organisation developed over fifty years ago mainly in the context of industrial management? The reason is that the aspirations and approach underlying the scientific management and classical management perspectives continue to be important influences on managerial thinking and behaviour, and on the operation of contemporary human service organisations. Organisation theory has developed, not by way of earlier theories being superseded by newer perspectives, but rather by way of additional ingredients being added to the existing concoction. While some elements of Taylorism, for example its theory of human motivation, have been largely superseded, the basic notion of viewing organisations as machines requiring careful design and fine-tuning is still influential, alongside other perspectives.

This influence has been particularly felt in public sector organisations during the last two decades. In this period, revised versions of scientific management have become fashionable in public administration, including human service administration. Workers in many organisational contexts find that their tasks and roles are shaped to a not inconsiderable degree by demands for performance measurement, programme budgeting, corporate planning, programme evaluation, outcome standards, effectiveness review, systems management, efficiency audit, management information systems, management by objectives, and so on. Patti refers to such management techniques as 'the new scientific management', arguing that they reflect the historical concerns of scientific management with rationalising organisational structures and processes to achieve efficiency and effectiveness (1978). Fabricant has argued that fiscal restraint and the dominance of Taylorist principles during the 1980s has led to the industrialisation of social work, that is its transformation from a craft activity to a form of repetitive, routinised people-processing (1985, p. 394). In the Australian public administration literature, commitment to the value of such techniques has been dubbed 'managerialism' (Considine 1988; Paterson 1988). The implications of managerialism for social and welfare workers are considered in detail in chapter 11.

Dominant values in social and welfare work sometimes lead workers to resile from viewing organisations in mechanistic terms. But if human service organisations are viewed in part as instruments to achieve certain desired social purposes, then it can be strongly argued that their effectiveness and efficiency are relevant and legitimate concerns. However, an unqualified mechanistic view of organisations is inadequate, viewed either from a managerial or a broader social science perspective. Mechanistic perspectives on organisations tend to treat organisational goals as unambiguous and mutually compatible, which is often not the case in human service organisations. They also tend to erroneously assume common goals and interests among organisational participants, and ignore or down-play their complexity of motives and aspirations. Organisations may, for some purposes, be usefully viewed as machines, but they are not only machines. Knowledge of other perspectives which draw attention to the complexity of social relations in organisations is also required.

Human relations

The prescriptions of Taylor and early scientific management were directed by a concern to maximise productivity and profits, maintain control over workers, and generally promote efficiency and effectiveness. These remain fundamental concerns of much organisation and management theory. However, in the mid-twentieth century the dominant position of scientific management was challenged by the human relations perspective.

The human relations approach emerged out of dissatisfaction with scientific management's theory of human motivation. Conventional accounts of the origins of human relations stress the importance of the experiments conducted in the 1920s in a factory of the Western Electric Company in Hawthorne, an area of Chicago (Etzioni 1964, pp. 32-41). The Hawthorne experiments, as they became known, were initially concerned with the relation between the physical working environment, for example lighting and worker productivity. However, their findings led the researchers to conclude that the key variables influencing output were not physical, but social. The researchers also concluded that social psychological factors were of greater significance than monetary rewards in motivating workers. Although more recently there has been considerable questioning of the methodology and interpretation of the Hawthorne experiments (Clegg and Dunkerley 1980, pp. 129-130; Perrow 1986, pp. 79-85), the central notion underpinning these studies—that social and psychological factors are crucial determinants of productivity—has sustained a great deal of the organisation and management theory written from the 1930s to the present day.

The human relations approach to the understanding of organisations can be summarised in terms of two main propositions.

The first is the need to distinguish between the formal and the informal structure and functioning of an organisation. The focus in scientific management and, in a different way, Weber's bureaucratic theory was predominantly on the formal aspects of organisations—rules, division of work, hierarchy and so forth. Human relations writers, by contrast, emphasise topics such as leadership styles, morale, and group interactions and relationships. Organisations, they argue, cannot be understood solely in terms of what appears on the organisation chart: the informal human relations in an organisation are critical determinants of organisational processes and outcomes.

There can be no argument in general terms about the need to understand and take account of social relations in organisations. This was an innovative idea in the 1920s and 1930s and is now accepted as commonplace. This fact alone testifies to the lasting influence of writers in the human relations tradition. However, the second main proposition that emerges from the writings of the human relations school is more contentious. Many human relations proponents present an ideal model of organisation and management, involving a perfect balancing of organisational goals and workers' needs. The task of management, as they see it, is to develop organisational structures and processes according to the supposed social and psychological needs of workers, so that workers thereby become more committed to organisational goals and to increasing effectiveness and efficiency (Holland and Petchers 1987, p. 206). In this approach, human beings are assumed to have a high capability for creativity and personal growth and to be strongly motivated by a desire for self-expression and self-actualisation (e.g. Argyris 1971). These qualities tend to be stifled, it is argued, by formal, bureaucratic organisations. Therefore, what is required is a more facilitative work and organisational environment, characterised by group participation in decision-making, and leadership styles that are democratic, permissive and considerate. Worker autonomy and participative management are key themes, and a wide range of organisational change techniques have been developed based on the human relations perspective, including T-groups, sensitivity training, survey feedback and other organisational development (OD) methods.

This model of management has often been stated in terms that sharply distinguish so-called classical management theory and the human relations approach. A good example is the dichotomy that has been drawn by McGregor, a prominent human relations theorist, between Theory X and Theory Y. Theory X, McGregor suggests, is the 'traditional view of direction and control' in organisations. This approach assumes that human beings have an inherent dislike of work and will avoid it if they can. As a consequence, it is held that most people need to be coerced, controlled, directed, and threatened with punishment to get them to put effort into achieving organisational goals. An implicit assumption is that people prefer to be directed, wish to avoid responsibility, have little ambition, and want security above all else. Most organisations, McGregor argued, make Theory X assumptions.

In contrast, Theory Y is based on 'the integration of individual and organisational goals'. It assumes that the expenditure of physical and mental effort in work is as natural as play or rest, and that people will exercise self-direction and self-control in the service of objectives to which they are committed. Human beings can learn, under proper conditions, to accept and seek responsibility, and managers should be constantly striving to utilise the human potentialities of organisational members (McGregor 1971).

The approach and prescriptions of the human relations school have considerable intuitive and ideological appeal to many workers. The optimistic value system and view of humanity, the emphasis on co-operation, participation and consensus, and the prominence given to interpersonal relations are all consonant with values widely held by social and welfare workers. While scientific management makes organisations sound like machines, human relations makes them sound like families or communities, far more familiar phenomena for social and welfare workers.

Undoubtedly, the prescriptions and insights of writers in this tradition are often helpful, and there can be no questioning of the importance of paying attention to the needs of the individuals that comprise an organisation. But how adequate is the human relations perspective as an overall framework for understanding the nature of organisations and organisational life?

Firstly, it needs to be stressed that while the focus of the human relations approach is, at first sight, on the needs of workers, the central concerns are traditional management issues, namely, productivity and control. The human relations approach, like scientific management before it, assumes or asserts that there is no fundamental conflict of interests between management and workers, or among any other groups or factions within the organisation. The message is that if everyone co-operates, everyone wins. This assumption of basic, common interests and goals within organisations is strongly challenged by other perspectives, which consider it to be manipulative. For example, group processes, consultation and participative mechanisms can be, and often are, used by managers as essentially symbolic activities. Induction programmes, socialisation processes and attempts to manufacture a 'corporate culture' are all management strategies that have as one central purpose the maximising of control. Clegg and Dunkerley argue that the main contribution of human relations theorists has been to 'produce a highly developed ideological apparatus of normative control . . . for the management of organisations' (1980, p. 135).

In addition, major questions have been raised about the major tenets of the human relations approach. The supposed empirical relationship between worker satisfaction and the quality and quantity of organisational outputs has not survived close scrutiny (for a trenchant critique see Perrow 1986, pp. 79-110). The quality of human relations in an organisation is no doubt a factor in effectiveness and productivity, although what constitutes 'good' human relations is an issue for debate. But other influences on effectiveness include the clarity of technology and procedures, the level of organisational resources and staff competency, economic reward structures, accountability procedures, and the quality of facilities and equipment, to name a few. Thus, a major difficulty with the human relations school is its narrow focus and concerns, and its implicit assumptions of the shared interests of all organisational participants.

Table 2.1 draws together the main propositions, discussion questions and implications of the three perspectives examined so far in the chapter. Bureaucratic theory, scientific management and human relations, although representing competing perspectives, can be viewed as the basic building blocks of twentieth century organisation theory. The issues they raise—authority, formal structure and human motivations and relationships—are fundamental elements in any comprehensive theory of organisations. However, other key dimensions need to be added to the picture.

Systems and ecological perspectives

Most contributors to the scientific management and human relations schools wrote from a managerial perspective. Their main concerns were productivity and efficiency. The emergence of systems perspectives on organisations in the 1950s and 1960s re-introduced a broader sociological focus. The systems view of organisations emerged from themes and perspectives then dominant in American sociology, particularly structural functionalism and general systems theory (Clegg and Dunkerley 1980, pp. 171-212). Underlying the systems perspective is a biological analogy:

> Social institutions, in much the same way as organisms, have needs of survival and adaptation to their environment which they satisfy by means of a particular pattern of interdependence between their parts. Viewed as Natural Systems, organisations are composed of an inter-related series of processes: it is the inter-relationship and the process . . . which should constitute the object of study (Silverman 1970, p. 27).

Whereas in scientific management the organisation is perceived as a machine, and in human relations a family, in systems theory the organisation is perceived as an organism.

The idea of viewing organisations in systems terms has considerable relevance for social and welfare workers. This perspective brings into focus three key issues: the emphasis on interdependency in

Table 2.1 Implications of bureaucratic theory, scientific management and human relations perspectives for social and welfare workers

Propositions	*Questions*	*Implications*
	BUREAUCRACY	
1 Legal–rational authority is fundamental to power relations in modern societies	1 Is bureaucracy necessary for efficient and equitable service provision?	1 Understand the nature of authority in organisations
2 Bureaucracy is the organisational form corresponding to legal–rational authority	2 Do writers on bureaucracy ignore informal processes in organisations?	2 Consider the relations between bureaucracy, efficiency and effectiveness
		3 Be concerned with harnessing and controlling the power of bureaucracies
	SCIENTIFIC MANAGEMENT	
1 Organisations can be thought of as machines requiring fine-tuning	1 Whose interests is scientific management concerned with?	1 Be aware of formal organisational structures and processes
2 Formal structures and processes are critical to organisational functioning	2 Does it ignore informal processes and conflicting interests?	2 Be concerned with issues of efficiency and effectiveness
	3 Does it have an adequate theory of human motivation?	3 Be able to critique and respond effectively to contemporary 'managerialist' demands
	HUMAN RELATIONS	
1 Social and psycho-logical factors are important in organisations	1 Whose interests are served by human relations theories?	1 Be aware of informal relations in organisations
2 It is important to distinguish formal and informal processes in organisations	2 What is the relationship between worker satisfaction and effectiveness?	2 Develop effective informal relations with other organisational participants
3 Organisations should be designed to meet the social psychological needs of workers		3 Understand the assumptions underlying human relations techniques

organisations, the idea of organisational needs, and the significance of organisational environment.

Fundamental to the systems approach is its stress on the interdependence of the various elements and units that comprise the organisation. This means that the internal operations and processes of an organisation should be viewed as

> a network of interacting, overlapping, conflicting or co-operating sub-systems or interdependent parts, each part receiving something from others, influenced by the behaviour of others, and itself behaving in ways which have consequences both for other sub-systems and for the organisation as a whole (Warham 1977, p. 72).

What this suggests to workers is that their actions and decisions are inextricably bound up with the actions of other organisational members and the overall organisation. They, in common with all other organisational participants, are not independent operators.

This proposition at first sight may appear unremarkable. However, this notion of interdependency challenges some widely held views in social and welfare work. Social work and organisations are sometimes portrayed dichotomously as having only conflicting or divergent interests. This is sometimes expressed in terms of tension between professional and organisational orientations (e.g. Briar and Miller 1971, pp. 99-102; Compton and Galaway 1989, pp. 483-484), and sometimes in terms of the worker as change agent in a largely hostile or recalcitrant organisational setting (e.g. Galper 1975, pp. 195-208; Compton and Galaway 1989, pp. 491-494). Both of these conceptions have some value and raise important issues, and are discussed in chapters 8 and 10. However, both views neglect or down-play the interdependence of social and welfare workers and organisations. The systems view of organisations suggests that there is a symbiotic relationship between organisations and workers, that is, their union is either necessary or advantageous to both. It suggests that workers need to view themselves as involved in organisations in a dynamic and interactive way, exercising influence and expecting, in turn, to be influenced by other organisational participants.

Another key element of the systems perspective is its emphasis on organisational needs. In the systems view, organisations are not viewed primarily as rational instruments to achieve specified goals, rather they are social systems which, like biological systems, need to survive, adapt and grow. Systems theorists have identified at a theoretical level the functional requirements (needs) that an organisation must meet in order to survive and grow (Mouzelis 1975, pp. 150-151). These include both external and internal requirements. External needs include the resources to carry out organisational functions (such as facilities, money, consumers) and the sanction of the community. Internal needs include the integration of the elements or units that comprise the organisation, the loyalty or commitment of personnel, and the technical and political capacity to mobilise and deploy resources.

The idea of organisations having needs has difficulties, which will shortly be discussed. However, the idea is useful for workers in two main ways. Firstly, it suggests some ways that workers can build their influence in organisations. It has been argued that one source of influence for individuals or groups within organisations is their contribution to the functioning of the organisation (Pfeffer 1981, p. 98). If this is so, it follows that if workers wish to extend their organisational influence, one important strategy is to identify organisational needs and endeavour to play a role in meeting these needs. For example, a worker may have skills in group processes which can be used to deal with inter-unit tensions within an organisation. Or a worker may develop skills in submission writing or media relations which could assist the organisation in dealing with its external needs. The reputation and standing acquired in these ways can be drawn on to influence other organisational processes.

An awareness of an organisation's needs also assists workers to understand processes of organisational change. It is often the case that organisational needs for survival and growth are in conflict with the ostensible purposes of the organisation. Organisational activities are shaped, not only, or even mainly in many cases, by formal goals and structures, but also by the 'myriad subterranean processes of informal groups, conflict between groups, recruitment policies, dependencies on outside groups and constituencies, the striving for prestige, community values, the local community power structure, and legal institutions' (Perrow 1986, p. 159). The systems view suggests that organisations, as living, dynamic systems, adapt to these factors and in the process often become diverted from their intended mission.

The last of the key issues raised by the systems perspective is the significance of organisational environment. In the systems perspective, organisations are portrayed as engaging in ongoing exchanges with the other organisations in their environment, taking in resources of various kinds, together with instructions both implicit and explicit, and transforming the resources into goods and services of various kinds (Warham 1977, p. 72). Adapting to the requirements of external groups shapes the goals, structure, culture and services of an organisation in ways that are often disputed, resented or resisted by groups and individuals within the organisation. These processes are examined in detail in chapter 4.

Systems theory provides a more dynamic, complex, holistic picture of organisations than either the human relations or scientific management perspectives. It provides social and welfare workers with important insights into the interconnectedness of organisations, organisational needs and the impact of environmental factors. But it too has shortcomings. Some writers have argued that the elements that comprise organisations are not necessarily as interdependent as the model suggests. Some parts of an organisation may have a relatively high level of functional autonomy, and may survive quite well even though separated from other parts of the organisation. The level of interdependence in any particular organisation is something to be investigated rather than assumed (Clegg and Dunkerley 1980, p. 208). It has also been claimed that the systems view underemphasises the rational and planned aspects of organisations. Many processes in organisations are rationally designed to achieve particular objectives, rather than simply being responses to organisational needs. As was suggested by Weber, this rationality can itself be a force leading to the growth and stability of organisations.

The systems approach can also be criticised for presenting an overly deterministic and reified perspective on organisations. While there may be value in thinking about organisations as if they are organisms with needs to be met, they are not in fact biological entities any more than they are machines or families. 'Organisations do not react to their environment, their members do' (Silverman 1970, p. 37). The actions of individuals in organisations are certainly influenced by their perceptions of the needs and circumstances of the organisation as a whole, as individual interests are bound up with the interests of the overall organisation. But the basic needs or requirements of the organisation can be met in a variety of ways. Different individuals and groups, with differing 'predispositions' (Silverman 1970, p. 36), will adopt a diversity of approaches to meeting these needs with varying consequences and degrees of success.

Finally, it should be noted that systems theory is concerned primarily with issues of integration and interdependence in organisations, rather than with issues of conflict and dissent. There is an underlying assumption that organisations seek to achieve balance and equilibrium, both externally with the environment and internally among the constituent parts of the organisation. This is, at best, only a partial picture of the functioning of organisations. 'An assumed tendency towards the resolution of conflict . . . need not operate if it does not suit the interests of the participants' (Silverman 1970, p. 39). Organisations, and groups within organisations, do not always adjust to changes to increase integration and balance, although extensive, ongoing, unresolved conflict usually has major costs in terms of organisational survival and growth (Bacharach 1983, p. 361).

A recent development in organisation theory, which shares some common themes with systems theory, is the ecological or human ecology model of organisations. In this perspective, organisations are viewed in ways analogous to the analysis of animal life by naturalists or bioecologists (Pugh and Hickson 1989, p. 67). The focus is on the ways that environments create conditions that result in certain populations of organisations either surviving and thriving or dying out. The theory is mainly concerned with populations of similar organisations, rather than with individual organisations. It examines such issues as the ability of organisations to adapt to changing environmental conditions, the competition for resources in a particular environment, and the 'carrying capacity' of each 'niche' in an environment. The environment is viewed as the main determinant of the kinds of organisations that exist in a particular society.

The ecological model could be applied to attempts to understand the emergence of new types of human service organisations, and the competitive struggle that often occurs among similar organisations in the human services field. For example, the proliferation of publicly funded community-based organisations during the 1970s and early 1980s could be described in terms of favourable environmental circumstances such as an expanding public sector, many gaps in the service network, availability of host organisations to sponsor services, and so forth. It could be argued that as growth in the public sector slows, it will be those organisations most adaptable to changing circumstances that will survive and grow. Hence, organisations able to act in more entrepreneurial ways to take advantage of trends towards the privatisation of human services may be best suited to the environment of the 1990s. The emergence of a new class of private sector human service organisations in niches created by these changed environmental circumstances could be predicted by the ecological model.

The criticisms th1at can be levelled at the ecological model in the context of human services parallel the criticisms of systems theory. Firstly, at a practice level, managers and workers in human service organisations should not be concerned simply with survival and growth of their organisations. For example, there may be important value, policy and political reasons why the members of a community-based organisation would not choose to adapt to the more entrepreneurial climate of the 1990s, preferring to take their chances in a hostile environment. Secondly, ecological theories tend to reify the environment, treating it as a unified whole which acts in some real sense. The alternative view, elaborated on in chapter 4, is that environment is a concept referring to a multiplicity of other organisations and circumstances. Finally, ecological theories tend to be determinist, and to neglect the capacity of organisations to shape and, in some cases, dominate their environment. We conclude with Perrow that systems and ecological perspectives can be useful, provided that 'the disabling assumptions of biology are removed' (Perrow 1986, p. 218).

Decision perspectives

Another way of looking at organisations is as decision-making systems. Decision theories of organisations were first formulated in detail in the late-1940s by Herbert Simon, and important developments in this approach have continued through to the 1980s. The idea of focusing on decisions as a means of understanding organisations has considerable appeal. Many of our experiences of organisations, especially human service organisations, involve decisions. Certainly, social and welfare workers, like many other participants in organisations, make decisions all the time. Should this sole parent be supported in her application for a pension? Should a court order be requested to remove this child from home? Should this young person with a drug dependency be admitted to the treatment programme? Should a recommendation be made for this prisoner to be paroled? Decisions are central in organisational life because of the intended, purposive nature of organisations. 'When people co-ordinate their activities for the attainment of a certain goal, they have continuously to take decisions, to choose among alternatives of action . . . A member of an organisation . . . is a decision-maker and a problem solver' (Mouzelis 1975, p. 123).

The decision perspective aims to elucidate the nature of decision-making in organisations. The importance of this topic for workers is apparent. As social and welfare workers are continually involved in making decisions, it is important for them to understand the nature of the process. Is decision-making in organisations rational, irrational or a mix of the two? What are the influences of organisations on decisions made by organisational members? Do the professional, 'textbook' models of how decisions should be made actually occur?

The decision-making literature is centrally concerned with the question of rationality. Scientific management and bureaucratic theory stress rationality as a central or defining characteristic of organisations. In contrast, human relations and systems theory present a rather more human, complex and messy picture. Decision theory suggests a middle course. It depicts organisations as comprised of individuals who are 'intendedly rational', that is they attempt to arrive at decisions based on clear goals and a comprehensive examination of the range of alternative means to achieve these goals. Complete rationality is, however, an impossibility. This is because individuals do not know the full range of alternative actions available to them, do not know the possible consequences of each alternative, and lack the resources (time, information, and knowledge of the future) to obtain this information. Their rationality is intended but bounded (Hasenfeld 1983, p. 29).

How then do individuals in organisations make decisions? The answer, according to Simon and other decision theorists, is that they develop routines and attempt to simplify.

. . . they conduct a *limited* search for alternatives along familiar and well-worn paths, selecting the first satisfactory one that comes along. They do not examine all possible alternatives, nor do they keep searching for the optimum one. Rather, they 'satisfice', or select the first satisfactory solution (Perrow 1986, p. 122).

To express it another way, individuals search for decisions that 'will do', rather than for the decision that is 'the best'.

This view raises a number of important questions about the nature of the decisions made by social and welfare workers in organisations. Professional models of practice prescribe a highly rational, often sequential, process of decision-making based on careful analysis of the problem from the consumer's perspective, and goal setting and intervention based on this information and the corpus of professional knowledge (e.g. Compton and Galaway 1979). But how common or typical is this process? Do workers really do what the theory says they should do? Faced with limited time and inadequate knowledge, do workers, like other members of organisations, make do with satisfactory rather than optimal decisions? If so, what influences their idea of what constitutes 'satisfactory'?

On this last question, decision theorists stress the key role of the organisation in determining the premises, or the basic assumptions, of decisions. While workers may be strongly committed to professional, consumer-centred decision-making, this perspective suggests that in actuality the parameters of their decisions are often defined by the organisation. Hasenfeld argues that the espoused models of the professional helping process, as found in the social casework literature, are myth:

Such a model ignores the fundamental fact that the entire helping process is anchored in an organizational context and that every decision made by the professional is influenced by such organizational variables as program content and structure, consumer eligibility criteria, organizational vocabulary, standard operating procedures, communication patterns, and the interdependencies of units within the organization (1983, p. 30).

The implications of this for workers are challenging and profound. Firstly, the argument, developed in chapter 1, that social and welfare work must be conceptualised as an organisational and a professional activity is underlined. The analysis suggests that workers usually operate in terms of procedures, concepts and criteria that derive from the organisation in which they work as well as from the profession to which they belong. Workers, it is argued, do not typically act as free-standing professionals with freedom to choose their consumers, their approach to defining problems and their therapeutic methods. This is particularly so in organisations where social and welfare workers are not dominant.

The role of the organisation in setting the parameters of workers' decisions is also important in understanding the nature of organisational control. The Weberian model of bureaucracy suggests that organisations control their participants through rules and commands based on and legitimised through rational–legal authority. Decision theorists add to this an emphasis on 'unobtrusive controls' (Perrow 1986, pp. 128–130). Individuals and groups in organisations are often controlled, not by the blunt and ham-fisted methods of orders and surveillance, but by control of the premises on which decisions are made. If organisations can induce individuals to voluntarily agree or acquiesce in treating certain issues as irrelevant or certain options as impossible, organisational control can be achieved with a high level of efficiency and effectiveness. It is essential for workers to be aware of this form of organisational control, to be able to make calculated and negotiated decisions about the parameters of their activities.

Workers in organisations are involved in making decisions not only about consumers (as discussed above), but also about organisational goals and processes and the allocation of resources. They attend staff meetings, sit on committees and boards of management, and get appointed to working parties to address organisational problems. These kinds of decision-making processes also are the concern of decision theories of organisations. In our experience, social and welfare workers often complain about the apparent irrationality of organisational decision-making processes. Decision theory suggests some of the reasons for this and proposes models of how organisational decisions are made.

One of the most evocative of these is the 'garbage-can' model. According to this model, organisations are often faced with great uncertainty, especially when their goals are vague and conflicting and their techniques are uncertain. In these circumstances, the decision-process resembles a garbage-can into which problems, solutions and interests are tossed, often in quite random ways. For example, funds may become available for a programme that does not of itself have a high priority in terms of consumers' needs, but which provides the opportunity to continue the employment of a valued staff member and to enhance the organisation's ailing public image. For these reasons, the funds are accepted. Over time, the programme becomes quite successful and this leads to organisational resources being channelled to the new programme area. These actions are then justified in terms of the organisation's flexibility in meeting new community and consumer needs.

Decision theories such as the garbage-can model can be criticised for over-emphasising the random, bargained and accidental nature of organisational decisions. In reality, organisations are constrained by such factors as their budget, their environment and their history (ever-present in the form of rules, records, and people with long memories and commitments), and most issues are not up for negotiation and decision-making at any one point in time. As an overall perspective on organisations, decision theory has other limitations. It does not explain why organisations are structured as they are, and pays relatively little attention to the impact of organisational environment. However, the idea of viewing organisations, and organisational participants such as social and welfare workers, as decision-makers coping as best they can with uncertainty is intriguing and not a little disturbing. It challenges the assumed rationality of such work as portrayed in some texts.

Market perspectives

A contemporary challenge to our implicit theories of organisations has come in the 1980s from economists arguing that we should view organisations from the perspective of free market economics. Expressed in basic terms, this perspective proposes that organisations can be best understood as comprising individuals competitively pursuing their self-interest (for a detailed discussion see Perrow 1986, pp. 219-257). Organisations consist in essence of a series of contracts, and organisational analysis is concerned centrally with the terms, conditions and circumstances of these contracts. On the basis of these propositions, economic analysts have constructed elaborate theories purporting to explain organisational behaviour.

Viewing organisations as marketplaces draws our attention to the role of transactions and individual interests in organisations. From a market perspective, relations within organisations involve economic-like transactions, in which the various parties, each pursuing their individual interests, give and receive benefits. Take the decision by a hospital to employ a social or welfare worker. A market perspective suggests that this decision is taken because it is believed that this will be of benefit to the organisation, or, more particularly, to groups within the organisation. That is, social and welfare workers employed by a hospital may be perceived as assisting other occupational groups, such as doctors, to perform their work more effectively or expeditiously. While the employment of the workers will be presented in terms of their usefulness in providing services to patients, the market perspective suggests that the real explanation is to be found in group and individual interests.

The worker accepting employment in the hospital will also bring a set of expectations to the relationship. At a personal level, the worker may be looking for a steady income, attractive working conditions, security and some status and privileges. Professionally, the worker may desire a relatively high degree of autonomy, the chance to work in his or her field of interest, the opportunity to practise certain kinds of skills or opportunities to supervise other workers. The market perspective suggests that the decision to join and participate in such an organisation is based on a calculation that this is personally worthwhile for some such combination of reasons.

The market perspective views transactions of this kind as the essence of organisational life. Sometimes these transactions take the form of a formalised, written contract, but more often they are implicit relations. They may be long-term, as in the example of the employment contract between a social worker and a hospital, or they may be 'spot' contracts, such as a brief interaction between a worker and a consumer. Individuals have contracts with all other parties that they deal with in the organisation. 'The [organisation] is little more than a bundle of bilateral agreements, free to be broken by any party and freely entered on' (Perrow 1986, p. 223).

The idea of viewing organisations as markets in which individuals pursue their self-interest does not sit comfortably with the personal and professional ideology of most social and welfare workers. Social and welfare workers tend to be uncomfortable with self-interest, particularly their own (we were recently told by the recruiting officer for a large government department that the question graduating social workers conspicuously fail to ask at job interviews is, 'How much will I be paid?'). It is important to recognise, however, that self-interested behaviour is a feature, to a greater or lesser degree, of all organisations. The organisational effectiveness of workers depends in part on their capacity to negotiate effective transactions with other groups and individuals in the organisation, based on a recognition of the interests of all parties concerned.

However, as an overall approach to understanding organisations, the market approach has major limitations. The underlying assumption that people are driven only by self-interest must be challenged. While self-interest obviously motivates everyone to some degree, it is also the case that the behaviour of almost all individuals is motivated to varying degrees by respect and concern for others. It can be further argued that the extent to which individual behaviour in organisations is self-interested or other-regarding is strongly influenced by organisational structures and conditions. Perrow raises the key issue:

> The principal assumption of [market] theory is that people maximize individual utilities, defined as reward (generally monetary) minus effort. I would . . . like to treat this assumption as a variable: Under what conditions will people in organizations maximize their own utilities regardless of the consequences for others, and when will they forgo an increase in utility or even suffer a loss because of the consequences for others? (1986, p. 232).

This is a key point to which we return later in the book. A considerable number of social and welfare workers are involved in organisations such as co-operatives, collectives and community-based organisations that are deliberately structured to enhance behaviour based on co-operation, reciprocity, trust and equality. Many others strive to develop collegial and co-operative relations within organisations where conditions favour and reward self-regarding behaviour. Reconciling these aspirations with the need to transact effectively with other organisational participants with differing interests and ideologies is a major issue for workers in many contexts.

A further fundamental flaw of the market perspective is its almost total indifference to issues of inequalities of power and resources in organisations. Even if it is accepted that it is useful for some purposes to seeing organisations as accumulations of transactions, it cannot be assumed that the marketplace is free or that participants trade on an even or a fair basis. As we shall see shortly, issues of power, authority and influence are considered by many analysts to be central in organisational analysis, and a perspective that neglects such issues is open to serious criticism.

Table 2.2 summarises the main propositions, issues and practice implications arising from the systems, ecological, decision and market perspectives on organisations. These approaches are similar in so far as they present a picture of organisational life focused on one key concept. Thinking of organisations as organic systems, decision-making mechanisms and sets of transactions adds to our understanding of organisations, provided we recognise the limits and difficulties associated with each approach.

Neo-Marxian perspectives

Marxian sociology had little impact on the study of organisations in the Western world until the 1970s and 1980s. Zey-Ferrell and Aiken argue that this was in large part a result of the kinds of questions dominant in writings on organisations prior to that time. Marxian analysis was not primarily concerned with questions relating to the internal functioning of organisations, or the relations between organisations and their immediate environments. However, 'as organisational analysts have begun to address societal issues of social change, social control, the consequences of domination of powerful economic organisations, class relations, and the like, the Marxian perspective has become increasingly relevant and important' (Zey-Ferrell and Aiken 1981, p. 230). The main strength of the Marxian perspective is its emphasis on the relations between organisations and dominant groups in the society and economy, and the ways in which these shape organisational processes.

Marx's account of the organisational changes that occurred in capitalist societies in the nineteenth century differs markedly from Weber's analysis which we considered earlier. Whereas Weber argued that modern forms of organisation could be understood in terms of the emergence of legal–rational authority, Marx emphasised that modes of organisation, as in, for example, the factory system, developed as means of exploiting and controlling workers and the labour process (Zey-Ferrell and Aiken 1981, pp. 121-122; Clegg and Dunkerley 1980,

Table 2.2 Implications of systems, ecological, decision and market perspectives for social and welfare workers

Propositions	*Questions*	*Practice implications*
	SYSTEMS PERSPECTIVES	
1 The elements and units that comprise an organisation are interdependent and interacting	1 Is interdependence over-emphasised?	1 Be aware of interdependence with other organisational participants
2 Organisations are social systems with needs (functional requirements) that must be met for survival and growth	2 Are rationality and planning under-emphasised? 3 Is the approach over-deterministic? 4 Is there too much emphasis on integration, and not enough on conflict and dissent?	2 Be aware of the organisation's 'needs', and of how influence can be acquired by responding to those needs
3 Relations with the environment are crucial		3 Understand environmental influences on the organisation
	ECOLOGICAL PERSPECTIVE	
1 The environment is the main determinant of the kinds of organisations that exist in a society	1 Should survival and growth by adapting to environmental circumstances be the primary considera-tion? 2 Does the approach neglect the capacity of some organisations to shape their environ-ment?	1 Be aware of the changing nature of the organisational environment, so that decisions can be made about adapting to new circumstances and opportunities
	DECISION PERSPECTIVES	
1 Organisations are decision-making systems	1 Is the random nature of organisational decision-making over-emphasised?	1 Be aware of 'unobtrusive control' via the premises of decision-making
2 Individuals in organisations make satisfactory rather than 'rational' decisions	2 Does the approach fail to account for key factors such as structure and environment?	2 Understand the actual nature of the decision-making process in the organisation

Propositions	*Questions*	*Practice implications*
3 Organisations determine the premises of decision-making		3 Develop skills in making professional decisions in an organisational context
4 Organisational decision-making resembles the 'garbage can' model		

Market Perspectives

1 Individuals in organisations pursue their self-interest	1 Are individuals in organisations motivated only by self-interest?	1 Be aware of the role of self-interest in organisations
2 Transactions between individuals are the essence of organisational life	2 Is the organisational marketplace free and fair?	2 Understand the influence of organisational factors on self-interested/other-regarding behaviour
3 The market in organisations is the best means of allocating resources	3 Is the market an efficient and equitable means of allocating of resources	
	4 Does this perspective neglect the central role of power, authority and influence in organisations?	

pp. 33-70). Similarly, in his theory of the state, Marx emphasised the ways in which the state serves the interests of the ruling capitalist class (Mouzelis 1975, pp. 8-11; Etzioni-Halevy 1983, pp. 9-13). Marx viewed the state bureaucracy as an instrument of capital, which would subsequently 'wither away' after the revolution, with the advent of a communist society. This is a different emphasis from Weber, who viewed bureaucracy as a necessary feature of all modern, industrialised societies.

Contemporary Marxian writers similarly emphasise the importance of analysing organisations in terms of their role and place in capitalist society. The defining characteristic of capitalist societies is the private ownership of the means of production. Classical Marxism postulated that private ownership gives rise to two main classes, the owners of the means of production and the workers, whose interests conflict. Contemporary Marxian analysis argues that, although class relations in modern capitalist societies have become far more complex than this, much social and organisational life can still be explained in terms of the conflicting class interests that stem from the capitalist mode of production (for a brief overview of Marxian and other theories of class see Western 1983, pp. 13-39).

The organisations in which most social and welfare workers are employed are generally not directly involved in economic production. However, neo-Marxians argue that, because human service organisations function within a capitalist system of production, they are structurally constrained to serve the interests of capitalism. Fundamental to this analysis is the argument that because of their dependence on a successful economic base for their existence, their functions are inevitably shaped by the interests of the capitalist system as a whole. Human service organisations, it is argued, serve these interests in a number of ways. They assist the processes of capitalist production and accumulation by ensuring a healthy, educated, and available labour force. They provide legitimacy for capitalist societies by conveying the appearance of a caring and humanitarian society despite the persistence of inequality and poverty. They contribute to the maintenance of the status quo by assisting in the processes of maintaining order and control in society, and through reinforcement of the norms and values of capitalist societies, such as the work ethic. Finally, they tend to reproduce and reinforce in their own hierarchical and non-egalitarian structures the overall patterns of domination in society (Ham and Hill 1984, pp. 32-36; Hasenfeld 1983, pp. 39-40).

This emphasis in neo-Marxist writings on the 'structural constraints' that operate in capitalist societies is an important contribution to the understanding of organisations. While systems theory drew attention to the importance of the immediate organisational environment, the neo-Marxian perspective goes further in emphasising the importance of the overall structural position of organisations in the society and the economy. This emphasis in neo-Marxist writings is not unique. Some systems theorists also focus on the structural position of organisations in society. Katz and Kahn (1966, pp. 111-114) argue that all organisations perform production, maintenance, adaption or management functions for the society as a whole. Health and welfare organisations, in this schema, are primarily concerned with maintenance: they 'help to keep a society from disintegrating and are responsible for the normative integration of society' (Katz and Kahn 1966, p. 112). However, this emphasis on integration and societal needs clearly differs fundamentally from the neo-Marxian perspective. The latter gives us the capacity to go beyond the abstract notion of societal needs to an examination of dominant political and economic interests. Whereas Katz and Kahn say that maintenance organisations are concerned with 'normative integration', a neo-Marxian perspective leads us to ask key questions such as whose norms are being applied to whom, and with what consequences for the various groups involved? The answers to these questions are complex and disputed. In particular, it should be noted that the neo-Marxian concept of an economically and politically dominant 'ruling class' is challenged by analysts proposing 'elite' and 'pluralist' interpretations of the distribution of political power (for the main issues see Parkin 1980, pp. 268-279).

The issue of the focus and distribution of political power is bound up with the related question of the extent to which structural factors constrain human service organisations and the individuals that work in them. How much autonomy from domination by powerful economic interests do human service organisations have in capitalist societies? This is an important issue. If human service organisations have a significant degree of power in their own right, they, and those that work within them, may well be able to carry out reforms and activities that are in the interests of workers or other groups, albeit within the framework of the capitalist system (Satyamurti 1981, p. 197). A Weberian analysis lends support to the position that large, state, human service bureaucracies tend to accumulate a high degree of power in their own right. 'State agencies derive power from their command of legal, financial and organisational resources and are not merely instruments of capital' (Ham and Hill 1984, p. 187). However, the Weberian perspective rather pessimistically suggests that such bureaucracies then tend to use this power in their own interests. These are complex issues raising fundamental questions about the relationship between economic and political power in capitalist societies.

Neo-Marxian analysts are also concerned with examination of intra-organisational processes. One line of analysis is that organisations are characterised by internal contradictions, and that these contradictions provide the impetus for organisational change and transformation:

> Many theorists see the organization as a reasonably coherent, integrated system, rationally articulated or functionally adjusted. This view . . . is an abstraction. If one looks at the organisation concretely and pays attention to its multiple levels and varied relations to the larger society, contradictions become an obvious and important feature of organizational life (Benson 1981, p. 274).

Benson goes on to argue that contradictions may be generated from within the organisation, or from the larger society, and imposed on the organisation. He gives the example of a prison's dual purpose of rehabilitation and punishment. 'This may produce inconsistent moves within the organisation yielding contradictory structures, competing interest groups, and occasional periods of crisis' (Benson 1981, p. 275). For Benson and other neo-Marxians (e.g. Heydebrand 1980), the interplay of these contradictions is fundamental to the functioning and historical evolution of organisations. This emphasis is consonant with the perceptions of many social and welfare workers, who often describe their experiences of organisations in terms of contradictions, for example care versus control, openness versus secrecy, professional versus organisational loyalties.

The neo-Marxian perspective is also valuable in drawing our attention to the structural position of workers in human service organisations. In chapter 1 we examined some of the limitations of viewing workers as autonomous professionals, and suggested they should also be viewed as members of organisations. A neo-Marxian analysis suggests that we should also consider their position as workers with class interests. Social and welfare workers are, in most cases, directly or indirectly state employees. As such, in Marxian terms, they are members of the working class or labourers, 'defined by non-ownership of the means of production and paid the equivalent of his or her labour power's value' (Clegg and Dunkerley 1980, p. 488). This view raises important issues. It suggests that social and welfare workers share important common interests with all workers, particularly those in the public sector, and with the labour movement generally. In terms of the structural and political location, it implies that social and welfare workers should be affiliated with and active in trade unions, and approach their organisational life and activities from the stance of an employee whose interests are often in conflict with the employing body.

Social and welfare workers should recognise that they are employees, as well as members of organisations and professionals. Each of these three roles shape their position and relations in organisations in different ways. Each can be seen as a source of power, authority and influence; each also has inherent constraints. All three dimensions need to be recognised if workers are to participate effectively in organisations. However, the idea that social and welfare workers share identical interests with all other workers also requires critical analysis. The growth of social and welfare work as an occupation can also be viewed as part of the emergence of a salaried, middle class whose interests are closely bound up with the growth of public sector human services and the existing capitalist structures (Jamrozik 1991, pp. 23-53). It can be argued that this new middle class has its own interests that are not necessarily subordinate to those of capital, other workers, or consumers of human services (Ham and Hill 1984, p. 186; Mishra 1984, pp. 95-96). Such an analysis raises important questions concerning the structural position of social and welfare workers in organisations, and in the society as a whole.

Political economy perspectives

Political economy perspectives share with neo-Marxian writers the view that organisations must be understood in the context of political and economic relations in society as a whole. This perspective also emphasises the centrality of power relations in the internal structures and processes of organisations (Gummer 1985). A central tenet of this perspective is that an organisation is 'an arena in which various interest groups, external and internal . . . compete to optimise their values through it' (Hasenfeld 1983, p. 44). Some writers refer to these various interest groups as 'stakeholders', that is person or groups who have an investment in the organisation, and have an interest in its operations (Abrahamsson 1977, pp. 117-118). In human service organisations, these may include professional workers, other occupational groups, trade unions, management, consumers, regulatory bodies, funding bodies and interest groups. Social and welfare workers are viewed as one group among many seeking to pursue their values and interests in and through the organisation.

This picture of organisational life has intuitive appeal for many workers, who often experience and interpret organisational life in terms of the conflicting interests and values of the different players. The task of charting a course through the turbulent waters of conflicting personal, professional and organisational interests is a commonplace experience. However, in considering the relevance of this perspective there are two key questions to consider. Firstly, what is meant by 'power', and how is this concept related to other terms such as 'authority' and 'influence'? Secondly, what are the factors that affect the power of groups and individuals in organisations?

The definition of power is a matter of considerable theoretical dispute (Parkin 1980, pp. 263-265). We consider it important to distinguish clearly between the concepts of power, influence and authority. Power refers to capacity to force compliance or to resist a demand for compliance. It is closely linked to the concept of domination. Thynne and Goldring express it thus: 'Power (is) the capacity of a person or persons (A) to achieve a result . . . in the form of action or inaction on the part of another person or other persons (B)' (1987, p. 2).

Influence, by contrast, is the capacity to have an effect on the actions or behaviour of others. It has been suggested that the relationship between power and influence be thought of in terms of a continuum of degrees of power, with influence (low) and domination (high) being the two poles (Thynne and Goldring 1987, p. 2). While this is helpful, we would argue for a sharper distinction with power being reserved for specific circumstances in which one person or group can compel, coerce, constrain—in short, dominate—another. Power is also about the capacity to resist such processes.

Both terms need to be clearly distinguished from authority, the concept encountered earlier in examining Weber's concept of bureaucracy. Authority can be thought of as a distinctive form of power, that is, legitimate or accepted power. Within modern organisations, the most important source of authority is legal–rationality, that is, the acceptance of known rules, laws and procedures, although the other bases of authority identified by Weber, charisma and tradition, may also be important in particular instances.

It needs to be stressed that the concept of power outlined above is different from the social psychological concept of empowerment currently popular in social and welfare work. The idea of empowerment in therapeutic practice refers essentially to the attainment of self-management competency (Furlong 1987, p. 25); individuals are presumed to be capable of developing a sense of control or power over their lives. By contrast, in political terms, power is held by one person or group over another or others. It is relationship specific, that is, a person is not 'powerful' or 'powerless' in general, but only with respect to other parties in the context of particular social relations (Pfeffer 1981, p. 3).

Another issue is the distinction between exercised power and potential power (Parkin 1980, p. 264). It can be strongly argued that the existence of power does not depend on it actually being exercised. A person or group may have power over others simply as a result of them believing or accepting that certain consequences would follow from acting or not acting in a certain way. An ability to understand and estimate the nature and extent of the potential, or latent, power of individuals and groups within an organisation is an important political skill as this defines the limits of the possible in any given situation.

The complexity of these issues can be illustrated by the case of a hospital social worker. She may well have considerable influence over, say, the nursing and medical staff on the wards in which she works, that is, a capacity to persuade, cajole, educate, and so forth. This influence may extend to the broader hospital around some issues. Her formal authority, in so far as it is based on the established rules of the hospital, is likely to be extremely limited: she may be able to direct the work of subordinate social workers or welfare staff, but she will not be able to exert authority over other staff, such as doctors, ward sisters and nurses, or patients. Indeed, she may well be subject to the authority of these other professionals. Certainly, in the medical treatment of patients her influence will be extremely limited and her authority, in all probability, nil. She may, however, have considerable capacity to shape her own work, and in so far as this has an effect on others this is a significant source of power. For example, she may be able to determine which patients she sees, what actions she will recommend, which organisational projects she will engage in, and so forth. This should be seen as the exercise of power.

A key concern of the power perspective is analysis of the factors which affect the power and influence of individuals and groups in an organisation. In the case of the hospital social worker, what factors affect her power and influence? Are these factors controlled, to some degree, by the worker herself, or is her power essentially determined by her position in the organisational and social environment?

In making this assessment, it is first important to distinguish clearly between the political nature of social and welfare work as an activity and the level of political power that workers, individually or collectively, can exercise (Adams and Freeman 1980). It can be convincingly argued that social and welfare work is a political activity, both in the sense that the values and commitments of workers influence the performance of their work, and in the sense that such work is inevitably linked to political functions such as social control. However, this is quite different from saying that social and welfare workers are politically powerful. 'The extent to which a job is "political" has no relationship at all to the political leverage the occupants of those jobs can exercise . . .' (Adams and Freeman 1980, p. 448).

What then are the determinants of political power and influence in organisations? Pfeffer suggests that 'the power of organisational actors is fundamentally determined by two things, the importance of what they do in the organisation and their skill in doing it' (1981, p. 98). The first of these factors draws our attention to the importance of structural position and functional relevance. Individuals and groups will have influence, it is argued, to the extent that their activity is important to the organisation. Groups that provide the organisation with legitimacy, that obtain resources for the organisation, that solve organisational problems, or that perform key or critical technical tasks will have a greater capacity for organisational influence (Pfeffer 1981, p. 127; Gummer 1978).

This capacity must, however, be mobilised. Organisational power and influence depend, not only on what a group does, but also on how well it performs its organisational functions. It is also dependent on the perceptions of other organisational actors of the significance of the group's functions and activities. In this sense, power and influence derive from 'the ability of the participants to convince others within the organisation that their specific tasks and their abilities are substantial and important' (Pfeffer 1981, p. 98). Moreover, the political capacities and capabilities of a group will be significant factors. Political resources include group cohesiveness, high morale, good leadership, established networks, developed information sources and a capacity to analyse the organisation in political terms.

Much analysis of organisational power focuses on these two factors: structural position and function, and political skills. As Gummer puts it, any group within an organisation 'must be able to "sell" itself and have something to "sell"' (1978, p. 358). Let us apply these ideas to the previous example of a hospital social worker. As discussed above, the limits to her authority are likely to be tightly drawn. Hence, her capacity to bring about changes in the hospital, outside of her areas of personal power and discretion, will usually depend on the degree of influence that she can muster. Such influence will depend on the importance of the functions that the worker plays in the hospital and the extent to which social and welfare workers, and no others, can perform these. This may well be problematic. Social and welfare work functions are often not perceived as being as important to hospital functioning as the work of other groups such as surgeons, medical technologists or nurses. Moreover, there is often a perception that social and welfare work tasks can be performed equally satisfactorily by other groups, such as nurses, volunteers and aides. Workers wishing to exert influence in the hospital will have to attempt to portray their activities as valuable to the organisation as a whole. This can be done by undertaking activities that bring prestige to the hospital, or that solve organisational problems, or that bring in or save resources. Moreover, the hospital social and welfare workers as a group will need to develop their political capacities and capabilities to be able to build on and utilise the influence that derives from their importance to the organisation. These strategic considerations present complex dilemmas for workers.

The literature contains many examples of social and welfare workers successfully pursuing strategies of this kind, although often these are not explicitly analysed in political terms. For example, Cleak describes the role of social work in the emergency department of an Australian hospital, showing how social workers developed a significant role in assessment and short-term management of patients' psycho-social needs and problems at the point of entry to the hospital system. The service enhanced the speedy resolution of problems for the patient, contributed to effective utilisation of in-patient beds in the hospital, and gave the social workers the legitimacy and opportunity to be involved in hospital policy issues (1988, pp. 23-28). In a different context, James and Jones describe how a social work service to support victims, witnesses, defendants and their families was developed between 1978 and 1988 in the Victorian Coroner's Court. This was done by convincing the coroner, the police, the Office of Corrections and Community Services Victoria that such a service would contribute to the effective operation of the court, as well as to the well-being of people involved in court proceedings (1988, pp. 31-34). In both of these settings, social workers were apparently successful in negotiating effective roles within the organisation and significantly influencing organisational processes. They achieved this (to re-use Gummer's phrase) by 'selling' themselves and, even more importantly, by having something to 'sell'.

The political power and influence of social and welfare workers, and of all other groups, in organisations is, however, dependent on factors additional to political resources and strategies. Account must also be taken of the context within which power relations occur. Zald suggests that organisations can be thought of as having 'constitutions' that provide the setting for political processes (1970, pp. 225-229). This constitution which may include, but is not the same as, the written constitution is 'a set of agreements and understandings which define the limits and goals of the (organisation) . . . as well as the responsibilities and rights of participants standing in different relations to it' (p. 225). These understandings, although not fixed, limit the range of matters that are open for negotiation at any particular time within the organisation. These constitutional norms, Zald suggests, 'are deeply embedded in the relationship of an organisation to the society of which it is a part' (1970, p. 27). This observation reminds us again of the neo-Marxian emphasis on the structural constraints on organisations stemming from the dominant power relations in capitalist society.

In some ways, Zald's idea of 'constitutional norms' is somewhat similar to Bachrach and Baratz's concept of non-decision-making in organisations (1980). They suggest that in any given political system, such as an organisation, there is a 'mobilisation of bias' that prevents certain issues from becoming matters of debate. Dominant individuals and groups 'limit decision making to relatively non-controversial matters, by influencing . . . values and political procedures and rituals, notwithstanding that there are . . . serious but latent power conflicts' (1980, pp. 370-371). Bachrach and Baratz, and Zald, are suggesting that to fully understand the distribution of power in an organisation we must look beyond the visible manifestations of power and conflict. We must, they argue, critically examine not only what issues are raised within the organisation, but also which issues are left unexamined. Zey-Ferrell and Aiken suggest that such an analysis should lead us to ask further related questions: How did the existing power relations among groups originate? What classes and groups benefit by the existing relations, and which are disadvantaged? What are the consequences of the present distribution of power in the organisation for present society and future generations (1981, p. 17). While the actions that social and welfare workers can undertake within organisations will be circumscribed by their political resources and skills, their analysis arguably should encompass these broader issues.

Finally, and relatedly, it should be emphasised that the power of individuals and groups within organisations is influenced not only by their political resources and skills, but also by their relationship to the prevailing patterns of social inequality in Australian society. The major dimensions of inequality in Australia are those related to social class, gender, Aboriginality, ethnicity, age, disability and place (Western 1983). These inequalities may be reflected, reproduced, or challenged within organisations. Many of the issues of concern to social and welfare workers in organisations revolve around these social inequalities, and much of their activity involves efforts to promote equitable relations in organisational settings. In this context, it is particularly important to consider the political resources of consumers of human service organisations, many of whom belong to groups which are relatively powerless in Australian society. The issue of their participation in organisational processes that affect their lives is considered in detail in chapter 9.

Feminist perspectives

Feminist perspectives on organisations are of central and special significance to social and welfare workers. One basic reason for this is that the majority of social and welfare workers are women, as are the majority of consumers of many human service organisations. Feminist writers place this reality at the centre of their analysis, arguing that the roles and relations of workers and consumers to organisations cannot be understood if gender relations are ignored. Gender relations are viewed as central in organisational life, as they are in the broader society. Other perspectives on organisational analysis are criticised for being gender-blind, and failing to consider, or even acknowledge, sexual domination in organisations and society.

Feminist perspectives argue that patriarchal, social, and economic relations, that is, male domination and power over women, permeate society and social institutions and are a basic source of political and social inequality.

> At the heart of feminism is a very simple idea: that there are not two sorts of people in the world . . . the dominant and the subordinate. We are all equal irrespective of our gender. Social relations that obliterate this fact must therefore be transformed and recreated in ways that reflect equality in terms of gender (Dominelli and McLeod 1989, pp. 1-2).

In their analysis of organisations, feminist writers have pointed to numerous ways in which gender structures and influences organisational life (Hooyman and Cunningham 1986; Ferguson 1984; Yeatman 1990). These include the dominant role that men have in senior and managerial positions in organisations, barriers to opportunities for advancement for women workers, the imposition of masculine culture in organisations, discrimination and sexual harassment of women workers, and insensitivity to the needs of women and children as consumers.

A major emphasis in feminist writings has been to show how male-dominated organisations reflect, reinforce and reproduce existing gender relations. Feminist perspectives have also underpinned many reform processes in mainstream (or 'male-stream') organisations that aim to restructure gender relations. For example, 'femocrats' have played a central role in the introduction and implementation of equal opportunity and anti-discrimination legislation (Yeatman 1990). Feminist writers and workers have also attempted to articulate and create alternative organisations, based on fundamentally different assumptions from mainstream organisations. Many of these organisations are 'women only' and are concerned with issues such as women's health and domestic violence. The structures and processes developed in these contexts pose important questions for all organisations, and these are considered in chapter 6.

Hooyman and Cunningham (1986) identify six main themes in feminist perspectives on working in organisations. In the first theme, there is an emphasis on the need to value women's perspectives and experiences. Female values that are seen as important for organisations include flexibility, capacity for intuitive awareness, empathy and nurturance (p. 167). It has been argued that women can be agents for transformational changes in organisational and managerial life, because of the values and qualities that they bring (Gummer 1990, pp. 112-115).

In the second theme, a feminist perspective involves a questioning of false dichotomies such as expert–non-expert, professional–non-professional, worker–consumer. Hooyman and Cunningham argue that these distinctions are often used to keep consumers separate and powerless, and they argue for a more holistic approach to defining and addressing problems, that integrates many different perspectives (p. 168).

The third theme is a re-conceptualisation of power. Although concepts of domination are central to feminist social analysis, there is an emphasis on attempting to create different kinds of power relations in organisations based on ideas of empowerment:

> In a feminist model, power is facilitative; empowerment to action occurs rather than domination. Personal power is then political, allowing people the ability to make decisions for themselves and to achieve self-determination and control over their own lives rather than over the lives of others (Hooyman and Cunningham 1986, p. 169).

The fourth theme is closely related to this theme as it emphasises democratic organisational structures. Feminist writers stress the need to modify organisational structures to facilitate empowerment of workers and consumers. Key elements of feminist structures include minimal hierarchy, fluid definitions of roles and responsibilities, rotation of tasks, accountability to peers, sharing of skills and consensual decision-making (Hooyman and Cunningham 1986, p. 170). Bureaucratic structures are viewed as male-based models of organisation and administration.

The fifth theme deals with the central emphasis in feminism on the importance of organisational process as well as product or output. Feminist values in management emphasise the need to deal with people as individuals, to respect individual's feelings, to deal with conflict as it arises, and to take the time to develop strong relationships among people who are working together. 'The feminist model is developmental, concerned with long-run effectiveness and the processes necessary to attain it, rather than only with short-term efficiency' (Hooyman and Cunningham 1986, p. 170). Feminist perspectives also emphasise the need for processes to reflect social goals. 'If feminists aim to create egalitarian social relations then these must be reflected in their practice' (Dominelli and McLeod 1989, p. 9).

The sixth theme deals with the feminist perspectives' emphasis on the need to draw links between the experiences of individuals, organisations and underlying social conditions. The expression 'the personal is political' encapsulates this theme. The connections between the experiences of women in particular organisations and patriarchal relations in the broader society are emphasised. The necessity of changing underlying social conditions as well as their manifestation in particular organisational contexts is stressed.

Feminist approaches to organisational analysis pose significant challenges to the perspectives that have been examined in this chapter. They question the values underlying the formal objectivity and impersonality of the bureaucratic model, and stress the role of bureaucratic organisations in maintaining patriarchal structures. They reject the detachment and focus on outcomes alone of the scientific management perspective. There are some commonalities with human relations in the emphasis on personal and inter-personal factors in organisational life. However, feminism, unlike much writing from the human relations perspective, is not managerialist in focus. Feminist views reject the emphasis in the market perspective on 'transactions' and self-interest, and stress the potential for creating relations of mutuality and sharing in organisations.

The relations between feminist perspectives and neo-Marxist views of organisations are complex. There is an extensive debate within feminism over the relationship between social divisions based on gender and other social divisions such as class (Dominelli and McLeod 1989, pp. 6-7). Many feminist writers acknowledge the contribution that radical and neo-Marxist perspectives have made to an understanding of the role of state organisations, but are critical of the lack of attention to the nature of women's experiences and gender questions in general. They are also critical of the lack of attention to the personal in neo-Marxist analysis: 'in failing to render a gender-specific account of dependency and caring, it has not . . . broached the question of how to develop a practice addressing the suffering of women, who form the majority as clients, carers and social workers' (Dominelli and McLeod 1989, p. 15).

Feminist perspectives share with the political economy approach an analysis of organisations in terms power relations, but object to the neglect of gender relations by many writers. The feminist emphasis on empowerment of individuals and groups differs from the more instrumental view of power, authority and influence of writers in the political economy tradition.

Feminist emphases on process and self-determination are themes held in common with the Aboriginal perspective on organisations, discussed below. Yeatman argues that femocrats, that is, women holding senior positions in state administration, have played a significant role as a brokers and mediators of the claims of groups such as Aboriginal people and people from non-English speaking backgrounds around issues to do with inclusion and exclusion from mainstream organisations (1990, p. 90).

Feminist perspectives on organisations raise key issues for both men and women workers. We would argue that it is as important for men to come to grips with feminist perspectives on organisations as it is for women. Men involved in social and welfare work need to be aware of the centrality of gender in organisational relations. Moreover, there is a convincing argument that men's interests as human beings, particularly their opportunities and capabilities for emotional engagement, are not served by patriarchal social relations. The increasing attention being paid to men's issues and the nature of masculinity is opening up important, additional perspectives on gender analysis.

Another central issue raised by the feminist perspective is the relations between different groups and classes of women. Although the feminist perspective stresses that gender pervades all social relations, women's individual circumstances are also shaped by their class position, their race and ethnicity, their geographic location and so forth. Yeatman suggests that this has been a particular dilemma for femocrats who attempt 'to speak on behalf of all women when their practical ideological commitments often best express the interests of women who like themselves are positioned within full-time primary labour markets' (1990, p. 81). This dilemma can also be understood in terms of the neo-Marxian perspective on the development of the 'new middle class', and its relations to state structures (Jamrozik 1991).

It is important to note that feminism differs from many of the other perspectives we have examined in that it seeks to link analysis and action. It also requires a personalised, rather than an analytically detached, response to organisational issues. It encompasses a framework for understanding the nature of organisations and a political agenda for organisational change.

Aboriginal perspectives

Aboriginal perspectives on organisations, unlike the other perspectives we have examined, are not based on a literature concerned with theoretical reflection on the nature of organisations, although there is a developing body of significant writings. However, in the Australian context it is vital to state that there is a distinctive Aboriginal view of organisations, and that social and welfare workers must be aware of this. This perspective is grounded in Aboriginal history, including the history of relations with non-Aboriginal people, and in particular the relations between Aboriginal people and state organisations.

This history is one of colonisation, dis-empowerment and dis-possession. Between 1788 and 1900 the population of Aboriginal people was reduced from approximately 750 000 to 100 000 as a result of introduced diseases, expropriation of land, and killings (Mulvaney and White 1987). Many Aboriginal people were gathered by force and herded into missions. Many found their traditional lands turned into pastoral leases, their presence tolerated solely as a source of cheap labour (Reynolds 1987).

During the twentieth century this systematic and deliberate dis-empowerment has continued. What began with the dis-possession of land has been extended to all other aspects of life. Aboriginal people were made dependent upon others for food, clothing, education, housing and health care. 'Decisions were made about them and for them and imposed upon them' (Royal Commission into Aboriginal Deaths in Custody 1991, vol. 1, p. 9). The consequences have been appalling. Charles Perkins summarised the position as follows:

> ...Aboriginal people, by any measure, are the most deprived and impoverished section of Australian society. Forgotten — or ignored — are these condemning statistics:
> • the average Aboriginal life expectancy is 20 years less than that for other Australians;
> • Aboriginal infant mortality is nearly three times that of non-Aboriginal Australians;
> • trachoma is seven times more prevalent among Aboriginal people [than in the general population];
> • Aboriginal unemployment is five time higher than the national average;
> • on average Aboriginals earn only half that of other Australians;
> • a large proportion of Aboriginal families live in sub-standard housing and temporary shelters made from scrap iron and timber, and
> • Aboriginal imprisonment rates are up to 16 times higher than for other Australians (Perkins 1986, p. 2).

Relations between Aboriginal people and mainstream organisations are graphically portrayed in the findings of the Royal Commission into Aboriginal Deaths in Custody. Between January 1980 and 31 May 1989, ninety-nine Aboriginal and Torres Strait Islander people died in the custody of prison, police or juvenile detention institutions. The circumstances of their deaths were varied, but in every case the victims' Aboriginality played a significant or dominant role in their incarceration and death (Royal Commission into Aboriginal Deaths in Custody 1991, vol. 1, p. 1). The Royal Commission's report demonstrates how Australian society, its institutions and organisations, have historically oppressed Aboriginal people, marginalising and excluding their needs and aspirations from the mainstream political agenda. This process has been described as one of 'institutional racism'. By this is meant:

> . . . a pattern of distribution of social goods, including power, which regularly and systematically advantages some ethnic and racial groups and disadvantages others. It operates through key institutions: organised social arrangements through which social goods and services are distributed. These include the public service, the legal and medical systems, the education system (Pettman 1986, p. 7).

Many commentators argue that contemporary changes in policy and terminology have had little impact on this pattern of relations. Policies of 'self-determination' have been developed as attempts by governments to 'recognise the unique position of Aboriginal people in Australia and to provide them with an effective basis for achieving real control over their own lives' (Royal Commission into Aboriginal Deaths in Custody 1991, vol. 2, p. 159). However:

> The perception of many Aboriginal people . . . is that too often policies are propounded, programmes put forward, assistance offered in a form which has been largely pre-determined in the bureaucracies of the departments concerned; that there is a process of consultation with relevant Aboriginal communities or bodies but that the parameters of the consultation have been set in advance; that the agenda is being fixed by non-Aboriginal people, not by Aboriginal people (Royal Commission into Aboriginal Deaths in Custody, vol. 1, 1991, p. 20).

Other studies have concluded that in contemporary society, Aboriginal people are as controlled by welfare organisations as they ever have been in the past, despite the superficial appearance of control of their own affairs (Collman 1988, p. 13)

The failure of mainstream organisations to respond to the needs of Aboriginal people, has led to the establishment of Aboriginal-controlled organisations (Perkins 1986). It is to these organisations and services that many Aboriginal people look to address their needs. The Royal Commission wrote of these organisations:

> The variety is endless, the energy is enormous. Some of course, fail. What is surprising is not that some fail but that so many keep going and even those that run down often come up again. All of these are dedicated in their own way to the empowerment of Aboriginal people, to raising self-esteem, demonstrating the ability to exercise control of their own affairs, attacking the legacy of the past (Royal Commission into Aboriginal Deaths in Custody 1991, vol. 1, p. 17).

The Aboriginal perspectives on organisations arises out of these various experiences with non-Aboriginal and Aboriginal organisations (these experiences are documented in detail in Royal Commission into Aboriginal Deaths in Custody 1991). The perspective is not couched in the accepted academic language of organisational theory, as this language is itself embedded in the political agenda of the dominant culture. Even words such as social justice, access, equity, equality, rights and participation are not culturally neutral, and when applied uncritically by non-Aboriginal organisations and workers to Aboriginal people constitute a form of cultural dominance. The Aboriginal view emphasises that the processes of self-determination are as important as outcomes, and that processes and outcomes must be measured in Aboriginal terms. The demands are for land rights, control and self-determination, compensation for past wrongs and a treaty to map out a new future. As one Aboriginal writer states:

> Blacks resent the child/ward status implicit in the continued denial of resources and remain embittered by the fact that these resources are, or stem from, their heritage and birthright—the land—stolen by the colonists two hundred years ago (Sykes 1989, p. 230).

It is crucial that social and welfare workers struggle to understand the Aboriginal view of Australian history, and the perspective on the role of the state, its institutions and organisations that flows from Aboriginal experience. The evidence demonstrating the failure of the majority of non-Aboriginal organisations to understand and respond effectively to the needs of Aboriginal people is irrefutable. Coming to grips with the Aboriginal perspective is, in the Australian context, a vital task for social and welfare workers, and a fundamental challenge to non-Aboriginal organisations. Developing such an understanding is an essential part of gaining a critical perspective on organisations.

Developing a 'critical' perspective

All of us, as a consequence of our daily contact with organisations as employees, consumers, members or simply observers, acquire ideas about what organisations are like, how they work, and what can be expected of them. In addition, our ideas about organisations are shaped by the media, by educational experiences, and by the experiences of others including family and friends. These ideas can be thought of as our received or implicit theories of organisations.

Our beliefs about organisations are also strongly influenced by organisations themselves. All organisations, to varying degrees, attempt to positively construct community perceptions (and the self-perceptions of their members) in ways that will enhance the organisation's fortunes. Gouldner has pointed out that one important aspect of this process is that organisations 'inhibit the flow of certain kinds of information about themselves, in short, they have secrets' (1963, p. 161). Social and welfare workers need to be able to question and challenge 'official' versions of the nature of organisations, as well as their own 'received' beliefs.

Table 2.3 Implications of neo-Marxian, political economy, feminist and Aboriginal perspectives for social and welfare workers

Propositions	*Questions*	*Practice implications*
	NEO-MARXIAN PERSPECTIVES	
1 Organisational structures and processes are centrally concerned with domination and control	1 Are capitalist societies dominated by a ruling class?	1 Be aware of the structural constraints and relative autonomy of the organisation
2 Organisations operate within the structural constraints of capitalism	2 What are the limits of structural constraints?	2 Understand the impact of dominant political and economic interests on the organisation, and your relation to those interests
3 Organisations are characterised by internal contradictions	3 Does the idea of contradictions encompass the diversity of interests in organisations?	
4 Employer–employee relations are central to organisational processes	4 What is the nature of class conflict within organisations?	3 Understand the implications of being a worker (employee) in an organisation
	POLITICAL ECONOMY PERSPECTIVES	
1 Organisations are political arenas in which stakeholders seek to maximise their values	1 How much of organisational life can be understood in political terms?	1 Be aware of the political nature of organisations
2 Power, influence and authority must be clearly distinguished	2 To what extent is the political arena in organisations structured and biased?	2 Understand the sources of power, influence and authority
3 It is important to distinguish between exercised and potential power	3 How do patterns of social inequality affect power relations in organisations?	3 Develop the skills to increase political capability and capacity
4 The determinants of organisational power include position and function, political skills and structural context		4 Develop sensitivity and skills in promoting equitable relations in organisations

Propositions	Questions	Practice implications
	FEMINIST PERSPECTIVES	
1 Gender relations are central to an understanding of organisations	1 What are the implications of a gender analysis for men and women workers?	1 Workers should be sensitive to gender issues in their practice in organisations
2 Women's experiences of organisations should be valued	2 How does a gender analysis deal with the issue of differences among women, including differences of class, race, ethnicity, and location?	2 Workers should be aware of the importance of process as well as outcomes
3 Process is as important as product		3 Workers should seek to understand the links between the personal and the political
4 Democratic structures should be fostered to facilitate empowerment of workers and consumers	3 What are the links between the feminist perspective and the other perspectives we have examined?	
5 The personal is political		4 Workers should be aware of how gender relations structure dependency and consumer roles
	ABORIGINAL PERSPECTIVES	
1 Institutional racism operates through key institutions and organised social arrangements	1 To what extent are organisations reflective of the interests of culturally dominant groups?	1 Be aware of how organisational processes are culturally bound and may dominate, marginalise or exclude certain groups
2 Self-determination and control are central to the Aboriginal perspective on organisations	2 How can non-Aboriginal organisations relate more effectively to the needs and aspirations of Aboriginal people?	2 Be aware that consultation is not the same as control and self-determination
3 Key concepts such as social justice, effectiveness and so on should be defined and measured in Aboriginal terms in the Aboriginal context	3 Does this require acceptance of different processes and outcomes than for others in the society?	3 Workers and organisations need to understand and accept the validity of Aboriginal definitions of desirable organisational processes and outcomes

As we have seen, organisation theory provides workers with many different perspectives from which to analyse the organisations in and through which they work. These perspectives provide a basis for re-appraisal of 'received' and 'official' ideas about organisations, and the development of a critical perspective. None of the approaches that we have examined provides an unambiguous, all-embracing framework for understanding organisations that can be adopted holus-bolus. The issue for workers is not primarily that of choosing among perspectives. Rather, the analytical process is one of developing an integrated approach to the understanding of organisations, based on a critical appraisal of organisation theory and experience of organisational life. This integrated approach should comprise ideas about the nature of organisations, the factors that influence organisational structures, processes and behaviour, and the implications for social work practice.

To assist in this process, we have summarised in Tables 2.1, 2.2 and 2.3 the main propositions, issues and practice implications raised by each of the perspectives that we have analysed. In Table 2.4 we pull some of the main themes of the chapter together in the form of a checklist of key questions for organisational analysis. This list can be used by workers wanting to critically examine, at a general level, their own organisational context. All of the issues raised are examined in more detail in later sections of the book; indeed, the book as a whole can be viewed as our critical analysis of human service organisations. The checklist should be viewed as a practice tool designed to provide a means of systematically applying the theoretical writings on organisations presented in this chapter to a practice context. We suggest that this exercise be undertaken as a way of grounding and reflecting on the material presented in the chapter.

Our own approach to organisational analysis centres on the political economy perspective. We view organisations as comprising individuals and groups with competing and often conflicting interests, existing within the broader political and economic structure. This perspective is fundamental to our analysis throughout the book. In particular, we emphasise the need for workers to analyse their own sources of power, authority and influence. We see this as basic to effective organisational work. Similarly, the political position of consumers in organisations needs to be carefully analysed as part of any process to improve organisational responsiveness to their needs.

Our overall approach, however, is influenced by many of the other perspectives outlined and critiqued in this chapter. We view the bureaucratic nature of modern organisations, as outlined by Weber, as the starting point for organisational analysis. Scientific management's concerns with efficiency and effectiveness, and its contemporary manifestation in 'managerialism', cannot be accepted uncritically. We examine this perspective closely in chapter 11. However, we readily accept the importance of efficiency and effectiveness in organisations

Table 2.4 Checklist of key questions for organisational analysis for social and welfare workers

---

1   What is the nature and basis of authority in the organisation?

2   What are the formal structures and processes?

3   What informal processes and relations are important?

4   What are the organisation's needs for survival and growth?

5   What are the patterns of inter-dependency among members and units?

6   What are the main environmental influences?

7   What is the nature of the decision-making processes?

8   Does the organisation tend to promote self-interested or other-regarding behaviour?

9   What are the structural constraints on the organisation?

10   Which are the main stakeholders, and what are their interests and values?

11   What are the sources and distribution of power, influence and authority? How might workers utilise power, influence and authority in organisations?

12   How are major social inequalities, in particular those based on class, gender, location, ethnicity and race, reproduced or challenged within the organisation?

13   What are the implications of this analysis for workers in their different roles as organisational members, professionals and employees?

---

providing human services to consumers, and the relevance of formal structures and processes. The emphasis in the human relations perspective on the informal, personal and inter-personal elements of organisational life are also incorporated into our analysis.

We have drawn on writers from the systems and ecological perspectives in terms of our emphases on the influence of environmental factors on organisations, and the importance of inter-dependencies among organisational participants. The market perspective draws our attention to the pervasive influence of self-interest in organisations, although we do not accept that organisations are simply collections of transactions between groups and individuals. Nor do we believe that organisations must be built around market-like relations; we are interested in the potential of alternative organisations based on values of mutuality, equality, openness and trust. Decision perspectives have been particularly influential in shaping our ideas about how organisations seek to exercise control over front-line workers.

Neo-Marxian perspectives have shaped our understanding of the structural constraints on human service organisations, and the relative autonomy of state organisations. They also show how conflicts within organisations reflect broader class interests in the overall society. Human service organisations perform specific functions in the society, economy and polity, and awareness of these is fundamental to organisational analysis and understanding. Similarly, an awareness of gender-based divisions in society, and the ways that these are produced, reinforced, reproduced and challenged in and through organisations is essential. We have attempted to incorporate such understanding drawn from feminist perspectives into our analysis. We do not claim to present an Aboriginal perspective on organisations. However, we have attempted to incorporate an awareness that there exists a distinct Aboriginal perspective on the questions and issues we examine.

Finally, underpinning our analysis is a belief that human service organisations are of central importance in the struggle to promote a socially just society. Our analysis is based on the belief that the attempt to pursue the social justice agenda of access, equity, equality, rights and participation for all citizens in and through human service organisations is possible, worthwhile and of fundamental importance.

Chapter review questions

1 Why do workers need a critical perspective on organisations? How can a worker develop a critical perspective on organisations?
2 What is meant by the term 'bureaucracy'? How can the bureaucratisation of modern society be explained?
3 Does the scientific management perspective on organisations have any contemporary relevance for social and welfare workers and human service organisations?
4 Do you agree with those writers in the human relations school who argue that organisational structures and processes should be developed to meet the social and psychological needs of workers? Why or why not?
5 Is it helpful to apply systems and ecological theory to the analysis of organisations? Consider this question in relation to the role of social and welfare workers in organisations.
6 What is meant by 'bounded rationality' in organisations? How is this relevant to social and welfare work?
7 What, if anything, is wrong with thinking about an organisation as a marketplace where individuals engage in transactions and negotiations in pursuit of their interests?
8 To what extent are human service organisations constrained by the structural requirements of the capitalist economy and society?

9 Social and welfare workers can be seen to relate to organisations in three main ways: as employees, as members of the organisation, and as professionals. What differences stem from viewing workers in each of these ways?

10 How powerful and influential can social and welfare workers in organisations be? How powerful and influential should they seek to be?

11 What are the differences between power, influence and authority?

12 What are the main elements of a feminist perspective on organisations?

13 What is your understanding of an Aboriginal perspective on organisations?

Further reading

Detailed accounts of the development of organisation theory, including the perspectives discussed in this chapter, can be found in Clegg and Dunkerley 1980, Mouzelis 1975, and Perrow 1986. Perrow's account is particularly lively and interesting. More summary accounts can be found in Hasenfeld 1983, pp. 12-49 and Perrow 1976. Hasenfeld's account focuses on human service organisations. Warham 1977, pp. 63-92 discusses some of the developments described in this chapter in relation to social work. A critical perspective on organisations is outlined in Zey-Ferrell and Aiken 1981, pp. 1-21. Feminist perspectives are outlined in Hooyman and Cunningham 1986, Yeatman 1990 and Ferguson 1984. An Aboriginal perspective is presented by Sykes 1989. See also the analysis in Bennett 1989. The Royal Commission into Aboriginal Deaths in Custody 1991, vol. 2 provides a detailed analysis of the issues underlying relations between Aboriginal people and non-Aboriginal organisations.

Case study

WELCOME TO THE ORGANISATION

Peter Madison waited expectantly for the session to start. He had graduated just two months earlier from the Whitlam University School of Social Work and Community Welfare Studies, and applied for a job as a child protection worker with the State Department of Community and Family Services. At the time, the department was experiencing a severe shortage of trained workers, due mainly to high turnover rates in the child protection area. Peter was immediately offered a position in an inner suburban area office of the department. He had started work two days ago. Today was day one of the three-day orientation programme provided for new graduate members of the department. The opening session, according to the timetable that had been distributed to the dozen or so social work, community welfare and psychology graduates who had by now assembled in the seminar room, was simply entitled 'A welcome to the organisation from the Deputy Director-General (Corporate Support and Services)'. A well-dressed, confident-looking woman entered the room and sat at the table at the front of the room, and the session began.

'On behalf of the Minister for Community and Family Services and the Director-General, I would like to extend to all of you a most sincere and warm welcome to the department. My name is Jill Johnson and I am the Deputy Director-General (Community Support). My colleague, who has responsibility for corporate support and services, was due to speak with you this morning, but he has been called by the Minister to assist with some pressing issues. I am very happy to step in for him. The Minister, and all of us in the Senior Executive Management Group, place a very high value on these orientation programmes. The department is entering into an extremely exciting and challenging period of growth and development, and we are conscious that it is the quality of our front-line workers that will, in the last analysis, determine whether or not we are able to meet the demanding goals we have set for ourselves as an organisation. Your commitment to the department and its goals is a key factor, and I personally am looking forward to talking with you about what we, as a department, can achieve together.

I feel I should begin by dealing with some of the misconceptions about the department that, in our experience, new graduates sometimes bring with them. While this may sound rather unduly negative, I believe that I do need to acknowledge that in the past the department has had an image problem in some sections of the community, perhaps most notably out at Whitlam University. Some schools and departments out there (I won't name them, but some of you have been closely connected with them for the past four years) persist in portraying this department as a conservative, hierarchical, irrational, impersonal, oppressive bureaucracy, that is hostile to the exercise of professional skills. I guess that what I want to do this morning, above all else, is to say that this is an outdated view. Whatever the department may have been like in the 1960s and 1970s, I can tell you that today it is striving to become a highly professional, caring, effective, service-oriented organisation. I personally have a background as a social worker, and I have found the department a highly rewarding and enjoyable place of employment. We are far from perfect, of course, but I can assure you that you are now part of a group of people dedicated to making a positive contribution to the social development of our state.

Let us take each of the five areas of criticism often levelled at the department, and compare them with the actual situation. Firstly, it is still sometimes said that the department is motivated by a conservative ideology. To destroy this myth, I think I need only refer you to the Departmental Goals

Statement that you will find in your folder. You will see there that as part of our new corporate plan, we have defined our goals as follows:

1 To increase the capacity and capability of families to provide care responsibly for their members;
2 to provide high quality environments which provide opportunities and security for children whose parents have been unable to care for them;
3 to increase the capacity of local communities to respond effectively to their own social needs;
4 to generate opportunities for young offenders and other young people requiring assistance and opportunities to participate appropriately in the community.

All departmental programmes and activities are oriented towards the purposes and philosophy stated in these goals. Naturally, there is plenty of room for discussion about the ways in which these goals will be pursued, and the work that can be done is always subject to the availability of resources. However, I am sure you will agree that our broad direction is positive and forward-looking, and we are sure that it has the backing of the community as a whole.

But what about the claim that we are hierarchical and bureaucratic? Again, I believe I can readily demonstrate to you that this is another outdated myth. The department has recently undergone a major re-organisation to ensure that our structures and procedures are appropriate to our tasks and circumstances. In place of the traditional hierarchy, we have adopted regionalisation, combined with a matrix style management structure and extensive lateral linkages. This has given us a remarkably 'flat' organisational structure. I understand that the organisational structure is to be discussed in detail this afternoon by John Simpson, the Director of Organisational Services. I will just say that the structure has been designed to facilitate good communication up, down and across the organisation, and to decentralise decision-making. We simply do not have a traditional hierarchical structure. We believe strongly in a participative management style. You can expect to be involved in decision-making in your area office or specialist unit from day one, and innovative ideas and suggestions are always welcome.

This brings me to discuss the suggestion that this is an impersonal organisation. I find this a particularly offensive suggestion. Of course, we are a big and busy organisation, and the personal needs of staff can sometimes be neglected. However, we believe that as a human service organisation we have special responsibilities to take a lead in personnel matters. We believe that people matter, and that people who are contented are productive workers. All of our managers are required to take special training in people management, and there is an open-door policy on people matters. This means that if you have concerns or problems in the job, or matters that are affecting your work performance in any way, your manager is available to talk the issue through. All units and offices have regular staff meetings and your contribution to problem-solving and organisational development is welcome.

There are also regular informal functions and plenty of opportunities to mix socially with other staff, if you choose to do so. While I am on the subject, we very much hope that you will all be able to join us for the lunch planned for tomorrow, where we will be joined by staff from around the department. We think of ourselves more as a big extended family than as a bureaucratic machine—so, welcome to the family!

Another criticism that sometimes comes our way is that we are an irrational organisation, prone to inconsistencies and political in-fighting, and not always in control of our decision-making. In the 'old' department, if I may use that term, this was certainly an issue. However, we now have systems in place to ensure a high level of rationality and efficiency. One of the key elements of this three-day orientation session is to introduce you to the operation of these systems. The department has recently completed the introduction of a programme management and budgeting system, including comprehensive performance indicators. This system works in tandem with our new management information system, which ensures that comprehensive records are kept on programmes, budgets, personnel, community needs, and consumers. All workers are required to keep records of their consumer work and other activity, according to our established forms and procedures. Training in these procedures will, of course, be provided. We see computer technology as a tool to assist us to achieve the efficiency and cost effectiveness that is required of a modern, accountable public service department.

Some critics of the department see these systems that I have been talking about as evidence of the essentially oppressive nature of the department. This again is nonsense, although clearly any planning and data management system needs adequate safeguards. You will find that we rely heavily on, and encourage the exercise of, your professional skills and judgement, within the broad context of departmental policies. You will also find that we are respectful of the rights of consumers. While we do have wide powers of intervention in family life in certain circumstances, we are aware of the need to exercise these powers carefully and responsively.

In conclusion, I draw your attention to the departmental symbol, a person inside a diamond shape. The four sides of the diamond represent the key elements of our social care strategy: the individual, the community, the family and the department. It is the partnership amongst these four elements that will result in sound social development. My talk this morning, and the sessions you will attend over the next few days, are designed to give you the understanding of this organisation that you need to work effectively with us, and with our partners in social development. Welcome again. Are there any questions?'

Key questions

What does this speech convey to Peter Madison and the other new workers about the nature of the organisation? Are there any key questions or issues that appear to have been omitted or misrepresented, or any misplaced emphases? How might Peter and the other workers proceed to develop their own critical analysis of the organisation?

Case discussion points

1 What questions, if any, would you ask the Deputy Director-General? Why or why not?
2 What other sources of information, if any, about the organisation should be accessed? How?
3 Analyse the deputy Director-General's speech from each of the perspectives on organisational analysis discussed in this chapter.

3

Human service organisations: purpose, technology and auspice

... what is needed by those who are going to work in an organisation, is some way of knowing what makes it distinctive: of conceptualising the differences between that particular organisation and another which may, or may not, be in the same line of business (Warham 1977, pp. 82-83).

In chapter 2 we examined analytical perspectives on the study of organisations in general, without distinguishing among different kinds of organisations. However, many social and welfare workers are inclined towards a view that the organisations in and through which they work have characteristics that set them apart from other kinds of organisations. We have seen that some workers describe their organisations as 'social work agencies', a term which suggests an organisation engaged in distinctive tasks of a professional nature (Warham 1977, p. 63). Writers sometimes seek to draw a distinction between 'people-serving' social welfare organisations and 'people-exploiting' business and industrial organisations (Austin 1981, p. 39). In a similar vein, there is sometimes considerable resistance to applying general administrative or managerial criteria of efficiency and effectiveness to organisations involved in social welfare, on the grounds that these are inappropriate for services to people. If the organisations in which social and welfare workers are employed do have distinctive characteristics, understanding these is clearly an important element of organisational analysis. These are the issues that we focus on in this chapter.

The term most commonly used which denotes the distinctiveness of the organisational settings of social and welfare work is 'human service organisation'. The use of this term suggests that there is a class of organisations involved in a distinctive set of activities with characteristic problems and issues. We use this term throughout the book to refer to the kinds of organisations in which social and welfare workers are located. In our view, human service organisations are, indeed, distinctive. But what exactly does the term mean? In what ways do human service organisations differ from other kinds of organisations? What are the implications of these differences for social and welfare workers?

These questions reflect a broader debate in organisation theory. One theme in writings about organisations, particularly in the management literature, is that all organisations resemble each other so closely that similar principles apply to understanding and working in all of them (e.g. Caplow 1976, p. 5). However, alongside this emphasis there has been an increasing recognition of the 'variety of the species' (Perrow 1970, pp. 27-49). This latter view holds that,

> different types of organizations have different processes, structures, environments, customers, clients, employee aspirations, and contingencies . . . it is considered more fruitful to try to understand organizations in terms of those elements that are unique or specific to them rather than in terms of those things that are general to all organizations (Zey-Ferrell and Aiken 1981, p. 16).

The difficulty with this approach lies in deciding which features of organisations will be used to classify them. There are numerous criteria for classifying organisations, including societal function, prime beneficiary, nature of compliance and type of technology (Etzioni and Lehman 1980, pp. 85-86). How can it be decided what is the best way of sorting out the similarities and differences among organisations?

These issues arise for anyone using the term human service organisation. The issue is complicated by the variety of organisations that comprise any given type. The organisations that employ social and welfare workers are a mixed bag, varying in size, auspice, service field, degree of professionalisation, authority structure, and so forth. Do these varied organisations have any common, key characteristics that set them apart from other kinds of organisations?

To address these questions we will examine the three criteria most commonly used in the literature, and in daily usage, to distinguish human service organisations. These are purpose, technology and auspice. Definitions of human service organisations sometimes combine these three criteria. For example, Hasenfeld denotes human service organisations as,

> . . . that set of organizations whose principal function is to protect, maintain, or enhance the personal well-being of individuals by defining, shaping, or altering their personal attributes . . . These organizations are distinguished from other bureaucracies by two key characteristics. First, they work with and on people whose attributes they attempt to shape. People are in a sense their 'raw material'. Second, they are mandated—and

thus justify their existence—to protect and promote the welfare of the people they serve (1983, p. 1).

This widely used definition includes elements of purpose (enhancing personal well-being), technology or technique (defining, shaping or altering personal attributes) and auspice (publicly mandated to protect and promote welfare). The usefulness of each criteria needs careful examination.

Purpose

It is common for human service organisations to be distinguished from other organisations in terms of their supposedly distinctive purposes. Human service organisations, it is argued, are those that aim to meet the needs and contribute to the well-being of their consumers, and to contribute to overall social welfare. These elements are stressed in formal definitions of human service organisations, such as Hasenfeld's cited above. Similarly, Martin's definition begins with the statement that 'the purpose of human service organizations is to meet socially recognised needs of people' (1985, p. 130). She, in common with many other writers and practitioners, explicitly distinguishes human service organisations from private production organisations, whose main purpose is assumed to be profit:

> Despite increasing social pressures on private sector production organizations to take into account the social consequences of their operations, a contrast can be drawn between them and public human service organizations, the mandate of which is the meeting of human need and the promotion of human well-being (Martin 1985, p. 129).

The strengths and limitations of purpose as a basis on which to distinguish human service organisations from all others, can be illustrated by an examination of Blau and Scott's widely quoted classification of organisations according to their 'prime beneficiary', that is, the person or group who is intended to benefit most from the organisation (Blau and Scott 1962). Blau and Scott suggest that organisations essentially comprise four main categories of persons: members or rank-and-file workers; owners and managers; consumers (patients, customers, prisoners, students, and so on); and the public-at-large, that is, the members of the society in which the organisation operates. Organisations, they suggest, can be usefully classified according to which of these groups is the intended prime beneficiary. 'Mutual benefit associations' are those where the prime beneficiary is the membership. 'Business concerns' primarily benefit owners and managers. In 'service organisations' the consumer is of paramount concern, and in 'commonweal organisations' it is the public-at-large.

Blau and Scott suggest that this is a useful approach to the analysis of organisations because different kinds of organisations have their own distinctive issues and concerns (Blau and Scott 1980, p. 103). For example, they suggest that the crucial problem facing mutual-benefit associations is that of providing for participation and control by the membership. These issues are familiar to workers in community-based organisations. In business concerns, by contrast, the overriding need is to maximise operating efficiency to beat the competition. Service organisations, they suggest, are characterised by endemic conflict between professions and administrators, while the crucial problem posed by commonweal organisations is that of developing mechanisms whereby they can be accountable to the general public.

This approach to understanding organisational issues has some value. It is certainly true that the purposes that organisations espouse mean that they must confront certain kinds of organisational issues. For example, many of the organisations in which social and welfare workers are located claim to be concerned above all else with consumer well-being—they are service organisations in Blau and Scott's classification. This claim means that issues of organisation–consumer relations will be central concerns. Such organisations have to decide what legitimacy to give to consumer definitions of their own needs as opposed to the definitions of others, such as professionals, workers, managers and the community. They also have to justify their operations in terms of the achievement of desirable outcomes for consumers, and develop fair or acceptable ways of working with consumers.

On close examination, however, attempts to distinguish human service organisations in terms of purpose present difficulties. These stem, essentially, from the multiplicity of purposes of all organisations. Organisations have many different goals and many different beneficiaries. The extent to which different groups actually benefit from an organisation is a matter to be investigated rather than assumed. Furthermore, we cannot assume that because an organisation says that its primary purpose is service, or meeting the needs of consumers, that this is in fact the case. There is a need to distinguish between the official or stated goals of an organisation and its operative goals, that is, what it actually does (these points are examined in detail in chapter 5).

These issues can be illustrated by considering the example of a hostel for people with psychiatric disabilities operated as a profit-making venture, with public subsidy and subject to governmental regulations. Who is the prime beneficiary of the hostel? No doubt the official ideology is that the hostel is a service organisation whose purpose is to provide accommodation and care for the residents. But it can also be argued that it is a commonweal organisation, in that it is dealing with the social problem of disability on behalf of the broader society, and receiving public funds to do so. At the same time it is also a business concern that aims to show a profit for those who have invested in the enterprise. There is also evidence that it is commonplace in residential organisations for staff to give higher priority to their own interests than to the interests of residents. Is the hostel a service organisation, a commonweal organisation, a business concern or a mutual-benefit organisation for employees? In fact, like many organisations, it is a mix of Blau and Scott's organisational types, and many organisational issues stem from the competing expectations of the organisation's potential beneficiaries.

The difficulties of distinguishing human service organisations by their purpose can also be approached by considering the place of these organisations in the broader society. There is a need to distinguish between the formal ideology of an organisation, its policy in operation, and its function in society (Smith 1979, pp. ix-xi). We saw in chapter 2, that the functions of human service organisations may be seen to include assisting the processes of capitalist production and accumulation, legitimising inequalities and inequities, reproducing and reinforcing gender relations, and maintaining order and social control. This presents a different picture from Hasenfeld and Martin, with their emphasis on meeting human needs and enhancing individual well-being. An organisation's purposes, we can conclude, do raise characteristic problems and issues that affect its operations and activities. But we must not make naive assumptions about the purposes and functions of organisations that claim human service as their domain.

Technology

The idea that human service organisations can be distinguished according to their technology, by which is meant 'the nature of their work', has developed into a substantial body of theoretical writings during the 1970s and 1980s (Sarri 1971; Vintner 1974; Hasenfeld and English 1974, pp. 1-23; Sarri and Hasenfeld 1978, pp. 1-18; Hasenfeld 1983, pp. 1-11). This emphasis on the role of technology in shaping organisational structures and processes is not new: the impact and implications of technology have been major concerns in organisation theory since the late 1950s (Silverman 1970, pp. 100-125). What is original is an emphasis on the distinction between work with physical and non-animate objects and work with people. For Hasenfeld and his colleagues it is this latter factor that gives human service organisations their distinctive character. Viewed from this perspective, human service organisations are those that are engaged in defining, shaping, or altering the personal attributes of individuals. Hasenfeld's use of the term human service organisation encompasses virtually all of the organisational settings for social and welfare work including schools, hospitals, welfare agencies, correctional institutions, mental health clinics, and employment agencies. These organisations, he argues, share a 'unique set of characteristics' (1983, p. 9) that give rise to distinctive organisational attributes and problems.

The most fundamental of these characteristic, according to Hasenfeld and his colleagues, is that human service organisations have people as their raw material. Although this terminology is redolent of a mechanistic, scientific management view of organisations in which people are reduced to objects, Hasenfeld is actually arguing the opposite. The distinctive attributes and problems of human service organisations arise, he argues, because their consumers have a moral, social and political identity, and are 'self-activating', that is, their responses are determined not only by what is being done to them, but also by their own desires, motivations and experiences (Hasenfeld and English 1974, p. 8).

The moral identity of consumers means that human service organisations must take into account prevailing community standards about what is a fair, just and reasonable way of working with people. They must make judgements about the morality and acceptability of organisational behaviour (for example, is corporal punishment acceptable in schools? Is it reasonable to check on the marital and living situations of social security recipients?) and of consumer behaviour (for example, what constitutes child abuse? What makes a person deserving of access to a nursing home or of receipt of emergency relief?). These value judgements have consequences for a consumer's self-identity and life chances. Consequently, human service organisations develop, and are heavily reliant on, ideological systems that provide their personnel with reference points for making and justifying their decisions and policies.

In addition, consumers have a social and political identity that shapes their relations to the organisation. Consumers have an identifiable social position based on such factors as class, gender, occupation, culture, ethnicity and race, and geographic location, and may have affiliations with organisations that represent these factors. They are also citizens or residents who have legal and political rights and responsibilities. Human service organisations must keep these matters of affiliation and status in mind when designing, allocating and providing their services. The decisions of human service organisations may contribute significantly to the social and economic opportunities available to people, or may marginalise and exclude them. Such processes of marginalisation are illustrated in Perrow and Guillen's account of human service organisation's responses to the AIDS crisis (1990), and Collman's account of the treatment of Australian Aborigines by mainstream human service organisations (1988).

Working with people involves not only moral and social ambiguities, but also technical uncertainties. Hasenfeld and English express this by saying that human service organisations are often characterised by relatively indeterminate technologies, that is, the links between what they do and the outcomes they wish to attain are relatively unclear. They identify several factors that influence the determinacy of an organisation's technology (1974, p. 13). The desired outcomes themselves may be unclear (this is discussed below). Consumers may vary greatly in their personal attributes, and in their attitude to the organisation: what works for one person may not work for someone else. The attributes of the people providing the service may also vary greatly. Furthermore, what an organisation does may be based on incomplete knowledge about cause and effect. All of these factors contribute to technical indeterminacy.

Human service organisations vary a great deal in the determinacy of their technologies. Some medical procedures, grounded on a well-established knowledge base, appear highly determinate, while technologies for the detection and prevention of child abuse appear relatively unclear and imprecise. The perception of technical indeterminacy is problematic for a human service organisation as it effects its standing and legitimacy, and organisational morale. For these reasons, most human service organisations attempt to standardise their technology and in various ways try to promote the belief within and outside the organisation that what they do really works.

One of the reasons given by Hasenfeld and others for the indeterminacy of the technology of human service organisations is that their goals are difficult to specify and measure. Partly, this is because their goals tend to be ideological in nature, that is, they are essentially about values, beliefs and norms. This creates problems for human service organisations as there is typically widespread disagreement both within and outside the organisation about these values and norms. These disagreements are strongest when the organisation is dependent on diverse outside organisations or groups holding differing views on the goals the organisation should pursue, and when there are differing views within the organisation associated with different professional, occupational and social groups. The personal goals of workers and consumers may be congruent or in conflict with dominant organisational goals. In either case, these individual goals will also affect the goals that are pursued in and through the organisation.

Perhaps the most problematic attribute of human service organisations is the difficulty that they have in demonstrating their effectiveness. The indeterminacy of technology, the difficulty in observing and measuring goals such as mental health, rehabilitation and family functioning, and technical difficulties of measurement all contribute to the lack of reliable and valid measures of effectiveness. How is it possible to measure an 'improved sense of personal well-being' arising from a counselling programme, in terms that are acceptable to all parties? Comparison is often drawn with organisations such as manufacturing corporations where success can be measured in terms of the goods produced and sold at a certain level of profit (Vintner 1974, p. 46).

This characteristic, it is argued, produces a number of difficulties for human service organisations. It is a major cause of the difficulty that they face in legitimating their activities and obtaining resources from the external environment. It may also lead to displacement of goals. In the absence of clear and measures of effectiveness, the organisation is prone to evaluate itself on criteria not directly related to outcomes, such as volume of work done, efficiency, or adherence to rules. Lack of clear measures of effectiveness also inhibits innovation and change; if new methods and approaches have difficulty in demonstrating superior effectiveness, and if the shortcomings of existing methods are difficult to demonstrate, change is hindered. 'Reasoned choice among alternative courses of action and development of more effective measures are rendered more difficult when crucial knowledge about consequences is lacking' (Vintner 1974, p. 49). Finally, human service organisations are prone to highly subjective and doctrinaire assessments of organisational effectiveness. There is a tendency for claims for success to be based on subjective evaluation by staff and testimony from consumers, and for the views of outsiders to be discounted. This results in reinforcement of existing services and organisational ideologies.

In organisations that work with people, the core activities of the organisations are staff–consumer relationships. It is through these relationships, constructed as roles such as teacher–pupil, doctor–patient, social worker–client, counter staff–applicant, that the organisation determines its responsibilities, assesses need, and undertakes its work with people. The success or failure of the organisation with respect to its ostensible goals are largely determined by the nature and quality of the relations between staff and consumers. These relations vary in duration, scope, frequency and intensity according to the kind of work to be done. Organisations hoping to bring about major changes in consumer attitudes and behaviour will typically require long, frequent and intensive relationships with them (Hasenfeld and English 1974, pp. 14-15).

One implication of the prime importance of these relations is the need to invest organisational resources in the employment, training and support of front-line workers. Another is the need to find ways of ensuring the quality and accountability of these workers. This latter issue presents major problems for many human service organisations. The quality of staff–consumer relationships is affected by people's personal attributes. Moreover, the visibility of these interactions is very low, and there are legal, ethical, technical, and economic reasons that make it difficult for the organisation to exert close supervision (Hasenfeld 1983, p. 10). There is often considerable conflict in human service organisations between senior administrative staff who are intent on maximising their control, and front-line workers who are equally intent on maximising their autonomy and discretion. These issues are discussed in detail in chapter 8.

This last mentioned conflict often involves issues relating to the role of professionals in organisations. Human service organisations typically rely heavily on professional staff to undertake work with people, and the trend towards increasing professionalisation seems to be continuing. Relations with professional groups such as doctors, lawyers, psychologists, teachers and therapists are an important part of the daily work of many social and welfare workers. Moreover, workers themselves often rely heavily on an assumed or claimed professional status to enhance their position, influence and autonomy within organisations.

There are a number of reasons for the widespread employment of professionals in human service organisations (Hasenfeld and English 1974, pp. 17-20; Vintner 1974, pp. 40-44). One ostensible reason is that these organisations require the codified knowledge and commitment to service ideals that are the hallmarks of a professional service. Certainly, many human service organisations rely heavily on the knowledge and skills that professionals are believed to provide. However, other functions served by the employment of professions include the legitimation of the organisation, the strengthening of organisational control over front-line work, and the attainment of relatively stable labour markets.

Extensive reliance on professionals, while necessary for the effective functioning of many human service organisations, also brings with it a number of organisational problems. Authority and control structures in highly professionalised organisations are often complex and cumbersome. The organisation's demand for compliance with its rules and procedures and the profession's demands for autonomy and discretion must invariably be negotiated and resolved. Organisations employing several different professions may face difficulties in integrating and co-ordinating their activities and providing a coherent, consumer-focused service. Some organisations become locations for the exercise of professional techniques and skills which are not closely related to organisational goals as perceived by other groups inside and outside the organisation. Highly professionalised organisations may get out of touch with the consumer groups the organisation wishes to serve. Friction between professional groups may generate conflicts that are wasteful of organisational resources, and that detract from services to consumers.

This analysis of the distinctive characteristics of organisations that work with people is based largely on the work of Hasenfeld and his colleagues. We are in agreement with their basic proposition that technology is one useful way of identifying the distinctive features of human service organisations, alongside purpose and auspice. However, one important criticism of this approach is that this concept of human service organisation is too general and all-encompassing to provide a sound basis for organisational analysis. Stein refers to the concept as a 'voracious shark, swallowing diverse organisations like so many schools of fish' (1981, p. 32). He suggests that the term, as well as including health, education and social work services, could also cover a dentist's office, a law firm, a maximum security prison, a public library, a for-profit marital counselling agency, a state public welfare system, and a barber shop:

> ... the use of the term to connote a defined type of organization with specific behavioural, functional, and management characteristics is confusing because it does not reflect reality. In current usage, it usually lumps together service agencies that differ markedly in function, auspice, relationship to marketplace, size and structure, and other critical variables, and therefore does little, when used as an analytic concept, to help in understanding organizational behaviour, management, or implications for service delivery (Stein 1981, p. 34).

Stein's criticism is countered by the argument that, although organisations that work with people have common or distinguishing characteristics, this does not mean that they are all alike. Technology, as well as being a means of distinguishing human service organisations from other organisations, can also be used to classify them. Hasenfeld suggests that there are two key dimensions for categorising human service organisations: the types of consumers that they serve and the procedures and techniques that they use to bring about changes in their consumers. He suggests that there are major differences in organisational functioning and societal expectations between organisations whose primary task is to enhance the well-being of persons judged to be functioning adequately in society, and those whose task is to deal with those judged to be malfunctioning or deviant (1983, p. 4).

Hasenfeld also suggests that we should distinguish between people-processing, people-sustaining, and people-changing technologies (1983, p. 5). People-processing involves providing people with a label or a status that leads to them being treated in certain ways by other organisations and social institutions. The acquisition of labels such as 'sole parent', 'disabled' or 'veteran' become prerequisites to receiving services or benefits. People-sustaining technologies provide personal welfare or care, without necessarily attempting to change the person's attributes. Support services such as child-care, accommodation, and home visiting may fall within this category. People-changing technologies attempt to alter the personal attributes of people. Examples are family therapy, budget counselling and educational programmes. We argue that a fourth category, people-controlling, should be added to Hasenfeld's list to cover the functions of organisations such as prisons, psychiatric institutions and correctional programmes which are often primarily concerned with control, restraint, or, in some cases, repression. This diversity of functions requires workers to maintain a critical view of the nature of service in their organisations.

Auspice

The third criteria that can be used to distinguish human service organisations is the nature of their auspice. By auspice is meant the patronage or mandate under which the organisation operates. The organisations that employ social and welfare workers in Australia operate under several different auspices including non-profit voluntary and community-based associations, profit-making ventures, and government organisations. These differences are important, and will be examined shortly. However, many writers have stressed that a central, defining characteristic of human service organisations is their public auspice, or, to put it another way, that they are part of the state. The existence of a public auspice or mandate is implicit in much of Hasenfeld's analysis of human service organisations (see especially Sarri and Hasenfeld 1978, pp. 1-18). Martin also argues that 'any attempt to define the peculiar features of human service organisations should give due weight to the public nature of their mandate and resource base' (1985, p. 128). In a similar vein, Austin defines human service organisations as 'the group of formal organisations under government and non-profit philanthropic auspices that produce public services' (1980, pp. 38-39).

From this perspective, it can be argued that the vast majority of the organisations that employ social and welfare workers operate under public auspice, and are, directly or indirectly, part of the state. Social and welfare workers in Australia are mainly employed either directly by government departments and agencies, or by non-government organisations that are funded and regulated to a significant degree by government. This way of thinking about human service organisations parallels our emphasis in chapter 1 on the need to link policy and practice. It means that workers need to think about their practice as taking place in and through the state. We will now examine some of the key characteristics of state organisations, and issues associated with working in them.

One fundamental characteristic of state, or public auspice, organisations is that they operate in a political environment, and are directly shaped by public policy processes. 'Fundamental to all public good provision is the fact that the determination of the amount and form of the public good to be provided, and the assessment of the service outputs and outcomes, is a collective or political process' (Austin 1980, pp. 57-58). This results in certain inherent vulnerabilities and uncertainties. Decisions about the goals and activities of the organisation are subject to pressure from groups such as legislators, political parties, pressure groups, the media and the electorate. Consequently, goals and objectives may be many, diverse and possibly conflicting. Economic and political changes will have a direct impact as human service organisations are often heavily or solely dependent on public resources. Organisations working with people are particularly vulnerable to these pressures given their often unclear goals and lack of clear measures of effectiveness.

A related characteristic of state organisations is that they experience tension between societal and consumer goals. Human service organisations typically provide services to individual consumers. However, these services are not solely, and in many cases are not primarily, designed with consumer preferences and satisfaction in mind. Economists have used the term 'merit goods' to refer to goods or benefits provided to a consumer in which the values and preferences of the provider, or a third party, determine the form and amount of the benefit provided. Many social services provided through human service organisations fall into this category. Many examples can be provided. The extreme case is that of mandatory 'services' such as correctional institutions, where notions of societal welfare take clear preference over prisoner preferences and satisfaction. Somewhat more blurred is the example of publicly funded marriage guidance counselling services. These are provided not only for the benefit of those couples receiving advice and support, but also because it is presumed to be in the interests of society as a whole to reduce marital disharmony and prevent family breakdown. Such services are provided for a combination of reasons to do with public expenditure, social stability and public morality.

The implication of the 'merit goods' characteristic of human services is that the operation of human service organisations involves ongoing ambiguities and uncertainties about the mixture of general welfare and individual benefit objectives. While the ideology of social and welfare work often stresses the primacy of consumer preferences and interests, the extent to which these are of foremost concern within the organisation is problematic. This is certainly the case when there is direct conflict between the interests of dominant societal groups and the interests of consumers. If human service organisations are seen (as in the neo-Marxian perspective) to be dominated by such goals and functions as assisting the process of capital accumulation, assisting the reproduction of labour power, and social legitimation and control (see chapter 2), then issues of consumer satisfaction may often be of only marginal concern.

The above factors often result in highly ambiguous professional roles in public sector organisations. This is because it is often unclear whether and to what degree professionals should identify with consumer goals, with broader welfare or societal goals, or with the goals of the organisation. Professionals may adopt the view that consumer needs and preferences should define their activities, as in the traditional model of private professional practice. But alternatively they may identify with broader societal or organisational goals, stressing the responsibilities of professional service to the larger society or organisation (Austin 1980, pp. 80-81). There is no unambiguous resolution of these issues. Each worker must deal with them in the light of their own personal and professional values.

A further characteristic of public sector organisations is that there may be relatively weak links between goals, techniques, outputs and outcomes. A commonly held view of policy-making and implementation is that policy decisions are made by legislators, ministers, or members of executive committees, translated into administrative directions by managers, which in turn shape worker activities. This leads, it is assumed, to organisational outputs that will have the outcomes intended by the original policy decision. In this model, workers have a relatively clear, albeit constricted, place in the policy process.

Our earlier discussion of the technology of human service organisations indicates a number of factors (such as unclear goals and indeterminate technology) that are likely to impede the operation of this model. However, there are also factors relating to the public auspice of human service organisations that make these linkages problematic. It can be argued that the key impediments to such rational implementation stem from the nature of political relations within public auspice organisations (Austin 1980, pp. 76-80). The processes of policy development and implementation are political, involving compromises between conflicting values, and among key interest groups. Moreover, the symbolic functions performed by a human service organisation may be of equal or greater importance than its substantive functions. The establishment and support of an organisation may demonstrate symbolic recognition of a problem or issue by a public body, and this, rather than any demonstrated outcomes, may be the political justification for its existence and the source of its political and community support.

Finally, it must be stressed that services that are provided under public auspice are subject to a range of public accountability requirements. This is the case whether the service is provided directly by a government department, or indirectly through a publicly funded or regulated non-government organisation, although the nature and scope of these requirements vary in different contexts. The mechanisms designed to ensure accountability include the legislation and regulations establishing the service, general legislation concerning the behaviour and actions of public sector employees, ministerial and administrative controls, financial accountability requirements, parliamentary processes, advisory and consultative mechanisms, and processes established under administrative law (for example, ombudsman, administrative appeals mechanisms, freedom of information legislation). Public auspice organisations undertake their often precarious balancing of social objectives and consumer satisfaction in this context of extensive formal accountability requirements.

Almost all social and welfare workers in Australia are employed in organisations that operate under public auspice, and are thus subject to the issues, structures and processes discussed above. However, as noted above, public auspice can take a variety of forms. It is important to examine the differences among these different forms, as each have distinctive characteristics and present different challenges, constraints and opportunities to the workers employed in them.

Many social and welfare workers are currently employed directly by government departments or statutory bodies. The essential feature of a government department in the Australian system of government is that it works directly for and to a minister, and is subject to his or her direction. The minister, who is a member of the majority political party or parties in the parliament, provides political leadership and control of the department. At the non-party political level, direction is provided by a senior official known variously as a permanent head, director-general or secretary. Departments are usually organised on an essentially hierarchical basis, with their functions being divided into divisions, branches, regions, areas and units. The formal and informal relations among these sections of the department are often quite complex. Social and welfare workers are usually located in sections of the department that also comprise other officials and professionals, but they may also in some circumstances be part of a unit with its own separate identity and function within the organisation. Some examples of departments that employ social workers are the Commonwealth Department of Social Security, and the various state departments of community and family services, housing and health.

Social and welfare workers are also located in government agencies which have been established by statute. Statutory bodies are an alternative organisational form to departments for achieving the purposes of government. While they vary considerably in organisational structure, generally they are managed by a governing body often called a commission or a board and have some greater degree of independence in their day-to-day operation than do government departments. Examples of statutory bodies that employ social and welfare workers are hospital boards, housing commissions, and corrective services commissions in various states. Local government authorities, which have become a significant employer of social and welfare workers, are statutory bodies in that they are created by and subject to state local government Acts and other legislation. They differ from other statutory bodies in that the councillors are elected, and in the breadth of their responsibilities.

The characteristics of public auspice organisations, outlined above, are typically experienced by workers employed by government departments and agencies in a quite direct fashion. Workers employed by government departments operate within policy, legislative and resource frameworks that are the outcome of complex political processes. These processes are ongoing, often involving many organisations, groups and individuals. As a result, the worker's context is often in a state of flux, with policy and resource guidelines subject to frequent change and revision. Moreover, the complexity of large government departments, and the public sector generally, means that social and welfare workers are but one group among many seeking to shape organisational activities. Professional and personal goals and aspirations must typically be transacted in the context of the responsibilities that the worker has as an official: to perform statutory duties, to act within established policies, and to be subject to requirements for public accountability.

Many social and welfare workers are also employed by not-for-profit organisations. These may be structured in a number of different ways. Often they comprise a membership or constituency that elects or appoints a management board (and sometimes a smaller executive), which in turn may appoint staff to undertake the day-to-day work of the organisation. The organisation has a constitution which outlines its aims and philosophy, and specifies the rules by which it will function. In its 'pure' form, the not-for-profit, or 'voluntary' organisation, is essentially a private body, that is not part of the public sector. Its membership provides its auspice. In reality, however, most not-for-profit organisations operate under public auspice to a greater or lesser degree. Most importantly, many are dependent to a considerable degree on public funding to carry out their functions. This funding often brings with it requirements and expectations that the organisation will operate within a particular policy framework, and meet certain requirements of public accountability. Not-for-profit organisations are also often required to meet certain regulatory requirements of government. This also brings them within the ambit of the public sector.

Because of these links to the public sector, many non-government organisations share many of the characteristics of public auspice organisations. They are susceptible to changes in their political environment, and are required to be accountable for their activities to funding and regulatory bodies. These demands must be balanced with the accountability that the staff and management of a non-government organisation have towards their membership or constituency. Workers in such organisations are often faced with complex situations which require them to develop services and activities and work in ways that take account of these diverse organisational pressures.

Human services are also provided by private sector organisations, also referred to as commercial or for-profit organisations. Private sector organisations have been a feature of human service provision for many years. Hospitals, nursing homes, medical services and child-care centres are examples of human services provided by the private sector, as well as other sectors. More recently, private provision has been extended into fields such as rehabilitation, counselling and prisons. Private sector organisations are constituted as companies. These may be owner-operated, such as private medical practices or small child-care centres, or they may be larger, more complex structures with shareholders, a board of directors, and employed managers and staff.

Like not-for-profit organisations, private sector human service organisations are often extensively funded, subsidised or regulated by the public sector. They must, therefore, deal with requirements for public accountability, and be responsive to the changing political environment. These pressures must be reconciled with their requirements to show a financial return on investment and to be a profitable enterprise. It is still relatively uncommon for social and welfare workers in Australia to be employed in private sector organisations, although this may change with increasing interest in the privatisation of human services.

Conclusions

There is no final, unambiguous and definitive way of distinguishing human service organisations from all other kinds of organisations. However, the three approaches to this issue that we have examined provide a basis for analysis of the distinctive nature of the organisations in which social and welfare workers are located. There are differences between working for, say, a Coca-Cola bottling plant and working for a youth refuge or a rehabilitation agency. The latter organisations are distinguished by the kinds of goals they espouse, the kind of work they do, and their auspice.

The theoretical analysis undertaken in this chapter provides a framework through which workers can examine the distinctive nature of their organisational context, and the ways in which this shapes their work. The issues and circumstances that workers face in organisations are not arbitrary; they stem from organisational characteristics that can be identified and analysed. Workers need to ask the question: 'What kind of organisation am I working in, and what are the implications of this for my work?' Often, the answer to this question will be complex.

Table 3.1 'What is distinctive about my organisation?': an analytical framework

Key questions	*Issues and implications*
PURPOSE	
1 What purposes does the organisation espouse?	i 'service' goals may compete with other purposes
2 What other purposes does the organisation serve?	ii stated purposes may differ from the organisation's operational purposes and from its broader societal functions
TECHNOLOGY	
3 What is the nature of the organisation's technology?	Consider the implications of the following characteristics:
4 Is it involved in:	i 'raw material' is people
i people processing?	ii indeterminate technology
ii people sustaining?	iii ambiguous goals
iii people changing?	iv staff-consumer relations are critical
iv people controlling?	v reliance on professionals
v combination of these?	vi poor effectiveness measures
5 Which of the characteristics of 'people' organisations listed opposite apply?	
AUSPICE	
6 What is the nature of the organisation's auspice?	Consider the implications of the following characteristics:
7 Does it operate under public auspice?	i dependent on complex environment
8 Is it a:	ii tension between society and consumers
i government department?	iii weak linkages between goals and outcomes
ii government agency?	iv ambiguous professional roles
iii not-for-profit organisation?	v public accountability requirements
iv private sector organisation?	
9 Which of the characteristics of public auspice organisations listed opposite apply?	
10 How do the purposes, technologies and auspice of this organisation interact and inter-relate?	

The espoused purposes, technology and auspice of a particular organisation interact in complicated and often puzzling ways. Nevertheless, an attempt to unravel this complexity will assist workers to become more effective in organisations.

In Table 3.1 we outline an analytical framework that workers can use to analyse the distinctive features of any human service organisation, including their own. The questions listed in the table provide a systematic approach to the question, 'What kind of organisation am I working in?' The kinds of issues and problems associated with different kinds of organisations can then be identified and appraised, using the material in this chapter. This table provides a summary of the main themes and issues raised in the chapter, and can be used as a practice tool in organisational analysis. The case study which follows provides an opportunity to examine the usefulness of the framework in understanding the kinds of organisational issues that confront workers.

Chapter review questions

1 What do you understand by the term 'human service organisation'?
2 Can human service organisations be distinguished from other kinds of organisations in terms of purpose? Why or why not?
3 What, if anything, is distinctive about the technology of human service organisations? What are typical characteristics of organisations that 'work with people'?
4 What are the differences between people processing, people sustaining, people changing and people controlling? What are examples of each of these processes? Is this a useful way of classifying human service technologies?
5 What are the main consequences of the public auspice of human service organisations?
6 What are some of the implications for social and welfare workers of the characteristics of human service organisations identified in this chapter?

Further reading

A good starting point is Hasenfeld's brief definition and elaboration of human service organisations (1983, pp. 1-11). An earlier, lengthier conceptual overview can be found in Hasenfeld and English (1974, pp. 1-23). For a critique of Hasenfeld's approach see Stein (1981) and Martin (1985). Vinter (1974) looks at the characteristics of organisations that attempt to change people classified in some way as deviant or malfunctioning. Austin (1981) analyses the implications of public auspice for human service organisations, see especially pp. 37-41, 51-61 and 76-86. A more straightforward approach is Warham's discussion of the implications of public sponsorship, financing, control and administration (1977, pp. 30-62). Although she is concerned mainly with social workers in the British social services, her analysis has general applicability. Etzioni and Lehman (1980, pp. 85-130) provide a selection of the classical readings on comparing organisations. Some of these classification systems are critiqued in relation to social work by Smith (1979, pp. ix-xi and 17-23).

Case study

THE OUTER NICKLIN REHABILITATION UNIT

The Outer Nicklin Rehabilitation Unit was recently established to provide a range of rehabilitation services in Outer Nicklin, a large, suburban area, population 200 000, located on the fringe of an Australian capital city. The Unit is part of the Commonwealth Department of Community Services, Housing and Health and is responsible for the provision of rehabilitation services to people with disabilities in the area. The Unit has been in its existing premises, a modern suite of offices in the main shopping plaza, for less than three months.

The Outer Nicklin area mainly comprises low to medium cost, privately owned, family dwellings built during the last fifteen years, and dwellings constructed and rented by the public housing authorities. There is above average unemployment and household incomes in the area are below average. The region is ethnically diverse, and there is a high proportion of sole-parent families. There is also a high proportion of young people in the area and unemployment is a major problem among this group. Major sources of employment include a large vehicle assembly plant, a major hospital, a government office complex, and a range of light industries. Many residents commute to work in other parts of the city.

The Unit operates under the provisions of the Disability Services Act of 1986. This Commonwealth legislation states that the eligibility group for Commonwealth-provided rehabilitation services (such as the Unit) is:

sect. 18 . . . those persons who—

(A) have attained 14 years of age but have not attained 65 years of age; and

(B) have a disability that—

(i) is attributable to an intellectual, psychiatric, sensory or physical impairment or a combination of such impairments; and

(ii) results in a substantially reduced capacity of the person—

   (a) to obtain or retain unsupported paid employment; or

   (b) to live independently.

The Act empowers the Unit to provide or arrange for the provision of rehabilitation programmes of many kinds. Those specifically mentioned in the Act include:

sect. 20 (5) . . .
(a) employment and vocational training, educational courses and programmes, and mobility and other independent living training;
(b) diagnostic and assessment services, medical services, occupational therapy, physiotherapy, speech therapy, and counselling and social work services;
(c) accommodation, transportation and personal support services;
(d) prostheses and aids;
(e) the repair of prostheses and aids;
(f) books, tools of trade and other equipment.

The Unit was established as part of a policy by the Commonwealth government to provide community-based rehabilitation for people with disabilities. Previously, rehabilitation services in the state were provided by the Commonwealth predominantly in large, centralised hospital-like settings. Regional Units such as the one at Outer Nicklin were developed to replace these large residential institutions, and were hailed by the Minister and senior officials in the department as examples of 'smaller, more accessible community-based services'. Critics argued that they were primarily a cost-saving exercise, and that their actual role and purpose was unclear. A number of goals for Regional Units were outlined in ministerial and departmental policy statements. In summary, these stated:

1 services should be relevant to the local context;
2 services should be accessible to those that need them;
3 services should be integrated with other local services;
4 consumer participation in service development should be promoted;
5 community awareness of the needs of disabled people should be increased;
6 services should be provided where possible in normal living situations;
7 the proportion of women, migrants, and Aboriginal people using the service should be increased.

The staff of the Unit comprises a psychologist, a physiotherapist, two rehabilitation counsellors, an occupational therapist, a social worker/ community welfare worker, two clerical assistants and an executive officer. The rehabilitation counsellors, the executive officer and the occupational therapist are experienced in the rehabilitation area, but all other staff are new to this field. Jennifer Martin, the social worker/community welfare worker, was appointed partly because of her experience in community work, which is seen as relevant to the Unit's goals. Other staff bring their own special interests. The occupational therapist is experienced in developing programmes for people suffering from chronic back pain, and is keen to continue her work in this area. One of the rehabilitation counsellors is particularly interested in and knowledgeable about services to people with hearing impairments. The Executive Officer is an occupational therapist who has taken the job to gain some administrative experience. None of the staff have worked in Outer Nicklin before their appointment to the Unit.

The Unit is structured on a multi-disciplinary team model. The Executive Officer has responsibility for administrative functions, but professional staff are not subject to this officer's direction in professional matters, and receive supervision from 'seniors' in their disciplines, who are located in state headquarters. It is envisaged that the Unit will operate on a collegial model with important Unit decisions being made at staff meetings, which are held each Monday morning from 9.00 to 11.00 a.m. The Unit is accountable to a manager in state headquarters, who also has responsibility for six other Units.

During the first three months of operation as a Unit a number of organisational issues have emerged. Staff have expressed difficulty in identifying and explaining their role in the community. Organisations that serve or potentially serve disabled people seem unclear about the Unit's function. There is some scepticism among staff and in the community generally about the whole idea of community-based rehabilitation, and whether it can be put into practice in any useful way. Morale has been affected by a recent circular from the Department imposing tight budget restrictions on the Units, and suggesting that the Units increase their proportion of 'compensable' clients, that is, those whose fees for the Unit's services will be met by a third party, such as workers' compensation or an insurance company. Units have also been told by the Department that they must show that their work with consumers results in 'demonstrable positive outcomes for consumers'. They have also been told that the cost-efficiency and cost-effectiveness of each Unit will be evaluated in a major review, to be undertaken in two years' time. There is already talk of Units being abolished and their functions being performed by private sector professionals and organisations.

Some tension is also emerging between staff members concerning the kinds of rehabilitation work that the Unit should undertake. Some staff are keen to follow their professional interests, and argue that the issues of what programmes to run and which consumers to accept should be left as a matter for their own professional judgement. Jennifer argues that the needs of the local community should be the prime consideration. The cost of different kinds of services is also a consideration. It is becoming increasingly apparent that the Department does not look favourably on Units that focus on providing a small number of high-cost services (for example, expensive equipment for people with severe disabilities), preferring to achieve a higher number of outcomes for a given expenditure.

One pressing issue for staff is the introduction of the new computerised management information system. This system requires the Unit to keep detailed records on consumer contact, expenditure, and unit plans and activities. Staff are worried about the amount of time they need to spend on filling out forms, and the extent of control that the system will give senior management.

A special all-day staff meeting has been convened to discuss current needs and future directions for the Unit. Jennifer sees this as an important meeting and decides to prepare for herself a written analysis of the issues. She sees her role as including working at an organisational level to achieve important goals. She believes that unless some of the organisational issues are addressed, the effectiveness of all workers in the Unit will be impeded. It seems to her that many of the problems facing the Unit are typical of those encountered by human service organisations, and she feels that understanding this will help the workers in the Unit to come to grips with the issues.

Key question

Analyse the distinctive nature and characteristics of the Regional Unit, and the organisational and practice issues that stem from this analysis. In the light of this analysis, what recommendations should Jennifer Martin bring to the meeting concerning the Unit as a whole and her role?

Case discussion points

1 Do you think it is helpful to view this organisation as a human service organisation? Why or why not?
2 The Unit is located in a government department. What implications flow from this?
3 Is this a 'service' organisation in Blau and Scott's terms?
4 Is this organisation concerned with people processing, sustaining, changing or controlling? What implications for the worker flow from this?
5 To what extent do you think the worker will be able to influence the activities of the Unit, and her own role in it? What factors will affect her level of influence?
6 Should organisational matters be the concern of the worker in this case? Why doesn't she just get on with her casework and community work?
7 How does a focus on organisational issues enable the worker to combine policy and practice concerns?

Understanding organisations

PART II

Understanding
organisations

Part II provides a theoretical framework to assist social and welfare workers to undertake organisational analysis. Four key concepts are introduced: organisational environment, organisational goals, organisational structure and organisational culture. Each of these concepts encompasses an aspect of organisational life that social and welfare workers need to understand in order to practise effectively.

Chapter 4 examines the environment of human service organisations. At a general level, the environment can be thought of as everything outside the organisation that influences the organisation, or that the organisation wishes to influence. The chapter examines different ways of conceptualising the environment, the nature of relations between organisation and environment, strategies and tactics for dealing pro-actively with the environment, and the implications for social and welfare work.

Chapter 5 focuses on organisational goals. These can be defined as the future state of affairs that the organisation is trying to bring about. The chapter looks at the nature of organisational goals, their determinants and their impact on organisational participants, especially social and welfare workers. The central concern of this chapter is to show how an understanding of goals can be used by workers to achieve desired outcomes in the organisation.

Chapter 6 examines the concept of organisational structure. This concept refers to the relatively enduring pattern of relations in the organisation, including the system of authority, the division of labour, and patterns of co-ordination, control and communication. These are key issues for workers as they delineate the nature and role of their work in the organisation, as well as impacting generally on organisational outcomes and the treatment of consumers. The chapter examines the factors that shape structures, the structural alternatives for human service organisations, and the ways that workers can use an understanding of structure to work effectively in organisations.

Chapter 7 introduces the concept of organisational culture. Culture is taken to be the beliefs, attitudes, practices, procedures, ideology, rituals and symbols that pervade an organisation. Awareness of the impact of culture is important for workers, whose training strongly emphasises values and attitudes and beliefs. The chapter examines the nature of organisational culture, its sources and consequences in human service organisations, and the practice implications of an awareness of cultural issues in organisations.

4

Organisational environment: context and target

Although many people employed in enterprises of every shape and size do feel that the world in the late twentieth century presents an appallingly complex and changeable jungle, only some of them would see the jungle as totally impenetrable (Dawson 1986, p. 113).

The central theme of this book is that social and welfare workers need to understand the organisations in which they work. However, to pursue this theme, it is necessary to examine a broader canvas. Organisations are not insular phenomena. They are embedded in and are part of complex societies, have their own unique histories, and continually inter-relate with individuals, groups and other organisations. These entities external to the organisation are often collectively referred to as the organisational environment. The environment has a profound impact on organisational goals, structures and processes, and is also the target of the organisation's endeavours. The aims of this chapter are to assist workers make sense of the environments of human service organisations, to identify and discuss the skills needed by workers to deal with organisational environments, and to show the relevance and value of this understanding for practice.

As we saw in chapter 2, the nature and influence of organisational environment is an important and recurring theme in organisation theory. Weber's account of the rise of bureaucracy in modern society is based on an analysis of the impact of changes in the broad social, political and economic environment on organisational structures and processes. The scientific management and human relations schools largely ignored the organisational environment, but the emergence of the systems, and later the ecological, perspective brought the environment to centre stage. Systems theory proposes that organisations be viewed as engaging in ongoing exchanges with groups in their environment, and that these exchanges are necessary for organisational survival and growth. These propositions are now central to our understanding of organisations. Political economy perspectives emphasise the political nature of these exchanges, and the high capacity for influence that is often held by external stakeholders. Neo-Marxian and feminist analysts, and the Aboriginal perspective, direct our attention to the relations between organisations and dominant groups in the society and economy, and the ways in which these shape organisational processes. We have also seen, in chapter 3, that human service organisations are often highly dependent on complex political environments. This chapter attempts to integrate and elaborate these various themes.

The concept of organisational environment is inherently artificial. Take the case of a worker employed in the community services section of a local government authority. He or she may identify strongly with the goals and ethos of the section, and feel a sense of common identity with other workers in the section. The section becomes his or her main point of reference in the organisation. The other members of the local authority—engineers, clerical staff, outdoor workers, and so on—are, from this perspective, part of the environment of the community services section. However, other participants in the local authority may see it differently. From the perspective of the city manager, for example, the community services section is likely to be viewed as a constituent part of the local authority as a whole, the environment of which comprises such entities as the state government departments, other local authorities, professional associations and trade unions, resident action groups, political parties, contractors, local traders, and so forth. Alternatively, from the perspective of a town planner, the planning section may be the key organisational point of reference. None of these perspectives is necessarily preferable to any other. The point is that the conceptualisation of what is 'inside' (part of the organisation) and what is 'outside' (part of the environment) is a matter of position and point of view.

There are two fundamental reasons why an understanding of the nature of organisational environments, and the relations between organisations and their environments, is needed by social and welfare workers. Firstly, for social workers the environment is target. Social and welfare workers profess a concern with social change. This typically involves attempting to work through an organisation to bring about changes in its environment. Take, for example, a worker employed in a women's health centre. As well as working directly with the women who attend the centre, the worker may be engaged in attempts to change the attitudes and practices of health professionals, make generic health services more accessible and responsive to women, change community attitudes around various health issues, and change government policies and funding patterns. She is working through an organisation (the centre) to change aspects of the organisation's environment (other organisations, funding bodies, professions, the community as a whole, and so on). Organisational skills, specifically the capacity to understand and deal with organisation–environment relations, are requisites for workers in such circumstances.

Secondly, and conversely, workers need to understand the environment because of its impact on organisations, consumers and workers themselves. To put it another way, the environment is context. The women's health centre, in the above example, is dependent on its environment for many things, including financial resources, staffing, consumers (referrals) and legitimacy. This dependency makes the centre subject to outside influence. There may be conditions attached to the funds that the centre receives. Other organisations may only make referrals if they are satisfied in certain ways of the quality of the service provided, for example that they are provided by qualified personnel. Attitudes and expectations that are prevalent in the society as a whole influence the ways in which the centre is perceived and dealt with by other organisations and groups. Developing the capacity to deal with these environmental influences is essential to achieving satisfactory outcomes for consumers, and to organisational survival, growth and effectiveness.

The complexity of organisation–environment relations stems from this reality that the environment is both target and context. Paradoxically, human service organisations, and the workers employed by them, are often seeking to bring about changes within the very organisations and groups on which they are dependent. The women's health centre, for example, is confronted with the task of both shaping and adapting to its organisational environment. Its success in negotiating this task will determine its survival and effectiveness. Undertaking this complex task requires a clear conceptualisation of the environment, and an understanding and awareness of the skills and strategies involved in organisation–environment relations.

Competence in the sphere of organisation–environment relations is an important skill for all social and welfare workers, whatever their formal organisational role. For workers with formal administrative responsibilities this competency is, quite clearly, required. Many workers, however, are involved in developing and implementing strategies for organisation–environment relations, even though they are not formally administrators. This is particularly the case in small not-for-profit organisations, and in decentralised units of large government and non-government organisations. Competency in dealing with environmental issues is also important for those involved in community practice. Brager and Specht refer to this as 'managing foreign affairs' (1973, pp. 188-212). Casework often involves direct relations with the organisational–environment. Caseworkers need to be able to access the resources of other organisations, develop collaborative relations, and advocate for consumers in their transactions with other organisations. A capacity to deal with environmental issues enhances the workers' value and usefulness to an organisation, and thus their own capacity for organisational influence. For all these reasons, all workers should make it their business to understand organisation–environment relations.

Conceptualising the environment

The environment can be thought of as everything outside the organisation that influences its operation, or that the organisation wishes to influence. For practice purposes, however, it is necessary to develop a clearer, more analytical, picture of the world outside the organisation. What exactly does the environment comprise? Do different organisations have different kinds of environments that call for different strategies and responses? Are some aspects of organisational environments particularly important or problematic?

Organisation theory provides many models and approaches to conceptualising organisational environments (e.g. Hasenfeld 1983, pp. 50-83; Jackson and Morgan 1978, pp. 229-255; Stoner, Collins and Yetton 1985, pp. 78-89). Our view is that for social and welfare workers there are four approaches that are especially valuable. We suggest that the environment of a human service organisation be thought of as comprising, firstly, a set of overlapping arenas, secondly, a task environment, and thirdly, a general environment. It can also be thought of, fourthly, as having certain definable qualities. Each of these conceptualisations contributes to our overall understanding.

Organisational arenas

All organisations are linked to, and are part of, broader fields of human endeavour. Identifying these fields and linkages, and exploring their implications, is a good starting point for environment analysis. We have called these fields of endeavour 'arenas', a term which suggests competition, conflict and resistance. But they can also be thought of as 'spheres of operation', a term suggesting collaboration and co-operation. Human service organisations can be thought of as taking part in up to five arenas, as portrayed in Figure 4.1.

Firstly, organisations have a geographic identity: they are part of a particular locality. For many human service organisations, locality is a central determinant of organisational functioning. Location influences such factors as consumer characteristics and needs, availability of resources (for example, funds, volunteers, complementary services), accessibility of the organisation's services, and the organisation's political, economic and cultural milieu. Social and welfare workers in

Figure 4.1 The arenas of human service organisation

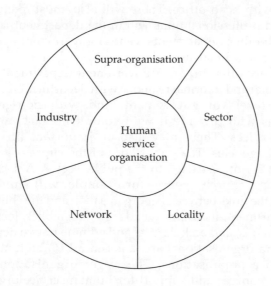

human service organisations need to be aware of and responsive to locality issues. The extent to which an organisation is perceived as identifying with or belonging to a locality influences its acceptance and effectiveness. Organisational linkages within local areas are expressed in part through formal, local organisations such as welfare councils, local councils of social service, local government authorities and progress associations. Equally important are an organisation's informal local links and contacts. Often an organisation has to give consideration to its relations with locality at several levels. For example, an organisation may need to identify with a suburb, a city, a larger region or the whole state or country.

Social and welfare workers have historically paid more attention, in theory at least, to locality than to any of the other arenas we have identified. This largely reflects the influence of community work within social and welfare work. Techniques for analysing the geographic context of practice, such as community profiles, are well known, and are covered in such well-known community work texts as Warren (1965) and Henderson and Thomas (1980, pp. 49-84). This material is extremely useful to analysis of the environment of human service organisations, provided that it is kept in mind that locality is but one of the arenas that workers need to understand.

Human service organisations are also often part of what might be termed a supra-organisational arena. For example, a worker employed in a local branch office of a government department needs to be aware of the complexity of the supra-organisational environment. The branch office may be part of a regional or district office, which in turn will have direct links with head office. There will also, most likely, be other specialist and professional units within the department, and further linkages with other departments, central government agencies and legislative and judicial agencies. The boundaries of the supra-organisation are often fuzzy. A government department may have extensive formal and informal relations with departments and agencies from other levels of government, and with non-government organisations who provide it with complementary, ancillary or necessary services. There may also be important linkages with international agencies. The importance of the supra-organisational environment is not restricted to the public sector. A social worker employed by a church agency, for example, will similarly need awareness of the links between her organisation and the church's social services department, its ruling synods and assemblies, local parishes and congregations, and ecclesiastical and administrative departments.

The supra-organisational arena is central to the functioning of human service organisations. The larger organisation provides legitimacy, resources and support for human service organisations operating under its authority. However, these are not given unconditionally. Perrow suggests that what we term the supra-organisational environment can be thought of in terms of a nested-box:

> . . . inside each box is a smaller box whose dimensions are constrained by the larger box. Each box is independent to some extent of the large boxes (and the smaller ones within it) and can be analyzed as such. But it is also quite dependent on the shape of those within and without it (Perrow 1986, p. 192).

It follows that an understanding of the other boxes in the supra-organisational environment (especially adjacent boxes) is of great importance.

The two arenas we have so far examined are sometimes portrayed as representing the horizontal (locality) and vertical (supra-organisational) dimensions of a human service organisation's environment. However, they are only two of the arenas in which human service organisations must function. Organisations are also linked to sectors. This term has become popular in the parlance of human service workers. There is talk, for example, of the non-government sector or the youth services sector. Other usages include the public sector, the private sector, the small business sector, and so forth. The term 'sector' is sometimes used somewhat imprecisely and inconsistently. We use the term quite specifically to mean organisations and individuals who are organised around common interests and concerns. Take, for example, the community welfare sector. This term is used to denote a broad range of organisations including church-based agencies, providers and consumers of welfare services, and professional associations in the social welfare field. These groups perceive themselves as having some interests in common, such as the need to influence government policy, and have become organised and identified as a sector. Specifically, the Australian Council of Social Service (ACOSS) claims to represent the community welfare sector, and receives wide recognition as such from government and other organisations. The affiliates of ACOSS are not bound by supra-organisational ties or by locality ties (other than by being part of the same nation). What brings them together is a perception of some degree of common interests, goals and concerns.

Human service organisations need to participate actively in the sectors to which they belong, and to encourage the development of sectional identity. Such an identity may be critical to their capacity to participate in political processes. Organisations in the human services area are often dealt with collectively in policy processes, and need to be able to act collectively on many issues of common concern. Organisational activities directed towards major policy changes and other environmental issues are typically co-ordinated and developed through the 'peak' organisations that claim to represent the sector's interests. An understanding of how the sector (or sectors) to which the organisation belongs are structured, how they function, and the implications of associating with them, are important aspects of the conceptualisation of the environment.

Closely related to the concept of sector is the idea that a human service organisation is also part of an industry, or of several overlapping industries. The concept of industry, as used here, refers to a grouping of organisations that comprise a system of production. Industries, considered broadly, can be of many different kinds. They may be highly competitive or dominated by a single, or a small group of organisations. They may be highly regulated and controlled or quite disorderly; tightly structured or loose.

All human service organisations belong to an industry, such as the child-care industry or the aged-services industry, although the extent to which the industry is formally structured and acknowledged varies. The characteristics of a structured and developed industry include consultative and decision-making processes, specialisation and division of labour, established linkages and routines around such matters as referral and intake of consumers and consumers, and formal processes for regulation, training, information production and dissemination, and standards and quality control. Informal processes are also important in industries. The structures that develop reflect political processes and ideological positions as well as the exigencies of production. It is important for social and welfare workers, together with other members of human service organisations, to be aware of the implications of their location in an industry. If their organisation performs key or valued functions this is an important source of influence in the industry as a whole. There are important strategic considerations involved in questioning, challenging or failing to acknowledge established industry structures. These are particularly important for social and welfare workers to understand, as their concerns are often focused on issues of industry structure, such as the role of volunteers in service provision, the role of consumers in decision-making, resource allocation processes, and so forth.

Finally, human service organisations, and the social and welfare workers within them, can be conceptualised as belonging to networks of other organisations and individuals. An organisation's network can be thought of as all the significant organisational linkages and relations that impinge on, or can be influenced by, the organisation. In this sense, the notion of network is multi-dimensional, embracing all the organisation's external relations including those specifically linked to locality, supra-organisation, sector or industry. The extended nature of organisational networks also needs to be understood. For example, the network of a women's shelter encompasses its direct links with the sponsoring body (say, a church) and with its funding bodies (say, the relevant state government department), but will also include relations that the members of the shelter are not directly involved in at all, such as negotiated arrangements between the Commonwealth and state governments. Workers seeking to understand their organisational environment need to be aware of the extended and multi-dimensional nature of networks.

This analysis of organisational arenas opens up important issues for social and welfare workers. To some extent, social and welfare work has tended to have a rather restricted view of the context of practice, focused primarily on locality. A broader view that locates workers in human service organisations that participate in multiple arenas, those of the locality, the supra-organisation, the sector and the industry is needed. Collectively, these arenas comprise the network of relations within which human service organisations and workers operate. Identifying these arenas, and locating oneself, and one's organisation in relation to them is a first step in environmental analysis.

The task environment

A second approach to environmental analysis is to examine the organisation's task environment. In the course of undertaking its work, a human service organisation necessarily engages in interactions with many other organisations, individuals and groups. Its task environment can be defined as 'all those elements in the organisation's environment that have the potential to influence its performance or survival' (Lauffer 1977, pp. 47-48). Clearly, it is of great strategic importance to social and welfare workers to accurately map this environment. If an organisation and its participants are not aware of the inter-organisational relations that influence organisational functioning and effectiveness, their actions are likely to have unintended, and often undesired, consequences.

A conceptual map of the task environment of a human service organisation is provided in Figure 4.2. Firstly, we can conceive of the task environment as comprising both direct and indirect elements (this distinction follows Stoner, Collins and Yetton 1985, pp. 78-79). The direct task environment comprises those organisations that are in direct, and often, frequent contact with the organisation. The most important elements are resource providers (especially fiscal resources), providers of legitimation, and providers of consumers. Other key elements are complementary services, competitors, targets, organisations representing consumers, regulatory bodies, and professional and industrial organisations. All of these categories of organisations can have a profound impact on organisational functioning.

Figure 4.2 The direct and indirect task environment

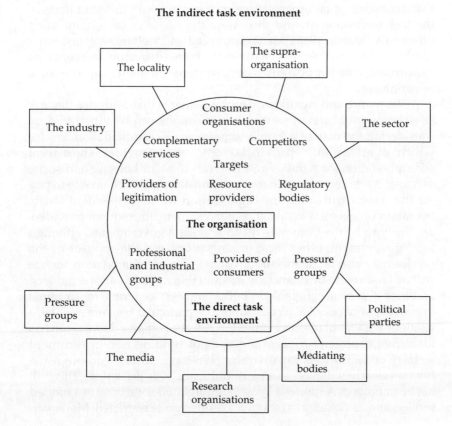

The indirect task environment comprises organisations and groups that the organisation is less likely to be involved with on a regular basis, but which affect the climate within which the organisation operates. It includes the four arenas discussed earlier, and specifically the media, political parties, pressure groups, research organisations and mediating bodies, that is organisations that represent groupings of organisations to government, other industries, and so forth. The line between the direct and the indirect environment is fluid. For example, an organisation working in a policy field that becomes highly contentious may need to have regular and close contact with the media. The media will in these circumstances be part of its direct task environment. Conversely, if an organisation has stable relations with its regulatory bodies, that require little attention, this may be best thought of as part of its indirect task environment.

Relations between an organisation and its task environment are two-way: an organisation is influenced by the groups in its environment that control resources, legitimation, referrals, and so forth, and in turn seeks to influence them. It is important to remember that all organisations are also part of the task environment of many other organisations, whose activities they will often wish or seek to shape. Different parts of an organisation have contact with different parts of the task environment, and thus view the needs of the organisation differently (Martin 1980). Managers, social and welfare workers, other workers and consumers will each have differing perceptions concerning the importance of different elements in the task environment.

The nature and significance of the elements that comprise the task environment of human service organisations can be illustrated by considering the case of a Family Emergency Accommodation Service which operates in a provincial city, and provides short-term accommodation for families and referrals to other housing and social services. As its consumers in most circumstances will be unable to pay for the service provided, the organisation will be dependent for its operation on external financial resources. Its main resource providers are likely to be the Commonwealth and state governments, although local government, other local organisations and the sponsor of the service may also be financially involved. The accommodation service will be required to be financially accountable to these various funders, and may also be accountable in policy and service terms, for example to provide services of a certain kind to a particular consumers. These relations with fiscal resource providers may be complex. Horsburgh has identified fourteen different methods of funding non-government welfare organisations in Australia (1980, pp. 26-29). Although the funders clearly will have extensive influence over the service, this will not be unlimited. A funder's knowledge and understanding of a funded service, and its capacity to monitor, are often quite restricted. Moreover, the political repercussions of reducing or ceasing to fund the accommodation service may be considerable, depending on its relations with other organisations in the task environment. Informal expectations concerning reporting and accountability will be at least as important as the formal requirements (Graycar 1982).

The accommodation service will also need non-fiscal resources, such as volunteers, equipment, buildings, and expertise of various kinds. If it relies for these resources on external bodies such as a volunteer's exchange, a local church, or the local authority, these also become part of its task environment. Small, not-for-profit organisations often rely heavily on local organisations for such resources, because of limited funding. This may have a significant impact on the organisation. For example, if the accommodation service relies heavily on a local church for its supply of volunteers, this will affect the nature and character of its services. Volunteers may bring with them cultural and moral views concerning the homeless and their needs, which will impinge on service provision.

As well as resources, the accommodation service needs legitimation, that is, a community perception that it is a suitable organisation to carry out its intended functions. An important provider of legitimation will be its sponsoring body, be it a church, the local authority, some other body, or the board of directors. Legitimation might also come from the employment of professionals, the receipt of public funding, referrals from other agencies, and endorsements and expressions of support from community leaders, service providers, the media, professional associations, satisfied customers and other groups with community standing. Ongoing legitimacy will in part reflect the quality of the organisation's services, but will also stem from the success of the organisation in presenting a public image of itself as a capable, trustworthy and acceptable service.

Relations with the providers of consumers are also critical. It is unlikely that the Family Emergency Accommodation Service will be short of potential consumers, given the prevailing need for emergency accommodation for families. However, the service may wish to control access to the service in certain ways. It may, for example, wish to give priority to certain kinds of families and needs. This will require effective links with referral agencies such as the Department of Social Security, the State Housing Department, the Family and Community Services Department, emergency relief organisations, and information and advice centres. These, and other similar organisations, may also provide complementary services. For example, the users of emergency accommodation will also need income support, child care or similar services available through other organisations.

The complexity of the task environment will be significantly heightened if organisations providing complementary services are also the targets or competitors of the Family Emergency Accommodation

Service. The organisation may be concerned about some of the policies of the State Housing Department concerning low income families, and have campaigned in the local press for these policies to be changed. It may also be in competition with other emergency accommodation services for public funding. Organisations in the task environment often have such multiple identities; it is not uncommon for the one organisation to be funder, regulator, complementary service provider and target. All these identities must be kept in mind by social and welfare workers if they are to assist their organisations to deal strategically and effectively with their task environments.

Other groups in the Family Emergency Accommodation Service's direct task environment may include organisations claiming to represent the interests of consumers, such as housing action groups; regulatory bodies such as the local council (health inspection, fire regulations, land use restrictions); and professional and industrial bodies, such as unions, who may have concerns about the pay and working conditions of staff, and service quality issues. Each of these kinds of organisations may, at certain times and in certain circumstances have a decisive impact on the organisation. A worker employed by the service should have an awareness of these key elements and their potential to influence organisational life, and a capability to deal in a pro-active manner with them.

The Family Emergency Accommodation Service will also be affected by organisations and groups with which it usually has less direct or frequent contact. In Figure 4.2 these are collectively depicted as the indirect task environment. Political parties and pressure groups concerned with housing issues may have an impact on policy that affects the Family Emergency Accommodation Service, even though direct contact with the organisation may be minimal. Research organisations may produce findings that impinge on the organisation's techniques or community perceptions about the need for emergency accommodation for families. Organisations claiming to represent an industry or a sector, described in Figure 4.2 as mediating bodies, may also impinge, by pressing certain claims on government or raising certain issues for public debate. For example, the accommodation service may be affiliated with a housing alliance, a network of supported accommodation services, or a local welfare council. The media, local and national, will shape public attitudes and public policy towards the issue of emergency accommodation. The local media may concern itself directly with the activities and operation of the service. All of these organisations comprise the indirect task environment, together with those elements of the locality, supra-organisation, industry and sector that impinge indirectly on the organisation.

Mapping the task environment is a prerequisite to dealing strategically with organisation–environment relations. It enables workers to identify key external organisations, and to begin to understand the nature and extent of their influence, and how they in turn can be influenced. Lauffer outlines a simple process that workers can use to begin to analyse their organisation's task environment (1977, p. 50). Firstly, list all the organisations with which the agency interacts, or that have an impact on the organisation. Secondly, categorise each of them under appropriate headings such as funder, competitor or target (they may appear in more than one place). Thirdly, draw a diagram of the task environment, using Figure 4.2 as a guide. Fourthly, systematically work around the diagram, highlighting those relations that are problematic, or potentially problematic, to the achievement of organisational goals. Pay particular attention to organisations that have multiple relations with your organisation, for example both funders and targets. This will provide a sound basis for the planning of strategies and tactics to deal with the organisational environment.

The general environment

An organisation's relations with its task environment do not take place in a vacuum. They are located in a broader societal context that can be referred to as the general environment of the organisation. This general environment comprises economic, political, legal, technological and societal dimensions. Its character is not fixed and static, and may sometimes change rapidly, although most of its elements are relatively enduring. Individual organisations, other than the large and powerful, usually have little impact by themselves on the general environment, although in concert with other organisations they may have a degree of influence. However, their own internal activities and their relations with the task environment are shaped by the general environment in many direct and indirect ways.

Figure 4.3 provides a framework for analysis of the general organisational environment. It suggests that there are five key dimensions. Firstly, organisations are shaped by the economic structures within which they operate, and prevailing economic policies and conditions. As discussed in chapter 2, human service organisations are influenced and constrained by their role and place in the capitalist economy (Hill and Bramley 1986, pp. 9-17). The level of fiscal resources available for human services is determined in large part by perceptions about the economic consequences of public spending. Funding for human services depends largely on judgements about whether they can be afforded, and in particular about the likely impact of expenditure levels on taxation, incentives, inflation, employment, the balance of payments, and overall economic efficiency (Hill and Bramley 1986, pp. 77-101). The economic structure of the human services sector itself also needs to be considered. Most human service industries in Australia are mixed economies, that is, they involve a complex amalgam of public, not-for-profit and private production. Understanding the nature

Figure 4.3 The general environment

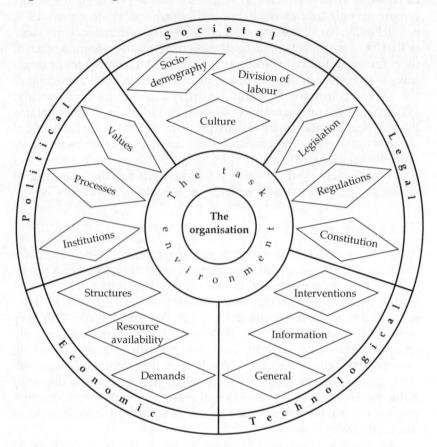

and consequences of these structures is important for those working in human service organisations.

Prevailing economic circumstances also have an important influence. When national, regional or local economies face difficult times, the impact on human service organisations is likely to be two-fold. Their capacity to attract resources may be reduced, as public and private funding sources are cut back, and the demands on the organisation may increase as a consequence of higher rates of unemployment, mental health problems, family crises, and other social problems stemming from the more difficult economic circumstances. Hasenfeld suggests that this puts human service organisations in a double-bind situation. 'The economic conditions that produce a high-risk population also adversely affect the capacity of human service organisations to mobilise resources to respond to their needs' (1983, p. 53).

Organisations are also shaped by the general political environment in which they operate. This comprises the general constitutional and institutional arrangements for political activity. In Australia the federal system of government, and the intricate system of inter-governmental relations which it spawns, have a major impact in all fields of human service provision. The roles, relations and impacts of major political institutions and actors such as parliaments, ministers, premiers and the prime minister, Cabinets, departments, the electoral process, and the courts need to be understood. Insight into political processes and the distribution of power are also needed. This involves analysis of the power of the institutions and actors listed above, together with the roles of political parties, pressure groups, the media, and major social groups such as manufacturers, employers, unions and professions.

Prevailing attitudes and values are a further key element of the general political environment. For example, an organisation providing support to unemployed young people will need to be aware of the role of dominant societal values concerning the work ethic, the family, and socially defined, acceptable social behaviour. Such awareness is particularly important where organisations challenge dominant attitudes and beliefs, and on issues where community opinion may be sharply divided. It is also the case that dominant attitudes can change markedly over time. For example, attitudes to the role of women in the paid labour force have changed significantly over the last twenty years. The links between values and the distribution of power must be understood. Political systems develop and endorse certain value systems in order to systematically benefit some groups at the expense of others. Structural racism and discrimination experienced by Aboriginal people and many people from non-English speaking backgrounds are examples of these processes.

Closely related to the political elements are the legal aspects of the general environment. All human service organisations operate in a legal context that provides both opportunities and constraints. Organisations are usually subject to legislative provisions relating specifically to the organisation's field of service. This legislation may define and control many aspects of its operation including funding and accountability requirements, client and consumer rights and eligibility provisions, programme goals, and administrative procedures. For example, Commonwealth government legislation and regulations governing grants to child-care services stipulate such matters as which consumers will have priority of access, the levels of subsidy, the levels of fees and charges, and matters relating to organisational structures. State government legislation applying to these services typically covers such matters as staffing qualifications and experience, numbers of children allowed per staff member, and the required standards for physical facilities.

Relatedly, human service organisations operate within a general regulatory framework that imposes a wide range of duties and obligations, ostensibly designed to protect the public interest and promote broad public policy objectives. Applicable regulations may relate to fire, safety and health matters, zoning and town planning requirements, conditions of employment of staff, and professional registration and practice. Public sector organisations in most states are also subject to administrative law covering freedom of information, appeals against administrative decisions, anti-discrimination and equal opportunity, and consumer protection. The legal environment also comprises provisions relating to the constitution and operation of the human service organisation itself. All organisations need a legal identity in order to receive funds, enter into contracts, hire staff and provide services. The laws of the various states and territories provide a number of optional organisational forms for human service organisations, including associations, co-operatives and companies. These organisational forms define the general structure of human service organisations, and specify decision-making processes and accountability requirements.

In any society, the nature and level of technology shapes many aspects of life including the goods and services produced and used, the nature of work, and the structure and character of urban and rural living. Human service organisations are shaped by technological changes in many significant ways. Firstly, many of the problems and issues that human service organisations deal with stem from technological change. For example, technological change often results in new patterns of employment and the displacement or redeployment of certain groups of workers. Human service organisations are then created to deal with the problems and issues stemming from unemployment. Similarly, many health and emotional problems result in part from the technologies used in the workplace, giving rise to rehabilitation and related services.

Secondly, the rapid changes that have occurred in the field of information technology have had a major impact on human service organisations, as on all organisations. Greater capability to collect, store and retrieve information has many benefits, but also poses many issues for social and welfare workers, together with other human service workers. Problems include the enhanced potential for organisational control of front-line workers and consumers, the potential for greater standardisation of organisational and professional work, fear of excessive time and resources being consumed in reporting and data gathering processes, and issues of privacy, confidentiality and the security of information.

Thirdly, technological changes affect the range of service options available to human service organisations. This is most apparent in the field of medicine, where the development of high tech diagnostic and treatment tools has a major impact on worker roles, expenditure levels and patterns, and relations between the organisation and consumers. Technological changes can also have a major influence in fields such as mental health, corrections and disability. The availability of drugs to control some forms of mental illness has made possible a much greater emphasis on community-based programmes. The development of electronic 'bracelets' and other surveillance devices has the potential to make corrections systems less reliant on prisons. New aids for people with disabilities have led to greater opportunities for independent living. Technical feasibility is only one of the criteria determining the adoption of new technology by human service organisations. Issues of costing, impact on organisational structures and power relations, and moral and ethical considerations are also factors. An awareness of these factors, and of the potential impact of changing technology on organisational functioning is integral to an understanding of the general environment.

The societal context is the final element of the general environment identified in Figure 4.3. This very broad category has many dimensions, from which a number of particular importance can be identified. The socio-demographic make-up of the overall society and the local community shape the social problems and needs that the organisation deals with, its access to resources, and its repertoire of services. Key socio-demographic variables include age, gender, ethnic composition, Aboriginality, family structure, income, employment, education levels, health status, the incidence of disability, and geographic location. The nature and composition of the labour force in the general environment also impinges on organisational functioning. Employment patterns and opportunities have a major bearing on many other aspects of social life. Workers in human service organisations need also to be aware of the ways in which prevailing cultural and value systems impinge on their organisation, and of the ways that the organisation may reflect, promote or challenge these systems.

Usually, when we conceptualise the general environment we have in mind the nation, or some large region such as a state. However, it is increasingly important to be aware of the international environment. Organisations with international affiliations may receive financial and other support from their international network. International agreements entered into by governments may impinge on organisational operation. For instance, international covenants on world heritage, human rights and the rights of children have all featured recently in the Australian context. The treatment of Aboriginal people has been raised in forums such as the United Nations, and is a matter affecting Australia's international reputation. It is also the case that new technologies or ideas often originate in other countries. For example, the idea of 'normalisation', which has been influential in disability policy and practice in Australia, was imported from Europe and North America. Finally, it is desirable for human service organisations and workers to develop an awareness of and links with similar or like-minded groups in other countries. The boundaries of the general environment are not drawn at national borders.

Environmental characteristics

As well as comprising arenas, a task environment and a general environment, the environment of a human service organisation can be thought of as having its own distinctive characteristics. Some organisations, for example, seem to have relatively easy environments: funds are readily available and expectations are clear and predictable. For others, the environment appears much more complicated, turbulent and antagonistic. It is necessary for workers to be able to systematically analyse these aspects of the environment, their causes and their implications.

There are many frameworks for analysing the nature and characteristics of organisational environments (e.g. Hasenfeld 1983, p. 65; Jackson and Morgan 1978, pp. 233-239). Collectively, these point to four key dimensions:

1   uniformity–diversity;
2   certainty–uncertainty;
3   richness–paucity;
4   hospitability–hostility.

The diversity–uniformity dimension refers to the range of expectations and challenges in the environment that the organisation must meet. An organisation dominated by one clear external set of demands has a uniform environment. By contrast, an organisation that must meet many, varied expectations is characterised by environmental diversity. There are two main sources of diversity. Different kinds of organisations in the task environment impose different expectations, as shown in Figure 4.4 (adapted from Stoner, Collins and Yetton 1985, p. 95). Moreover, an organisation may operate in field of service characterised by conflicting and contentious community values. Diversity is heightened when there is interplay between these two factors. For example, an organisation providing emergency accommodation for victims of domestic violence will need to meet the diversity of expectations of funders, sponsors, the victims, other service providers who wish to access the service, regulatory bodies including the local health, fire and town planning authorities, the police, unions and professional associations representing the interests of the workers, and interest groups concerned with the issue of domestic violence. All of these pressures are heightened by the divisions in the community generally about the causes of domestic violence, the needs of victims and the locus of responsibility for the issue.

Figure 4.4 Differing expectations of a human service organisation

External Source	Criteria of organisational performance
Funders	Are funds being utilised efficiently and effectively, according to policies, programme goals and guidelines?
Sponsors	Are sponsors' goals, values and interests being pursued?
Consumers	Are services meeting needs and demands as defined by consumers?
Professional Organisations	Is the position of professional members secure and are professional standards being maintained?
Industrial Organisations	Are staff interests protected, working conditions and remuneration satisfactory?
Competing Service Providers	Are there any environmental, programme or image weaknesses which can provide us with opportunities?
Complementary Service Providers	Are our interests and image protected in the joint arrangement? Are working relationships satisfactory and programmes effective?
Regulators	Is the regulatory framework adhered to and are minimum standards being met?
Interest Groups	Are key interests recognised, pursued and protected?

Diversity of criteria → Potential for conflict

Relations between the accommodation service and its environment will also be influenced by the certainty–uncertainty of the environment. Certainty is a function of two factors: the rate of change in the environment and the quality of information that the organisation possesses about these changes. Examples of factors producing significant changes in the environment of human service organisations are changes in government and the patterns of political influence, revised funding priorities and programme guidelines, new technologies, trends in community attitudes and opinion, the emergence of new needs and shifts in the composition of target groups. In the case of the domestic violence service, political changes at state and Commonwealth levels and changing community perceptions of the issue are factors that may result in uncertainty. The level of uncertainty will depend, in part, on whether the organisation has developed effective means of obtaining information about such changes.

The operations of the domestic violence service will also be affected by the overall availability of resources in the sector, locality and industry in which it is located. We refer to this as the richness–paucity dimension. Fields of human service vary considerably in the availability of resources, and this changes over time as problems, issues and consumer groups rise and fall in political and community prominence and concern. Clearly, an organisation competing in a resource poor context will experience different pressures from one operating in a context where resources are relatively abundant. There will also be periods when resources for a certain sector or industry are expanding, and times of cutback and consolidation.

Finally, the environment of a human service organisation can be considered in terms of hospitality–hostility. A hospitable environment is one which enables an organisation to achieve a high level of autonomy in its goals and activities. A hostile environment severely limits the organisation's activities, leaving little room for choice and decision (Hasenfeld and English 1974, p. 99). It can be argued that, in these terms, human service organisations are often faced with hostile environments. This is because they are often not-for-profit, deficit operating organisations, with limited or no capacity to produce a financial surplus from their operations. This in itself leads to high dependency on external organisations. Moreover, their activities typically involve contentious social values. This means that the goals, technologies and general operations of the organisation will be constrained by dominant community value systems. Add to this the fact that, as public sector or quasi-public sector bodies, human service organisations are subject to a range of accountability requirements, which also limit their freedom to set their own course. It has been argued that many non-government organisations, because they lack both a legal mandate and guaranteed access to public funds, are particularly insecure vis-a-vis their environment (Tucker 1981). All of these factors characterise the case of the domestic violence service, discussed earlier.

The ideas considered thus far collectively provide a comprehensive framework for environmental analysis. We argue that a sound grasp of this framework is a useful prerequisite to consideration of strategies and tactics for dealing with the environment, and to organisational analysis and practice in general. The framework is summarised in Table

Table 4.1 Ways of conceptualising the organisational environment

1 What are the arenas in which the organisation participates (or should participate)? What are the implications of being part of:
  i   the locality?
  ii the supra-organisation?
  iii the sector?
  iv the industry?
  v the overall network?

2 What are the key organisations in the task environment? How important to the maintenance and effectiveness of the organisation are they?

DIRECT		*INDIRECT*	
i	resource providers	i	mediating bodies
ii	providers of legitimation	ii	the media
iii	providers of consumers	iii	pressure groups
iv	professional/industrial groups	iv	political parties
v	regulatory bodies	v	research organisations
vi	consumer organisations	vi	'the industry'
vii	target organisations	vii	'the locality'
viii	competing services	viii	'the supra-organisation'
ix	complementary services	ix	'the sector'

3 What is the nature and impact of the general environment?
  i   economic?
  ii political?
  iii legal?
  iv technological?
  v societal?

4 What are the characteristics of the organisational environment?
  i   uniformity–diversity?
  ii certainty–uncertainty?
  iii richness–paucity?
  iv hospitability–hostility?

5 Overall, what are the most significant and problematic features of the organisational environment?

4.1. This summary can be used as an analytical tool by social and welfare workers considering the development of strategic initiatives and responses to environmental issues and circumstances.

Dealing with the environment

The complex nature of organisation–environment relations requires social and welfare workers, together with other professionals and administrators, to give careful consideration to strategic and tactical matters. As a consequence of their dependence on elements in the environment, human service organisations and workers often find themselves reacting to external pressures rather than dealing positively with the opportunities and constraints posed by the environment. To deal effectively with the environment:

> There is a need to be proactive rather than reactive—that is, to try to sense or project what might happen and to plan for the implications of such changes for the organization. Further, in true proactivity, an attempt to positively influence the environment's elements should be made through assertive, organized behavior (Abels and Murphy 1981, p. 71).

A proactive approach to the organisational environment involves three key elements:

1 constructing and reconstructing the environment;
2 developing an overall strategy;
3 choosing tactics and techniques.

An understanding of these elements, and their inter-relationship, provides a sound basis for practice in this area. Table 4.2 provides an operational framework for a proactive approach.

Constructing and reconstructing the environment

All organisations inhabit an organisational environment that can be described and analysed using the terms and categories summarised in Table 4.1. However, it is important to remember that the environment of an organisation is not wholly fixed or given. Members of an organisation have the capacity, in varying degrees, to create and change its environment (Dawson 1986, p. 106). This process can be illustrated by considering the actions of powerful organisations, such as multi-national corporations. Clegg and Dunkerley show how multi-national companies, in the pursuit of corporate goals, are able to change and manipulate their environments by influencing government policy and legislation, creating markets for goods and services through advertising, suspending markets through agreements with competitors on price and product, ensuring supplies and markets through takeover and ownership of other companies, and moving in and out of different markets according to judgements about financial strategy and profitability (1980, pp. 385-395). For these companies, the environment is not something to which the organisation simply responds or reacts. Rather, it is something to be shaped and influenced in the pursuit of corporate goals.

Human service organisations similarly have considerable capacity to create their own organisational environments. Some large, powerful human service organisations dominate whole sectors or industries and

Table 4.2 A practice guide to dealing with the organisational environment

---

1 Clarify the goals and objectives of the organisation

2 Analyse the current composition and character of the environment (see Table 4.1)

3 Assess the potential and desirability of reconstructing the organisational environment to best accomplish organisational purposes. In particular, is there a case for considering:
    i relocating in sectors?
    ii restructuring locality relations?
    iii moving to a new industry?
    iv extending networks?
    v restructuring resource provision?
    vi restructuring the bases of legitimation?
    vii reorganising service arrangements?
    viii retargeting services?
    ix influencing external perceptions?
    x changing the general environment?

4 Determine an overall strategy for maintaining domain consensus. Bear in mind the following considerations:
    i the need for an overall acceptance of the role of the organisation
    ii the need to make choices about the overall level of domain consensus
    iii the unequal nature of many exchanges and negotiations
    iv the changing nature of an organisation's domain
    v the need to consider the stances the organisation will take: authoritative, co-operative, competitive, disruptive

5 Determine the repertoire of tactics and techniques to be utilised:
    i gathering information
    ii networking
    iii marketing and public relations
    iv resource mobilisation
    v lobbying
    vi collaborating
    vii co-opting
    viii disrupting

---

mould the environment around themselves and their interests. Their influence extends to many areas of the general environment including legislation and government policy. Examples are to be found in large, central government departments or non-government organisations that are the dominant service provided for particular consumer groups, such as people with an intellectual disability. For smaller organisations, the construction of the general environment is largely beyond organisational control and influence, but many aspects of the direct and indirect task environment can be shaped and moulded. The key question is: in what ways can the environment of the organisation be constructed and reconstructed to best accomplish organisational purposes, and particularly service to consumers? Ten specific methods can be identified.

Relocating in sectors

All human service organisations are part of at least one sector, for example, education, youth. However, the sector with which an organisation identifies and is identified is partially a matter of organisational choice. Take the example of an organisation providing women's health services. Historically, it may have identified strongly with the women's sector, receiving its funding, philosophical base, and political support from other organisations and groups in the sector. However, the organisation may at some point find the need to reconstruct its environment by developing stronger links with the health-care sector. This may be for many reasons—better funding sources, a need for greater legitimacy, more or different referrals from health organisations, and so forth. Alternatively, the organisation might decide that its current location in the women's sector should be re-affirmed for reasons of clear identity, philosophical position, political backing, and so forth. Making decisions about sector location is one of the key ways in which organisations construct their environment.

Reconstructing locality relations

All human service organisations serve a particular geographic area, be it small such as a neighbourhood, or large such as a state. Organisations can decide to change the location they serve (for example, move to a new suburb) or change the scale of their activities (for example, concentrate on one part of the state). Such changes might occur as a result of changing perceptions of needs, or of changing opportunities and constraints in different places. More commonly, organisations will seek to change the nature of their locality relations. For example, a suburban office of a large government department providing community services may decide to develop its links with other organisations in the locality by obtaining information about their activities, developing collaborative activities, or appointing local individuals to an advisory committee. Alternatively, an organisation may decide to distance itself from other local organisations. Such initiatives would markedly change the environment by making local linkages more or less significant.

Moving to a new industry

Human service organisations can change their environments by moving into new service fields. For example, a church social service department may decide to extend its activities in the field of aged care and cut back in the area of emergency relief. Such moves may be motivated by philosophical concerns, but they may also mean the organisation is operating in a more hospitable environment, for example, more funding, greater opportunities, and so on.

Extending networks

An organisation can make a deliberate attempt to extend its network of relationships, in order to explore new opportunities, obtain better information, exercise influence and promote acceptance of the organisation's ideas and services. This will often involve contact with organisations in the indirect task environment, such as other parts of the industry, sector and supra-organisation, the media and research and political organisations.

Restructuring resource provision

Reliance on external funding is a significant constraint on many human service organisations, particularly non-government, not-for-profit organisations. One way of dealing with these constraints is to diversify funding sources. This can be done by increasing the range and number of external funding bodies and by developing internal funding sources. Many non-government welfare organisations have diverse funding patterns, with sources including Commonwealth, state and local government, the sponsoring body, private firms and trusts, investments, fund-raising and donations, membership, and charges for services (Graycar and Jamrozik 1989, pp. 146-147). However, the relative autonomy that, in an overall sense, may flow from a diversity of funding sources has to be balanced against the pressures of attempting to meet numerous, competing external expectations. Diversity brings with it its own operating problems.

Restructuring the bases of legitimation

Organisations receive their legitimation from various sources, most notably as a result of their relations with sponsoring and funding bodies. Just as the funding base of an organisation can be restructured, so can its pattern of legitimation. For example, a church welfare organisation providing services to people with a disability may decide to appoint representatives of consumers, professional groups and residents of a particular geographic locality onto its board of management to demonstrate that it is a widely supported, community-based organisation, not just a 'church agency'. Community organisations and notable individuals may be requested to provide public statements of support for the organisation for the same reasons.

Reorganising service arrangements

Most organisations develop relatively enduring arrangements with organisations providing complementary services. Certain patterns of referral and procedures for dealing with particular circumstances become part of the organisation's routines, and a critical aspect of its relations with the environment. Organisations can seek to rearrange these patterns and procedures to take advantage of new opportunities, develop more stable sources of consumers, move into different fields of activity, and so on.

Re-targeting services

Organisations can take steps to focus their services on a different target group. A rehabilitation service, after studying its consumer profile and community needs, may decide that it should extend its activities to include more women, people from ethnic backgrounds, and Aboriginal people. Re-targeting is often a strategic issue in gaining access to new resources. Most human service organisations are faced with demands that far outstrip their capacity to supply services. This gives these organisations the responsibility and opportunity to make careful decisions about which needs emanating from the environment will, and will not, be met.

Influencing external perceptions

All organisations are perceived in certain ways by the organisations, groups and individuals in their environment. Many factors shape these images: direct experiences of the organisation's services, opinions and beliefs spread informally through networks, information provided by the organisation, and the symbols and messages through which the organisation communicates its goals and activities. These perceptions have a major influence on the ways that the environment deals with the organisation. Organisations may or may not receive funding, referrals and support depending on whether or not they are seen by groups in the environment as reliable, ideologically sound, established, conforming, competent, innovative, or whatever quality it is that is viewed as desirable. These perceptions are not fixed or static, although once established they are difficult to shift. Attempting to change these perceptions is a key aspect of constructing and reconstructing the organisational environment.

Changing the general environment

The approaches to constructing the environment examined so far relate, mainly, to influencing aspects of the direct and indirect task environment. However, as mentioned above, large and powerful human service organisations also have considerable capacity to change the general environment of areas of human service provision and social life, and from time to time attempt to do so. For example, in the mid-1980s, the Commonwealth Department of Community Services and Health initiated and implemented major changes in the funding of services in the fields of aged care and disability. These initiatives were aimed at changing service philosophies, community attitudes and values, methods of service delivery and the distribution of services to various target groups. The changes resulted in a new legislative, policy and administrative environment for human service organisations operating in these fields.

Overall strategy

Implementing a proactive approach to the organisational environment is far from simple. It requires full awareness of the opportunities and constraints imposed by the general environment, the level of organisational dependence on the task environment, and the characteristics of the environment. Most importantly, it requires a holistic perspective on organisation–environment relations, that is the whole picture needs to be considered and taken into account. Another way of expressing this is to say that an organisation needs an overall strategy for dealing with the environment. Following Brager and Holloway, we use the term 'strategy' to refer to the organisation's longer term game plan. Strategy incorporates consideration of what to do about a problem and how to go about doing it. 'Tactics', a term used later in the chapter, are the short-range and specific activities that are linked together in an overall strategy (Brager and Holloway 1978, p. 131).

Developing a strategy for organisation–environment relations resembles a delicate balancing act, in which equilibrium has to be maintained in the face of a diversity of competing and changing pressures and influences. This equilibrium is described by some writers as 'domain consensus', that is overall acceptance of 'the claims that the organisation stakes out for itself in terms of human problems or needs covered, population served, and services rendered' (Hasenfeld 1983, p. 60). This equilibrium is often precarious, particularly for organisations seeking to bring about significant and unpopular changes, or whose values and activities are opposed by powerful interests. However, to maintain their balance and survive, all human service organisations seek or are forced to arrive at some degree of accommodation with their task environment. This can be thought of as creating a 'negotiated' environment with other organisations based on exchanges that involve some mutual reinforcement or reward (Cook 1977, pp. 66-67). It can also be described as 'forming domain consensus':

> ... forming a domain consensus encompasses a process of negotiations, compromises, and exchange agreements between an organization and elements in its task environment that reflects their respective calculations of the costs and payoffs to be derived from an organization (Hasenfeld 1983, pp. 63-64).

There are strong pressures and incentives for human service organisations to negotiate stable, ongoing relations with other organisations, including in some circumstances those perceived as targets of the organisation and hostile to its aims. Failure to do so may result in the organisation's demise, or it may be left vulnerable to outside forces, and consequently prone to frequent changes of purpose, ongoing crisis, poor morale and overall ineffectiveness. However, domain consensus does not necessarily, or even typically, involve agreement with all groups in the task environment. An organisation may be strongly supported by some groups, but have an uneasy or hostile relationship with others. Domain consensus refers to an overall and sometimes uneasy, acceptance that the organisation has a role to play, and a place that it rightly occupies, that is that it has a domain.

All organisations make choices about the level of domain consensus at which they will operate. Some organisations pursue a conservative strategy, in which they attempt to maximise their acceptability and indispensability to the organisations around them. The cost is reduced internal organisational control of goals and activities, as they construct their goals and activities to meet external demands. Others, particularly those with a strong sense of mission, may adopt more risky or adventurous strategies which involve ascertaining and meeting only minimum external expectations. This gives the organisation greater control of goals and activities, but at a cost of potential instability and strain. Strategies that have such risks require especially careful management and planning, and regular re-appraisal.

It should also be noted that the negotiations and exchanges that organisations engage in with other groups are not necessarily, or even typically, fair and equal. The playing field is rarely level. For example, it can be the case that a government funding body has a virtual veto power over the activities of small, non-government organisations, particularly if there are no readily available, alternative funding sources. In such circumstances, it is especially important for members of such organisations to take a proactive approach to environmental relations. However, an organisation's domain is not fixed and constant. The organisational environment changes in ways that may provide opportunities to expand or change the domain, or that may create difficulties or challenge the existing domain consensus. The organisation may itself be influential in bringing about some of these changes. All organisational domains are susceptible to changes in the general or task environment.

Organisations have the choice of several general stances in their dealings with organisations in their task environment (Hasenfeld 1983, pp. 70-82). An organisation in a dominant position may adopt an authoritative stance towards other groups. For example, a government department responsible for funding non-government organisations may specify expectations and require compliance, and generally portray itself as in command. Alternatively, it may adopt a co-operative stance, stressing the partnership between government and the non-government sector in achieving mutually agreed purposes. A non-government organisation similarly may choose to co-operate with other organisations in its service field, but in some circumstances it may adopt a more competitive stance, by trying to make its activities more desirable and attractive to funders, potential customers and the community at large. In other circumstances, organisations may adopt a disruptive stance to a particular organisation or group of organisations, in an attempt to force a change in policy or extract concessions or resources. Typically, an organisation will have different stances at different times with different parts of its task environment, although it may also have a prevailing 'style' that characterises most of its relations. We would argue that organisations that are flexible in their stance have a greater chance of maintaining domain consensus over time than those that are locked into one style and approach in their dealings with other organisations.

The complexities of establishing and maintaining domain consensus is illustrated by the following story about an organisation providing a service to 'street kids' in an inner city area. The organisation was established by a group of highly committed youth workers, with close church connections, concerned about the problems faced by homeless young people in the inner urban area. The group had strong and clear views about the kind of service they wanted to provide: a practical, informal, supportive, non-judgemental, engaging service that related to young people on the young people's own terms. The organisation was incorporated as a non-profit association with the assistance of a local church, which had representation on the Board and provided a small amount of funds. However, it was clear that further financial support was needed for the organisation to function at an effective level of operation. A grant, renewable annually, was obtained from the State Government Family and Community Services Department. The grant application was successful largely because of the widespread public concern about youth homelessness, and the 'respectability' given to the group by the involvement of the church.

For two years the organisation operated on a shoe string budget, heavily dependent on state government funds and the willingness of workers to work long and irregular hours for low pay. Little attention was paid during this time to administrative matters, due to the lack of resources and the higher priority given to work with the young people. During this time the organisation had apparently negotiated a reasonably enduring domain consensus. The state government was happy to be seen to be tackling a social issue attracting much media attention, other social agencies were pleased that someone else was addressing a difficult and in many ways unrewarding problem, and the church's governing body was happy to maintain its support particularly as the organisation had attracted public funds. However, the precariousness of these organisational arrangements was exposed by one single event. The Minister of Family and Community Services, a person of well-known, strong conservative views on moral issues, received a complaint from departmental workers about a publication of the youth organisation describing, in 'street' language and explicit detail, how young people should protect themselves from contacting AIDS and other sexually transmitted diseases. The chairperson of the Board, a church elder, was summoned to the minister's office where he was told that if the publication was not withdrawn immediately, and an undertaking given that no similar material would be issued, funding would cease at the end of the financial year, a mere two months away. It was rumoured that the minister had held preliminary discussions with another youth service, run by an evangelical church, about the provision of a more 'acceptable' youth service in the inner city area.

The Board considered their options. They could simply refuse to comply and see if the minister would carry out the threat (they thought this was likely). They could seek alternative funding (a slow and uncertain process, likely, in any case, to involve the same difficulties). They could mount a public campaign against the decision, stressing the importance of the organisation's activities, but the organisation was not geared up for such activities, and in any case, would they get public support around this particular issue? Or they could agree to withdraw the publication, and re-assess the organisation's relationship with its environment.

Because little, prior attention had been paid by the organisation to developing external support and legitimacy, it found itself vulnerable to this sudden change in circumstances and left with little option but to comply. They withdrew the publication. Issues the Board resolved to consider as part of their re-assessment in the wake of these events were: how could we have better negotiated and maintained our relationship with the state government to make us less vulnerable? How can we better manage our acknowledged, risky organisational strategy? Should we accept that we are in competition with some other youth organisations, or should we emphasise co-operative and collaborative arrangements with all other organisations in the field? Should we be geared up for conflictual and disruptive actions, given the likelihood that a similar situation may recur? In effect, the Board resolved to reconsider the ways that the organisation could rebuild and retain its place in the domain consensus.

Tactics and techniques

Constructing the organisational environment, and developing and implementing an overall environmental strategy, involve a number of specific tactics and techniques. To put this another way, there is a repertoire of skills and tasks that social and welfare workers involved in organisation–environment relations need to acquire. All organisations need the capacity and capability to perform these tasks, and workers are often called on, or wish, to undertake them. The main elements of this repertoire are listed at the end of table 4.2 and are discussed below.

All organisations need to develop ways of systematically gathering information about key changes in their task and general environment. This is sometimes referred to as 'boundary scanning', that is, regularly examining changes and developments in the environment that may be creating opportunities or difficulties for the organisation. All organisations need systems to ensure that this activity takes place. These can be of many kinds. Records can be maintained on other organisations in the task environment, on changes and trends in the local socio-demographic environment, on developments in public policy, on new technologies and service types, and on the nature of the demands being made on the organisation by customers and potential customers. Many records will be ongoing and in need of regular updating. Other information gathering exercises may be one-off, such as a community needs survey.

Networking is the process of extending the formal and informal set of contacts that the organisation and its members have with other individuals and organisations. This is an important part of the information gathering process, and is also important as a way of disseminating information about the organisation and its services and building goodwill. Networks can be extended through informal interactions and through more formal events and processes such as participating in conferences and committees, and taking part in consultations.

Marketing is the process of determining what 'product' will be provided by the organisation, in what place and at what price, and promoting its acceptability. As such, it is an important element of what was earlier discussed as 'creating the organisational environment'. The applicability of business marketing concepts and techniques to human service organisations is discussed in detail by Holmes and Riecken (1980). Closely related to marketing is promotion and public relations. Public relations is the process of influencing public knowledge and perceptions of the organisation. Steiner (1977, p. 160) has identified the purposes and functions of public relations in the human service setting as including:

1 informing the public about the scope, purpose and impact of service programmes;
2 obtaining support for continued programme operation from the public, legislatures, clients and interest groups;
3 providing data on public opinion and prevalent attitudes towards the agency, and its various services;
4 developing formalised communication networks with opinion leaders, mass media, and potential funding sources for the purpose of influencing favourable and beneficial actions;

5 instituting a feedback mechanism allowing for community input and decision-making;
6 gaining acceptance for the implementation of new services or the reduction and termination of ineffective ones;
7 informing the public about the types of programmes and services available and eligibility requirements for participation.

Because most human service organisations are dependent on external funding, the capacity to mobilise resources is highly valued. Fund-raising for non-government organisations has become a large and complex activity with its own developed techniques and technologies (Abels and Murphy 1981, pp. 159-165). Large organisations often employ professional fund-raisers or development officers. However, social and welfare workers are also sometimes given responsibilities in this area. Skills in writing and negotiating submissions for funding are commonly expected of social workers.

Lobbying is the process of systematically campaigning to change the attitudes and decisions of important individuals and organisations in the environment. Most lobbying activity by human service organisations is directed towards government, and is concerned with changing public policies, funding arrangements and regulatory processes and structures. Like fund-raising, lobbying has become a highly organised and specialised activity. Some non-government organisations employ professional lobbyists to act on their behalf. Others rely on the lobbying activities of peak organisations such as the Councils of Social Service, or on their own resources. Lobbying involves a wide variety of skills including use of the media, the ability to present ideas convincingly, and an understanding of the nature of the policy and political process. Successful lobbyists rely heavily on establishing and developing a network of contacts in government, political parties, the industry and the media.

Collaborative activities are of great importance to human service organisations seeking to secure their place in an environment. By engaging in joint, co-operative activities, organisations increase their value to other organisations, extend their networks, acquire valuable information and build up goodwill. Lauffer (1978, pp. 187-238) describes the available repertoire of collaborative activities in detail. These can be summarised as follows:

1 joint funding arrangements among service providers such as pooling of resources, purchase of services, and combined funding applications;
2 joint administrative arrangements between services in a similar field or locale. Examples are joint sponsorship of studies or research, combined publicity and public relations, integrated record keeping, combined premises and administrative support;

3 linkages involving sharing or exchange of personnel. Examples are staff transfers, out-stationing of staff, combined staff training, and the use of volunteer bureaus;
4 linking of consumer services, such as case conferences and co-ordination, joint projects and multi-purpose centres;
5 participation in joint planning and co-ordination mechanisms. For example, participating in local welfare councils, the planning activities of local, state and Commonwealth government, councils on the ageing, and so forth.

All of these linking methods provide organisations with opportunities to secure their place in the locality, industry or sector in which they have chosen to operate.

Co-option is the process of incorporating important elements in the environment into the organisation itself, to reduce opposition or gain valuable resources and support. The composition of Boards of non-government organisations often reflect processes of co-option. For example, it is common for funding bodies, sponsors and consumer groups to be given representation on management committees, to give decisions made by the group greater legitimacy and standing. Similar processes are at work when government agencies appoint advisory committees or institute consultative processes (VCOSS 1981). Co-option can also involve less formal processes, for example obtaining public endorsements of the organisation's activities from notable or powerful individuals.

In some circumstances, human service organisations will want to bring pressure to bear on other organisations in ways that go beyond the tactics and techniques we have outlined. These should not necessarily be viewed as more or less 'radical' that the other techniques mentioned; disruptive tactics are employed by many groups in the society both radical and conservative. Examples of disruptive tactics are strikes, lock-outs, overloading of facilities, stall-ins, speak-ins, demonstrations, pickets, and threats of all of these (Sharp 1977). Disruptive activities, like all the tactics we have discussed, require careful consideration and calculation. In essence, the target must be vulnerable to disruption, the organisation engaging in the disruption must have the resources to sustain its actions, the organisation must be able to withstand counter attack, and the disruptive activities must receive significant support from other groups and organisations. Most organisations providing mainstream human services are dependent on ongoing co-operative arrangements with the organisations in their task environment, and their use of disruptive tactics will usually be small-scale and temporary. Organisations that are out of the mainstream, and that have less to lose and few resources, are more likely to use disruptive tactics. As Saul Alinsky said, 'Tactics means doing what you can with what you have' (quoted in Cox et al. 1977, p. 153).

Conclusion

The concept of organisational environment refers to all the phenomena outside the organisation. The environment is both target and context. Social and welfare workers aspire to changing many aspects of the world outside their organisation. But the environment is also the context which is the main source of the resources, legitimacy and consumers needed by human service organisations. The complexity of organisation–environment relations stems from this duality.

The knowledge and skills required by workers relating to the organisational environment are two-fold. Firstly, they need to acquire a conceptual framework for describing and analysing the environment of their organisation. We have proposed that the environment of a human service organisation be thought of as comprising a set of overlapping arenas, a task environment and a general environment, and as having certain definable qualities. These are portrayed in Figures 4.1–4.4 and summarised in Table 4.1. Workers need to be able to describe the environments of their organisation using these concepts, and be able to understand the implications for their organisation, for themselves and for consumers.

Secondly, workers need to be able to deal with the organisational environment in a proactive fashion. This involves three elements: constructing and reconstructing the environment, developing an overall strategy for organisation–environment relations, and selective use of the available tactics and techniques. The environment of an organisation is not wholly given; it can be constructed and reconstructed to maximise the organisation's and workers' purposes, particularly responsiveness to consumer needs. There is also a need for an overall strategy. Organisational environments are negotiated, or, to put it another way, organisations need to develop domain consensus. Finally, these processes involve knowledge and judicious use of specific tasks and techniques. Table 4.2 summarises the options and choices facing workers attempting to come to grips with organisation–environment relations.

Chapter review questions

1　What do you understand by the concept of 'organisational environment'?
2　Why do social and welfare workers need to be concerned with the organisational environment? What knowledge and skills do they need in the area of organisation–environment relations?

3 What do you understand by the concepts of organisational arenas, task environment and general environment? Using the frameworks developed in this chapter, apply these concepts to a human service organisation with which you are familiar.
4 What are the characteristics of the environment of this organisation?
5 What is meant by constructing and reconstructing the environment? How realistic is it to suggest that human service organisations can reconstruct their environments?
6 What is involved in the process of developing domain consensus?
7 What is the repertoire of tasks and techniques available to a worker for dealing proactively with the organisational environment? Consider the relevance of each of these to a human service organisation with which you are familiar.

Further reading

Hasenfeld (1983, pp. 50-83) provides a good overview of the theory of the environment of human service organisations. Materials written from a more general managerial and organisational perspective include Stoner, Collins and Yetton (1985, chapter 3) and Dawson (1986, chapter 5). Cook (1977, pp. 64-84) provides an overview focusing on exchange and power, which addresses some of the theoretical complexities. Perrow's chapter on 'Environment' (1986) critiques the development of thinking about environment in organisation theory. Abels and Murphy make a strong case for a proactive approach to environment (1981, chapter 4).

Lauffer (1977, pp. 47-54) outlines a useful practice guide to studying the task environment, and Martin's (1980) model of the multiple constituencies of human service organisations is also useful. There are a number of introductions to the tasks and techniques for dealing with the environment: collaborative activities (Lauffer 1987, chapters 10-12); disruptive tactics (Sharp 1977); marketing (Holmes and Riecken 1980); public relations (Steiner 1977, chapter 7) and fund-raising (Abels and Murphy 1981, chapter 10).

Perrow and Guillen's account (1990) of organisational failure in the face of the AIDS disaster would be useful background reading for the case.

Case study

MANAGING A COMPLEX ENVIRONMENT:
THE CASE OF AIDS

Maria Mendelson sat in her office reading the introduction to the recently issued 1988–89 annual report of the AIDS Council of Eastern Australia:

Acquired Immune Deficiency Syndrome (AIDS) first emerged as a health issue in Australian society in 1983. By the end of 1986, 360 persons in Australia were diagnosed as having AIDS. By January 1989, Australia had 1168 notified cases (forty-two female) and 564 known deaths (twenty-five female). In the early stages of the pandemic a number of community groups were established to respond to the social and political issues arising from AIDS, and to provide assistance and support to people with AIDS. One of these was the AIDS Council of Eastern Australia, formed in 1985 by a group of homosexual men who felt that existing government health and welfare services were not responding to the needs of men suffering and dying as a result of the disease.

At that time, AIDS was widely perceived in the community as a male, 'homosexual' disease. Public debate in the State of Eastern Australia linked AIDS policy to the issue of the morality and acceptability of homosexual behaviour. However, the failure of the Red Cross Blood Bank to detect the AIDS virus prior to providing blood for transfusions led to AIDS being transmitted to a number of non-homosexual people, including women, young babies, haemophiliacs and people undergoing routine surgery. It also became clear that AIDS was being transmitted via the sharing of needles by intravenous drug users, and that it was spreading into the heterosexual community. Awareness that AIDS was a public health issue of concern to the whole community began to emerge.

Since its beginnings in 1985 the AIDS Council has rapidly expanded its services and operations. It now has offices in eight provincial centres, as well as its main office in the capital city of Eastern Australia. It is now a major service provider, assuming many roles not provided by mainstream health and welfare organisations. These include public education, professional and volunteer training, home-care services for people with AIDS, emergency financial relief, counselling services including grief and family counselling, day-care centres, visiting services to hospitals and prisons and research into the incidence and transmission of AIDS.

The AIDS Council is a community-based organisation with a membership base of over 400 individuals including health and welfare professionals, families and friends of people with AIDS and members of many religious groups. The seven-person executive is representative of these different groups. The Council is currently working with over 300 people with AIDS throughout the State. The Council's professional staff train and co-ordinate several hundred volunteer workers. The Council's current client profile parallels closely the epidemiological distribution of AIDS in the State. Some 82 per cent of clients are homosexual or bisexual men, with the remainder mainly intravenous drug users or haemophiliacs. Over 60 per cent of AIDS-related deaths in the State have been cared for through the Council's home care service.

Maria joined the AIDS Council in 1987 as a Home-Care Co-ordinator. She had been a volunteer in the home-care programme in 1986, during her final year of studies. At the end of the year she was offered, and accepted, full-time employment, and she had been with the Council ever since. She was the first social worker/community welfare worker employed by the organisation. She thoroughly enjoyed her two years in the job, which had been one of the most exciting, although frustrating and sad, experiences of her life. She found the work challenging, but enjoyed developing her expertise and standing as an AIDS worker. She was now recognised as a person with considerable knowledge and skills, and was active in the development of new programmes and services in the Council. One important aspect of her professional development had been coming to terms with dominant community attitudes towards AIDS. When she was first employed by the Council, she was surprised to find that the stigma applied to people with AIDS also extended to their families and friends, and to the people who worked with them. She had developed very strong view about the need for much greater public acceptance and understanding of people with AIDS, as well as the need for preventative programmes.

Maria's study of the latest annual report had a specific purpose. The Council was facing a crisis point, and Maria was trying to work out her position on the difficult decisions that would need to be made in the weeks ahead. The crisis concerned the Council's funding. The Council's services and activities were dependent on funding from the Commonwealth and State governments. This funding had enabled the Council to employ a range of full-time staff including an administrator, a psychologist, a community education co-ordinator and four social workers/community welfare workers, including Maria, who acted as service co-ordinators. The funding was also necessary to support the Council's operations in provincial areas, which was co-ordinated by part-time workers. The funds received from the Commonwealth and State governments comprised 95 per cent of the overall operating budget of the Council.

Funding had been a continuing difficulty for the AIDS Council. The State government, which espoused a strongly conservative perspective on so-called issues of 'family values' and 'moral questions', for several years refused all approaches for funding from the Council, which it perceived as a 'gay' organisation. Members of the Council campaigned to force the State government to support the Council, and as the full extent of the health and social impact of AIDS became clearer, the State government was increasingly pressured to take a more active and sympathetic stance.

Much of this pressure came from the Commonwealth government. The Commonwealth's policy on AIDS funding was to provide funds to the States on a matching basis, that is for every dollar of State expenditure, the Commonwealth would provide one dollar. This could be for direct expenditure by the State or for State funding of non-government organisations such as the Council. Commonwealth funds were available up to an amount determined by a formula based on the number of notifications of AIDS cases, overall State population and the size of the Aboriginal population in the State. The Commonwealth also required that half of its grant be spent on prevention, education and counselling, and half on treatment and support services outside hospitals. The AIDS Council was the major provider of these services in the State.

After much negotiation, the Commonwealth and State governments had reached a compromise. The State agreed to match Commonwealth funds for the AIDS Council, provided the joint funds were channelled through an 'acceptable' church organisation. This was agreed to by the Commonwealth government and the AIDS Council. In 1988-89 the Council received $400 000 of joint funds through this circuitous route.

One of Maria's recent tasks had been to assist in the preparation of the Council's 1990–1991 budget submission as a member of the Council's budget committee. The demands on the Council were increasing rapidly with the rise in the number of people with AIDS in Eastern State, and the Council's submission reflected this increase. In preparing their budget submission, the Council took into account the Commonwealth's funding formula. On the basis of their projections of the growth in notification rates, the need for expanded public education programmes, and the Council's role as the major community service provider, the Council applied to the State government for approximately one million dollars for the forthcoming year.

To the Council's surprise, the State government responded with an offer of only $412 000, an increase of only 3 per cent on the previous year's allocation. This did not even keep pace with inflation and would mean major cutbacks in the Council's activities at a time of increasing demand for services. Clearly, the State government had either decided not to match Commonwealth funds up to the maximum available under the formula, or to use the Commonwealth funds to support its own services for people with AIDS (mainly hospital-based, medical services), or to fund other groups.

The State government's offer was considered at a meeting of the AIDS Council's executive. Maria attended in her capacity as a member of the budget committee. It was an angry meeting and feelings ran high. One member asked, 'What have the bastards done with the rest of the Commonwealth money? On the basis of the formula they've collected about two million dollars and now they're sitting on it while people are bloody well dying!' Another member demanded to know what the Council was going to do: 'It's the same old story. We got nothing originally until we took some social action. You have just got to continually keep the public pressure on them. I think we should get some people with AIDS together and picket Parliament, get a ministerial delegation up, get some media coverage. They've got to know we are not going to accept this quietly'.

The President of the Council asked for a bit of time to try to negotiate with the State government. The Executive decided to take no immediate action and to meet again the next day inviting all full-time staff to be present. The next day the President reported that he had been told by the State government official responsible for AIDS funding that he had discussed the issue with the Minister and there was no question of negotiation: 'It's take it or leave it'. The official had also indicated, off the record, that the State Minister had made the following points:

1 He felt that there was no need for funding increases in the education programmes targeting homosexual and bisexual men because the figures showed that notifications had levelled out.
2 He was afraid of a backlash from other welfare agencies and community groups if increased expenditures continue to be directed to people with AIDS.
3 'In any case, people with cancer or liver disease and so on don't get all these extra services that the AIDS Council wants to provide' (home-care programmes, funeral benefits, extra pharmaceutical costs, twenty-four-hour home nursing, twenty-four-hour phone support line, counselling services etc.)
4 He believed that money should be put back into established mainstream services such as hospitals, psychiatric services, community health and domiciliary care services. In his view, volunteer-based services in this area are not reliable and are incapable of maintaining the longer term commitment necessary.

Once again, the meeting was angry and there were calls for the Council to undertake some public social action to try to force the State government to reconsider. This was argued strongly by some of the staff and committee members who had been with the Council since its inception. However, two members of the executive, one representing haemophilic groups, the other a person with close church connections, thought this approach was unwise. They noted that there was an election due shortly and argued that the issue could well become a 'political football'. The need for a moderate approach was also supported by the administrator. He argued that most existing services could be maintained on the grant offered to the Council, provided cuts were made to the research programme and the proposed expansion of the educational programmes. However, under pressure he conceded that the twenty-four-hour home-care service might also run into problems, given the 150 new cases likely to come on stream throughout the year.

The administrator's comments caused a furore. The community education co-ordinator questioned the administrator's commitment to the preventative approach to AIDS: 'Its all very well nursing dying people, but surely its more important to stop people getting AIDS in the first place. Without that extra funding we will have more people than ever with AIDS. If we cutback anywhere, it should be on the welfare side. It's about time the hospital system lived up to its responsibilities to AIDS sufferers. All we do is to make it easier for them to avoid dealing with the issues.' One influential and well-regarded homosexual member of the executive, who had been actively involved in setting up the Council, was so angry he walked out of the meeting, saying, 'This organisation was set up by gays for gays suffering from AIDS because the existing system wouldn't do anything for them. Now its been taken over by professionals and administrators whose only concern is where their next pay packet is coming from!' He slammed the door behind him, leaving the rest of the group in stunned silence.

The President was the first to speak. He pointed out that being angry with one another was not going to solve the problem of what to do next. He asked that the meeting be adjourned until the end of the week, and that everyone give some thought about the next step. He asked each group in the organisation to prepare a brief detailing the implications of a no-growth budget for their particular area. As Maria had been closely involved with the budget committee, he asked her to prepare a strategy document that would consider the short term and longer term options faced by the Council.

Key questions

What factors in the organisational environment should Maria take into account in preparing her strategy document? What action strategies, short and long term, are available to the Council to deal with the issues raised in the case, and what are the implications of each?

Case discussion points

1 What are the main components of the Council's organisational environment? Analyse both its task and its general environment.
2 What are the characteristics of the Council's environment?
3 What opportunities exist for the Council to construct or reconstruct its environment?
4 How can the Council achieve a high level of domain consensus? Should this be an organisational goal?
5 What tactics and techniques are available to the organisation in its negotiations with the environment? Which of these, if any, should Maria recommend?
6 What does the case illustrate about the impact of the environment on organisations, and organisation–environment relations generally?

5

Organisational goals: banners or guiding principles?

In order to understand the complexities [of organisations] we must abandon the simple notion of organizational goal as a defining characteristic. We must adopt models which pay more attention to the interests of different groups within the organization ... the way in which [they] define their own interests, pursue their own goals and ... implement their own definitions of the situation (Smith 1979, p. 15).

The concept of organisational goals is central to organisational analysis and practice. All organisations lay claim to being goal-directed enterprises, and social and welfare workers often join an organisation because they are attracted by its espoused goals. In human service organisations, these goals are almost always couched in the language of service. The annual reports of human service organisations are often brimming with virtuous statements proclaiming goals such as 'increasing the capacity of families to care responsibly for their members, strengthening the capacity of communities to address their own social needs, generating opportunities for people with disabilities to maximise their independence and integration into community life and providing developmental opportunities for children'. Such goals are often highly compatible with the values and principles enunciated by social and welfare work. Indeed, if the professed aims of human service organisations and social and welfare work were both taken at face value, fundamental harmony between workers and their host organisations could be expected.

In reality, however, the experience of many workers is that the espoused goals of human service organisations are a poor guide to day-to-day activities and practices. Organisations that proclaim their commitment to the needs of consumers are often found to be more concerned about the needs of staff, the demands of funding bodies, or their political image. Organisations that claim to respect the rights and wishes of consumers are frequently found to abuse those rights, and treat their consumers with scant respect. Organisations that purport to support families sometimes seem to act in ways that are disruptive and destructive of family life. Often the survival and growth of the organisation itself, and the well-being of its members, seems to take precedence over its substantive goals and objectives. Social and welfare workers, drawing on their practice experience, can provide many examples of such slippage, and often direct conflict, between stated goals and actual organisational activities.

This perceived gap between purpose and practice often places workers in a quandary. How can workers be effective in a context replete with such discrepancies? Our experience is that this is a common dilemma for workers seeking to achieve their personal and professional goals through organisations. However, it may be that the issue itself needs reframing. Specifically, it may be necessary to question the expectation that organisations have clear goals that steer and guide organisational activities. Do organisational goals provide guiding principles, or are they vague abstractions, or is it possible that they may be both of these? Does it make sense to take the official goals of an organisation at face value? If not, what is the significance of organisational goals, for the organisation as a whole, for social and welfare workers and for consumers? To begin to answer these questions we need to know where goals come from, who influences their formulation, and how they change. We need to explore how goals can be analysed, and understand the functions they play in human service organisations. With this knowledge, we can examine how workers can strategically use an understanding of organisational goals, and goal-related processes, to maximise desired outcomes for consumers. Our starting point, however, must be the most basic question of all: do organisations have goals?

Do organisations have goals?

This question may, at first glance, appear frivolous. As we have already noted, most human service organisations espouse a set of goals which often occupy a prominent place in the official publications of the organisation, and are repeatedly enunciated in the speeches and public pronouncements of the organisation's leadership. Members of organisations from time-to-time undertake and participate in goal-setting and goal-clarification exercises. Moreover, in everyday language we often refer to the goals of organisations. Part of our 'common-sense' view of organisations is that they comprise people who have come together to achieve some common purposes, which are the organisational goals.

This view is confirmed by many sociological definitions of organisations. For example, Etzioni defines organisations as 'social units (or human groupings) deliberately constructed and reconstructed to seek specific goals' (1964, p. 3). In this view, an organisational goal is 'the state of affairs which the organisation is attempting to realise. Organisations are thus seen as "instruments": rationally conceived means to the realisation of a single, specific stable and generally accepted group goal' (Smith 1979, p. 3). This way of thinking about goals, sometimes referred to as the orthodox model, also underpins a great deal of management thinking and advice. Human service organisations are regularly exhorted to develop clear goals and objectives to guide their activities and operations (e.g. Senate, Standing Committee on Social Welfare 1979, pp. 63-72).

Despite this apparently, wide consensus about the centrality of goals, many writers have questioned the meaning of statements that organisations have goals. It has been argued that to attribute goals to an organisation is to fall into the trap of reification, that is 'the attribution of concrete reality, particularly the power of thought and action, to social constructs' (Silverman 1970, p. 9). Clearly, individuals can have goals, but what exactly do we mean when we say that a community health centre, a competitive employment service or a family centre have goals? Silverman suggests that 'It seems doubtful whether it is legitimate to conceive of an organisation as having a goal except where there is an ongoing consensus between the members of an organisation about the purposes of their interaction' (1970, p. 9).

Ongoing consensus about goals tends, however, to be a rare commodity in many human service organisations, other than at a very high level of generality. Take the case of a social work department in a university. The members of that department may have a broad consensus that one of its goals is to 'produce highly competent social work practitioners'. However, as soon as analysis and interpretation of this goal is undertaken, cracks, and often deep fissures, in the apparent consensus begin to appear. Different members of staff are likely to hold strong and varied convictions about the nature of social work itself, of what constitutes good practice and competency, and of how these should be taught. For some, a good practitioner is a person with finely tuned therapeutic skills; others will stress the importance of generic skills, including community and organisational work and policy analysis. Some staff will emphasise the acquisition of technical skills; others the need to explore personal beliefs and values. These different perspectives shape the behaviour of staff: they operationalise the broad goal in quite different ways. However, in this example, staff are not the only players with strong and legitimate views about the goals of the organisation. Field-work educators, students, outside employers and other members of the university all have their own perspectives on the goals that the organisation should pursue. Goal consensus in this setting, as in many others, tends to be somewhat illusory. In what real sense would such a department have goals?

Individuals in organisations will not only have different perspectives on the goals that should be pursued, but also different perceptions of what the current goals are. Studies of welfare departments, schools and police departments show that when members of staff are asked about the current aims of their organisation they give markedly different responses (Smith 1979, p. 6). These differences of perspective and perception reflect the multiplicity of goals and their often conflictual nature, particularly in human service organisations (Etzioni 1964, pp. 14-16; Smith 1979, pp. 4-5). In the example discussed above, the goal of producing competent graduates probably vies with many other departmental goals such as producing research and publications, maintaining the organisational image in the community and contributing to the development of the profession. These goals may, to a degree, complement one another, but it is also true that they may conflict. There is likely to be competition over the allocation of resources to different goals, and the pursuit of one may jeopardise the pursuit of another. For example, if the department pursues the goal of acting as a vocal, independent critic of government policy, it may offend key organisations in the task environment and hence put at risk the department's capacity to attract external research funds and obtain student placements.

The stated goals of human service organisations also tend to be vague and highly general. In chapter 3, we saw that this stems from the indeterminate nature of human service technologies, and from the need to appease many interests both inside and outside the organisation. This latter factor is especially significant. It is relatively easy to achieve consensus on the goal of, say, 'promoting the value of family life', but as the implications and elements of such a broad goal are specified and elaborated, the more likely it is that various groups inside and outside the organisation will perceive that their interests conflict. Given the diversity of interests both within an organisation and in its environment, there are often strong reasons for goals to be enunciated at a high level of abstraction.

Further complexities arise when we look at organisational goals over time. Organisational goals are not static. Changes come about because of many factors such as changing personnel, changes in the organisational environment, and political changes within the organisation. Changing goals are sometimes acknowledged formally by changes to the constitution or statements in official publications. But more often they are not well defined, representing more a process of organisational drift than of deliberate planning.

These criticisms of the orthodox model of organisational goals, particularly as they apply to human service organisations, can be summarised in the following statements:

1 the idea of organisational goals is a reification. People have goals, but abstractions like 'organisations' cannot;
2 there is no ongoing consensus in organisations about goals. Different individuals and groups, inside and outside the organisation, have different perspectives and operationalise goals in different ways;
3 members of organisations differ in their perceptions of organisational goals;
4 organisations have multiple goals which often are in conflict with one another;
5 goals are often vague and enunciated at a high level of abstraction;
6 organisational goals are not static.

Collectively, these point to the need to abandon the idea that human service organisations have goals in the sense of clear, agreed on, consistent, durable purposes. As Smith states, 'The orthodox model does not present a picture of re1al organisations but only of hypothetical or ideological future situations'(1979, p. 7). For workers seeking to understand and reconcile the gap between the espoused goals of organisations and the daily reality of organisational life, this is a crucial point. Stated organisational goals should not be taken to represent the clear commitments of all organisational members and constituencies; in this sense, they cannot be taken at face value. Complex organisations, by their very nature, are replete with discrepancies and contradictions. The worker's task is not to merely denounce, bemoan or rail against these inherent complexities, but to understand and analyse them, in order to find ways of working constructively within and through them.

This perspective on organisational goals has been derived from a consideration of the reality of human service organisations. However, similar conclusions stem from our review, in chapter 2, of different perspectives on the study of organisations. The orthodox goal model is underpinned by the scientific management perspective, which views organisations as machines or instruments to achieve clearly defined purposes. However, we also know that organisations need to respond to the needs of individuals (human relations), that organisations themselves have 'needs' for survival and growth (systems theory), that decision-making processes typically do not resemble the 'rational model', and that individual self-interest is an important factor in organisational life (market perspective). We also know that organisations operate within the structural constraints of a capitalist society (neo-Marxian perspective), and that they are political arenas in which stakeholders seek to maximise their values through exercising influence and using authority (political economy perspective). The issue of who participates in goal-setting activities is central in determining the content of goals. Organisations that exclude women, Aboriginal people, people from non-English speaking backgrounds and other groups from goal-setting processes are likely to develop goals that do not reflect their needs or interests (feminist and Aboriginal perspectives). Taken together, these perspectives point to the inherent complexities of organisational goals.

Abandoning the orthodox view of organisational goals does not mean abandoning the notion of organisational goals as such. Although most organisations do not have clear, unchanging, agreed on, mutually complementary goals, there is, nevertheless, a sense in which goals are central to the nature of organisations and organisational life. 'The whole point about organisations is that they, in part, comprise planned and coordinated activities. Since these activities do not occur randomly there must be some agreed-upon basis for them' (Clegg and Dunkerley 1980, p. 317). One solution to this conundrum is provided by Albrow. He suggests that 'organisations are social units where individuals are conscious of their membership and legitimise their cooperative activities primarily by reference to the attainment of impersonal goals' (quoted in Smith 1979, p. 7). Goals are indeed central to organisations, even though they are often multiple, vague, conflicting and in a constant state of flux. However, to understand this, workers need to go beyond a rudimentary notion of goals, and analyse the distinctions that can be made among various kinds of organisational goals.

Analysing organisational goals

Much discussion of organisational goals is clouded by a failure to draw key distinctions between different types of goals, and different ways of using the concept of goals. We will draw attention to three such distinctions, and discuss their implications for social and welfare workers. These are:

1 official and operative goals;
2 mission, goals and objectives;
3 outcome, system and service goals.

Official and operative goals

Analysis of organisational goals often centres on the organisation's 'official' goals. These are the goals that are stated in annual reports and other official publications, and that often figure prominently in public speeches and statements by the organisation's leadership. It is necessary to distinguish between these official goals and the 'operative' goals of the organisation. 'Operative goals designate the ends sought through the actual operating policies of the organisation; they tell us what the organisation actually is trying to do, regardless of what the official goals say are the aims' (Perrow 1974, p. 216).

This distinction is critical. Much confusion concerning organisational purpose stems from the mistake of taking official goals at face value, that is as representing what the organisation is really trying to do. This is not necessarily the case. This is not to say that the official goals are unimportant. Testimony to their significance and importance is the prominence they often have in organisational publications, and the care that is often taken in their framing. However, this importance stems from their utility to the organisation, and to groups within the organisation, rather than from their accuracy as guides to the actual functioning of the organisation.

These functions of official organisational goals can be illustrated by an example of a goals statement of a government department in the human services area, as shown in Table 5.1. This goal statement has a number of characteristic features. It presents to the reader an idealised image of the organisation; it comprises multiple goals; and it is couched in highly generalised and abstract language. The statement serves a number of important organisational purposes. Most importantly, it contributes to the legitimacy of the department. Like all organisations, the department is concerned with its standing with other groups in its task environment such as non-government welfare organisations, churches, other government departments, the government of the day, opposition parties, professional groups, and the media. Phrases such as 'strengthening the capacity of communities and families', 'generating opportunities' and 'demonstrating excellence' convey a message to these external groups that the department is an organisation with a philosophy and orientation befitting its functions, and that it is worthy of support. The goals also provide guidelines for organisational activities. They indicate, to people and groups both inside and outside the organisation, the main fields of activity of the organisation, and the nature of organisational activities. Thus, each of the goals listed corresponds approximately with a field of organisational activity: family support, disability programmes, substitute care, juvenile corrections, community development and organisational management.

The goals are also important in the orientation and socialisation of members of the organisation. They convey the dominant ideology of the organisation, as well as the style of its operations. For example, the goal statement has a dominant theme of individual and community self-help. Such themes set the tone and orientation of the organisation, and may become the underlying premises of organisational decision-making. As such, goals may be one of the means by which the organisational leadership attempt to assert compliance and control over organisational members. Goal statements are also means of establishing, at a broad level, standards of achievement for the organisation. They can also be used for planning purposes, in that they may provide an overall idea of the direction in which the organisation sees itself heading.

Table 5.1 A typical official goals statement of a government department in the human service area

---

The purpose of the Department is to contribute positively to the social development and well-being of the ... community through services responsive to identified needs which:

- strengthen the capacity of communities to address their own community needs;
- protect, assist and support individuals and families.

Within the framework of Government policy, State/Commonwealth responsibilities and the availability of resources, the Department will promote or, where necessary deliver services to:

1 increase the capacity of families to care responsively for their members;

2 generate opportunities for people with physical, sensory or intellectual disabilities to maximise their independence, integration into community life, and access to services and appropriate care;

3 achieve safe, responsive environments which provide developmental opportunities and security for children whose parents have been unable or unwilling to protect them;

4 generate opportunities for young offenders or youth whose behaviour or life circumstances are such that they require assistance to participate appropriately in the community;

5 increase the capacity of local communities to respond effectively to their social needs and to the emergent needs of their members;

6 demonstrate excellence in all areas of service to ensure the achievement of operational and strategic objectives.

Source: Queensland, Department of Family Services and Aboriginal and Islander Affairs, *Annual Report 1987-88*, p. 7.

The official goals may, of course, accurately portray the real or operative goals of the organisation, as well as performing the functions that have been described. However, this cannot be assumed. To identify the operative goals of the organisation it is necessary to look closely at the activities of organisational members, and at the allocation of resources within and by the organisation. 'Operative goals reflect the organisation's actual commitment of resources. That is, allocation decisions of available resources indicate what members of the organisation intend, in fact, to accomplish' (Hasenfeld 1983, p. 87). Hasenfeld gives the example of a psychiatric hospital, where most of the money, personnel and time are given over to the physical care of patients, the prescription of drugs and the hiring of attendants. Its operative goals, irrespective of any fine words in the annual report, can be deduced from this allocation of resources to be the custody and control of patients. Identifying operative goals is more difficult than identifying official goals, often requiring careful research or inside knowledge of organisational processes.

Perrow suggests that there are two main kinds of operative goals (1974, pp. 216-217). The first are those that stem from the official goals, but represent choices among competing values. Often these amount to issues of priority. For example, the goals listed in Table 5.1 encompass six fields of organisational activity. In actual practice, the bulk of resources of the organisation may be devoted to two or three of these areas, with other areas getting relatively little. There are also other important priority questions. Does the department emphasise preventive, protective or remedial family services? Does it give priority to urban or rural areas? Does it give a high priority to work with particular sub-groups within the population such as Aboriginal people or people from a non-English speaking background? Does it emphasise social support or social control? All of these options are consistent with the broadly stated official goals. The priority of choices that are made and implemented become the operative goals of the organisation.

The second kind of operative goals are those that are tied directly to group or individual interests, and bear no necessary connection to the official goals. For instance, the minister of a government department is likely to view it, to a greater or lesser degree, as a vehicle for her political ambitions and as an instrument to secure the re-election of her party. If departmental funds are allocated according to such political criteria (for example, priority to projects in marginal electorates), then this becomes, in fact, one of the operative goals of the organisation. Similarly, the department may be used by a rapidly rising public servant to advance his or her career. Social and welfare workers, or other occupational groups, might use the department to practice a particular therapeutic technique that interests them or to advance certain personal or professional values or beliefs. If they use their time on these activities, and commit departmental resources to them, these too become part of the operative goals of the organisation.

Mission, goals and objectives

Analysis and understanding of organisational goals also requires clear differentiation between the concepts of mission, goals and objectives. These terms are used extensively within organisations, although there is considerable inconsistency in the meanings attributed to them, and other terms such as purposes, principles and aims are also in common use. It is important to understand the conceptual distinction between the terms, and the ways in which the terms are used in practice.

An organisation's mission sometimes referred to as its purpose can be thought of as the broadest aim that an organisation defines for itself. Mission statements often contain two elements: a statement of the organisation's broad purpose in the society, as defined by the organisation, and a statement of the organisation's particular aims that set it apart from other organisations in the same field. The mission statement at the beginning of Table 5.1 contains both of these elements. The societal purpose is defined as 'contributing to the social development and well-being of the . . . community'. The particular aims are defined in terms of 'strengthening the capacity of communities' and 'protecting, assisting and supporting individuals and families'.

Organisational goals can be thought of as broad statements of intent. Examples are the six statements of intent in Table 5.1. In theory, they can be distinguished from mission statements in that they are somewhat more specific, often referring to particular areas of organisational activities. In practice, as in Table 5.1, there is often considerable overlap between the broad mission and specific goals. For example, 'strengthening the capacity of communities' appears as part of the mission statement and as the fifth goal.

Organisational objectives need to be distinguished clearly from both mission and goals. Objectives are statements of specific intent that describe target groups or desired achievable results within specified time-frames (Senate Standing Committee on Social Welfare 1979, p. 63). Objectives can be thought of as 'the targets that must be achieved if the organisation is to achieve its goals . . . they are, in fact, the translation of the mission into specific, concrete terms against which results can be measured' (Stoner, Collins and Yetton 1985, p. 119). For example, organisational objectives relating to goal three (Table 5.1) could be:

- to establish fifty new family group home places by June 1990;
- to recruit and train twenty new foster parents in the north-west region by April 1990;
- to revise the manual of service standards for foster homes in consultation with the Foster Parents Association by December 1990.

It is increasingly common for human service organisations to develop official mission, goals and objectives statements. In large organisations, particularly in the public sector, these processes can be extremely elaborate. For example, all Commonwealth government departments are required, as part of the annual budget process, to develop detailed programme statements setting out the departmental mission, the goals of each of the main programme areas of the department, and specific objectives and plans for all sub-programme areas. In the case of the Commonwealth Department of Community Services and Health this comprises a document of over 200 pages (Australia, Budget Related Paper No. 7.4A, 1989-90). Similar processes are followed in most state governments. It is also increasingly common for non-government human service organisations to have established processes, although not as elaborate, for formulating statements of mission, goals and objectives, and relating these to organisational activities.

There are a number of reasons why human service organisations are increasingly interested in identifying mission, goals and objectives.

Mission and goal statements, as we have seen, serve several important organisational purposes, including enhancing organisational legitimacy, providing guidelines for organisational activities, and orienting and socialising staff into the organisation. Their weakness, however, is that they are usually too general to provide effective standards for appraising organisational effectiveness and for organisational planning. Stated objectives complement the mission and goals by providing specific standards of achievement by which performance can be planned, monitored and evaluated. The formulation of clear objectives is most commonly justified in terms of public accountability and efficiency. It is argued that unless precise and testable objectives for organisational activities are set, it is impossible to evaluate whether or not they are successful and worthy of public funding and support (Senate, Standing Committee on Social Welfare 1979, pp. 63-71). This is an attractive proposition. However, it should also be recognised that precise and testable objectives are also important to administrators and external funding and monitoring bodies, as means of ensuring compliance with directions and achieving control over organisational activities. Such control may not be perceived by recipients of funding to be in their, or their consumers', interests. Consequently, when there is disagreement, as there often is, about the objectives that an organisation should pursue, some groups may be strongly motivated to keep goals and objectives fuzzy and imprecise.

The relations between mission, goals and objectives are shown in Figure 5.1. Conventionally, the connections are often portrayed as hierarchical, with a set of goals flowing from the organisational mission, and objectives similarly stemming from the goals (the formal model in Figure 5.1). These are often viewed as means–ends relationships. Objectives are the means of attaining goals (ends), which in turn are the means of attaining the organisation's mission (ultimate ends). However, in practice, this means–ends distinction is often blurred. The 'fit' between mission, goals and objectives is not always, or even typically, clear-cut. Processes designed to produce clear statements of mission, goals and objectives often result in products that more resemble the operative model in Figure 5.1.

This does not necessarily reflect on the skills of those formulating the mission, goals and objectives statements, although this may be a factor. The complexities of organisations and their tasks, rapidly changing circumstances, and competing interests within and outside the organisation, all impact on attempts to clarify organisational directions, and are reflected in mission, goal and objectives statements. As portrayed in the 'operative' model, goals do not always relate directly to the overall mission. They may be related to a specific organisational objective. Objectives may relate to more than one goal. Goals and objectives may sometimes be transposed, with achievable,

Figure 5.1   Relations between mission, goals and objectives

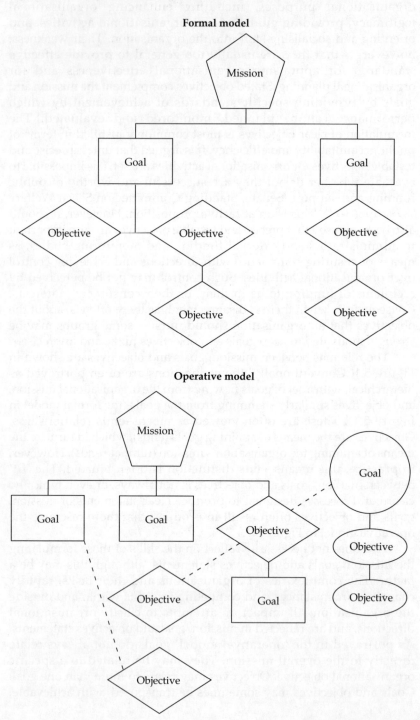

short-term, concrete objectives replacing the broader goals. The imposed or assumed rationality of the formal model rarely reflects the complex reality of the typical organisation.

Outcome, system and service goals

The goals that organisations espouse and pursue are of many different kinds. An understanding of the different categories of goals, their nature and inter-relationships, will be of considerable assistance to workers in coming to grips with the complexities of organisational life. The literature on organisations provides several ways of classifying organisational goals (e.g. Perrow 1970, pp. 133-174). For our purposes it is sufficient to group them into three categories. Outcome goals can be thought of as the intended impacts of the organisation's outputs on its environment, including its consumers. System goals relate to the efficient functioning of the organisation, and its survival and growth. Service goals are concerned with the characteristics of the service produced by the organisation. Much organisational life involves a process of interplay, negotiation and tension among these different kinds of goals.

These goal categories, and their significance for organisational analysis and practice, can be illustrated by the case of the Department of Social Security, the organisation with responsibility for the payment of income security benefits and pensions throughout Australia. The outcome goals of the Department are those directly concerned with the organisation's impact on Australian society, and on people in need of income support. It has been suggested that the Department has three main outcome goals:

- poverty alleviation—ensuring at least a minimum acceptable income for all Australians;
- income maintenance or protection—encouraging people's efforts to maintain and restore their income . . .;
- income redistribution—ensuring . . . a more equal distribution of resources and life chances . . . (Donald 1986, p. 2).

The nature of the outcome goals of human service organisations is always subject to analysis and debate. Different ideological perspectives lead to quite different analyses of a government department such as Social Security. For example, neo-Marxians would argue that the main operative goals of the Department are to legitimise and reinforce economic inequality, bolster work incentives, circulate money in the economy and generally maintain the social and political status quo. Market liberals, by contrast, would argue that organisations such as the Department of Social Security are in fact dysfunctional to the capitalist economy, in that in practice they destroy work and investment incentives, erode personal freedom and create a new privileged class of self-serving bureaucrats and professionals (for these various perspectives see Watts 1987, p. xii). An important task for social and welfare workers is to develop their own critical analysis of the outcome goals of the organisations in which they work.

The two other kinds of organisational goals are illustrated by a Department of Social Security document entitled *Corporate Direction into the '90s* (September 1989). This publication claims to outline the 'purpose, aims and priorities of the Department of Social Security'. Under the heading 'Our Aims', there are five points:

> **Client service**: We strive to provide high levels of service to clients, seeking to be fair, courteous and efficient at all times.
> **Staff support**: We aim to give all staff the opportunity to advance based on individual abilities, performance and potential. We aim to provide a quality work environment which gives personal recognition and job satisfaction.
> **Quality**: In all aspects of our work we seek to achieve the highest possible standard, prompt delivery, consistent quality and technical competence.
> **Innovation**: We encourage new ways of thinking among our staff. In this way we can continue to introduce necessary change and improve client service.
> **Accountability**: We recognise that we have to maintain the integrity of the social security system and be fully accountable for the funds we distribute.

Interestingly, none of these are outcome goals, as defined above. Rather, they are a mixture of 'system' and 'service' goals. The statements about staff support, innovation and accountability are examples of system goals: they are concerned with the efficient functioning of the organisation. The statements about client service and quality are service goals: the focus is the nature of the delivery of services to consumers.

Being able to distinguish among these three categories of goals serves a number of analytical and practice purposes for social and welfare workers. Firstly, all human service organisations should identify goals relating to outputs, systems and services. Goal statements that omit one or more of these components are incomplete. Workers involved in goal setting, or in appraising the performance of an organisation, should attempt to ensure that all three elements are satisfactorily considered.

Categorising goals in this way also helps us in understanding key aspects of the nature of goal conflict in organisations. A significant source of conflict in organisations relates to the competing demands of outcome, system and service goals. Different groups within organisations are typically associated with these different goal categories. Administrative staff often have responsibility for, and interest in, the efficiency of the organisation, and thus tend to stress the importance of system goals. Professional staff, as a consequence of their training and organisational role, are often more concerned with issues of service quality. While many groups inside and outside the organisation may from time to time express commitment to the organisation's outcome goals, often these are not an overriding priority for any one group. Concern with outcome goals tends to rest with senior management (or management committees) who are answerable to external bodies for organisational performance, and with individuals and groups with strong personal beliefs or external allegiances. Often it is groups external to the organisation, such as those representing consumers and various community interests, who have the strongest commitment to outcome goals.

The conflicting demands of outcome, system and service goals are often experienced as struggles over scarce organisational resources. Administrators may demand more funds and staff for training, information systems, planning and other elements of system effectiveness. Professional staff will counter with calls for more elaborate services, employment of more direct service staff, better consumer support facilities, and so forth. More fundamentally, the different categories of goals provide different criteria for organisational effectiveness. Is the success of the Department of Social Security to be measured primarily in terms of poverty alleviation (an outcome goal), technical competence (a systems goal), or 'fair, courteous and efficient' service delivery (a service goal)? All human service organisations may be evaluated on the basis of all three types of goals, and the main focus is ever-shifting.

Social and welfare workers need to appreciate the importance of all three kinds of goals for human service organisations, and to encompass concern with all three in their work. Social and welfare workers, in common with other professionals, often focus their concerns on issues of service delivery to consumers. This is entirely appropriate, but system goals are also, in our view, equally fitting concerns. If social and welfare workers dismiss system goals as mere 'administrative' matters, they open themselves to criticism from other organisational members of having a narrow, professional outlook and of being indifferent to broad organisational concerns. Moreover, opportunities for interesting and effective practice, such as in the area of staff support, will be missed. Concern with organisational outcomes ought also to be a major focus of social and welfare workers in organisations. Workers ought to concern themselves with the appraisal of the organisation's achievement in meeting stated outcome goals, and with discrepancies between the stated and operative outcome goals of the organisation.

Goal analysis: summary

An ability to analyse organisational goals is central to social and welfare work. One analytical approach to assist workers in this is summarised in Table 5.2. Fundamental to organisational goal analysis is an

Table 5.2 A framework for organisational goal analysis

Concept	Definition	Questions
Official goals	The stated goals of the organisation	1 What purposes do the official goals serve? 2 How accurately do they describe what the organisation is 'really' trying to do?
Operative goals	The ends sought through the actual operating policies of the organisation	1 How are resources and rewards allocated in the organisation? 2 Do operative goals reflect priority choices stemming from official goals, or the interests of individuals and groups?
Mission	The broadset aim that the organisation defines itself	1 Does the organisation have a stated mission? 2 Does the stated mission accurately portray the social role and distinctive character of the organisation?
Goals	Broad statements of intent	1 How do these relate to the mission and the main areas of organisational activity?
Objectives	Statements of specific intent that describe desired achievable results within specified time-frames	1 Are objectives clearly stated? Why or why not? 2 How 'tight' are the relations between mission, goals and objectives? Could they be tightened? Should they be?
Outcome goals	The intended impacts of organisational outputs on the environment, including consumers	1 What are the operational outcome goals of the organisation?
System goals	The efficient functioning of the organisation, and its survival and growth	1 Are system goals and objectives clearly enunciated? 2 What priority is given to system goals? What priority should be given?

Concept	Definition	Questions
Service goals	The characteristics of the service provided by the organisation	1 Are service goals and objectives clearly enunciated?
		2 What priority is given to service goals? What priority should be given?
		3 Is there conflict between outcome, system and service goals? What is the nature of this conflict? How can it be dealt with?

understanding of the distinctions that can be made between official and operative goals, between mission, goals and objectives, and between outcome, system and service goals. Summary definitions of these terms are provided in Table 5.2. The 'questions' column provides a systematic approach to critically analysing the goals of a human service organisation, and can be used by workers for this purpose. Careful and critical analysis of organisational goals is a prerequisite for effective participation in organisational goal processes, which we will now consider.

Where do goals come from?

In addition to being able to critically analyse organisational goals, social and welfare workers need to understand the processes that result in organisations adopting and pursuing certain goals and rejecting others. These processes can be understood from a variety of perspectives. However, the political economy perspective provides a particularly useful framework. Within an organisation, operative goals emerge out of political interactions among organisational groups and individuals, all pursuing their own views of what the organisation should be trying to achieve. Individuals and groups with power and authority use their position to define the official and operative goals of the organisation. Others seek to acquire influence over the direction of organisational activities by mobilising their own political resources, such as expertise, prestige, organisational location, networks and so forth. Much of this process involves the negotiation of agreements and compromises that represent an acceptable reconciliation of the interests of the various stakeholders. However, this may lead to the emergence of a dominant coalition within an organisation, that is a grouping which can exercise control or a prevailing influence over the direction and nature of the organisation's activities (Hasenfeld 1983, p. 96). In such circumstances, the goals may reflect not so much a reconciliation of interests as an imposition of the interests of dominant stakeholders. These processes will reflect, reproduce and, in some cases, may challenge structural inequalities within the organisation, such as those based on gender, ethnicity, race and class.

It is often the case that individuals or groups in positions of authority within the organisation have considerable control over organisational goals. Senior management, the board of directors, the minister and others in positions of authority can often control key processes, such as the allocation of resources, that determine the organisation's operative goals. However, many other organisational groups can also exercise extensive influence. Groups that perform key functions for organisations, particularly vis-a-vis the external environment, are often well positioned to influence organisational goals. Individuals and groups, including social and welfare workers, working at the front-line of human service organisations are able, by virtue of their strategic location, to shape the operational goals and activities of organisations (see chapter 8). Consumers, by contrast, are often poorly placed to influence organisational directions. They are often unorganised and unable as a group to negotiate with the organisation. They may possess relatively few political resources, and may be viewed by dominant groups in the organisation as deviant, dependent and ill-equipped to participate in organisational processes. They may belong to groups that have long been excluded from decision-making processes, such as women, people with disabilities, Aboriginal people and people from ethnic minorities. We would argue that one of the major contemporary challenges for social and welfare workers in human service organisations is to develop mechanisms which will enable consumers to participate effectively in goal determination, and related decision-making processes. These issues are considered in detail in chapter 9.

These intra-organisational processes are only a part of the overall goal-setting process. The goals of human service organisations also derive from the organisation's need to meet the expectations of key groups in the task environment, particularly funding and legislative bodies, the suppliers of consumers, and groups with the potential to provide or withhold legitimation. 'While the motivation of (organisational personnel) . . . may be profits, prestige, votes, or the salvation of souls, their efforts must produce something useful or acceptable to at least a part of the organisational environment to win continued support' (Thompson and McEwen 1980). Goal-setting is in large part a process of determining the relationship of the organisation to its task environment and to the larger society. Changes in the task and general environment always give rise to the need to review organisational goals and objectives. For example, organisations will find themselves needing to respond to the creation of competing or complementary organisations, modifications in public policy, demographic shifts, new technologies and other external changes that render existing goals and objectives outmoded or unacceptable. Organisations that are significantly dependent on external resources, but fail to monitor the environment and adapt their goals and objectives to changing circumstances, are likely to suffer decline and even demise. Organisational goal-setting is not, therefore, an open-ended process, in which organisational participants have unlimited choices of what the organisation will do. Social, economic and political structures, and the immediate requirements of the task environment, provide the setting within which the intra-organisational politics of organisational goal-setting occurs.

These goal determination processes within organisations are ongoing. This often may not be fully appreciated by organisational participants. Many organisations will undertake formal planning processes to develop statements of goals and objectives, and to clarify the goals and objectives of the various constituent parts of the organisation. Social and welfare workers need to understand these processes, and be able to utilise the opportunities they present. However, formal planning and goal-setting exercises are but a part of the overall goal formulation process. The operative goals of the organisation are established through ongoing decision-making processes as well as through these formal planning exercises, and the actual direction of organisational activities may vary significantly from the formal plan. Decisions about the allocation of resources, the hiring and firing of staff, the choice of projects and service technologies and the selection of consumers, are the main determinants of operational goals, and these may or may not be consistent with the formal statements of goals and objectives.

It follows, then, that the processes of developing organisational goals are dynamic, and that goals are frequently in a state of flux as the organisation responds, through complex decision processes, to both internal political changes and external circumstances. One consequence is that the initial goals specified by the founders of the organisation and enshrined in the written constitution or similar documents, may be a poor guide to contemporary goals and activities. In some organisations there is strong commitment to the 'founding principles', and any deviation from the original goals, methods and activities is treated as apostasy. Nevertheless, most organisations find it necessary to change direction over time. Three different kinds of change processes relating to goals can be distinguished: displacement, succession and adaptation.

Goal displacement refers to the process whereby an organisation, perhaps unwittingly, substitutes for its 'legitimate' goal some other purpose for which it was not created (Etzioni 1964, p. 10). A common form of goal displacement is the substitution of system goals for

Table 5.3 What factors shape organisational goals? An analytical framework

---

1 What are the goals of the organisation? (see Table 5.2)

2 Who are the significant individuals and groups within the organisation
   that seek to influence organisational goals?
   a   What goals do they seek to achieve through the organisation?
   b   What political resources can they bring to bear?

3 How significant are social and welfare workers in the goal development
   process?
   a   What goals do they seek to achieve through the organisation?
   b   What political resources can they bring to bear?

4 How significant are consumers in the goal development process?
   a   What goals do they seek to achieve through the organisation?
   b   What political resources can they bring to bear?
   c   What structures or processes exist to enable them to participate in goal
       formulation?

5 What is the composition of the 'dominant coalition' (if any) in the
   organisation? Which groups participate in, and which groups are
   marginalised or excluded from, the coalition?

6 What groups in the task environment, and what characteristics of the
   general environment, shape the organisation's goals? Whose interests do
   these groups tend to represent?

7 How are the goals of the organisation shaped by the social, economic and
   political structures of society?

8 What formal goal determination processes occur in the organisation?
   How significant are they in determining the operative goals of the
   organisation?

9 What other decision-making processes are significant in setting
   organisational goals and directions?

10 How can the changes in the organisation's goals over time be
   characterised? Is the organisation experiencing goal displacement,
   succession or adaptation?

---

outcome goals. That is, the survival and growth of the organisation
itself becomes the primary goal, and the ostensible outcomes become
means to that end. Another circumstance is to be found when the
procedures designed to administer a goal become the goal itself (Smith
1979, p. 6). Goal displacement in the non-government sector commonly
occurs in situations where organisations, under the pressure to obtain
resources, conform to the expectations and demands of the external
funding source (Berg and Wright 1980).

A different process of organisational goal change is goal succession. This occurs when an organisation has successfully accomplished its original outcome goals and has been able to move on to new outcome goals. A classic example of goal succession is the experience of the American Foundation for Infantile Paralysis which, after successfully leading the campaign to find a vaccine for polio leading to an elimination of the disease, turned its attention to the combating of birth and genetic defects among infants. In similar fashion, the Red Cross, initially founded to respond to human suffering in wartime, and finding itself 'underemployed' in the post-First World War and post-Second World War periods, moved into the fields of public health and blood donor programmes (Etzioni 1964, pp. 13-14).

Goal adaptation is a similar process to succession whereby an organisation modifies its outcome goals, not because they have been achieved, but because new circumstances have generated new challenges for the organisation or made the earlier goals inappropriate or impossible. In Australia, Family Planning Associations have expanded their activities to include sex education, human relationships and basic preventative health for women, as well as birth control. Similarly, many non-government organisations in Australia in the late-1980s working in the areas of disability adapted their goals and activities in response to new policy directions and changing community expectations that people with disabilities should live, to the greatest extent possible, in normal community situations.

It is essential that social and welfare workers develop skills which allow them to understand and unravel the processes that influence goal-setting in their organisation. A guide to these processes, which summarises the ideas presented in this section, is provided in Table 5.3. The table presents a series of questions for workers to ask about goal processes in their organisation. Reflection on these questions will provide workers with an understanding of the derivation of their organisation's goals. Such an analysis will provide a sound basis for strategic involvement in organisational goal determination processes.

The strategic use of goals

Social and welfare work is a practice-oriented activity and as such is concerned with analysis primarily as a basis for action. In this chapter so far, we have provided a framework of ideas to enable workers to analyse the goals of their organisation, and understand the processes and factors that have shaped these goals. It is this analytical capacity which, we argue, is critical and underpins effective human service work in organisations. In addition, it is essential that workers understand the direct relevance of goal analysis to practice. We refer to this as the 'strategic use of goals'. There are four key areas:

1 capitalising on the complexity of goals;
2 utilising official goals;
3 participating in planning processes;
4 involving consumers in goal processes.

Capitalising on the complexity of goals

Our analysis thus far of the nature, types and origins of goals in human service organisations points to their complexity, fluidity and diversity. Organisations are not machines dedicated to clear, common purposes which are rationally and relentlessly pursued. Rather, they are collections of individuals and groups with varying values and interests, working around stated or assumed purposes, which are often competing or conflicting. The actual nature of these purposes will be shaped by political interactions both within the organisation and between the organisation and its environment.

It is therefore of great importance that workers understand and accept this as being one of the realities of organisational life, and view it as providing significant opportunities for the exercise of influence and the creation of personal and professional autonomy. Clearly, there are situations in which it is necessary for organisations to clarify their goals and objectives, and workers should be skilled participants in these processes, as discussed below. However, clarification of official goals and objectives is not, as such, a particular concern of social and welfare workers. Their primary concerns are with the operational goals and outcomes of the organisation, particularly as these relate to consumers. That is, social and welfare workers, in the last analysis, are more concerned with what organisations actually do than with what they say they do.

The complexity of goals, if acknowledged and understood, provides workers with many opportunities to influence operational goals and outcomes. The complexities of decision-making processes mean that there are many decision points, some of which workers may be able to influence or even dominate. For example, many social and welfare workers are strategically placed to influence consumer intake processes. Because decisions about which potential consumers are and are not served are important determinants of operative goals, this should be viewed as a key opportunity. Often, workers need to position themselves to be able to exercise influence, such as by participating in budgetary and planning processes, accepting membership of decision-making committees, and being active in bodies such as unions and professional associations.

The complexity of goals, and the associated difficulties of enforcing a regimen of goals across the whole organisation, may also open opportunities for workers to establish areas of 'goal autonomy'. This means that workers, while unable to have a major influence on the overall direction of the organisation, may be able to control particular organisational activities, processes or units, particularly those in which they are directly involved. It is quite possible that these may have goals that differ considerably from official or dominant organisational goals. For example, in the 1970s some Department of Social Security social workers adopted a 'community work' approach to their work that was not officially sanctioned or approved, and that did not conform to formal departmental expectations of extensive client contact. For a time, organisational circumstances were such that they were free to pursue their own goals, even though these were not derived from, and meshed only loosely with, official goals. There can be a range of costs associated with such an approach, such as losing contact with the larger organisation or sacrificing opportunities for wider organisational influence. Nevertheless, it is not especially unusual for organisations, particularly large organisations, to accommodate or tolerate for considerable periods of time activities that diverge from the official goals, particularly if there is no direct or public challenge to the dominant goals of the organisation.

Utilising official goals

As we have seen, an organisation's official goals may or may not be an accurate guide to operational policies and activities. However, official statements about mission, goals and objectives may be of considerable use to social and welfare workers in achieving their professional and personal aims through organisations. In the first place, official goals provide legitimation for activities and programmes that workers, among others, may wish to undertake. The highly generalised, lofty language of annual reports, ministerial statements, planning documents and the like can provide ideological patronage and protection for beleaguered projects and for new projects and ideas seeking organisational support. Indeed, it can be argued that no change proposal or innovation should be introduced into an organisation without connecting it to the organisation's mission and goals (Brager and Holloway 1978, pp. 61-66).

Official goals can also be used to hold the organisation, and groups within the organisation, to account. Because goals are typically broad and high-minded, it is almost always possible to point to the failures of a human service organisation to achieve its mission and goals. This situation is often used by external groups, including legislative and review bodies, the media and consumer advocacy groups to highlight their case. Internally, groups such as social and welfare workers can use ambitious goal statements to press for more resources, better facilities, programme extensions and the like.

It follows that social and welfare workers need to keep track of official statements of goals and objectives, and to become skilled in formulating and presenting their ideas and proposals in language that signals symbolic allegiance to dominant goals. It may be that for some purposes and on some occasions, professional language should be replaced with the terminology dominant within the organisation. For example, if the term 'community development' is out of favour, a community development activity may need to be presented as a project contributing to the 'outreach' goals of the organisation. If more than one stated goal can be harnessed to a proposal, so much the better. It is often the case that certain buzz-words or phrases gain currency within an organisation for a period of time. Use of these words connects a proposal, at a symbolic level, to dominant organisational goals and may thus assist its acceptance. For example, in one organisation concerned with post-graduate medical education, the use of phrases such as 'summative assessment', 'a patient-oriented approach' and 'adult learning' came to connote the organisation's educational approach, and were widely used to secure agreement for new ideas. Sometimes, organisations spell out explicitly the elements that will contribute to a proposal's acceptability. For example, an internal memorandum to staff of one government department headed 'Key issues to be considered when suggesting policy changes', listed (among others) the following:

- whether the change is consistent with the Social Justice strategy;
- what impact the change would have on the Government's economic objectives;
- whether the change would achieve a significant improvement in client service;
- whether the change would create any positive (or negative) financial or other incentives for clients to work or serve;
- whether the change improves the integrity of social security programs (unpublished internal document).

Clearly, workers proposing or resisting a change proposal should use such officially sanctioned criteria to legitimise their case.

Participating in planning processes

Although we have emphasised that the operative goals of organisations emerge out of complex organisational processes, the value of participation in explicit, deliberate planning exercises should not be underestimated or dismissed. Human service organisations utilise a number of management techniques and processes to clarify organisational direction and build a sense of common purpose. While these may be viewed, from a power perspective, as attempts by those in authority to exercise control, they undoubtedly can also serve valuable organisational functions. They can assist the organisation to respond to changes in the environment, contribute to the development of morale and shared purpose among organisational members, address and solve problems and achieve greater efficiency and effectiveness. For these reasons, and for others specific to social and welfare work discussed below, workers need to be able to participate effectively in these formal planning processes.

Organisational planning is a large and complex area of management theory and practice. However, the main techniques and approaches that social and welfare workers are likely to encounter or to use can be briefly and simply described. Goal analysis is the process of clarifying organisational goals and objectives through processes of structured group discussion, consultation and analysis of organisational circumstances (Mager 1972; Bresnick 1983, pp. 16-25). It is usually intended to produce both a clear statement of organisational goals and objectives, and a sense of common purpose and group cohesion among organisational members. Strategic planning is a more elaborate process which both defines goals and sets out the means by which they will be achieved. A strategic planning process may involve a number of elements or stages including environmental analysis (see chapter 4), organisational resource analysis (which is concerned with identifying the strengths and weaknesses of the organisation), goal analysis and formulation, strategic decision-making (the process of selecting programmes and projects to achieve goals and objectives), strategy implementation, and monitoring and control of progress (Stoner, Collins and Yetton 1985, pp. 116-150). Many organisations have an annual strategic planning cycle, involving regular review of organisational directions and activities.

Programme budgeting is a widely used technique that attempts to link planning and resource allocation in organisations. Organisational goals and objectives are formulated for a specified time period, and a series of programmes or projects are devised to achieve the designated objectives. The organisation's financial planning is then designed around these programme activities, so that it is possible to link expenditure to programmes, and hence to objectives. The annual planning and budgetary cycle consists of reviewing the success of programmes in meeting their objectives, reformulating organisational goals and objectives in the light of the previous year's activities and other changes in the organisation's circumstances, and revising programmes accordingly in the context of available financial resources. A central aim is to reduce the gap between the stated goals and objectives and the operative goals and objectives, as gauged by the allocation of resources (Macleod 1978).

A closely related set of techniques are those widely known as management by objectives. Essentially, management by objectives can be viewed as a way of linking strategic planning to the organisational structure and the individuals who comprise the organisation. It is a means of assigning responsibility for the achievement of objectives, and motivating individuals to work towards these objectives. Agreement is reached, at all levels of the organisation, on a person's areas of responsibility and expected results (objectives). Individuals are given extensive leeway to work towards these objectives in whatever way they see fit, but there is agreement that their performance will be appraised on the basis of the achievement of results (Bresnick 1983, pp. 25-33; Wiehe 1978; Raider 1978).

A key element of management by objectives is that individuals in organisations are able to plan the activities, programmes and projects for which they have been assigned responsibility. Commonly used techniques for project planning include Gantt charts, PERT (Program Evaluation and Review Technique) and CPM (Critical Path Method). These are all essentially methods of breaking down an organisational activity into its individual tasks, linking these tasks in a logical and sequential way, and estimating and scheduling the time and resources necessary to complete the activity (Bresnick 1983, pp. 53-66; Stoner, Collins and Yetton 1985, pp. 240-246). Social and welfare work in organisations often involves project activity. Examples are setting up a volunteer programme, establishing a service in a new area, or undertaking a piece of action research. Workers are also quite often required to develop their own programme of activities, or to create procedures for standard organisational activities. Project planning techniques are highly relevant in these circumstances.

There are a number of strong arguments for social and welfare workers to become skilled and to participate actively in these various planning techniques and processes. As we have seen, official goals and objectives can be used to legitimise change proposals, to resist change viewed as undesirable, and to hold organisations to account. Planning skills are highly valued within organisations, and workers who demonstrate capability in this area are likely to increase their standing generally within the organisation, and hence their capacity for influence. Planning processes also provide opportunities to build links and networks with individuals and groups across the organisation. Finally, workers, whether or not they hold management positions, may wish to use planning processes to assist the organisation of which they are a part to reassess purposes and direction, and to respond proactively to changes in the organisational environment.

Involving consumers in goal processes

We have already noted that consumers are often poorly placed to influence the determination of organisational goals, as they lack the political resources to participate effectively in these processes. This is particularly the case for those groups that are structurally marginalised or excluded from such processes such as women, Aboriginal people,

people from non-English speaking backgrounds, people with disabilities and other groups. A major challenge for workers is to identify and develop effective ways of maximising the effective representation and participation of consumers in goal determination processes. There are two main avenues. Firstly, social and welfare workers, in their advocacy role, should attempt to ensure that the interests of consumers are given full consideration when goals are being developed. Consumer interests are frequently overlooked in the processes of negotiation and bargaining leading to operative goals. A common situation is for consumers to receive poorly integrated and discontinuous services as a result of deals negotiated between other more powerful organisational groups. Hasenfeld gives the example of patients in a psychiatric hospital who may be encouraged by ward attendants to be passive and conformist, by social workers to express their feelings and hostility in group sessions, and by doctors to accept psychiatric treatment based on medication (1983, p. 102). Each occupational group may have negotiated its approach in accordance with the general goal of treatment and rehabilitation, but the overall impact on patients is a confusion of expectations. Social and welfare workers should strive to understand the overall impact of organisational activities on consumers, and to bring this perspective to bear in processes of goal determination.

Social and welfare workers' perceptions of consumers' goals, no matter how well-intentioned, may, however, be at variance with those that consumers would express were they able to participate directly in goal processes. Secondly, therefore, workers should press for direct consumer representation and participation in decision-making processes. Consumers need access to decision-making forums, and the resources to participate effectively in these forums. The issues associated with consumers acquiring an effective voice in organisations are complex, and are given detailed consideration in chapter 9.

Conclusions

The concept of organisational goals is complex. All organisational activities are undertaken and legitimated in the name of certain stated goals. Yet there is often no ongoing consensus about goals among organisational members, and goals are often multiple, conflicting, abstract, vague and changing. This makes organisational life confusing and contradictory, often resulting in social and welfare workers being perplexed by the gap between the rhetoric of the official goals and their own experiences of organisational life. To unravel the tangle of organisational goals, workers must first distinguish between official and operative goals, and then between organisational mission, goals and objectives. It is also important to be aware of the differences between outcome, system and service goals, and the tensions and conflicts among them. Equipped with these concepts, workers can analyse the goals of any human service organisation with which they are familiar.

Organisational goals emerge out of complex political processes, both within the organisation and between the organisation and its environment. Workers need to understand how goals develop, to be able to participate strategically in these processes. They need to be able to capitalise on the complexity of organisational goals, utilise official goals to legitimise their own goals and objectives, participate effectively in planning processes, and maximise the involvement of consumers in goal processes.

Chapter review questions

1 In what sense can it be said that organisations have goals?
2 Would you expect there to be a high level of consensus about the goals of a human service organisation among organisational members? Why or why not?
3 Think back to the perspectives on organisational analysis introduced in chapter 2. What would each of them lead you to expect about the nature of organisational goals?
4 What is the distinction between official and operative goals? Why is this an important distinction to make when analysing the goals of a human service organisation?
5 What are the differences between organisational mission, goals and objectives? What is the relationship between mission, goals and objectives in a human service organisation?
6 What are the distinctions between outcome, system and service goals?
7 What factors account for the influence that some individuals and groups within organisations are able to exercise over the operative goals of an organisation?
8 How influential can and should (a) social and welfare workers and (b) consumers be in determining the goals of a human service organisation?
9 How important are social, economic and political structures, and the task environment, in shaping organisational goals?
10 Through what organisational decision-making processes are goals determined?
11 What is meant by goal displacement, goal adaptation and goal succession?
12 How can social and welfare workers use official goals to achieve their professional and personal goals in organisations?

13 Is it important for social and welfare workers to participate in formal planning processes? Why or why not?

14 What responsibilities do social and welfare workers have towards consumers in organisational goal processes?

Further reading

There are several excellent, brief introductions to the theory of organisational goals including Etzioni (1964, chapter 2), Smith (1979, chapter 1) and Hasenfeld (1983, chapter 4). Hasenfeld is especially strong in relation to the political processes resulting in organisational goals. Readers wishing to explore the theoretical issues at greater depth could consult Clegg and Dunkerley (1980, chapter 8). The key distinction between official and operative goals is outlined in Perrow (1974). A valuable introduction to the various kinds of organisational goals is Perrow (1970, chapter 5). A clarion call for the formulation of clear goals and objectives in human services can be found in a report of the Australian Senate (Standing Committee on Social Welfare 1979, chapter 5). General overviews of the planning techniques discussed in the chapter are provided in Stoner, Collins and Yetton (1985, part II) and Bresnick (1983, chapters 2 and 4). Mager (1972) provides a highly readable introduction to organisational goal clarification. There are several useful readings in Slavin (1978) dealing with specific techniques, in particular Macleod (1978) on programme budgeting, and Weihe (1978) and Raider (1978) on management by objectives.

Case study

GOAL CONFLICT IN THE SOUTHSIDE EMERGENCY YOUTH SHELTER

Ann Killen slowly climbed the front stairs of the weatherboard house at 43 Kingsford Avenue, South Wilmott, an upwardly mobile, inner-city suburb of the state's capital city. 'Pretty classy area for a youth shelter', she thought to herself, looking around at the neighbouring houses, many of which were recently renovated, displaying wooden verandahs and a profusion of landscaping. She paused on the top step, enjoying the warmth of the morning sun, before ringing the bell.

Suddenly the front door flew open, and a young woman, probably no more than about thirteen-years-old, emerged. Before Ann had time to say

'Hello', the woman turned her back to the open door and shouted through it. 'And another thing . . . you can stick yer rules on swearing up yer arse too!' She turned to Ann, and with a contemptuous sneer muttered, 'Fuckin' youth workers'. And then she was down the stairs, out of the gate, and gone.

Ann turned back to the door which now framed a man she recognised as Shane Williams, one of the workers at the Shelter. He shouted past her, 'Susanne . . . hang on a minute . . . let's talk about it'. Then, noticing Ann, he added 'Welcome to the mad house. I'll be back in a minute . . . make yourself coffee'. Then he in turn was running down the stairs, still calling out to Susanne to come back and try and work things out.

Ann made her way into the house and found the kitchen. It looked like a disaster area. Dirty plates and dishes were piled up in the sink. The table was covered with half-filled cups, spills of milk and coffee, an overflowing ashtray and the remnants of a bowl of cornflakes. Stuck to the fridge door was a large piece of paper with 'kitchen roster' written across the top. In the column marked Monday and the box marked 'breakfast clean-up', was written the name 'Susanne'. Ann looked in vain for a clean cup. With a sigh of resignation, she filled the sink with water and began to wash up. Susanne had obviously made other plans.

It was Ann's first day as joint co-ordinator of the Southside Emergency Youth Shelter. Shane was the other co-ordinator, and there were two other paid youth workers on the staff, and a pool of some twenty volunteers. She was looking forward to the job. She had just recently graduated, and had done her final placement with the Inner City Youth Streetwork Programme. She had become active in the Southside Youth Accommodation Coalition, and wanted to work in the area of youth policy and services. The Shelter job seemed a good opportunity to gain practice experience and a better understanding of the problems of youth homelessness.

Ann's first day in the new job passed very quickly. The kitchen turned out to be a good place to start to get a feel for the organisation. It was the hub of most activity in the shelter. Throughout the morning, residents, volunteers, members of the management committee and other visitors to the shelter, passed through the kitchen, and Ann was able to introduce herself and get an idea of what was going on.

During the afternoon, Shane and Ann had a long discussion about the shelter, its problems and issues, and how Ann and Shane might best work together and with the other staff. Ann discovered that Shane liked to talk. He had worked in the shelter for five years, longer than anyone else other than a handful of volunteers, and had strong views about what was going on. He seemed very keen to give Ann his version of events. 'There are four things you need to understand if you are going to work effectively in this place', he declared. 'They are its history, its funding, the bloody management committee and the kids'. Ann sipped her coffee, lit another cigarette, and sat back to listen and reflect.

'When this place started five or six years ago,' Shane began, 'there was nothing at all for young, homeless people on the Southside. Bill Cousins, the local Catholic priest (who is still on the Management Committee by the way), got together a group of committed local people who, without any government support, rented and staffed a house for young people who had absolutely nowhere to go. I will never forget those early days. Things were pretty chaotic and we had all sorts of hassles—trouble with the police, trouble with neighbours, problems with the council . . . the whole thing. But we knew what we were trying to do and where we were going. One thing we did in that first year was to become incorporated, and as part of that process we had to spell out our philosophy and goals in our constitution. I reckon these are still a pretty good statement of what we should be on about and I've got a copy for you to have a look at. I'll read out the key bits:

The mission of the Southside Emergency Youth Shelter is to provide a place of safety and protection for all young people who are in immediate need of shelter and support.

The goals of the Shelter are:

1   To open our doors to all young people, giving the highest priority to those who are rejected by and unacceptable to other organisations and the society as a whole.

2   To assist young people, where possible, to reunite with their families, or, in other ways, to meet their longer-term needs for accommodation and support.

3   To respect the individuality of all young people, and develop respectful and significant relationships with them.

Shane paused for breath, then continued. 'Now, I'd be the first to acknowledge that we don't always achieve all of that. But as far as I am concerned that's what we should be on about, and I do what I can to make sure the Management Committee, staff and volunteers don't forget it.'

'The other thing you need to know about is our funding situation. We couldn't keep running on charity the way we did in the first year. So, for the last few years nearly all of our money is provided by the Supported Accommodation Assistance Programme (SAAP), which, as I am sure you already know, is a joint Commonwealth-State funding program for crisis accommodation services. I've got a copy of the relevant aims for you.'

He handed a sheet to Ann. She quickly glanced over the section concerned with purpose:

The provision . . . of a range of supported accommodation services and related support services, to assist . . . persons of not less than 12 years of age nor more than 25 years of age, and their dependants who are homeless as a result of crisis and who need support to move towards more appropriate accommodation, including independent living where possible and appropriate.

Shane continued to speak. 'Now when you read that it sounds lovely. What it doesn't say, though, is what the funders expect to get for their money—which, I might say, barely covers our costs. The Commonwealth isn't too bad—they mainly just want pictures in the paper of the local member of parliament announcing our annual grant. But the State is a different story. Do you realise that at least 50 per cent of our residents are actually kids who are in the care of the Department of Family and Youth Services? The Department are forever ringing us up to look after one of their kids who is in a spot of bother, and we see some of these kids time and time again. Essentially, I think they see us as just a cheap alternative to detention centres!' Ann nodded, and Shane, without pausing for breath, carried on.

'One person whom I reckon believes that should be our major role is Lyn Birrell, the child protection worker who is the Family and Youth Services' representative on the Management Committee.' 'I know Lyn', interrupted Ann, 'We met on the Youth Accommodation Coalition. She seems to have lots of good ideas and really knows what's going on.' Shane did not seem pleased with this. 'I think you should know, Ann,' he replied, 'that she and I, to put it mildly, fight rather a lot. We seem to have very different views. She is always talking about the need for "closer integration and co-ordination between the shelter and the work of the department". What I think she means by that is that we should do their work for them. The rest of the committee aren't much better. In the old days, the committee was the volunteers, with Bill Cousins as the informal chairperson. Meetings were fun, and the committee were involved and knew what was happening on a day-to-day basis in the shelter. It's not like that any more. I am the only paid worker who sits on the committee, and I am supposed to liaise between the committee and the staff. Bill is still there, but he is not very involved these days. We have got an accountant (someone said we needed one), a couple of ex-volunteers, the Federal member of parliament (who doesn't get to many meetings), the local Uniting Church minister, and an academic psychologist from the College as chairperson. They are not a bad bunch in a way, but I'm worried about Lyn's influence. I don't think she has ever really understood what we have been trying to do these last five or six years.'

'Finally, there are the kids themselves. Basically, they are great. But some of them will push you just as far as you are prepared to go, and then a bit more. That's when it is essential to keep calm. They will test you. They want to find out whether you are serious or not, and whether you are like many of the other adults in their lives. Some of them have had a really bad time from their parents, their families, the police, or just adults in general. Some of them have been really badly abused by people they trusted, sexually, physically, emotionally. You name it . . . they've had it done to them. Until you prove otherwise, you're just another adult. They'll find out what makes you angry, what makes you sad, and then they will push all the buttons to see what sort of response they get. Above all keep cool, relax, keep listening, keep responding . . . but don't feel you have to personally resolve every issue or problem they throw at you. As I said this morning, welcome to the madhouse.'

Ann found it really interesting to listen to Shane, but she also felt she would need to find things out for herself. She started off on the day roster to enable her to know the routine of the shelter, and in turn to become known. She spent time with the residents, listened to their stories, and began the long process of trying to develop relationships based on trust and mutual respect.

In her third week in the job she moved on to the night roster duties. From Monday to Saturday, 6 p.m. to 8 a.m., she slept and ate at the shelter. The shelter at night was quite different from the day. Sometimes, especially on the evenings when people had run out of money and were waiting for their next social security payment, the house was full. There were people watching television, playing cards, or just sitting around talking or listening to music. Occasionally, some conflict and or tension would break out. This was hardly surprising given some fourteen people living in a house designed essentially for five or six.

Late on her second night on roster, Ann had to turn away two boys because the shelter was full. She rang round the other shelters first, but they, too, were full. They nearly always were. Eventually she sent the boys off to the Salvation Army Hostel for Homeless Men. It was not the sort of place that you would choose to send children. She tried not to think about where they would sleep if they didn't get in. Some of the other residents had argued with her about her decision, trying to persuade her to let the boys sleep on the floor. 'Come on Ann, its pissing down out there, you're not gonna make them go in the rain are you? Who's going to know?' Ann and the rostered volunteer pointed out that the shelter had made it a rule to take no more than fourteen people. They had all been through this before. A couple of residents then become angry. One girl, whom Ann thought was probably a friend of the boys, became really angry saying 'If you two just pissed off home, instead of playing prison guards, there would be two extra beds here that they could sleep in' She then went and collected her things and left with the boys. Ann hardly slept at all that night. She lay awake struggling with the irony. All over the city there were kids who needed a bed for the night and here she was, the co-ordinator of a crisis accommodation shelter for homeless kids, with an empty bed. It just didn't make sense.

As the weeks passed Ann settled into the routine and life of the shelter. Most nights that she was on duty she had to turn young people away, or try, usually unsuccessfully, to refer them on to another shelter. Other times they might turn someone away because they were drunk or obviously disturbed. Sometimes the shelter was full, other times people were turned way because they were too old. On a couple of occasions Ann had made the decision to ask people to leave, mainly for reasons concerning their behaviour or rule breaking. These incidents could turn quite nasty, and she worried about the process going wrong, particularly, where someone was obviously drunk, doing drugs or psychologically 'disturbed'.

It was a couple of weeks later, when Ann was back on the day roster, that Shane burst into the kitchen, livid with anger and brandishing a piece of paper which he thrust in front of Ann's face. 'Look what Lyn Birrell's done now,' he shouted, 'that woman can't be trusted. She is totally out of touch with reality. How can she make these criticisms. Look around you . . . this isn't an ideal world, but we do lots of good things. The kids need a bed . . . we can provide it. They need a sympathetic ear . . . we can provide that too within limits. But apart from that, we are up to our ears just keeping this place operating on a daily basis. We just don't have the resources or staff or time to do all that other stuff. What is she trying to prove?'

Ann took the sheet of paper from Shane and read the following:

Review of Goals of Southside YAS
After discussions with several other committee members, I am requesting a special management committee meeting to re-examine the appropriateness of the existing directions and programmes of Southside YAS. This is needed, I believe, because of a number of concerns raised by the recent Commonwealth review of the needs of homeless young people, which seem to bear out the concerns that many of us have had about the operations of our own shelter. Matters falling into this category that I wish to see discussed include:

1   The fact that of the 324 young people using the shelter last year, only 30 per cent were young women.
2   The fact that we turned away 165 young people last year because there were no beds available, and a further 134 due to them being ineligible, 'difficult' or 'disruptive'.
3   The fact that we only provide crisis accommodation—shouldn't we be looking at longer term accommodation needs.
4   The fact that we don't really help young people to get permanent accommodation or to re-unite with their families.
5   The need to work more closely with the programmes and activities of the State Family and Youth Services Department, one of our major funders.
6   The need to respond to the needs of Aboriginal young people, young people of non-English speaking backgrounds, young people with disabilities and emotionally disturbed young people. What are we doing for these groups?
7   The need to respond to the problem of 'refuge-hopping'—we know that many of our residents simply move from one shelter to another, without any of their longer term needs being addressed.
8   The problem of lack of expertise of shelter staff in dealing with the complex emotional and social problems experienced by residents.
9   The need to set specific objectives for the shelter on an annual basis.

I am firmly of the opinion that unless we address these issues, the credibility, funding and future of the shelter is seriously at risk. A new direction is called for.
Lyn Birrell

'Hey, calm down,' said Ann. 'Stay cool, just relax! Let's look at this carefully and work out just exactly what needs to be done.'

Key question

Critically analyse the goals of the organisation, using the concepts introduced in the chapter. Include an analysis of the factors shaping the goals of the shelter. How should Ann deal strategically with the letter from Lyn Birrell?

Case discussion points

1 Are there any discrepancies between the official and operative goals of the shelter? Explain any discrepancy.
2 Does the shelter have a clearly defined statement of its mission, goals and objectives? Is such a statement helpful or potentially helpful for the shelter? Why or why not?
3 Is there any tension between the outcome, system and service goals of the shelter?
4 What are the most important factors shaping the operative goals of the organisation? Consider the influences of groups in the organisational environment, consumers, the 'dominant coalition' (if any), interest groups within the organisation, and broad social, economic and political structures.
5 Is this organisation experiencing goal displacement, succession or adaptation? What are the implications of your answer?
6 How influential in setting the organisation's future goals can and should the worker be?
7 Is this a situation in which the worker might consider: (a) capitalising on the complexity of goals; (b) utilising official goals; (c) participating in planning processes; (d) involving consumers in goal processes. If so, how might she do this?

6

Organisational structure: roles, relations, rules and records

> Organisational structures are constantly evolving as a consequence of the activities that take place within them (Hall 1987, p. 56).

Imagine a social or welfare worker arriving for the first day of work in an unfamiliar organisation. What are the questions that are likely to be running through his or her mind? Most likely, they would include some of the following:

- What are my responsibilities and duties?
- To whom am I accountable and who is accountable to me?
- How do I find out the information that I need to do my job?
- What rules, regulations and organisational practices do I need to be aware of?
- Who is responsible for the various jobs that need to be done to make the organisation function?
- Who do I work with?
- How does the whole organisation fit together, and how do I fit into the organisation?
- How is work allocated to me?
- How much do I control my own work?
- How much is my role determined by other people in the organisation, and how much do I determine my own role?

These are all questions about the structure of organisations. The term 'organisational structure' needs careful definition. 'Structure' often carries connotations of building and construction. When applied to an organisation, there is a tendency to think in terms of formal, static, clearly delineated and enduring arrangements, such as those portrayed on organisation charts. This perspective is also found in some definitions of structure in the literature on management and organisation theory. Thus, Stoner, Collins and Yetton define organisational structure as 'the formal arrangement and interrelationship of the component parts and positions of a company' (1985, p. 301).

We argue that this view of structure as the 'walls, floors and ceilings' (Hall 1987, p. 56) of an organisation presents only a partial, and somewhat misleading, picture. The alternative is to view the structure of an organisation as 'the socially created pattern of roles and relationships that exist within it' (Dawson 1986, p. 41). Implicit in this definition are the ideas that organisational structure is not static, and that structure stems from decisions made by individuals. Structure, from this perspective, derives from ongoing attempts by all participants to pursue their own interests in the context of the organisation's history, environment and tasks. This dynamic, interactive view of structure is our starting point in this chapter.

All organisations have structure. An unstructured organisation is a contradiction in terms, although organisations certainly vary considerably in their level of formality, complexity and centralisation. Social and welfare workers need to understand structure. Structure shapes the ways consumers are treated, the nature of professional work, and social and political relations. Relating to structure is a central and complex practice issue for all workers. There are, in essence, four inter-related questions for social and welfare workers to consider:

1 What are the elements that comprise the structure of an organisation?
2 What are the different types of organisational structure?
3 What influences structure in human service organisations?
4 How can an understanding of organisational structure be used by workers in practice?

Aspects of these questions have already been addressed, albeit in passing, in earlier chapters. The nature and determinants of organisational structure are central concerns of organisational theory, and many of the perspectives examined in chapter 2 contribute to our understanding of structural issues. Weber's theory of bureaucracy points to the relationship between the circumstances of modern societies and the structure of organisations. Scientific management is concerned with principles to direct the structure and design of organisations. The human relations perspective stresses the importance of the informal structure, arising out of the interpersonal relationships of organisational members. Systems theory asserts the role of structure in maintaining the internal coherence of organisations, and ensuring successful adaptation to the environment. Neo-Marxian and political economy perspectives emphasise the structural position of organisations in the society and the economy, and how organisations reproduce and reflect structural divisions and inequalities in the larger society, including class, gender and ethnicity. These perspectives also explore the relations between organisational structure and the exercise of power, influence and authority. The feminist perspective points to the possibilities of alternative structures, based on different assumptions about the ways that individuals can relate to one another in organisations. The Aboriginal perspective points to the ways in which structures can act to exclude certain groups from full citizenship. This chapter draws these themes together, and links them to the distinctive characteristics of human service organisations and the practice concerns of social and welfare workers.

The elements of structure

A conventional approach to organisational structure usually begins with the construction of an organisation chart. Typically, this comprises boxes representing sections (for example, regional offices) and key positions (for example, State manager) joined together by lines. Such charts can be developed for all kinds of human service organisations, and two examples, one for a government department and one for a non-government human service organisation, are provided in Figures 6.1 and 6.2.

Organisation charts can be useful ways of depicting the various sections of an organisation, and their inter-relationships. However, as a guide to structure, in the sense that the term is used here, they have two major shortcomings. Firstly, they are incomplete. There are important aspects of structure that simply do not appear on organisation charts. We conceptualise organisational structure broadly as comprising four elements: roles, relations, rules and records. It is necessary to grasp the complex ways in which these four key elements inter-relate, and collectively give structure to organisations.

Secondly, organisational charts are limited by their focus on the official structure, and their neglect of the operative structure. The official structure (sometimes called the formal structure) is that portrayed by the organisation itself. It is found in official job descriptions, formal rules and regulations, terms of reference for committees and groups, annual reports, and similar officially sanctioned documents, including the organisation chart itself. The operative structure, by contrast, is the pattern of roles, relations, rules and records that occurs in practice. For example, a social or welfare work position may be described in an official job description, but operationally consist of quite different tasks and responsibilities.

Figure 6.1   Chart of a public sector organisation

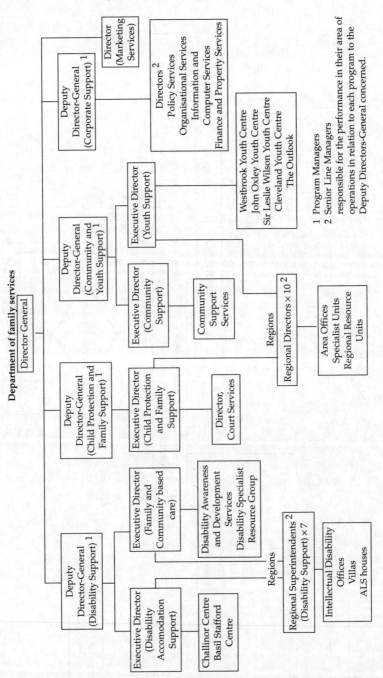

Source: Queensland, Department of Family Services and Aboriginal and Islander Affairs, *Annual Report 1989–90*.

Figure 6.2   Chart of a non-government organisation

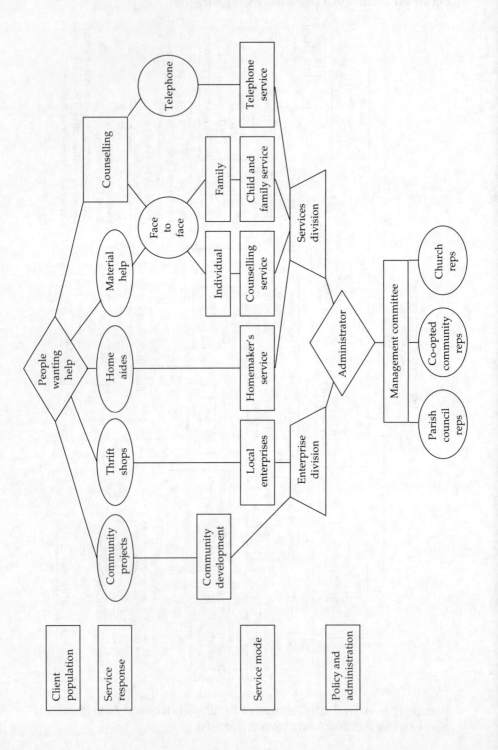

Similarly, the portrayal in official organisational charts of a flow of authority from the top to the bottom of an organisation, does not accurately represent the complexities of power, influence and authority relations.

Some of these limitations can be overcome by portraying organisations in a different manner. Tropman, for example, suggests abandoning 'boxcharts' in favour of 'organisational circles' (1989). This involves depicting the components of a human service organisation as a series of orbits revolving in complex ways around the 'executive core'. Such approaches to re-conceptualising human service organisations are useful, although it is necessary to be aware that they may contain implicit assumptions about relations of power, authority and influence. However, we argue that a framework for analysis of structure must go beyond organisation charting, to take into account all elements of structure, and operational as well as official dimensions. Table 6.1 depicts these various factors, which we will now discuss in more detail.

Roles

The term 'role', in the context of organisations, can be defined as the set of expected behaviours for a particular job-holder or group of job-holders. Formal roles for individuals in organisations are specified in 'job descriptions'. These set out the official expectations of the organisation of the incumbent of the job. Job descriptions typically outline the tasks to be undertaken, the person or persons to whom the job-holder is responsible, and the people whom the job-holder will work with in undertaking the tasks. But many other factors can be included such as the methods to be used, the sequencing of the work, the expected pace and quality of the work, performance standards and accountability requirements (Dawson 1986, p. 42). Job descriptions vary considerably in scope, that is the variety of tasks encompassed by the job, and depth, that is the extent to which an individual controls the nature of his or her work (Stoner, Collins and Yetton 1985, p. 293).

In practice, there is often considerable discrepancy between official roles, as written down in job descriptions, and on-the-job expectations and practices. Such discrepancies reflect the impossibility of encompassing all circumstances and situations in one statement, prepared at one point of time. All official roles unavoidably leave some scope for individual discretion. Individuals use this discretion in different ways, as they bring their own hopes, expectations and idiosyncrasies to the job. Moreover, once in the job, an individual is likely to be strongly influenced by his or her perceptions of the expectations of colleagues and consumers. These pressures can be understood in terms of inter-personal relationships, such as the influence of group norms (Mitchell and Larson 1987, pp. 259-280). However, a political analysis is also applicable. The ways in which a person operationalises her or his job affect the interests of professional colleagues, consumers, supervisors and administrative superiors, boards of management and other groups and individuals inside and outside the organisation. Negotiating these pressures may entail considerable conflict, involving adjustment and re-interpretation of the official job design. The official job description itself originates from such political processes, and, given the nature of these processes, can quickly become outdated.

Organisational roles are constructed around groups as well as individuals. The boxes on organisational charts depicting departments, sections, areas, management committees and so forth, are all examples of group roles. In addition to these major groupings, organisations comprise other official groups, such as standing (that is, ongoing) committees, task forces, advisory bodies and teams. The actual operations of these groups may depart from official expectations. Moreover, within organisations there exist a multiplicity of informal groups, which emerge whenever people interact on a regular basis. These informal groupings should also be viewed as part of the socially created pattern of roles that constitutes an organisation's structure.

Relations

The individual and group roles described above are linked in organisations in complex ways. On organisation charts these relations are represented by lines linking the various boxes. However, it is rarely made clear what these lines represent, and they are, in most cases, a gross simplification of intra-organisational relations. Structural relations are of essentially five kinds.

The most fundamental are those of power, authority and influence. Within all organisations certain individuals or groups are given the authority to direct and control others. The exercise of authority and control is seen most clearly in a hierarchical organisation such as a government department. Authority is centralised in the form of the director, and then delegated through the levels of the organisation. However, all organisations, including those organised as co-operatives or collectives, need, and exert, some level of control over organisational members. What distinguishes these latter organisations is not the absence of control, but a markedly different patterning of authority and control (for example, authority vested in the collective itself).

The operative counterparts of official authority and control are the alternative sources of authority in the organisation, and processes of influence and non-compliance. While legal–rational authority is fundamental to human service organisations, authority based on tradition or personal charisma may also play a significant part. For example, the founder of an organisation may continue to hold great authority long after the reins of office have been formally passed on to others. Moreover, individuals and groups without authority can exert influence over organisational decisions and activities, and some individuals and groups comply only partially, or not at all, with directives from those in positions of authority.

Closely linked to relations of authority and control are those of decision-making and planning. As discussed in the chapter on goals, all organisations have official processes for making decisions and setting organisational directions. Because there are so many decisions to be made in complex organisations, responsibility for making certain kinds of decisions is distributed around the organisation. For example, in a non-government human service organisation it may be formally agreed that broad policy decisions are the responsibility of the board of directors, administrative decisions are the responsibility of the executive director in consultation with senior staff, and decisions about individual consumers are to be left to front-line workers. Furthermore, there may be a planning process established which gives all staff and members of the organisation an opportunity to contribute formally to the determination of the future directions of the organisation.

Such decision-making processes are an important part of the official structure of an organisation. However, operative decision-making may involve considerable modifications to the official picture. Informal processes of consultation and discussion may be of great significance. Individuals may by-pass official channels in order to seek different or speedier decisions. People may exceed their official decision-making powers, or attempt to expand their area of discretion. Moreover, there will be significant aspects of organisational life that are areas of non-decision-making, that is assumptions that are not questioned and which, therefore, do not get raised as decisions.

Relations in organisations are also structured around the division of work. The tasks of complex organisations are typically too varied and too many, to be accomplished by one person, and must therefore be allocated to different individuals and groups. Efficiency can be achieved by dividing tasks in certain ways, and by specialisation. There are many different ways of dividing the work of human service organisations (see Healy 1988). The official division of work and operative practices may differ. For example, a group of professionals, including social and welfare workers, may officially work according to an inter-disciplinary team model, but in practice operate largely independently of one another, or under the control of one member of the team.

Relations among individuals and groups in organisations are also about communications. All organisations have official channels through which information can flow or be impeded. These channels include official publications and other missives (for example, newsletters, memoranda, reports), meetings, rules concerning the reporting and non-reporting of activities (for example, giving or denying certain people access to information, requiring or prohibiting the dissemination of information), and organisational records.

Information is a critical resource in organisational life, and an individual's role in creating, accessing and disseminating information is central to her or his organisational effectiveness. The volume of information in complex organisations is so great that individuals have to be highly selective in the information they process. Individuals acquire a considerable part of their information through non-official sources such as tea-room gossip, and discussion with friends and acquaintances. Sometimes individuals attempt to deliberately undermine official communication systems, by 'leaking', withholding or deliberately distorting information. Such practices raise significant ethical questions for social and welfare workers who often feel strongly committed to the principle of open relations with colleagues and consumers.

The most hidden elements of organisational relations may be the social relations among the individuals and groups comprising the organisation. By this we mean the ways in which the organisation reinforces, reproduces or challenges social divisions in the broader society in which the organisation is located. Historically, many organisations have officially distinguished and discriminated among organisational members and consumers on such bases as gender, race and ethnicity, religion, class, disability, age, and geographic locality. These official practices are currently under challenge, to some extent, by legislation concerned with equal employment opportunity, anti-discrimination and the protection of human rights. At the operational level, social relations are structured by the attitudes and beliefs of organisational members, and by indirect, societal constraints. An example of the latter is the impact of the limited availability of child care which limits the opportunities for women working in organisations. The structure of social relations in organisations should be of particular concern to social and welfare workers, because of the significance of gender divisions for a predominantly female occupation, and because of social and welfare work's professed commitment to socially disadvantaged groups. A major concern of workers should be to promote organisational practices that challenge and change, rather that reflect and reproduce, unequal and inequitable social relations.

Rules

All modern organisations have rules. Complex organisations tend to develop a large volume of rules, and there seem to be inexorable pressures for the rule book to expand. In large organisations, such as the Department of Social Security, the 'Manual of operational procedures' or equivalent, which codifies precedents, procedures and practices, is typically a massive tome which is added to on an almost daily basis. In such situations it is virtually impossible for any one member of the organisation to keep up-to-date with the rules. Small organisations also experience rule proliferation. For example, an account of the early years of a women's refuge collective details the development of a quite complex set of rules covering such matters as the conditions of membership, the rights of members and non-members, decision-making procedures, the responsibilities of action groups, the organisation of meetings, the duties of rostered women, methods of internal and external communication, the admission of residents, the democratic running of the house, the allocation of financial resources, the collection of information, and speaking on behalf of the collective (Women's Liberation Halfway House Collective 1976).

Organisational rules serve a number of purposes. Fundamentally, they are a form of organisational control. But they may also provide predicability, continuity, and protection for organisational members and consumers. They are necessary to ensure due process and equitable treatment. Organisational efficiency and effectiveness also require rules governing processes of production and uses of organisational resources. Rules can be divided into two broad, overlapping categories. Firstly, there are those governing roles and relations. Rules specify what individuals and groups do in the organisation, and establish structures of authority and control, planning and decision-making, the division of work, communications and social relations. Secondly, rules govern the delivery of services. They specify eligibility requirements, the nature, location and amount of services, and the rights and responsibilities of consumers. They lay down who gets what, when, where and how. Just as importantly, from a social and welfare work perspective, they determine who is excluded from the organisation and its services.

Rules come in many forms. All organisations are subject to the general laws of the nation or jurisdiction in which they are located. These include laws relating to the rights of citizens, labour relations, contracts, administrative law, local planning ordinances, and so forth. There are also laws that govern the formation of the organisation itself. Thus, all formally constituted, non-government organisations are subject to the requirements of such legislation as a Companies Act, an Associations Act or a Co-operatives Act. Public sector boards and corporations are subject to the legislation under which they are established, and government departments to the terms of the executive orders bringing them into being. Organisations are also subject to specific legislation concerning their area of operation. In the case of a government department, this will be the Acts and Regulations that they are responsible for administering. For a non-government organisation this may include legislation laying down funding or regulatory guidelines. External rules such as the above are, to a considerable extent, imposed on organisations. However, there are also rules that are devised predominantly within the organisation. In non-government organisations, the constitution establishes certain basic rules of organisational functioning, to which all activities and actions must conform. Subject to its constitution and to the external rules described above, an organisation frames internal rules to guide its day-to-day operations. These may be given the status of official rules, or they may simply be decisions of authoritative bodies that are recorded and communicated to organisational members. There may also be established precedents, that is decisions made in the past on specific cases that are routinely cited as the basis for decision-making in similar circumstances.

Like the other elements of structure, these official rules have an operative counterpart. Firstly, rules have to be interpreted and applied, and these processes provide extensive opportunities for 'rule making' by professionals and officials. Moreover, organisations have established practices which, while they may have no legal basis, are part of the expected and demanded behaviour of organisational members. When a worker is told that 'this is the way we do things around here', he or she is experiencing an established practice which is effectively part of the organisational code of behaviour. Some practices may be in conflict with the formal rules, but nevertheless sanctioned by those in authority: they 'turn a blind eye'. But others are unofficial practices, sanctioned neither by official rules nor by authority. Unofficial practices can be thought of as routinised rule-breaking. For example, the official rules may require that all consumers be given certain information about their rights to certain services, but in practice, for reasons of expediency or attitude, this information may routinely not be offered.

Records

The fourth, basic element of structure is the organisation's system of records. Weber pointed out that one key feature of modern organisations is that administration is based on written documents. The remarkable changes in information technology in the latter part of the twentieth century have elevated records to an even more central role. Computers and electronic data processing mean that organisations are now able to compile, collect, create, retrieve and communicate information on a hitherto unimaginable scale. Human service organisations increasingly have the capacity to access detailed data on consumers, staff and work units, work processes and activities, resource utilisation, the organisational environment, and organisational outputs and outcomes.

The files are a central element of organisational structure and have a considerable impact on relations and roles. Organisational decision-making is profoundly shaped by what appears in the files. Decisions about consumers are influenced by their previous history in the organisation (or in other organisations) as it appears in their official record. What is recorded, and equally significantly, what is not recorded, is likely to have a major bearing on a consumer's future treatment by the organisation. Similarly, the official identity of staff is shaped by the records that are maintained on them. Records are an important means of maintaining organisational and social control. The forms that professionals and front-line staff fill out, detailing the processes and outcomes of their work, are one of the means whereby management monitors organisational performance. Particularly in large, complex organisations, these official records may be the main or sole basis for key decisions.

The files are also important in creating the organisation's history. Files record the decisions and discussions that occur in meetings, the positions taken by various groups and individuals on key issues and noted in minutes or position papers, the official reasons for taking certain actions, contacts and discussions held, and so forth. When individuals or groups wish to justify their actions, or to take issue with others, this history is often retrieved. What is written in the records, particularly if it has been ratified as an accurate account, often becomes the authoritative version of events. Because files are sometimes restricted or closed to outsiders, and often to many organisational members, they may also be important repositories of organisational secrets.

The official files are not the only records held in organisations. Individuals and groups may also keep their own, unofficial written records. Workers may keep their own written records of what 'really' happened at a meeting, or of what a consumer is 'really' like, or of what the position of a particular group will be on a forthcoming issue. The memories of individuals in an organisation are also part of the operative records of an organisation. One outcome of a trend towards freedom of information in organisations, that is viewing the official records as public and common property, has been an increasing tendency to store and transmit information informally via 'personal' records, memory and word-of-mouth. Myths, anecdotes and stories about consumers, staff and events, transmitted in conversations among organisational members, are important parts of the operative record system.

Changes in information technology have a profound influence on the nature and role of organisational records, and on overall organisational structure. The capacity to create, store and transmit large quantities of information using sophisticated telecommunications, photocopiers, computers, facsimile machines, electronic mail and the like have multiple effects on structure. Many of the social implications of these technologies are still unclear. However, access to these means of communication is clearly an important source of power and influence in organisations. They may be used to increase central control, or as a tool to enhance democratic participation in decision-making. They may result in increased responsiveness to consumer needs, or they may lead

Table 6.1 The elements of organisational structure

Element	Official	Operative
ROLES		
Individual	Job descriptions: • task allocation • responsibilities • relations to other workers and processes • time allocation	The individual's expectations and performance of the job Social-psychological pressures on the job-holder Political negotiations concerning the nature of the job
Group	Departments, units, sections, etc.	Actual operations of formal groups i.e. what they really do
	Standing committees	Informal groups
	Task forces, teams, etc.	Political coalitions
RELATIONS	Power, authority and influence systems: • legal–rational authority	• traditional and charismatic authority • the exercise of power and influence • non-compliance
	Decision-making and planning systems: • allocation of responsibility • formal delegation • planning processes	• informal decision-making • exercise of discretion • by-passing official channels • non-decision-making
	Division of work: • specialisation • allocation and sequencing of tasks	• informal work practices • unauthorised work practices
	Communication systems: • official publications and reports • meetings • rules about information dissemination • management information systems	• informal communications • unauthorised communications • selection of information • 'leaking', withholding and distorting information
	Social relations: • personnel systems • opportunity structures • organisation-consumer relations • official anti-discrimination	• personnel practices • practices relating to consumers

Element	Official	Operative
RULES	General legislation	Rule interpretation and application
	Specific legislation	Professional and administrative
	Written constitution	discretion
	Internal rules	Established practices
	Manuals of operations	Unofficial practices
	Formal precedents	
RECORDS	Official files:	
	• consumers	• personal records
	• staff	• individuals' memories
	• organisational work	• myths, anecdotes and stories
	• outputs and outcomes	• conversations
	• the environment	
	• organisational history	

to infringements on privacy and less personal treatment. The nature and role of records are central issues in all contemporary organisations, and should be of major concern to social and welfare workers.

Summary

If social and welfare workers are to work effectively in organisations they require an understanding of organisational structure that goes beyond and behind the organisational chart. This understanding begins with an ability to recognise the main elements of structure—roles, relations, rules and records—and their inter-relationships. Table 6.1, which summarises these elements, can be used by workers as a basis for identification of the main elements of their organisation's structure, and of their own place in that structure. However, dissection of the elements of structure is only the first stage of analysis. The next task is to examine more closely the nature of structure in human service organisations.

Organisational structure: types and characteristics

While all human service organisations have common structural elements, these can be combined and assembled in many different ways. One way of thinking about these differences is to distinguish among different 'types' of organisational structures. Another approach is to identify 'characteristics' of organisational structures. We will proceed with a combination of both approaches.

There are a number of typologies of organisational structure in the literature on management and organisations (for example, Burns 1971; Ross and Murdick 1979). In the context of human service organisations, it seems useful to identify three kinds of structures: classical, organic and alternative.

Classical organisational structures are those based on the principles of classical management theory and scientific management discussed in chapter 2. Defining characteristics include a hierarchical system of control and authority, unity of command (that is, control at each level vested in one person), clear demarcation of tasks and responsibilities, a high degree of specialisation, an emphasis on vertical (that is, between superior and subordinate) rather than horizontal interaction, and downward rather than upward or lateral communication. Sometimes this kind of structure is described as 'mechanistic' (Burns 1971, p. 49) or bureaucratic (Stoner, Collins and Yetton 1985, p. 415). In human service organisations, such structures are most likely to be found where there is a management ideology that stresses the importance of centralised authority, where there are strong demands for external accountability, and where the tasks to be performed are of a relatively routine and standardised nature.

The perceived rigidities of classical organisational structures has led to a great deal of interest in, and experimentation with, organic structures. Organic structures, sometimes called behavioural (Ross and Murdick 1979, pp. 206-207) or organismic (Burns 1971, pp. 50-51), are typically described in terms such as adaptive, temporary, democratic, participative, fluid and flexible. They are characterised by flexible roles and relationships among staff, collegial rather than hierarchical relations, extensive lateral linking and communication across the organisation, decentralised and participative decision-making, commitment to the goals and ethos of the organisation as a basis for motivation, and differentiation among staff on the basis of knowledge and skills rather than rank or role. Organic structures are associated with extensive reliance on teams, relatively open communication, participatory decision-making processes and worker self-management. Whereas the theoretical underpinnings of classical structure lie in scientific management, organic structures are based largely on the approaches and assumptions of the human relations theorists. The emphasis in systems theory on the need for organisations to be adaptive to their environment is another underlying influence. Organic structures are often considered appropriate for organisations with a significant proportion of professional staff, and where decisions and tasks are non-routine and complex, requiring judgement, flexibility, adaptability and collaboration among staff with varying skills.

Alternative organisational structures, while sharing some common elements with organic structures, are differentiated from them in terms of basic philosophy and purpose. Both classical and organic structures are based on notions of managerial efficiency in the context of prevailing societal values. The choice between classical and organic structures is often couched in terms of what is 'best' for the organisation, as well as for workers. Alternative organisational structures, whose theoretical underpinnings lie in part in the feminist perspective, are often based on principles and practices which aim to challenge dominant societal values. Dominant values and conditions that are questioned may include inequalities of power and authority, professionalism, hierarchy, the separation of public and private spheres, impersonality in social relations, trends towards large organisations and social institutions, and separation of people into providers and consumers. Some characteristics of alternative structures include collective decision-making; deprofessionalisation; smallness of size; an expanded idea of 'membership' to include consumers, staff and supporters; greater equality of rewards and status; an emphasis on co-operative and other-regarding behaviour rather than self-seeking and competitive behaviour; undifferentiated organisational roles; and a mission to bring about such changes in the broader social and organisational environment. Many alternative organisational structures in the Australian context have emerged out of the women's movement, Aboriginal organisations, ethnic organisations, local community movements, and organisations concerned with green or environmental issues and alternative life-styles. In Australia and worldwide, such structures are a significant segment of the human services system, and are increasingly a focus of practitioner and academic interest (e.g. Powell 1986; Perlmutter 1988).

The three categories of organisations outlined above are ideal types. No particular human service organisation fits precisely into one of them. A hospital may be based on a classical management structure, but rely heavily on teams and collegial relations in certain areas of its operations. Similarly a government department, such as the Department of Social Security, may be basically structured according to principles of hierarchy and specialisation, but encourage decentralisation of some organisational processes and upward and lateral communication through the organisation—both features associated with organic organisations. A collective providing emergency shelter may be based on the principle of power equalisation, but due to the demands of an external funding body and the exigencies of the work, be required to give some members of the collective who have professional skills and qualifications the authority to make certain kinds of decisions in some circumstances. The typology of classical, organic and alternative structures provides an indication of 'basic organising principles', rather than providing a basis for definitive classification.

An alternative approach to understanding the differences among organisational structures is to identify certain basic characteristics of organisational structure and describe particular organisations in these terms. There are a number of different approaches to specifying these characteristics (e.g. Clegg and Dunkerley 1980, pp. 219-221; Hall 1987, pp. 56-97). The three concepts that we use are complexity, formalisation and centralisation.

Complexity refers to the number of sub-parts that comprise the organisation and the ways in which they are related. Terms sometimes used to refer to aspects of complexity are differentiation and specialisation. Complexity has a number of dimensions (Hall 1987, pp. 58-64). One aspect is the number of different skills that the organisation requires to perform its tasks, referred to by Clegg and Dunkerley as the 'number of specialisms' (1980, p. 219). As the number of different tasks increases, individual roles become more complicated, and there is a greater likelihood that the organisation will employ a wide range of specialist personnel and divide the organisation into specialist units and roles. A highly complex organisation is one where this process of role specialisation is at an advanced level.

The number of specialisms and the extent of role specialisation are aspects of horizontal complexity, that is the division of the work of the organisation. Vertical complexity refers to the sub-parts of the authority structure of the organisation. Organisations vary in terms of the number of levels or layers of authority, that is the number of positions between the director and the front-line workers. This is sometimes referred to as the difference between a 'tall' and a 'flat' organisational structure. Organisations also differ in terms of whether the authority structure is unified or fragmented. A unified structure (unity of command) is one where all workers are officially responsible to only one superior, the whole structure peaking with the chief executive. In a fragmented structure, there are multiple sources of authority, and workers may be responsible to different superiors for different aspects of their work. An example of this is when social or welfare workers are responsible to both a professional supervisor and an administrative director.

The extent of organisational complexity is related to organisational size, to the nature of the tasks to be performed, and to geographic spread. Human service organisations vary considerably in the extent and nature of their complexity. A large hospital, for example, is likely to be highly complex as it will comprise a wide range of specialist skills, grouped into separate administrative units. It may also have a fragmented authority system to accommodate both professional and administrative authority. The Department of Social Security is also highly complex, although in somewhat different ways. It has a tall hierarchy and the complexities of administering income security over a large geographic area results in a proliferation of regional organisations. However, the authority structure is quite unified, reflecting the relatively minor role of professionals and the relatively uniform nature of the service provided by operational units. The non-government organisation depicted in Figure 6.2 is also quite complex, both vertically and horizontally, even though it is fairly small. An example of a human service organisation of relatively low complexity might be a small child-care centre. The range of specialisms needed in such a centre is narrow; there is typically only a small number of operational units, and the authority structure is unified and flat, with the director having direct supervision of all staff.

The second structural variable is formalisation. We use this concept to refer to two aspects of organisational structure. Firstly, it signifies the extent to which rules, roles, relations and records are codified in writing. Secondly, it indicates the extent to which these elements of structure are standardised in the organisation. In all organisations there is a complex mix of formal elements such as written rules, standard forms, laid down procedures, duty statements and manuals, and informal elements such as unwritten rules, accepted practices, operative roles, and so on. A highly formalised organisation is one in which there is a relatively high level of codification and where this exercises a relatively strong influence on organisational activities.

The extent of formalisation depends on the nature of organisational tasks and on managerial ideologies relating to organisational control. In organisations where the work to be done is non-routine and is viewed as requiring initiative or innovation, and where workers are considered capable of exercising discretion and self-management, formalisation will tend to be minimal. Routine work performed by workers who are viewed by management as needing rules to guide their behaviour is likely to result in a highly formalised structure. In human service organisations, strong requirements for public accountability and procedural equity, often result in high levels of formalisation. Requirements to account for use of resources and for performance, also lead to strong pressures for standardisation of roles, rules, records and procedures. Environmental pressures for equitable treatment of consumers and employees add to demands for increased formalisation.

A high level of formalisation in human service organisations is often viewed by workers as inappropriate, notwithstanding these equity, efficiency and accountability considerations. This view is understandable, stemming as it does from the humanistic values of social and welfare work and the human relations tradition in organisational analysis which reject standardisation of human beings. It also reflects concerns about 'bureaupathology', that is excessive and irrational compliance with and dependence on organisational rules. Studies have found that professionals in general feel alienated from highly formalised organisations, which sometimes give little scope for the exercise of professional judgement (Hall 1987, pp. 81-87).

Human service organisations also vary in their degree of centralisation. This refers to the locus of authority within the organisation. Organisations in which the authority to make most decisions is maintained by top management or other central decision-making bodies, such as management committees, are highly centralised. Those in which decision-making authority is extensively delegated to subordinates, including front-line workers, are decentralised. An important element is the breadth or narrowness of the parameters of delegated decision-making powers. Many human service organisations require extensive decision-making authority to be delegated to the front-line, but if the scope for discretionary judgement is limited, the level of decentralisation is more apparent than real. Centralisation in terms of authority needs to be distinguished from spatial centralisation or decentralisation. An organisation may 'decentralise' by setting up regional and local offices to improve access and service delivery. But this may or may not be accompanied by decentralisation of decision-making authority.

Issues of centralisation and decentralisation are most apparent in large, public sector, human service organisations where size and complexity necessitate extensive delegation of authority. However, this dimension of organisational structure is equally relevant to the analysis of small, non-government organisations. It is not uncommon for decision-making authority in such organisations to be highly centralised in the management committee, director or, even, the 'team meeting'. All organisations can be analysed in terms of their degree of centralisation, irrespective of size, number of sites, or formal ideology.

These three concepts—complexity, formalisation and central-isation—provide a framework for description and analysis of the structure of human service organisations. All organisations can be represented as high or low in complexity, formalisation and central-isation. For example, a community centre may be highly centralised in that key decision-making is the preserve of a small, inner group on the management committee, but low on formalisation in that there are few written-down rules, and low on complexity in that there are only one or two layers of authority and little role specialisation. It is important to understand the complicated inter-relationships among these characteristics. For example, increasing organisational complexity may give rise to greater formalisation, but lead to decentralisation due to the greater difficulty of controlling the activities of organisational members. Analysing human service organisations in these terms is more productive than simply applying stereotyped and generalised labels such as 'bureaucracy' or 'collective'.

What influences structure?

All organisations have their own unique structure. The precise patterning of roles, relations, rules and records varies markedly from organisation to organisation. The distinctions drawn above between different types and characteristics of organisations provide an overall framework for analysis. However, each organisation has its own individual configuration reflecting its singular history and circumstances. If social and welfare workers are to relate effectively to organisations, they must understand the factors that give each organisation its distinctive structure. These factors, some of which have already been alluded to, include the organisation's environment, technology and size, together with the values and interests of influential and dominant groups within the organisation itself.

The influence of environment, and specifically the general environment, on organisational structure is a theme that was first introduced in chapter 2. A Weberian analysis suggests that bureaucratic organisational structures, based on legal–rational authority, are an outcome of the conditions and requirements of complex, industrialised societies. Neo-Marxian writers stress that the hierarchical, non-egalitarian structures of modern organisations reflect and reinforce overall patterns of domination by class interests in capitalist societies. Feminist writers similarly draw links between male dominance in the society and patriarchal relations in organisations (Hooyman and Cunningham 1986, pp. 167-171).

The impact of the general environment on the structure of human service organisations is indisputable, although this can be described and explained from several perspectives. However, to understand the structure of any one particular organisation we need to look closely at its relations with its task environment. The requirements, demands or expectations of key organisations in the task environment have a major influence on an organisation's structure. For example, it is common for public sector funding bodies to require non-government organisations in receipt of funds to meet certain constitutional requirements, to keep records of certain kinds, to employ workers who have certain qualifications or characteristics, and to conduct their business according to certain rules. These requirements are often stated formally in writing, but there may also be informal expectations that influence funding decisions. Non-government organisations will often modify their structure to take account of such requirements. There may be similar demands from providers of consumers. An organisation considering making referrals may stipulate that certain consumer records be kept, that certain procedures are followed, that certain kinds of staff deal with certain kinds of cases, and so forth. If there is dependence on this organisational source of consumers, these adjustments to structure may well be made.

Difficulties arise for human service organisations that find themselves faced with conflicting demands and expectations in their task environment. For example, organisations may be closely linked to a sector which is strongly supportive of decentralised, participative, informal, organisational structures. At the same time, it may be heavily dependent on public sector funding which carries expectations of formal reporting and accountability, procedural precision and care, and conventional decision-making processes. Negotiating and accommodating these pressures places a great strain on organisational structure. Similar pressures are placed on some units of government departments in the human service area that must respond, on the one hand, to the demands of funded, non-government organisations for autonomy and flexibility in their mode of organisation, and, on the other hand, to pressures from many other units and departments within the public sector for formality, standardisation and public accountability. Alternative organisations, which by their very nature are attempting to challenge dominant modes of organisational structure, experience ongoing conflict between environmental expectations and their own structure.

The structure of a human service organisation is also affected by the characteristics of the task environment. Organisations operating in hostile environments tend to 'tighten up' their structures, that is to increase central control and to standardise and formalise procedures (Hall 1987, pp. 111-112). Thus, a human service organisation under criticism concerning the quality, desirability or efficiency of its services may attempt to protect itself through stricter reporting requirements, closer control of staff activities, and the like. However, other characteristics of the task environment may be pushing organisational structures in the opposite direction. Hasenfeld argues that many human service organisations need to respond to multiple and varied demands in their environment, and that this diversity requires 'loose' structures which enable the different groups within the organisation to respond to these varied demands (1983, pp. 152-154). For example, a non-government organisation providing a range of different services such as depicted in Figure 6.2, would need to operate in a decentralised fashion to respond effectively to its wide variety of external constituencies.

Structure is also linked to the nature of an organisation's technology (Hall 1987, pp. 105-110). It is widely suggested that classical structures fit organisations engaged on relatively routine tasks, while organic structures are linked with activities requiring frequent exercise of judgement and discretion (Stoner, Collins and Yetton 1985, pp. 426-428). Hasenfeld argues that the technological characteristics of human service organisations (as outlined in chapter 3), together with environmental complexity, often result in 'loosely coupled organisations, in which work units preserve considerable autonomy and identity, and respond to each other in a circumscribed, infrequent, slow, or unimportant manner' (Hasenfeld 1983, p. 150).

The idea that human service organisations are typified by loosely structured work arrangements has important implications for social and welfare workers and will be examined further in later chapters where we look at the nature of front-line work in organisations. Essentially, the argument is that a combination of indeterminate technologies, vague and multiple goals, ambiguous evaluation criteria and reliance on professionals, produces weak authority structures in human service organisations. Faced with these circumstances, organisations tend, in practice, to accept high levels of autonomy for professional groups and for units working at street-level, provided this is negotiated with other groups in the organisation and 'managed' with respect to the groups in the external environment (Hasenfeld 1983, pp. 154-156). If this is the case, it suggests that social and welfare workers will often have, or be able to create, considerable latitude within which to develop their own organisational roles and relations.

Another factor often viewed as a major influence on structure is organisational size. A direct relationship between increasing size and increasing formalisation and centralisation is often assumed (Vintner 1974, pp. 460-464). For example, in our experience many workers are negatively disposed towards working in large bureaucracies, due to their supposed greater impersonality and routinisation than small organisations. However, research on organisations suggests a need for a more complex analysis, in which size may be seen as a consequence of organisational complexity rather than a cause of bureaucratisation (Dawson 1986, p. 58; Hall 1987, pp. 101-105). In other words, organisations grow in size because of the increasing complexity of what they do, but size as such is not as important in explaining structure as factors such as environment and technology.

Finally, organisational structures are influenced by the values and interests of groups within the organisation itself and in particular the values and interests of those who control the organisation. The structure of an organisation is largely shaped by environmental and technological factors as discussed above. But within the context of these factors, groups and individuals within the organisation seek to structure it in ways that meet their personal and group purposes. Structures are the outcome of ongoing political processes within the organisation and between the organisation and its task environment. Central aspects of these processes are the ongoing attempts by those with formal authority to assert and effect their control of the organisation, and the counter attempts by workers, and sometimes consumers, to influence organisational processes or resist control. This political analysis of organisational structure underlies the following discussion of the strategic use of organisational structure in practice.

The strategic use of structure

For social and welfare workers the central purpose of analysis is to inform and to guide action. The key question is: how can this analysis of structure be used strategically in practice? The importance of structure for workers is indisputable. Structure has a major bearing on the capacity of organisations to provide high quality services to consumers and on the standing of consumers in the organisation. It also bears on the role and position of social and welfare workers in organisations, includ1ing their capacity to work effectively as professionals. Structure is also central to other concerns such as authority relations and distribution of opportunities and resources within and by organisations.

More contentious is the stance that workers should take in relation to structure in their practice. This issue is sometimes posed as a choice that individual workers have to make between working within established structure and working outside or against those structures (e.g. Bailey 1980). We view the issues as more complex. The reality is that workers in different situations and at different times need to adopt differing approaches to organisational structure. The range of possible approaches or stances, and specific competencies associated with each of them, are outlined in Table 6.2. Some workers make a choice to relate to organisational structure primarily from the perspective of one or another of these stances. But all workers, we would argue, need to be able to move strategically between approaches, sometimes working within established structure, sometimes modifying, sometimes conflicting, and so forth. A worker in a particular organisation can move between modes, as different issues and circumstances require. The strategic use of structure involves matching the right approach to the right circumstances. This conceptualisation gives workers a flexibility and freedom to relate to structure in a dynamic and creative manner, rather than binding them to a correct line.

Working in and through structure

All social and welfare workers are involved in working in and through established organisational structure on a daily basis. Structure provides the legitimacy, mandate and resources for practice. It is through structure that services are provided to consumers and that professional roles are established and maintained. Working in and through structure has many dimensions. In 'loosely coupled' human service organisations it may mean recognising and developing the opportunities for autonomy available to front-line workers. It may also mean seeking to attain positions of authority in organisations and using such positions to direct and influence organisational activities. These aspects are examined in detail in later chapters.

One way of providing an overview of the competencies and issues associated with working in and through structure is to examine what this involves in relation to each of the four basic elements of structure: roles, rules, relations and records. In the first place, workers need to grasp the implications and possibilities of their individual and group

Table 6.2   The strategic use of structure

	Roles	*Rules*	*Relations*	*Records*
Working in and through structure	Understand organisational expectations: • of workers • of others	Know the rules Develop skills in rule interpretation application	Understand and exercise legitimate authority Exercise power and influence via established systems and processes	Understand the significance of records and recording Develop skills in accessing, creating and interpreting information
Building and modifying structure	Negotiate different roles: for social and welfare workers, other workers, and consumers	Work towards changing rules Establish new precedents	Change relations involving consumers, professionals, opportunity structures and participation	Develop different record systems Use existing records in innovative ways
Bending and side-stepping structure	Perform roles in non-conforming ways	Fail to disclose rule-breaking Use rules 'creatively'	Delay compliance Conform in token fashion Fail to co-operate	Fail to record information Covert use of records
Confronting and conflicting with structure	Refuse to perform specified roles Take industrial action Resign from the organisation	Refuse to comply with rules Encourage non-compliance with rules	Disrupt service provision and organisational processes	Whistle-blowing Withholding and distorting information
Creating alternating structures	Personalise roles Equalise roles Minimise distinctions among roles	Design rules to reflect and promote desired relations	Create equitable and participative relations	Create open and accessible records

roles in organisations. This means obtaining as clear a picture as possible of the behaviours and activities that are expected of them by other individuals and groups in the organisation, particularly those in positions of authority. Obtaining this picture may not be straight-forward, as role expectations are a product of ongoing, social and political processes, and official role descriptions and prescriptions may be a poor guide. A worker should not, of course, feel bound by prescribed roles. But efforts to change a role should be undertaken with full comprehension of prevailing expectations. As well as under-standing their own role, workers should also have a strong grasp of the roles of other individuals and groups, and their relations to the worker's own position and activities in the organisation.

Workers also require a knowledge and understanding of organisational rules, and skills in rule interpretation and application. A detailed knowledge of rules can often be used to make an organisation more responsive to consumers. This is particularly the case in complex, highly formalised organisations involved in people processing, where it can be virtually impossible for consumers to understand the profusion of rules that may apply to them. Knowing the rules enables workers to fully explore the potential for consumer service in the context of existing policies. Familiarity with rules, and proficiency in their interpretation and application, is often a highly valued and rare commodity in complex organisations, and skills in this area contribute to a worker's general standing and influence.

Working in and through structures also involves understanding and using the organisations's authority and influence systems. On the one hand, this means acknowledging legitimate authority. A cavalier approach to authority is difficult to sustain organisationally over long periods, and ultimately can be damaging to individual and group reputations within the organisation. Workers who persistently flout regulations, ignore established procedures, resist or fail to comply with directions, or choose not to participate in established processes, are in danger of losing the respect of their colleagues and their standing in the organisation as a whole. However, at the same time, workers should not 'yield unnecessarily to the requirements of administrative convenience' (Pruger 1973, p. 30). Unquestioning conformity to official directives and procedures, without considering the impact on consumer service, relations with other staff, or the achievement of organisational goals, is incompatible with professional practice and with a critical perspective on organisations.

A social or welfare worker should also be concerned with utilising all opportunities to influence organisational processes and outcomes, within the context of existing structural arrangements. These opportunities arise within both the official and operative structure. Within the official structure, workers can exercise influence via decision-making processes in which they participate on a formal basis such as staff meetings, committees, task groups, planning bodies, and so forth. Some human service organisations formally seek input from staff concerning organisational policies and practices, and these processes may provide important channels for influence. Workers may also seek to become key players in informal decision-making and communication processes.

A capacity to understand, utilise and contribute effectively to an organisation's record system is a further aspect of working in and through structure. Workers, in common with other organisational members, often spend a considerable portion of their time recording. Continuous requirements to keep case notes and other records up-to-date are common sources of frustration and annoyance for human service workers. However, workers must maintain awareness of the important role of records in constructing the organisational identity of consumers and other organisational participants. What workers write on records, and what they omit, is likely to shape the ways in which consumers or fellow workers are perceived and treated. Recording should be viewed as an organisational as well as a professional activity, and should be undertaken with an awareness of how information will be used by the organisation. It must also be noted that an ability to maintain accurate and useful records may enhance an individual's reputation, particularly in highly formalised organisations where such skills are valued.

Equally important is a capacity to access and interpret the large volume of information available in organisational records. The information collected by organisations may be of great value to workers, for both consumer advocacy and organisational change. Understanding the nature of organisational records, and having the technical and analytical skills to utilise and interpret information, are central facets of working through structure.

Although working in and through structure is an integral part of the daily working life of a worker, equally common is the experience of dissatisfaction with received or prevailing structure. Structures often impede rather than enhance service to consumers. They may create inequalities of opportunity and authority, rather than enhancing equity and participation. They may thwart rather than sustain good professional practice. They may be perceived as excessively centralised, complex and formalised, or, alternatively, as too loose, sloppy or relaxed. In such circumstances, workers will need to go beyond working in and through, and towards building and modifying, structure.

Building and modifying structure

Building and modifying structure can be viewed as the first level of response to dissatisfaction with working in and through established structure. Faced with aspects of structure that impede service to consumers, adequate participation in decision-making, good professional practice, or some other desired value, workers can attempt to modify existing structure or build a new structure. We have conceptualised organisational structure as a fluid, active phenomenon, involving ongoing change to roles, rules, relations and records. This suggests that social and welfare workers, along with other organisational participants, may be presented with many opportunities to participate in structural change.

Processes of structural change occur at both official and operative levels. At the official level, most organisations are continuously 'tinkering' (Pawlak 1976) with their structure. For example, a non-government agency over time may re-define the roles of programme managers, set up a task force on fund-raising, change rules concerning eligibility of a certain client group, increase the number of consumer representatives on the board, or introduce a new system of computerised consumer records. These are all cases of building and modifying official structure. Social and welfare workers should be involved in these processes if key concerns are at stake. For example, a process of increasing consumer representation on an authoritative decision-making body is a modification of structure that is likely to be of central concern, and the worker may wish to be actively involved in the change processes.

Workers will also find themselves in situations where they are called on to initiate or to advise on modifications to structure. For instance, a worker employed in a small non-government organisation is likely to be consulted, formally or informally, on such matters as the relations between the management committee and workers, the respective roles of paid workers and volunteers, inter-professional relations, intake processes, the kinds of information that should be recorded on clients, the rules that should govern staff and consumer activities, and many other structural issues. This has been described as the 'diagnostician' role. 'The most effective clinical social workers are those who are as adept at diagnosing organisational obstacles to good service as they are at diagnosing client problems' (Weissman, Epstein and Savage 1983, pp. 9-48).

Many organisations, particularly those in the public sector, periodically undergo a major re-organisation (Radin 1988). Such processes are organisation-wide attempts to build and modify structure, often involving re-allocation of organisational tasks and modifications to authority relations. These large-scale, usually management-initiated exercises can have major implications for workers and consumers, and workers need to appreciate their significance and participate in them to the fullest extent possible. The concerns of social and welfare workers in these exercises are many, but are often likely to focus on implications for their own roles, the resources available to front-line workers, the accessibility and quality of services to consumers, and opportunities for participation in decision-making. Re-organisations are invariably promoted in terms of greater equity, efficiency and effectiveness, but they may have other goals such as the cutting back of services or greater central control. From a critical perspective, they must be seen as reflecting the interests of various organisational participants, particularly senior management. Workers must be especially attentive to the interests of consumers and front-line staff in these processes.

It should be remembered that structure is also modified informally through the activities and exchanges of organisational members. The role that a worker plays in an organisation may be modified extensively without any changes to the official job or unit description. Similarly, recording may be done in ways that participants find appropriate or convenient, even though quite contrary to official prescriptions. It can be argued that workers should often work at the operative level in modifying structure, as change can be accomplished more readily and without formalising the process. This is particularly so when a worker is operating in a 'hostile' context, where the desired modifications to structure are unlikely to meet with the approval of people in authority. However, such changes to structure have the disadvantage of being inherently unstable. They usually rely either on negotiated agreements among individuals within the organisation, or on secrecy. Both of these may be readily disturbed. If it is intended that a particular structural change should last, then there is a strong case for seeking to formalise it.

Most of the change agendas of social and welfare workers in organisations focus on structure. The range of structural issues is legion, and spans roles, rules, relations and records as shown in Table 6.2. The involvement of workers in building and modifying structure tends to cluster around four main areas. First, there is the structuring of organisation–consumer relations. Here the worker is interested in the ways in which structure facilitates or impedes good service to consumers, and the participation of consumers in the organisation. Second, there are the structures that pertain to the standing of the social and welfare worker: the relationship of workers to power and authority, professional autonomy and discretion, relations with other professions and teamwork. The third set of issues are those concerning opportunity structures within organisations (Gummer 1988). Workers are concerned with the ways in which structure has the capacity to reinforce, reproduce or challenge social and political inequalities. Each of these three sets of structural issues are examined in later chapters.

The fourth cluster of issues are those of power and authority relations within organisations. For many workers the centralisation of power and authority within an organisation is an issue of basic concern. Many human service organisations, both public and non-government, are highly centralised, with participation in key decisions limited to a small group at the centre or top of the organisation. Workers are often attracted to attempts to decentralise authority, and to bring a wider range of organisational members into decision-making processes. Such proposals are often labelled participatory management (Fallon 1985; Weatherley 1985). They may involve such structures as group or collegial decision-making forums (Kahle 1969), self-management of work groups (Gummer 1988), inter-disciplinary teams, and quality circles, that is groups that are set up to examine specific organisational issues, outside of the established authority structures of the organisation (Lawler and Mohrman 1987).

The development of structures that encourage and support participatory management is a legitimate and significant issue for workers. Much contemporary management literature, stemming from the human relations school, stresses the importance of structures that spur creativity and innovation. Furthermore, structure needs to reflect the fluid environment and the complex tasks performed in many human service organisations. Minimising inequalities of authority and participation in organisations can also be promoted as goals in their own right. However, the propositions and promises of participatory management should be analysed from a critical perspective. Workers need to distinguish between participatory management as a set of management techniques to maximise productivity, and participatory management as a form of power and authority re-distribution. The former is more common, both in theory and practice, than the latter. The claims of staff for greater control of decision-making must also be considered alongside the rights and demands of consumers, members and sponsors to influence or control the same processes.

We can conclude that there are many circumstances in which building and modifying structure will be central tasks for workers in organisations. However, workers also face situations in which key values are threatened, undermined or neglected by human service organisations, yet the possibilities for organisational change are limited or non-existent. In such circumstances the worker may need to consider bending and side-stepping organisational structure.

Bending and side-stepping structure

All individuals who work in human service organisations experience some discrepancy between their personal values and the demands and expectations of the organisation in which they work. This issue is heightened when an individual identifies with a profession or occupation that provides a strong, alternative reference point to that of the organisation. The ethical stance of social and welfare work stresses the primacy of clients' interests (Loewenberg and Dolgoff 1985, p. 135). Yet, the everyday experience of many workers is that the interests and needs of consumers are, at best, only partially met by the organisation through which they work. Often, as we have suggested, such concerns can be resolved by working through or modifying structure. But what options do workers have when faced with conflicts that appear unresolvable through existing structure?

The first set of these options we describe as bending and side-stepping structure. Essentially, this means 'finding ways around' the official structure, but without directly confronting or conflicting with it. This usually involves activities that are not officially sanctioned, and may involve actions of questionable legality, according to a strict or literal interpretation of the law. Table 6.2 summarises what this may entail in relation to roles, rules, relations and records. Workers may decide to operationalise their role in ways that markedly vary from official prescriptions. They may decide to surreptitiously ignore orders to undertake certain actions. They may deliberately delay implementation of certain policies, act in unco-operative or obstructive ways, conform in a token fashion to organisational requirements, or work to rule. They may fail to record information that the organisation requires them to keep, or alternatively record information or construct records that include materials that the organisation would prefer not to be written down. They may disclose information to consumers about operative organisational processes, in order to assist the consumer to make effective demands on the organisation.

There is evidence that such practices are quite common in some areas of practice (Pearson 1975, pp. 24-32), and that they are widespread in human service organisations generally, particularly in those involved in 'people processing' (Painter 1980, pp. 266-269). Many instances of bending and side-stepping structure involve organisational rules and procedures. Pearson gives the example of social workers who, faced with formal requirements to undertake regular and frequent supervision visits to consumers, but lacking the resources to do so in any meaningful fashion, 'fiddle their books' and case-records in order to appear to comply with official requirements. They justified this as a re-arrangement of work to enable them to spend more time with those needing help more urgently. Pearson also gives examples of workers turning a blind eye to information that would disadvantage consumers. This often involved not disclosing minor breaches of social security regulations or probation orders, on the grounds that reporting these matters would add to the difficulties facing the families or individuals concerned (1975, pp. 25-29). It has been argued that the complexities of some human service organisations are such that ongoing, infringements of this nature are necessary for systems to be able to work at all (Taylor and Walton 1971).

A somewhat different situation is the creative use of rules to advantage consumers. Pawlak gives the example of a vocational rehabilitation counsellor who claimed to have improved the dental health of many consumers by liberally interpreting a rule providing dental treatment for consumers, if their appearance and dental problems were an impediment to them being considered for employment involving public contact (Pawlak in Weissman, Epstein and Savage 1983, p. 207). A related practice is providing information to consumers about how they should frame their applications for services or benefits. For example, the authors were told of a common practice of applicants for unemployment benefits in an area of high unemployment being told by Commonwealth Employment Service officers to randomly phone five local employers requesting work. This action would constitute 'evidence' of actively seeking work and would allow a positive assessment of the claim for benefit to be made, even though the officer and the applicant were both aware that the chances of actually finding work were virtually non-existent.

Bending and side-stepping structure in these ways raises complex ethical issues. Professional codes of ethics often provide little guidance. For example, the Australian Association of Social Workers' code simply states that 'where policies or procedures of the employing organisation contravene professional standards, the social worker will endeavour to effect change through appropriate organisational channels' (AASW 1988, p. 5). This avoids the central issue that for all individuals working in organisations there are, or should be, limits to obedience, that is circumstances in which official duties and obligations are over-ridden by other moral considerations (Harris 1983). Defining these circumstances is difficult, partly because organisational structure serves a multiplicity of purposes. Take the example of rules governing the payment of social security benefits. One purpose of these rules is to set limits to the re-distribution of income. But they also aim to ensure equity of treatment to people in different circumstances, and to establish consumer rights. Bending the rules for some individuals, but not for others, is clearly inequitable.

Moreover, bending and side-stepping structure is not necessarily done for the benefit of consumers. Indeed, it can be argued that the beneficiaries of such practices are more commonly the workers or the organisation itself. Painter points out that bending of rules is often done to make life easier for workers faced with difficult circumstances or difficult consumers. He gives the example of counter staff bowing to the demands of troublesome applicants, while more submissive consumers go without (1980, p. 268). Rules may also be interpreted more narrowly or harshly than intended by law, particularly if vigorous rationing of services is encouraged within the organisation. The issue of consumer rights is also problematic. Pearson gives the example of social workers in mental health interpreting the concept of emergency more broadly than intended in legislation, to enable a person to be compulsorily admitted to a mental hospital on the strength of one medical certificate rather than the usual two. This occurred, Pearson argues, to make the job easier for the workers involved in the admission process, and it was justified in terms of making the process of hospitalisation more rapid and smooth, and hence less distressing for the patient's family. Nevertheless, the practice clearly infringed on the rights of the patient.

Bending and side-stepping is not only ethically complex, but also politically hazardous. People in positions of authority in organisations place a high value on conformity with official or officially sanctioned structure. Deviance, if detected, may result in censure or disciplinary action, which may be directed at workers or consumers. Clearly, the stakes are highest if illegal practices or activities are exposed. Partly for these reasons, and partly because changing structure is a more enduring response to organisational shortcomings, we argue that workers should attempt to work through or change structure prior to considering less conventional options. Nevertheless, workers are involved continuously in situations where the contradictions and limitations of human service provision are exposed, and in such circumstances a strong moral case can be made for bending and side-stepping structure. We argue further that there are situations in which workers will need to consider actions that go beyond bending and side-stepping and into confrontation and conflict with structure.

Confronting and conflicting with structure

In one sense, confrontation and conflict are part of everyday life in organisations. Some degree of disagreement and discord over the multitude of issues addressed every day in human service organisations is to be expected. What we are referring to here goes beyond such commonplace occurrences. Confronting and conflicting with structure means a conscious and strategic decision to go outside and beyond established roles, rules, relations and systems of records. It implies a belief in the illegitimacy of existing structure or at least in the inability of existing structure to deal satisfactorily with a key issue or issues. Confrontation and conflict, in this sense, may be overt or covert. While some forms of confrontation and conflict are within the law, others are clearly illegal and contrary to the terms of employment in the organisation. The range of possible actions is summarised in Table 6.2.

One way of confronting structure is to refuse to perform a role or task that is expected and demanded by the organisation. Bailey gives the example of the role of social workers in English Social Service Departments in the provision of emergency accommodation (1980). He argues that workers have fallen into managing the homelessness problem on behalf of the state and society, rather than confronting the system with the reality of chronic, widespread homelessness. He argues that workers should be motivated by no consideration other than the needs of the homeless person, and that by implementing organisational rules and procedures designed to test eligibility, ration services and deflect demand, they are failing to live up to their professional code. Rather than conforming with official and operative expectations that they apply the rules, social workers should systematically use each case to apply pressure on the their organisation to provide adequate services. Bailey's position is that confronting and resisting structure is the central task of social and welfare workers.

Industrial action, such as stop-work meetings, strike action, picketing and refusing to undertake certain tasks or duties, is another form of confronting structure. Industrial action is usually organised by a trade union, although professional bodies are also sometimes involved. Industrial action can be an effective approach to confronting structure, drawing its strength from collective endeavour. However, there are some inherent difficulties with industrial action in the context of human service organisations. Full or partial withdrawal of services impacts most sharply on consumers, and often only indirectly impinges on managers and policy-makers. Workers are susceptible to charges of lack of concern with consumers, and their service ethos can make it difficult to sustain a campaign.

Another way of confronting structure is through whistle-blowing. This term refers to a situation where a member of an organisation brings some aspect of organisational practice or process out into the open. She or he 'blows the whistle' on organisational activities that are viewed as being wrong or illegitimate (Near and Miceli 1987; Gummer 1985). There are many different forms of whistle-blowing. Some whistle-blowing is formally sanctioned by legislation protecting the whistle-blower. Some occurs within the confines of the organisation, for example, a person reporting to senior management about practices that they are aware of within the organisation. More dramatic is the situation of material being disclosed in the public arena, through leaks to the media, pressure groups or politicians. Whistle-blowing can be an effective means of drawing organisational or public attention to an issue of great concern. However, unofficial whistle-blowing is often viewed by people in organisations as a direct challenge to their authority, and whistle-blowers who are detected can expect their allegations to be challenged, and to be punished in various ways including isolation, impugning of their character and motives, or expulsion from the organisation (Gummer 1985, pp. 97-99). For these reasons, whistle-blowing should not be undertaken frivolously or without careful planning.

The use of disruptive tactics constitutes a further set of approaches to confronting and conflicting with structure. Essentially, disruption involves preventing the target organisation from continuing to operate as usual (Specht 1985, p. 342). Such actions are intended to create disorder in the organisation, generate discomfort and guilt among its managers and members, draw public attention to issues, and generate solidarity among the protesters. Tactics include boycotts of services, non-compliance with rules (e.g. rent strikes in public housing), public demonstrations against the organisation, occupation of organisational premises and overloading of facilities (Specht 1975, pp. 342-344; Sharp 1977). The obvious difficulty in the use of these methods is that they are typically initiated outside the organisation by consumer and other interest groups, and directed at the organisation that employs the worker. The degree to which an individual worker can participate in such strategies is limited by their organisational membership. Workers using these tactics are most likely to be working to bring about changes in some other organisation, rather than in their own. The structural position of workers means that, in general, they are more likely to be the targets than the instigators of disruptive tactics.

Ultimately, confronting structure can mean resigning from the organisation or threatening resignation. If personal and professional values cannot be reconciled with organisational requirements this may be perceived as the only possibility. However, as Pruger points out, this still leaves the worker with an important choice: whether to go 'clean' or 'dirty' (1979, p. 453). To go clean means resigning without using the departure as an opportunity to raise the issues of concern. To go dirty means resigning in protest, and either privately or publicly making known the reasons for the resignation. Pruger suggests that there are many reasons resigning in protest is a rare phenomenon: the difficulties of obtaining outside support and interest; concerns about future career; loyalty to some continuing members of the organisation; and the capacity of the organisation to nullify the protest (1979, pp. 455-463). Perhaps the most important point, from a strategic perspective, is that the person who resigns immediately ceases to be a player, at least as far as intra-organisational processes is concerned. Once you have resigned, your capacity to work through, to modify, to bend or to confront structure from within is immediately terminated and the issues are left to those that you have left behind.

Confronting and conflicting with structure is one of the range of strategic approaches to structure available to social and welfare workers. Arguments that workers should always confront structure are as inflexible and unworkable as the contention that they should always work within structure. Some of the interventions described in this section, particularly 'disruptive tactics', often need to be organised from a position outside of the target organisation. Confronting and conflicting with structure often involves 'raising the stakes'; the penalties for failure can be very serious. The need for action to be preceded and accompanied by thorough organisational analysis is, therefore, particularly relevant.

Creating alternative structures

The final set of strategies available to social and welfare workers is the creation of organisations with markedly different structure to mainstream organisations. The broad characteristics of alternative organisations were described earlier in the chapter. They can be thought of broadly as those that depart significantly from conventional organisations in terms of goals, modes of operation, philosophy or structure (Hooyman, Fredriksen and Perlmutter 1988, p. 19). Three main forms of alternative organisations can be identified: community-managed organisations, co-operatives, and collectives.

Community management is a term that has passed into widespread usage, despite ongoing ambiguity about its precise meaning. In essence, community management means an organisation in which a high degree of control is exercised by local community members, often including local users of the service. The typical structure of a community-managed organisation is a management committee elected by community members and users of the service, with overall responsibility for the organisation, including the employment of staff. The rationale for community management is that local community members and users have a right to control local services, that community-managed services are more accountable and responsive to users, that such structures provide opportunities for personal and community development, and that community participation provides a strong basis of political support for the services provided by community organisations. Users and local community members are viewed as having an important role in service provision, alongside paid staff. Users are also viewed as active consumers, who should be given full information and opportunities to express their views (Jones and Nailon 1984). Many human services in Australia are provided through community-managed organisations, including child care, neighbourhood centres, supported accommodation, Aboriginal services, family support and women's emergency services.

Collectives are organisations distinguished by such characteristics as absence of formal hierarchy and leadership, emphasis on equal participation by all members of the organisation, sharing of knowledge and skills, consensus decision-making, and non-specialisation of roles and tasks (Melville 1985; Women's Liberation Halfway-House Collective 1976). Collectives are based on, and seek to develop, a strong sense of group identity, philosophy, solidarity and commitment. In the Australian context, most organisations espousing collectivist principles have emerged from the women's movement, and are based on a feminist analysis of society and organisations. Collective structures are particularly to be found in areas such as women's support and emergency services and women's health.

Co-operatives are organisations in which 'members own and democratically control the organisation in which they work and benefit from any surplus (profit) generated on the basis of work input rather than capital input' (Carruthers quoted in Halladay and Peile 1989). Primary producer co-operatives, housing co-operatives and credit unions have a long history in Australia, and are recognised in legislation governing their operation. Alongside such established groups, there has emerged a significant number of locally-based work co-operatives concerned with local production and consumption of basic goods, and with developing employment options for groups that are disadvantaged in or excluded from the labour market. Underlying ideals include mutuality of respect and dignity, co-operation, industry, economic justice, democracy, solidarity, and local community control. They are viewed by their proponents as 'potentially a superior approach to helping people than some of the strategies which have been developed under the aegis of the welfare state and professional social work practice' (Halladay and Peile 1989, p. 71).

Collectives, co-operatives and community-managed organisations are all attempts to create structures that address the perceived shortcomings of conventional structure. All workers should be aware of these alternatives, and their potential for consumer service. Significant numbers of social and welfare workers actively participate in the creation and development of alternative organisational structures. It is important, however, to apply a critical perspective with equal rigour to these alternatives as to mainstream organisations. This is widely recognised and acknowledged by the proponents of alternative structures, and a valuable, critical literature is emerging from practice, both local (Social Research and Evaluation Association 1980; Halladay and Peile 1989; Melville 1985) and overseas (Freeman 1972; Rothschild and Whitt 1986; Perlmutter 1988; Wilkerson 1988; Powell 1986; Schwartz, Gottesman and Perlmutter 1988; Hooyman, Fredriksen and Perlmutter 1988; Hyde 1989).

The issues facing organisations based on alternative structures can be roughly divided into two categories. Firstly, there are those arising from the environment in which the organisations operate. Alternative organisations are often faced with funding uncertainties, and with external hostility to their goals and structure. This is particularly the case if the organisation's ideology, membership or mission is perceived as contentious within the larger society. Relations with the environment are especially problematic when alternative organisations become heavily dependent on external funding and when they are drawn into established service networks. The conditions, both formal and informal, of external funding and participation in service delivery systems, present challenges to the organisation's autonomy, identity and structure, particularly if organisational members continue to identify strongly with the social movement from which the organisation originated. Establishing domain consensus in these circumstances is a difficult task, demanding a high level of organisational skills.

The second group of issues are those concerning intra-organisational structures and processes. Many issues have been identified in the writings cited above. These include: balancing process and task orientations; maintaining high levels of commitment from members, while ensuring that members do not burn-out; dealing with issues of specialisation and professionalism; maintaining processes of democratic decision-making and control; responding to pressures for increasing formalisation; defining the nature of leadership and authority; and dealing with industrial issues.

These issues are not, in essence, dissimilar to those facing mainstream organisations, even though they may be dealt with in different ways. All organisations have structure and all workers must choose how to relate to structure. The choices made by organisational participants, including social and welfare workers, about working through, building, modifying, bending, side-stepping, conflicting, confronting and developing alternative structures, contribute significantly to the ongoing processes of changing structure in human service organisations.

Conclusions

The structure of an organisation can be thought of as its socially created pattern of roles, relations, rules and records. Structure is dynamic rather than static, is created by organisational participants, and is shaped by the organisational environment and the tasks that the organisation has to perform. There are four basic elements of structure, each of which has an official and an operative component as shown in Table 6.1. Roles are the set of expected behaviours for a particular job-holder or group of job-holders. Relations are the linkages between roles. Five kinds of relations can be distinguished: power, authority and influence; decision-making and planning; division of work; communications; and social relations. Rules are the principles governing organisational processes and services. Records are the organisation's collective memory. Social and welfare workers, in order to work effectively in organisations, need the ability to identify these four elements of structure and understand their bearing on practice.

It is also useful to make distinctions between organisational structures, and to be able to describe and compare organisations in a systematic fashion. The typology of classical, organic and alternative structures provided in the chapter is built around the basic organising principles underlying an organisation's structure. The concepts of complexity, formalisation and centralisation provide a means of describing and understanding structural differences and similarities between organisations. The overall combination of these characteristics can be thought of as an organisation's configuration. Each organisation has its own individual configuration reflecting its own history and circumstances. The key factors that influence an organisation's structure are its environment, technology, size, and the values and interests of influential and dominant groups within the organisation.

Social and welfare workers need to be able to use organisational structure in their practice. This means adopting a strategic approach to structure. Five different approaches to structure can be distinguished. These are working in and through structure, building and modifying structure, bending and side-stepping structure, confronting and conflicting with structure, and developing alternative structures. The interventions associated with each of these approaches are summarised in Table 6.2. Workers must be able to move strategically between approaches in response to differing issues and circumstances.

Chapter review questions

1 Is it helpful to think of structure as the 'walls, floor and ceiling' of an organisation?
2 What does it mean to have a 'dynamic, interactive' perspective on organisational structure?
3 What are the four basic elements of organisational structure?
4 What is the difference between the official and operative structure of an organisation? Give examples of these differences in relation to the four basic elements of structure.
5 What are the five different kinds of relations within organisations?
6 What are the main differences between classical, organic and alternative organisational structures?
7 Explain the concepts of complexity, formalisation and differentiation in relation to human service organisations.
8 What are the main influences on the structure of human service organisations?
9 Why is organisational structure important for social and welfare workers?
10 What does it mean to 'strategically use structure'?
11 Drawing on your knowledge and understanding of human service organisations, give examples of each of the following:
  a working in and through structure;
  b changing and modifying structure;
  c bending and side-stepping structure;
  d challenging and confronting structure;
  e developing alternative structures.

Further reading

Excellent introductions to the concept of organisational structure can be found in Hall (1987, chapters 3 and 4), and Dawson (1986, chapter 3). A managerial perspective is provided by Stoner, Collins and Yetton (1985, part III). A theoretical introduction to structure in human service organisations is Hasenfeld (1983, chapter 6). Contributors to the social and welfare work literature take many different stances to organisational structure. On working within structure see Pruger (1973). On building and modifying structure read the materials brought together by Weissman, Epstein and Savage (1983), especially chapter 1'Diagnostician', chapter 2 'Expediter' and chapter 7 'Organizational reformer'. Pearson (1975) provides many good examples of bending and side-stepping structure, and Bailey's (1980) strongly worded case for ongoing confrontation of structure by social workers should be carefully appraised. Gummer (1985a) on whistle-blowing, Sharp (1977) on disruptive tactics, and Pruger (1979) on resigning in protest should be read by any social or welfare workers contemplating these courses of action. Jones and Nailon (1984) introduce the ideas underlying community management, as do Halladay and Peile (1989) for co-operatives. A special issue of Administration in Social Work in 1988 examines the experiences of a range of human services organisations based on alternative, mainly collectivist, principles.

Case study

THE WESTBANK FAMILY ACCOMMODATION AGENCY

The Westbank Family Accommodation Agency was established three years ago to provide emergency housing for families in Westbank City, a sprawling outer suburban area of a large Australian city. The agency was initially sponsored by the Westbank City Council, with funding provided by the joint Commonwealth–State Governments' Supported Accommodation Assistance Program (SAAP). The agency is located in a shopfront in the main street of Westbank, provided at a nominal rental by the Society of St Vincent De Paul. Services include four units used for short-term emergency housing, a 'bond money scheme' to assist families without cash to obtain rental accommodation, and a 'homeless families advocacy project'. The advocacy project aims to support families in their negotiations with home owners and the Housing Commission, and to raise housing issues in the community. Some short-term family counselling is also available through the agency. The agency has developed a strong interest in assisting women to escape from situations involving domestic violence, and the emergency accommodation units are primarily used for women and children in these circumstances. Much of the work of the Agency is with sole parents, mainly women.

Westbank City Council, as the sponsoring body, initially appointed a management committee comprising a Chairperson, Treasurer and Secretary, five appointed community members and three ex-officio members: a representative of the Westbank Office of the State Community Services Department, the Chairperson of the Westbank City Council Community Services Committee (a councillor), and the Westbank City Social Planner. This committee invited concerned individuals in the community to become members of the agency. The role of members is to generally support the work of the agency, and to attend quarterly meetings and the annual meeting. In fact, there are usually only about fifteen active members at any one time, mainly people who are working as volunteers or part-time workers in the agency. For the last two years it has been the practice for the positions of Chairperson, Secretary, Treasurer and community members on the committee to be elected at the annual meeting, and for their appointment to be ratified by the Council's Community Services Committee.

The Council's initial submission for funding covered the rental and operating costs for the four accommodation units, and the salaries of an accommodation co-ordinator and an assistant co-ordinator. The submission stated that, 'paid staff will be graduates of an approved tertiary-level course in social work or community welfare, and eligible for membership of their professional body'. The SAAP funding is supplemented by an annual grant from the Westbank City Council to cover operating expenses, including secretarial support.

The Council's decision to sponsor the Family Accommodation Agency was prompted by a campaign by local community service organisations, backed up by the local press. The City Social Planner and several councillors on the Community Services Committee of Council strongly supported the establishment of the service. The shortage of emergency accommodation for families in the area was widely recognised, and the Council's initiative was generally praised. In general, the agency is perceived as providing a needed and important community service.

The Council's initial intention was that after a short period of sponsorship by the Council, the agency would seek incorporation as an association in its own right. The Council's role would then be limited to that of a funding body. However, this plan has now run into difficulties. During the past twelve months a split developed on the management committee between the ex-officio members (a minority of three) and those elected by the annual meeting. The main issue in dispute is the structure of the organisation. The small group of staff, committee members, volunteers and other members of the agency have become increasingly attracted to the idea of operating as a collective. Almost all of the active members of the committee are women, who have a strong commitment to feminism and the women's movement. Most of those who use the service are women. The establishment of the agency has involved a great deal of difficult work, and the group of active members have become very close to one another through this experience. The group increasingly feels that a collective organisational structure would reflect and reinforce the relationships that sustain the work of the agency.

On a day-to-day basis, the agency is already attempting to work on the basis of collectivist principles. Meetings of the management committee have become largely formal, with most important discussions and decisions taking place at the weekly members' meeting, now called the meeting of the collective. It has been decided to pool all salary funding and pay all workers an equal hourly rate, irrespective of whether they are staff or volunteers. All formal distinctions of role and task among members, have been dropped, and there is a strong emphasis on workers learning from one another and sharing skills. The tasks associated with the positions of Chairperson, Treasurer and Secretary are shared on a roster basis. To ensure that all members are able to participate equally in the decision-making processes the service closes its office one day per week for the meeting of the collective.

These developments have been viewed with great concern by the ex-officio members of the management committee, although it is acknowledged that the agency is providing a needed service at relatively little cost to the community. The ex-officio members of the management committee are keen to press ahead with the plan for incorporation of the Agency as an association, despite their misgivings about the emerging collective structure. There is support for this view on the Community Services Committee of Council. However, the collective has taken the view that, however desirable incorporation may be in principle, it must take place on the collective's own terms. This view was expressed in a letter from the collective to the Westbank City Council:

We are unwilling to have a legal structure imposed on us, which while it may suit the purposes of 'mainstream community' organisations, does not suit us. In our struggle for a socially just society, we recognise that 'inequality' is not merely about the maldistribution of material resources, but is also about the unequal access of people to those structures in society which distribute 'power' as a resource. Collectivist principles, which we endorse unanimously, are concerned to challenge the idea that social life should be organised on a hierarchical basis. We reject the notion that it is appropriate for some members of our group to occupy 'power' positions, such as Chairperson, Treasurer or Secretary, and thus exclude other members from equal participation in the social life of our group. On balance, therefore, we wish to continue to operate the agency under the present arrangements, until we have had time to examine more fully the best way of organising a legal basis for our collective structure.

This letter brought matters to a head. The Chairperson of the Council's Community Services Committee requested the Westbank City Social Planner to present a report on the situation, and make recommendations to Council. The main points of his report were:

1 The Westbank Family Accommodation Agency is still a Council sponsored activity and a Council responsibility.

2 The management committee no longer effectively controls the agency, and ex-officio members of the committee have been excluded from any meaningful role.

3 A number of administrative irregularities have eventuated. The agency has consistently failed to provide financial and other required reports to the Council as agreed under the sponsoring arrangements. There have also been difficulties faced by the Council on a day-to-day basis in working with the agency, as no one individual seems to be responsible for administrative matters.

4 There are concerns that important conditions of the funding agreement have been breached, in particular the stated undertaking that workers will be qualified in social work or community welfare.

5 There have been complaints by ratepayers about a Council sponsored service closing its doors for one working day every week.

6 There have been a number of complaints made to the Council by ratepayers regarding the almost exclusive focus on services to women and children, to the neglect of married couple families.

7 The Local Government Employee's Association has expressed concerns that award conditions are not being adhered to in the Family Accommodation Agency.

8 The State Department of Community Services representative on the Agency's Management Committee shares many of these concerns. The Department has been unable to obtain information regarding decisions made at meetings of the collective, and is concerned at the usurping of the role of the Management Committee.

9 It is recommended:

a) That the agency return to the original community management structure. This means that the Committee of Management initially put in place by the Council resume full responsibility for the operation of the agency, and that there be an identified Chairperson, Treasurer and Secretary.

b) That the agency take immediate steps towards becoming an incorporated, non-profit association, with a membership structure, a board of management, and designated office-bearers.

c) That more emphasis be placed on service delivery and less on decision-making processes. In particular, that the office remain open during normal office hours from Monday to Friday.

d) That, in accordance with the approved submission guidelines, paid staff be professionally qualified.

e) That the accommodation co-ordinator position be expanded to include day-to-day management responsibility for the agency, and for that person to regularly report to the management committee on the operations of the agency.

f) That the record keeping and reporting systems of the agency be reviewed with a view to ensuring full financial and service accountability to the sponsoring and funding bodies.

g) That the meetings of the collective, while valuable, be viewed as the equivalent of staff meetings. The management committee, not the collective, is the authoritative decision-making body.

h) That the priority of service to women, rather than married couple families, be reviewed.

i) That if the agency is to remain under Council sponsorship for any significant period, the issue of the payment of award rates and associated conditions of employment be addressed.

The Social Planner's report generated considerable discussion at the Community Services Committee of Council. While there was general support for the recommendations put forward, it was also argued that the proposals should be discussed with representatives of the collective prior to a decision being made. The Social Planner was asked to convene a meeting involving five representatives of the collective, three members of the Community Services Committee of Council, the representative of the State Community Services Department, and the Social Planner. The meeting is to be chaired by the Chairperson of the Community Services Committee.

You are the accommodation co-ordinator in the agency. You have been in the job for two years, and are strongly committed to the work of the agency. You are a qualified social worker or community welfare worker. You are a woman, you espouse a feminist perspective on your work, and are strongly supportive of the move towards a collective structure for the agency. A meeting of the collective is to take place tomorrow to discuss the Social Planner's report and the invitation to the meeting with the members of the Council committee. You are trying to work out what to do.

Key question

Analyse the issues of organisational structure facing the agency. What will be your position at the meeting of the collective based on your understanding of these issues? What is the best strategy for the members of the collective to take in these circumstances?

Case discussion points

1 What does the case illustrate about the nature of organisational structure?
2 Analyse the structure of the agency using the 'four r's': roles, relations, rules and records, and distinguishing between the official and the operative structure.
3 What different kinds of structural relations are at issue in the case?
4 Does the agency have a classical, an organic or an alternative type of structure, or are there elements of all three? In your view, what kind of structure is most appropriate for the tasks and circumstances of the organisation?
5 Describe the agency in terms of complexity, formalisation and centralisation?
6 What factors are influencing the structure of the Westbank Family Accommodation Agency? Consider the impact of environment, technology, size, and the values and interests of influential and dominant groups within the organisation.

7 How have members of the collective strategically used structure in the recent history of the organisation? How are other participants, such as the Social Planner, strategically using structure to achieve their goals?

8 How would you conceptualise the strategic choices facing the accommodation co-ordinator? Would you agree or disagree with the proposition that she needs the skill to move strategically between working within, building, side-stepping, confronting and creating alternative structure?

9 What are the implications of this organisation's structure for 'professional' decision-making?

7

Organisational culture: shared and contested meanings and symbols

> What ever else they may be, organisations are . . . social creations and creators of social meanings (Allaire and Firsirotu 1984, p. 216).

What is organisational culture?

The process of entering an unfamiliar work setting can be likened to that of visiting a foreign country for the first time (Louis 1985, p. 27). The information in the guidebooks, the stories and photographs of friends who have visited previously, the advice of travel agents—all these somehow seem to fail to convey the feel of the place that comes with actually being there. In a similar way, in the first few days and weeks in a new job a worker,

> . . . gradually gains a sense of the feel, the smell, the personality of a workplace, a way of working, or a kind of work—though it may be difficult to translate . . . this into words that an outsider could grasp (Louis 1985, p. 27).

This sense of what an organisation is really like is an important aspect of our perception and experience of organisations. As we come to know an organisation better, we tend to gradually develop a sense of 'being at home' in it. We increasingly feel that we 'know' the organisation. Many different terms or labels are used to describe these feelings and impressions. People talk of the personality, the image, the style, the climate, or the character of an organisation, or of prevailing attitudes, norms, or group dynamics. However, during the last decade or so, organisational culture has emerged as the most common term used in the organisational and management literature to describe the feel or flavour of organisational life (Hofstede 1986, p. 253). Our aims in this chapter are to clarify the meanings and elements of organisational culture, to explore its origins and effects, and to show how an understanding of culture can be of value to workers in human service organisations.

The concept of culture has been imported into organisation theory from social anthropology. At a general level, culture can be defined as the way of life of a people. 'It consists of conventional patterns of thought and behaviour, including values, beliefs, rules of conduct, political organisation, economic activity, and the like, which are passed on from one generation to the next' (Hatch 1985, p. 178). Common elements of all societal cultures include age and gender differentiation, property rights, courtship rituals, funeral rites, religious beliefs and rituals, sexual mores, ways of dressing, and penal sanctions, to name but a few (Fincher 1986, p. 327). The concept of culture, as elaborated in social anthropology, has become extremely complex. As many as 164 different definitions of culture were identified by one writer, and there are many different theories concerning the creation, diffusion and impact of culture, and the relations between culture and society (these are summarised in Allaire and Firsirotu 1984).

The culture of a society is an influential element of the general environment of a human service organisation. We discussed this briefly in chapter 4, and the impact of the surrounding culture on organisations is an established theme in the organisational literature (Smircich 1983, pp. 343-344). Practices, norms, beliefs and ideologies that prevail in the society as a whole are imported into organisations, via the members of the organisation and through the structural relations between organisations and the larger society. For example, it can be argued that the work ethic is viewed as an important part of the culture of Australian society, and that this has an impact on the way that the Department of Social Security deals with its consumers. This occurs in part because the workers within the Department carry with them in their daily work the beliefs and attitudes that they hold as members of the larger society. It also occurs because the organisation's rules, policies and official ideology tend to reflect, reinforce and reproduce the dominant culture. Similar examples could be given of the ways that other elements of the societal culture such as dominant attitudes towards human service provision, gender relations, the treatment of ethnic minorities, attitudes towards elderly people, views of the family and the responsibilities of family members, and the role of professionals, impinge on human service organisations.

The influence of societal culture on organisational life is, however, only one aspect of the phenomenon of organisational culture. When we say that an organisation has a culture, or cultures, we imply that organisations are themselves culture-producing phenomena (Smircich

1983, p. 344). This means that the members of organisations inherit, create and sustain their own way of life, which interacts with the surrounding societal culture in complex ways. Attempts to define organisational culture in a precise and unambiguous fashion are bedevilled by the complexities of the concept of culture itself. However, there are some useful starting points. Smircich suggests that organisational culture be thought of as the 'fairly stable set of taken-for-granted assumptions, shared beliefs, meanings, and values that form a kind of backdrop for action' (1985, p. 58). Similarly, Dick conceives of organisational culture as 'the more pervasive set of patterns underlying the behaviours that express (the organisation's) sense of identity and unity' (1988, p. 3). Culture can thus be thought of as the 'social or normative glue that holds an organisation together' (Smircich 1983, p. 344). Blunt similarly suggests that organisational culture consists of a system of shared perspectives: 'it refers . . . to the company way of doing things or its philosophy, style, or spirit. It is implicit in the minds of organisational members; it is shared by them; and it can be transmitted by a process of socialisation (1986, p. 115).

These perspectives suggest to us that organisational culture has to do with shared meanings, and with the ways that these are created, expressed and reproduced within an organisation. We would add to this the important idea that culture is contested, changed and challenged, as well as being shared, within organisations. In this sense, an organisation may be multi-cultural. An organisation may have a dominant culture, but this may be challenged by other groups in the organisation which have or develop their own sub-cultures or alternative cultures. While culture may be 'social glue', 'cultures are just as likely, if not more likely, to act as centripetal forces that encourage . . . disintegration' (Van Maanen and Barley 1985, p. 48). It is to capture this key point, that we portray culture as involving both shared and contested meanings and symbols, and that we refer to organisational cultures, as well as to organisational culture as a whole.

Organisational culture has obvious and indisputable significance for social and welfare workers. At a personal level, workers often experience some degree of conflict between their own values and way of life and that of the organisation in which they are working. Dealing with this conflict is often a significant and difficult personal and professional issue. Moreover, the beliefs, meanings and values that permeate an organisation shape the activities of social and welfare workers in many ways. They influence the scope and boundaries of organisational endeavour, the ways in which work is done, relations among workers, and the treatment of consumers. Relations among different professional, occupational and social groups in human service organisations often involve clashes between different sub-cultures. From a political perspective, organisational life can be viewed, in part, as a struggle among different groups and interests to achieve cultural dominance. Understanding the nature of culture, and developing ways of working within, capitalising on, or changing culture are valuable competencies for social and welfare workers.

From these starting points, we are led towards three related questions:

1 What is the range of elements that collectively comprise organisational culture or cultures?
2 What are the origins of organisational culture and cultures, and how is culture disseminated, reproduced, challenged and changed in organisations?
3 How can social and welfare workers use an understanding of culture to achieve their goals and to improve service to consumers?

What are the elements of organisational culture?

Organisational culture, we have suggested, is about what it means to be a member of an organisation. But what does culture consist of? If we are attempting to identify or analyse the culture of a particular human service organisation, what exactly are we looking for? Table 7.1 is an attempt to unravel and lay out the basic elements of culture. As portrayed in that table, organisational culture comprises shared meanings, which may be values, beliefs, ideology and norms. These are given expression through shared symbols, notably myths, stories, rites, language and artefacts. These cultural elements may be overt or covert, official or operative. An organisation may have one dominant culture which pervades all areas of the organisation, or numerous cultures or sub-cultures co-existing in varying degrees of harmony or disharmony. The culture or cultures of the organisation may be strong or weak. We will now explain these concepts and distinctions in greater detail.

Being a member of an organisation necessarily involves relating to the shared meanings of that organisation. People who work for or participate in an organisation tend, to varying degrees, to view the world, especially the world of work, as members of that organisation. Sometimes this is referred to as identifying with the organisation. For example, some people working in non-government welfare organisations may develop strong beliefs about the greater effectiveness and desirability of their services, and the greater dedication of their personnel, compared to people in the public sector. Similarly, many people working for private enterprise take on the view that the private sector is inherently more efficient. At conferences and public forums, and in inter-organisational negotiations, individuals tend to act as organisational members, viewing issues and debates from their own

Table 7.1 The elements of organisational culture

Element	Definition	Overt	Covert
SHARED MEANINGS			
Values	what the organisation esteems and prizes	mission and goal statements, codes of ethics	spoken or unstated values
Beliefs	assumptions and understandings about the world, and particularly about the organisation, its work, and its consumers	written creed	informal, unratified or unstated beliefs
Ideology	a system of beliefs providing explanations of social reality, and how to act in the world	formal, written statement	informal, unratified or unstated ideologies
Norms	acceptable behaviour and action	standards, rules, policies	group expectations, taboos, styles of behaviour
SHARED SYMBOLS			
Myths and stories	narratives that express the meanings of organisational life	official history	anecdotes, gossip, parables
Rites	activities and events that sustain and transmit shared meanings	formal ceremonies	'functional' processes that serve symbolic purposes
Language	words that express shared meanings	the names of organisations, mottos, titles, acronyms	jargon, 'in-words', codes
Artefacts	physical, tangible objects that convey meanings	trophies, logos, letterheads and newsletters, pictures, visitors books	equipment, furniture, office layout, architecture

organisational perspective. There is, of course, great variation from person to person in the extent of this process. At one extreme, a person whose whole adult, working life has taken place within the one organisation is highly likely to have incorporated the shared meanings and view of that organisation. At the other extreme, an individual who joins an organisation with the intent of subverting or undermining it, is least likely to take on the organisation's world view. Factors such as the level of significance that an individual places on their organisational participation and the extent to which they possess other world views will also have an impact on the extent of their identification with the organisation.

Central to the systems of shared meanings that organisations may possess are the prevailing organisational values. Values, in this context, can be thought of quite simply as what the organisation esteems and prizes (Egan 1985, p. 278). They may concern organisational processes, ways of treating consumers, broad social goals or specific objectives. Overt values in human service organisations are almost always couched in highly positive terms, and may include such things as staff participation in decision-making, courteous and fair treatment of consumers, community involvement, confidentiality, commitment, honesty, openness, efficiency, team work, professionalism, and so forth. Such values may appear in written statements of the organisation, such as mission and goal statements and codes of ethics, or may be repeated regularly, almost ritually, in organisational meetings and public forums. Covert values of the organisation are those that are less readily acknowledged by the organisation, or that may indeed be deliberately hidden. For example, loyalty to the organisation may in fact be prized more than accountability to consumers, even though the latter is an officially espoused goal. Covert values are often the ones that have the most impact on the behaviour of organisational members. Counter-cultural behaviour is that which goes against dominant values, whether overt or covert.

Shared meanings also comprise beliefs and ideology. The culture of an organisation includes the beliefs, assumptions, and under-standings that prevail or predominate within it. These may be beliefs about the organisation itself, the nature of its work, the characteristics of its consumers, the traits of the organisational environment, or any other significant organisational factors (Egan 1985, p. 277). Beliefs may be stated explicitly in the form of a written or spoken creed, or they may be transmitted and reinforced through social relations within the organisation. When a series of organisational beliefs are linked together in a more or less coherent fashion, we can talk of an organisational ideology. Allaire and Firsirotu define ideology as 'a unified and systematic system of beliefs which provide encompassing, compelling, often mythical, explanations of social reality; it legitimises present social order or proposes radically different goals (1984, p. 213). Organisational ideologies are sometimes stated explicitly in official publications and statements, or they may be held implicitly or unofficially by workers in the organisation.

Further element of the culture of an organisation are the prevailing norms. Egan defines these as:

> the 'oughts', 'shoulds', 'musts', 'dos', 'don'ts' . . . standards, policies, rules, principles, regulations, laws and taboos that govern the behaviour of the system as a whole, of the sub units within the system, and of individual members of the system (1985, p. 279).

All organisations, either officially through standards, rules and directives, or informally through group processes (Mitchell and Larson 1987, pp. 268-278) develop norms about how organisational members should behave. These norms can cover a wide range of behaviour and action including how to dress, how to address people, how to relate to superiors and sub-ordinates, what forms of communication to use, how hard to work, how to treat consumers, how to interpret organisational rules, and so forth.

Of particular importance are norms relating to interpersonal relations, and the interpretation of roles. Often, organisations develop certain styles of personal and interpersonal behaviour that pervade much of the organisation's life. These may be constructive or destructive of organisational functioning. For example, a norm of 'encouragement of autonomy and entrepreneurship' may be of great value in a human service organisation needing to respond in innovative ways in a complex and changing environment. By contrast, a norm of 'depersonalisation of problems', that is the unacceptability of formal criticism of individuals (as distinct from gossip and back-biting), may lead to a dysfunctional conspiracy of silence regarding attributing problems to particular people (Blunt 1986, p. 120). Other styles of organisational behaviour that have been identified as being common and dysfunctional in many organisational contexts include unemotionality, that is the expression of feelings is to be avoided at all times; sub-ordination, that is always do what is expected of you and if in doubt wait for direction from above; conservatism, that is change is more likely to make things worse than better; isolationism, that is do your own thing and do not trespass on other people's territory; and antipathy, that is assume that most people will oppose you and do not trust anyone (Blunt 1986, pp. 119-120). An important part of comprehending an organisation's culture lies in identifying such styles of personal and interpersonal behaviour, and understanding the impact on organisational functioning and performance.

The shared meanings that comprise an organisation's culture, made up of values, beliefs, ideology and norms, often are expressed through symbols that give them substance, form and emphasis. By symbol we mean 'any object, act, event, quality or relation that serves as a vehicle for conveying meaning' (Beyer and Trice 1987, p. 6). Shared symbols, sometimes called 'cultural forms', can take many forms, and are themselves part of the culture of the organisation. Of particular importance are myths and mythical stories. A myth can be defined as a substantially fictional narrative of events related to origins and transformations, expressed in symbolic terms and endowed with a sacred quality' (Allaire and Firsirotu 1984, p. 213). All organisations, including human service organisations, have an abundance of such stories, which are used by organisational members to give expression to and define the meaning of their organisational actions. Some stories are about the origins of the organisation, or of key events in the organisation's history. Others are about competing organisations, significant personalities, or consumers. They may be sagas describing the heroic accomplishments of the organisation and its leaders, or legends of previous events. Stories get told in tea-rooms, in staff meetings, in annual reports, in official histories, and in many situations in which organisational members try to give and convey meaning about what they do. The role of mythical stories in social work has been elaborated by Rein and White (1981). They point out that 'like workers in any profession, social workers constantly exchange their own special set of stories—histories, anecdotes, gossip, parables—with interest, energy, and feeling. The stories are rarely pointless. They serve an essentially mythical function because they relate meaning to action' (Rein and White 1981). The key issue, from an organisation culture perspective, is not whether such stories are true or false, but that they express the meaning that individuals give to organisational life.

Shared meanings within organisations are also sustained and transmitted to organisational members by customs, rituals and ceremonies. These organisational rites can be thought of as activities and events which affirm and communicate shared organisational meanings. These rites sometimes take the form of special events that are explicitly ceremonial. A university graduation ceremony is a good example: the procession, regalia and songs, and the embossed certificates are an open display of the values, beliefs, ideology and norms of the organisation. But many of the more explicitly functional events and processes of organisational life also have symbolic significance. Take, for instance, the annual meeting of a non-government organisation. It serves the practical purposes of enabling the executive to report to members about the activities of the organisation, and of fulfilling accounting and constitutional requirements. Over and above this, however, it is an organisational rite that communicates and sustains shared meanings. In itself it symbolises the democratic constitution of the organisation. It is also a forum where organisational beliefs and ideology are reiterated, and core values re-affirmed.

Many organisational activities have an expressive as well as a practical dimension, and can thus be thought of as rites. Many different kinds of organisational rites can be identified (Beyer and Trice 1987, p. 11). When individuals join an organisation, the formal induction processes together with the informal meetings with new colleagues collectively can be viewed as rites of initiation into the organisation. They are the means whereby values, beliefs, ideology and norms are communicated to new members. Enhancement rites, such as awards and special lunches for members who have done well, similarly communicate and reinforce the organisational culture. The widespread organisational practice of establishing committees to deal with difficult or contentious issues is made more understandable if such committees are seen, in part, as rites of conflict resolution. 'Committees do not need to make substantive changes in order to reduce conflict because their very existence and their activities symbolise the organisation's willingness to cope with problems and discontent' (Gummer 1990, p. 140). Other important kinds of organisational rites are rites of renewal, for example the weekend workshop to re-assess goals, and rites of degradation, for example the discrediting of an individual or a programme, perhaps via elaborate evaluation and review processes.

Language also plays an important role in conveying shared organisational meanings. At the official level, organisations sometimes adopt mottos that are intended to convey, succinctly and powerfully 'what the organisation stands for'. Thus the motto 'sharing community care', adopted by the Commonwealth Department of Community Services and Health in the late-1980s, concisely imparts the idea of an organisation engaged in a partnership to provide caring services. The titles and official designations given to individuals and groups within the organisation should be understood as symbolic of the status or role that groups within the organisation attach to them. For example, small community-based community centres often prefer the title co-ordinator to that of manager, as more in keeping with their democratic and decentralised ethos. The very names of organisations have symbolic significance. An organisation calling itself 'The Independent Living Programme' is conveying a quite different meaning to one calling itself 'The Spastic Welfare League'. The terminology applied to users of services is also of considerable significance. Whether users are termed consumers, clients, patients, customers or some other term is an important indicator of organisational values and ideology. The way in which people are addressed within the organisation carries strong meanings. For example, whether 'inmates' (residents?) in a prison are called by their first name or by their surname is a significant indicator of how they are viewed and treated by the prison authorities. Body language, or gesture, used consciously or unconsciously, is also a way of communicating organisational meanings.

Often there are specific words and phrases that carry important meanings for organisational members, and which are therefore often used as a means of identification with the organisational culture. Common examples in human service organisations are words and phrases such as community, social justice, patriarchal society, and consumer rights. Such words have substantive and complex meanings, of real significance to the organisation. However, their widespread use also needs to be seen as a symbolic representation of organisational culture. Organisations also have taboo words. Words such as efficiency and effectiveness are not as highly prized in some welfare organisations as equity or justice, and the reverse may be true for many business organisations. An important aspect of the language of organisations is the use of jargon. The use of specialised, uncommon or unfamiliar words, including acronyms, can be an important means of asserting organisational identity. Jargon sometimes is used as a sort of secret code: the use and acknowledgment of particular in-words or phrases conveys shared membership of the organisation, or of a particular group.

Organisational culture is also shared and communicated by way of artefacts, that is physical and tangible objects that are expressive of organisational values and ideology. Most organisations have some artefacts that serve an explicit, official symbolic purpose. Logos, for instance, are often designed to convey key organisational values in diagrammatic form. Some organisations display photographs of significant events such as the opening of buildings, visits by important people, or the first meeting of the board. These serve as representations and reminders of what the organisation stands for. Trophies, framed certificates and letters, memorabilia of all kinds, and visitors' books are further examples of tangible, organisational symbols.

Organisational culture is also expressed through objects that serve functional purposes, the symbolic significance of which may be less consciously acknowledged. The architecture of organisational buildings clearly serves symbolic, as well as practical, purposes. Buildings can convey many messages about an organisation: whether it wishes to be perceived as powerful, whether it welcomes non-members, how formal or informal relationships should be, and so forth. Office layout, including the waiting rooms, similarly convey meanings about such matters as the nature of authority and decision-making, and attitudes to consumers. Office furnishings, the types of equipment on display, the style of letterheads and newsletters all convey messages about the way of life of the organisation.

This detailing of the ingredients of organisational culture provides social and welfare workers with a framework for examining and identifying the elements of the culture of the organisation in which they work. However, several key distinctions must be added to the picture painted thus far. Firstly, the distinction between the overt and covert elements of culture, as shown in Table 7.1, must be recognised. Egan suggests that the overt culture is that which is 'written down in public documents, discussed in a public forum, celebrated publicly, and open to challenge, at least within the organisation' (1985, p. 280). Covert culture refers to those elements that 'are not written down, tend towards the unawareness end of the continuum, are only partially understood, and remain for the most part undiscussed in the public forums of the organisation' (p. 281). There are various levels of covertness. Different aspects of culture may be undiscussed, unable to be discussed or, indeed, unconscious in the sense that most people in the organisation are unaware of them (Egan 1985, p. 281-282). Many organisational secrets (Gouldner 1963) relate to aspects of culture that organisational members have difficulty acknowledging and addressing.

It is also important to distinguish between the official and the operative culture of an organisation. Egan refers to this as espoused culture versus culture-in-use (1985, p. 282). The official culture can be thought of as a 'for-public-consumption' culture, deliberately designed by those at the top of the organisation to be passed down through the organisation, and to be presented to outsiders (Louis 1985, p. 79). Sometimes this is referred to as the corporate culture. As we will show later in the chapter, top management often attempt to shape culture as a form of organisational control. If they are successful in this attempt the official or corporate culture becomes the dominant organisational culture. Operative culture is the meaning that organisational members actually give to their participation in the organisation. In some circumstances this may differ substantially from the official culture. An organisation in which the official and operative cultures largely coincide can be said to have a strong or a homogeneous culture, that is the official culture has a major impact on the behaviour of organisational members. When the two are divergent or even conflicting, we can describe the culture as weak or heterogeneous.

This raises again the key issue of the multi-cultural nature of many organisations. Although in outlining the main elements of culture we have referred repeatedly to 'the culture' of an organisation, we do not wish to assume or imply that organisations have only one, distinct culture that pervades all aspects of organisational life and is held by all organisational participants. Rather, as already indicated, organisations, particularly complex organisations, are likely to be characterised by multiple and competing cultures, which vie for ascendancy in the organisation as a whole or for dominance in particular parts of the organisation. Particular professional or consumer groups, hierarchical levels, geographic units, or functional sections of an organisation may develop their own culture, complete with shared meanings and symbols, which then interacts with other parts of the organisation in complex ways. The circumstances leading to the development of multiple cultures in organisations, and the practice implications of this for workers, are addressed later in the chapter.

A capacity to identify and unravel the elements of an organisation's culture and cultures is fundamental to effective organisational practice. To summarise, a worker seeking to understand the culture and cultures of her or his organisation must first address the issues identified in this section, namely:

1 What are the shared and contested meanings and symbols in this organisation?
2 What are the overt and covert elements of the culture or cultures of an organisation?
3 Is there an official culture? To what extent does it coincide with the operative culture? To what extent is it dominant within the organisation?
4 Are there multiple cultures within the organisation? What are they? What are their relations to one another and to the official or dominant culture?

Addressing these questions leads to a further level of analysis: what processes shape organisational culture and cultures?

How is organisational culture created, sustained, reproduced, challenged and changed?

Organisational culture is not static. Just as the goals, environment and structure of organisations are continuously in flux, so are the elements that comprise their culture. Social and welfare workers need to have some understanding of the factors and processes that contribute to these ongoing changes. Whether they want to work through culture, create and sustain the existing culture, challenge and change culture, or develop organisational sub-cultures or counter-cultures, an awareness of how culture is made is critical. Our general view is that the development of culture in organisations fundamentally needs to be understood and explained from a political, as well as a social–psychological perspective. We see culture as being created by individuals and groups within organisations, but in conditions that are not entirely, or even substantially, under their control. These conditions include the competing cultures of other individuals and groups in the organisation, particularly those of management, the structure, processes and technology of the organisation, the inherited history of the organisation, and the organisational environment. Each of these factors will now be considered.

Every individual who participates in an organisation brings to it his or her own experience, personality, skills, beliefs and values. These are shaped by many factors including childhood and family background, social class position, gender, ethnicity, religion, education and professional training, and previous organisational experiences. Joining and working in an organisation involves finding meaningful or workable ways of relating one's individuality to the perceived reality of the organisation. 'All actors . . . strive to construct a coherent picture to orient them to the goings-on in the organisation' (Allaire and Firsirotu 1984, p. 215). These processes are central to and inherent in the development of organisational culture. Individuals are not simply empty vessels into which organisational values, beliefs, ideology and norms are poured. On the contrary, culture cannot be separated from the people who convey it. 'While a group is necessary to invent and sustain culture, culture can be carried only by individuals' (Van Maanen and Barley 1985, p. 35).

For social and welfare workers, an appreciation of the role of individuals in carrying organisational culture is essential. A major concern for many workers entering human service organisations, particularly large, public sector organisations, is that their individual and professional identity will be overwhelmed. We do not underestimate the pressures that organisations can and do exert on their members' actions and interpretations of the world. Indeed, much of this chapter is devoted to describing and understanding these processes. However, it must also be recognised that individuals themselves are contributors to and carriers of organisational culture and cultures. The ongoing contest over organisational values, norms, beliefs and ideologies occurs, in the final analysis, in the minds and through the actions of individuals.

Although individuals must make their own meanings out of their organisational experiences, culture is about meanings that are held in common. Organisational culture needs therefore to be understood as a group phenomenon. Complex organisations are characterised by numerous sub-groupings of many kinds. Take, for example, a state government department concerned with the care and protection of children. It will most likely group its employees into regional, area or district offices serving different geographic locations. There will also be groupings based on particular specialist activities such as adoptions assessment or child abuse prevention, as well as on technical functions such as accounting, information management and policy development. Other identifiable groups within the organisation will be the different hierarchical levels: senior management, middle management, supervisors, front-line workers, and consumers. Intersecting these divisions will be groupings, of varying levels of formality and official recognition, based on common membership of professional and industrial bodies, shared characteristics such as race, ethnicity or gender, and personal and social ties.

Each of these groupings can be considered as a site, or potential site, for the development of an organisational sub-culture (Louis 1985, pp. 78-80). Shared meanings and common frames of reference emerge out of relatively frequent and intense interactions and communications within a grouping of individuals (Van Maanen and Barley 1985, p. 34). Partially, these shared meanings occur through social psychological processes of enforcement of conformity to group norms (Mitchell and Larson 1987, pp. 268-278). But they also reflect the shared political interests and values of groups within the organisation. For instance, a regional office may develop a strong identification with its local area and see itself as representing the interests of that area in the organisation as a whole. A set of beliefs ('"the North" is always overlooked'), values ('the interests of remote areas must be protected') and norms of behaviour ('always advocate strongly for "the North"') may develop to underpin and sustain the regional office's position. Similarly, an occupational group, such as social and welfare work, may develop its own culture or sub-culture in the context of seeking to establish and maintain its organisational position. This might include beliefs such as 'we are the only workers who are truly concerned with consumer well-being', values such as 'consumer interests must always come first', and norms such as 'client work must always have higher priority than organisational demands'. Our point is neither to endorse nor to question such beliefs, values and norms, but rather to illustrate how sub-groups within organisations develop such cultures as they seek to define and sustain organisational roles and influence organisational processes.

The example we have been considering is of a highly complex human service organisation. However, many social and welfare workers are employed in small, relatively non-complex organisations providing a single service from one location. In such organisations, a relatively uniform organisational culture may well prevail. It has been suggested that a unitary organisational culture tends to evolve when all organisational members face similar problems, when everyone communicates frequently with everyone else, and when everyone accepts a common set of understandings about proper organisational behaviour and values (Van Maanen and Barley 1985, p. 37). In many alternative organisations, as discussed in the last chapter, the maintenance and development of such a shared organisational culture is seen as an essential task.

Our emphasis so far has been on the role of individuals and groups in the creation and sustaining of organisational culture. However, culture is also a structural phenomenon. Culture does arise out of individual and group action, but it is also shaped, to varying degrees, by the structured nature of organisational and social life. People create culture, but culture also impinges on them. 'It is in this sense that culture mediates between structural and individual realms' (Van Maanen and Barley 1985, p. 35).

What, then, are the structural factors that shape organisational culture? Firstly, the role of management, or the ruling coalition of the organisation, must be understood. Much of the current interest in culture stems from the idea that the creation of a particular kind of organisational culture by management is the key to enhanced organisational performance. This view has been popularised in best-selling management books such as Peters and Waterman's *In Search of Excellence* (1982). The secret of business success and excellence, they argue, is to create a strong corporate culture throughout the organisation (1982, pp. 75-78 and pp. 103-106). Specifically, they prescribe that staff should stay close to the customer, that there should be an ideology of creativity and initiative, and that there should be ample room for autonomy and individuality, within a context of clearly defined corporate goals and values. Organisational culture, from this perspective, is the key to greater managerial control and effectiveness: if you want to control the organisation, control its beliefs, values, ideology and norms.

Within human service organisations, management similarly seek to shape the culture of the organisation. This is done in many ways. Increasingly, human service organisations adopt mottos and logos signifying the key values that senior management wish to see promoted within the organisation. Explicit statements of goals and objectives, seminars and retreats for middle managers and other workers on organisational goals and practices, messages and homilies in staff newsletters, induction procedures, visits to front-line offices by ministers and directors—all these are, in part, attempts by management to exercise control through culture. The extent to which these attempts are successful depends on many factors. Senior management usually have many resources at their disposal including control of formal channels of communication, the capacity to reward and punish, high status, and access to all parts of the organisation. However, if there are strong sub-cultures within the organisation it may be that the official, corporate culture will 'trickle down the hierarchy with at least as much difficulty as other perspectives trickle up' (Van Maanen and Barley 1985, p. 47).

Culture also needs to be viewed as being embedded in and reproduced through the structures and processes of an organisation. The nature and form of the structural elements of an organisation, discussed in the last chapter and summarised in Table 6.1, often embody and reinforce culture. For example, in a women's refuge organised on collective principles the regular meeting of the collective is both a functional part of the organisational structure and an expression of the organisational ideology. The structure expresses and reinforces the culture. Similarly, the management committee of a not-for-profit organisation not only performs a management function, but reinforces the organisational belief in the accountability of the organisation to its membership. The relations between organisational structure and culture can be extremely complex. The above examples are of mutually supportive relations between structure and culture, but this is not always so. Consider the case of a community centre in which there is a strong belief in the autonomy of workers and volunteers, but in which there is in practice a high degree of centralisation of control and decision-making by an inner group on the management committee. In this situation, there is great potential for conflict and stress due to the imbalance of structure and culture. The resolution of this situation could result in change to the organisational structure, or culture, or both.

The nature of the organisational technology is another influence on culture. It can be argued that one of the consequences of the indeterminacy of technology in many human service organisations is that values, beliefs and ideology are elevated to a particularly significant position. Because the organisation suffers from uncertainties about what it is doing, and whether what is done really works, there is a strong need for the organisation's existence to be justified in terms of its belief system. Culture, in such organisations, may provide the conviction and motivation that in some other contexts derives in part from more demonstrable measures of organisational worth and effectiveness.

Finally, culture needs to be seen as located in an organisation's history and environment. Often an organisation's founder and early history play an important role in creating culture. Historical origins are often referred to in some organisations when key issues are under consideration. The role of environment in shaping culture was referred to earlier in the chapter. Organisational culture is shaped both by the general environment, that is dominant values, norms and ideologies in the wider society, and by its task environment, that is the expectations, demands, and social organisation of the groups on which the organisation depends and which it attempts to influence. There are, in effect, layers of culture: the broad societal culture, the dominant organisational culture (if any), and the sub-cultures within the organisation. These overlap, challenge, conflict, and reinforce one another in complex ways. It is out of these interactions that culture and cultures are created and developed.

Developing cultural competence

Culture impacts on many aspects of the functioning of human service organisations. The values, beliefs, ideology and norms that prevail within an organisation influence the motivation, attitude and actions of workers, organisational priorities, relations among organisational members, relations with consumers, and overall organisational effectiveness. The question therefore arises: what can and should social and welfare workers do to influence, and to respond to, the cultures of the organisations in which they work?

The broad answer to this question is that workers need to acquire 'cultural competence' (Allaire and Firsirotu 1984, p. 215). By this we mean the ability to relate to the cultural system of an organisation in a conscious and strategic manner. The range of specific competencies involved are outlined in Table 7.2 and are discussed below. Not surprisingly, much of the discussion of culture in the management literature has a 'top down' managerial perspective: managers are encouraged to create a strong culture as a means of increasing organisational effectiveness (Turner 1986, p. 103). Implicit in the ideology of the management perspective is the quest for control of the workplace and those who work there. By contrast, our perspective is 'bottom up'. Our concerns are the ways in which workers, wherever they are located in the organisation, can use their knowledge of culture to achieve their personal and professional goals. Broadly, we see cultural competency as involving intervention at four main levels: personal, group, consumers and the overall organisation.

Table 7.2 Cultural competencies for social and welfare workers

Point of intervention		Type of competency
1 Personal	i	Know your own and other individuals' values, beliefs, ideology and norms
	ii	Be aware of your own and other individuals' cultural impact in the organisation, and use this awareness to act in a strategic manner
2 Group	i	Be able to critically appraise the sub-culture of organisational groups, especially your own
	ii	Be able to participate in creating, sustaining, challenging and changing group culture
	iii	Be able to work cross-culturally within the organisation
3 Consumers	i	Be aware of the culture of individual consumers, and the implications for organisational processes
	ii	Be able to make organisations more responsive to the culture of individual consumers
4 Organisation	i	Be critically aware of the prevailing corporate culture
	ii	Be able to survive within and use the prevailing corporate culture
	iii	Be able to modify and work towards change of the prevailing corporate culture
	iv	Be able to resist and conflict with the corporate culture
5 General	i	Recognise the limits of culture and cultural intervention

The personal level

Cultural competency of necessity starts with oneself: it is in the first instance to do with self-reflection and self-understanding. Specifically, cultural competence is predicated on knowing your own and other individuals' values, beliefs, ideology and norms, and understanding their organisational significance. Key issues for workers to continually consider include:

- What does my personal, social and political ideology mean in the context of this organisation?
- What are my personal beliefs about the nature of organisational life, and how does this influence my actions and behaviour in the organisation?
- What are my own norms of behaviour, and my personal style, in this organisation?
- What are the factors that have shaped and continue to shape my cultural identity in the organisation, such as my gender, social class, ethnicity, and professional training?

Awareness of the personal cultures of other individuals in the organisation, and the points of similarity and difference with oneself, are important parts of such self-understanding.

Closely linked is the need for social and welfare workers to be aware of their own and others' cultural impact in the organisation, and to be able to use this awareness to act in a strategic manner. There are two aspects to this. Firstly, workers need to accept that they share, to varying degrees, the responsibility for making organisations the way that they are. All workers, by their actions, share in the process of making the world of the organisation. Organisational culture, as we have seen, is not simply fixed, received, or handed down. Rather, it is continuously being made and remade by the participants in the organisation, in the context of the given structural and managerial constraints. We all bear some responsibility for making our organisational lives the way they are (Smircich 1985, p. 71).

Relatedly, workers need to be aware of how their personal culture impinges on and is perceived by other people in the organisation. Matters such as dress, language and personal style are not, in organisational contexts, simply matters of personal taste. They are, inevitably and unavoidably, expressions of personal culture that are perceived and interpreted by other organisational members in ways that have organisational consequences. Take, for example, the matter of dress. Most organisations have, either formally or informally, dress rules that are observed by most organisational members. In such organisations as the police service, the armed forces and some religious communities this takes the form of a uniform, and failure to dress in the appropriate attire is treated as an explicit breach of the rules. In other organisations the dress codes are less explicitly prescribed, but none-the-less involve clear organisational expectations. Senior male public servants in most parts of Australia, excepting the tropics, are expected to wear suit and tie. Youth workers, by and large, are expected to dress informally. Mode of dress is important, then, not only for its obvious functionality, but also for what it symbolises. The power dressing of senior and middle-level public sector management indicates some level of identification with or acceptance of the mores, aspirations and status of the executive service. The jeans and T-shirts of the youth or community worker may symbolise identification with the consumers. Dress can be an important symbol and statement of attitude to the organisation. It can be used to identify with, or to assert separateness from, or rejection of, prevailing organisational values.

Similar considerations apply to such matters as the use of language, and personal style. The extensive use of jargon by a professional group in communicating with other individuals and groups is likely to be perceived as a sign that the group wishes to assert its separateness and, possibly, its superiority. The use of the dominant terminology of the organisation as a whole, on the other hand, may symbolise the professional group's interest in and willingness to identify closely with the larger organisation. If punctuality, and careful and accurate recording, are part of the dominant organisational style, conformity with or neglect of these matters by an individual will have an impact, irrespective of how effective that individual is in other aspects of his or her work. A key aspect of cultural competence is being aware of how our presentation of self influences the ways we are perceived within the organisation.

The group level

Self-knowledge and awareness are the first steps towards cultural competence. But cultural competence is also about understanding and intervening at a broader organisational level. For many workers the primary points of intervention are the units or groups to which they belong within the organisation, such as the regional office, the ward, the division, or a particular professional group. In small, non-government organisations this immediate work group may be the organisation as a whole. In some situations individuals view themselves as belonging to more than one grouping. Thus, a child guidance worker in a school may see herself as part of the school where she is primarily located, but also part of the welfare resources group within the education system as a whole. Each of these groupings, as we have seen, will have its own culture or sub-culture. An important competency for social and welfare workers is to be able to critically appraise the sub-culture of organisational groups, especially their own. Groups within organisations develop values, beliefs and norms, and ways of expressing these, which have consequences for the group's relations with other parts of the organisation, and for service to consumers. Social and welfare workers need to be able to identify, describe and understand the culture of a group, and assess its impact on the group's effectiveness.

Take, as an example, the case, mentioned earlier in the chapter, of a regional unit of a large public sector organisation, located in a remote part of a state. Such a unit may develop a strong belief that they, and the area they serve, are neglected and misunderstood by the metropolitan authorities. This belief may, or may not, be grounded in reality. Whether it is or not, the belief itself will have an impact on the operations of the unit. This impact may be positive and negative. On the positive side, it may result in a strong sense of common purpose and group identification, and may cement links with the local community. But on the negative side, it may result in a stereotyped view of central office and those who work there, a lack of awareness of the circumstances facing other parts of the organisation, or excessive belligerence and hostility in dealing with outsiders. The ability to identify such group values and norms, and critically appraise their impact, is a key element of cultural competence.

To identify and analyse group culture requires, in the first instance, an understanding of the elements of culture, such as that provided in Table 7.1. It is necessary to know what it is you are looking for. Additionally, observation and analytical skills are required. Organisational culture is often manifested in the language used in the group, in the stories that are told, in group rites and other symbols. By being aware of what is being conveyed in these ways, and of what is being hidden, a picture of some of the central elements of the culture of a group can be developed. It is also necessary to develop and maintain a constructively critical stance within the group. This involves the ability to step back from the group to appraise the significance and consequence of its values, beliefs, ideology, and norms, while at the same time maintaining active and committed membership. This task may generate a range of personal tensions for workers, as they attempt to resolve the often conflicting and contradictory demands of self versus group.

The purpose for a worker of critically appraising the culture of a group to which he or she belongs is to be able to create, sustain, challenge or change group culture. The development of group culture can be thought of as a dynamic learning process (Gagliardi 1986, p. 120). A unit within an organisation develops norms and beliefs that enable it to deal with the supra-organisation and other external demands, and that enable members of the unit to work together reasonably satisfactorily. However, these norms and beliefs may be challenged by changing circumstances, and by the experiences of the unit in dealing with them. If these changed circumstances bring into question values, beliefs, ideologies or norms that are deeply rooted within the group, there may well be strong resistance to criticism and discussion of them. Individual workers need to be able to contribute to ongoing processes in which groups create and re-create their ways of understanding and acting, in the context of ever-changing political, economic and social circumstances.

A central element in the process of building and challenging group culture is consciousness-raising. Many people in organisations do not deliberate explicitly on culture. Individuals, in the main, are inclined to accept, rather than critique, the received culture of the group or the organisation. Consciousness-raising involves arousing awareness of the nature and consequences of a group's culture. This may involve complex and difficult educational processes, as people are not always eager to examine their behaviour, its meaning, and the premises on which it is based (Egan 1985, pp. 285-287). Working with the sub-unit or group of which you are a part in ongoing re-examination of values, beliefs, ideology and norms can be a thankless task. This is particularly the case when such a re-examination leads to a challenging of strongly held values and beliefs. It is made more difficult by the exigencies of daily life in organisations: staff turnover, lack of resources, status differences, organisational demands, and so forth. Yet activity of this kind can and should be an integral part of human service work. Staff meetings, committees, tea-room discussions, and informal meetings with colleagues all provide opportunities to build, sustain, and challenge aspects of the group's way of doing things. Rapid, fundamental change in a group's culture is rare, and the extent to which even highly planned, conscious attempts to mould culture are successful is a matter of debate (Dalmau and Dick 1987, pp. 24-28). Nevertheless, a 'culturally competent' worker should be strategically considering ways of assisting his or her group to explore aspects of the group culture. This is particularly the case when a worker is engaged in organisational development and change, a topic we examine in detail in a later chapter. Techniques for assisting groups to engage in explicit consciousness-raising processes have been described by Gumprecht (1986, pp. 220-222) in relation to women's groups in organisations, and Dick (1988, pp. 17-28) in relation to organisations at a general level.

A further element of cultural competency is the ability to work cross-culturally within the organisation. This means the ability to work effectively with other sub-cultural groups within the organisation, such as other professional and occupational groups, or groups performing particular functions. This requires developing an understanding of the values, beliefs, ideology and norms of such groups, identifying the key points of agreement and divergence with one's own culture, and exploring opportunities for effective collaboration, while recognising areas of potential conflict. The ability to cross sub-cultural boundaries in organisations is of great value, as it potentially provides workers with important sources of organisational information and political support.

The consumer level

As well as being about personal and group culture, cultural competence is centrally concerned with the relations between human service organisations and consumers. Workers need to be aware of the culture of individual consumers, and the implications for organisational processes. It is frequently the case that the personal culture of an individual seeking or receiving service from a human service organisation is quite different from that of the organisation and those who work for it. Such differences can be of many kinds. Clearly, cultural differences based on gender, ethnicity, Aboriginality, age, class, disability and place have major implications for the nature and appropriateness of services provided to consumers. But there are also less conspicuous ways in which consumers may find themselves as cultural outsiders in respect to the organisations with which they need to deal. A few examples of the types of situations in which cultural awareness is critical will illustrate the kinds of matters of which workers must be aware.

Cultural awareness is a central issue in the treatment of women consumers in male-dominated settings. Feminist writings concerning the treatment of women in childbirth have stressed that mothers and doctors have contrasting frames of reference for this experience. Obstetricians, most of whom historically have been men, have tended, it is argued, to treat childbirth primarily as a medical process. For the majority of women, however, childbirth is viewed primarily as a natural event of great personal significance, in which her status as a 'patient' is problematic (Pascall 1986, pp. 171-174). Cultural awareness, in this organisational situation, involves being aware of the meaning of the childbirth experience for women, and of the differences between their interpretation and construction of the event, and that of the predominantly male professionals. Changing practices and procedures during the last decade in many maternity hospitals, in so far as they have tempered some of the extremes of medical management, exemplify a developing awareness of the cultural meaning of the childbirth experience for women. Indeed, with moves to encourage fathers to attend neo-natal classes, be present at the birth, and assume a greater role after the birth, many formally accepted cultural norms which separated men from the birth experience are changing.

The treatment of ethnicity by human service organisations provides many examples of the need for awareness of consumers' culture (Cox 1989). In many parts of the Australian public sector there is an official goal of providing services that are sensitive to the culture of ethnic minorities (Sanders 1984, pp. 276-278). However, putting this goal into practice requires a high level of cultural awareness at all levels of organisations, including awareness of implicit and explicit discrimination and racism being practiced by the organisation. One area of particular relevance to social and welfare workers is that of ethnocentric cultural values concerning families and relations within families. It is often the case that individuals from ethnic minorities hold beliefs that are markedly at variance with the dominant Australian culture and with the service ideology of the organisation to which they have come for help. These might include a strong belief in male domination in marriage, a cultural taboo against wives participating in the paid labour force, or enforcement of strict control over adolescent children, particularly young women (Cox 1989, pp. 119-126). Ensuring that organisations are made fully aware of these complex, cultural issues, and that they are dealt with in a sensitive fashion is a key ingredient of cultural competence.

Undoubtedly, the area of greatest cultural insensitivity in human service administration in Australia is to be found in the treatment of Aboriginal people. For many decades, official policies of protection and assimilation denied the desirability of recognising Aboriginal culture in human service provision, and public policy generally (Coombs 1978, pp. 6-7). The official adoption of policies of self-determination since the early and mid-1970s, and official acceptance of the rights of Aboriginal people to retain and develop their own culture, have not, however, been readily translated into culturally sensitive services and policies. On the contrary, in fields such as corrections, housing, child and family welfare, and health-care, the record is one of ongoing cultural insensitivity. The operative culture of many human service organisations, despite official statements to the contrary, continues to be dominated by values, beliefs and practices which exclude Aboriginal people from a quality of life experienced by the majority of Australians. The shortcomings of attempts by mainstream human service organisations to implement policies based on the ideology of Aboriginal self-determination have been extensively documented (e.g. Edmunds 1990; Collman 1988; Sanders 1987). While the roots of cultural insensitivity towards Aboriginal people are deep and complex, social and welfare workers need to develop a fuller understanding of Aboriginal culture and its relations to mainstream human service organisations. They also need to be willing and able to engage in organisational processes which will produce services which are culturally sensitive and relevant to the needs of Aboriginal people.

Other significant cultural groupings in our society are those based on age, class, place and disability. Workers in organisations serving youth need to be aware of youth cultures and the importance of such cultural expression for young people. Similarly, workers in nursing homes need an appreciation of the values and norms of the elderly people who are their residents. Workers from middle-class backgrounds need to be aware that the values and norms of families and individuals who are largely excluded and marginalised from social participation are unlikely to reflect the worker's own values. Organisations need to be aware that there may be significantly different norms and values in rural and urban Australia that need to be taken into account by human service providers (Gregory 1977). In recent years we have become aware that people with disabilities may develop their own culture, including in the case of people with deafness, their own language (Sacks 1990). All human service organisations, not only those in the disability area, need to be aware of these aspects of cultural identity for people with disabilities.

All our examples so far concern situations in which consumers have markedly different personal characteristics from those of social and welfare workers. However, more broadly, the issue of cultural awareness in relation to consumers can be thought of as one involving organisational insiders and outsiders. Take the case of a community centre which has developed a strong sense of unity and belonging among its members. This shared culture may be a source of great strength, be nurtured and fostered, and be perceived positively by members. However, it may also have the hidden or unintended consequence of tending to exclude other community members who are not party to these 'shared understandings' which come from participation in the organisation. This may be detrimental to the centre's espoused goals of outreach to the overall community. A similar point can be made concerning the relations between highly formalised organisations and their consumers. Requirements for the completion of application forms and the provision of personal information through prescribed administrative processes are major cultural hurdles for some consumers (Cox 1989, pp. 194-196). They feel like outsiders, and remain so unless they adapt to the organisation's ways of doing things or until the organisation itself changes.

Social and welfare workers, as well as being aware of consumer culture, need skills in making organisations more responsive to the culture of individual consumers. Cox (1989, pp. 186-194) outlines a number of useful strategies which, though developed specifically to address issues of ethnic diversity, have general applicability to the broad issues of responsiveness to consumer culture. Firstly, organisations need to pay close attention to the felt and expressed needs of consumers and to continuously re-examine professional and organisational perceptions of consumer needs. Definitions of need in human services policy and practice rely heavily on prevailing professional and organisational ideology (Martin 1982). Workers need to create opportunities for consumers' understandings of their own needs to be articulated within the organisation. This might involve such actions as facilitating consumer representation and participation in planning and decision-making, developing forums for consumer consultation, encouraging research into consumer needs, and fostering an organisational culture that includes belief in the value of listening to consumers. These activities will be discussed in greater detail in chapter 9.

Organisational responsiveness to consumer culture may also involve the development of culture-specific programmes and services or adaptation of mainstream services to the cultural needs of particular consumers. The recruitment of workers and volunteers from the same cultural background as consumers is another important approach. This serves two purposes. Firstly, that the worker may be able to deal in culturally appropriate ways with the consumer because of common language, and shared values and experiences. Equally importantly, 'indigenous workers' can perform educational, liaison and advocacy roles for consumers from minority cultures within the organisation. We stress that these considerations are not restricted to the fields of ethnicity and Aboriginality. Thus, a community-based organisation may decide to employ a local on the grounds that personal identification with the needs and aspirations of other local people may help the organisation to become culturally sensitive.

Responsiveness to consumer culture also involves issues of access. Cultural differences between the organisation and its intended consumer group may result in lack of take-up of the organisation's services. Social and welfare workers need to address cultural barriers to service usage. Language is particularly significant. At one level this may involve the use of interpreters, bilingual staff, and multi-lingual publicity materials. But more subtly, it involves careful attention to the language and terminology used by organisational members in their dealings with consumers. If organisations speak a foreign language, as far as the consumer is concerned, the accessibility and effectiveness of organisational services will be seriously limited. Similar considerations apply to the presentation of the organisation, its architecture, the style of dress of staff, the layout of reception rooms, the manner of reception staff, and so forth. Collectively, these matters have been termed 'cultural accessibility'. Organisations should accommodate, as much as possible, the consumers' preferred language, value system, behavioural norms and belief systems (Cox 1989, p. 192).

Another approach is to encourage interaction between staff and consumers whose culture differs from their own. This may be done relatively formally, for example by arranging meetings to exchange views with organisations representing consumer interests, or it may involve informal, social meetings between staff and consumers. An important tactic may be to get management and staff to meet consumers on the consumer's own turf, rather than in the office. Oliver Sacks illustrates this graphically in *Seeing Voices: A Journey into the World of the*

Deaf. He provides an account of his first visit to Gallaudet University, a university for the deaf where sign language is used universally for the study of mathematics, poetry, chemistry, philosophy and all other university activities. He writes, 'I had to see all this for myself before I could be moved from my previous "medical" view of deafness (as a "condition", a deficit, that had to be treated) to a "cultural" view of the deaf as forming a community with a complete language and culture of its own' (Sacks 1990, p. 127). Cross-cultural interaction is complex and personal contact is an important part of cultural learning.

The organisational level

The emphasis thus far in our examination of cultural competence has been at the level of the individual worker, her or his primary group within the organisation, and the consumer. This, however, is only one part of the picture. We stressed earlier in the chapter that while culture is created by individuals and groups within organisations, this occurs in conditions that are not entirely, or even substantially, under their control. In particular, there is likely to be a prevailing or dominant, corporate culture, espoused by the senior management or ruling coalition of the organisation. The key point is that this corporate culture is, explicitly or implicitly, a form of managerial control. Effectively, 'the top management team aims to have individuals possess direct ties to the values and goals of the dominant elites in order to activate the emotion and sentiment which might lead to devotion, loyalty and commitment to the company' (Ray 1986, p. 294). Workers need to be able to relate strategically to the prevailing corporate culture.

Firstly, this requires workers to be critically aware of the prevailing, corporate culture. The ability to identify the values, beliefs, ideology and norms espoused and promoted by management or the ruling coalition is fundamental to effective work within organisations. It is a vital part of the process of learning 'what the game is like'. We have stressed that organisations are not value-neutral; they are not empty shells within which individuals and groups can pursue their personal and collective goals. Awareness of the prevailing values, their strength and effects, is basic to effective practice.

Critical awareness of the prevailing organisational culture can be acquired through careful and systematic observation of the shared meanings and symbols listed in Table 7.1. If the prevailing corporate culture is largely overt, and official statements and symbols can be relied on as accurate indicators of dominant cultural values, then the process is relatively straightforward. Explicit attempts by management or the dominant coalition to create corporate culture via seminars, workshops, company magazines, weekend retreats, mission statements and the like provide important opportunities for workers to understand the official corporate culture. Developing critical awareness of corporate culture is, in part, simply a matter of being aware of official, organisational statements and activities, and appraising these according to one's own perspectives.

However, the process is rarely as clear cut as this. The prevailing culture is usually to some degree covert, partially hidden to outsiders and even to members of the organisation. Knowledge and awareness in these circumstances can only come via ongoing participation in the organisation and contact and interaction with organisational members. In some cases, the dominant organisational culture is almost entirely covert, at least as far as outsiders are concerned. For example, the Fitzgerald Commission of Inquiry into the Queensland Police Force identified a dominant, covert 'police culture', sustained by an elite group within the force, which included 'contempt for the criminal justice system, disdain for the law and rejection of its application to police, disregard for the truth, and abuse of authority' (Queensland Commission of Inquiry 1989, p. 200). These cultural norms were, of course, never officially acknowledged, although, as evidence to the inquiry demonstrated, they provided the backdrop to the daily experience of members of the police force. They were, to some degree, camouflaged, as far as the general public was concerned, by the organisation's official symbols and statements which sought to preserve the image of a dedicated and responsible police force. We can conclude that developing an awareness of the prevailing organisational culture, in its covert as well as overt manifestations, requires both systematic observation and sustained participation in the organisation over a period of time. It is not a simple matter of reading a mission statement, valuable though that may be. One of the pitfalls in the first few weeks and months after joining an organisation is to make premature judgements or assumptions about the prevailing culture. It is often wise to spend some time 'soaking up' the culture and getting the feel of the organisation.

Given an awareness of the prevailing culture of their organisation, workers need strategically to be able to take different stances at different times in relation to it, depending on circumstance and personal conviction. Sometimes, the need is simply to be able to survive within and use the prevailing culture. Surviving within an organisational culture, particularly one perceived as hostile, is in itself an important practice skill. Workers may experience considerable tension between their own personal and professional culture and the dominant organisational culture, yet not wish, or be in a position, either to resign from the organisation or to take it on. In such circumstances, survival is the name of the game. This may involve attempting to create areas of autonomous practice within the organisation, token acquiescence with aspects of organisational activity, covert non-compliance with organisational directives, or turning a blind eye to some organisational practices. Such strategies, which undoubtedly pose difficult ethical questions, are part of the everyday reality of many social and welfare workers, faced as they often are with organisational contradictions and tensions that cannot be effectively confronted, at least in the short term.

More positively, social and welfare workers need to develop skills in using the prevailing culture to achieve positive outcomes for consumers. Much of this involves the use of organisational symbols, particularly language, to achieve personal and group goals within the organisation. Thus, workers wishing to promote a certain kind of programme within an organisation that uses the language of efficiency and effectiveness may be well advised strategically to couch their proposal in such terms even if other words and values underpin the proposition. Similarly, a proposal to expand community development activities may be more positively received in some organisational contexts if described as community outreach or community liaison. Of course, it may be decided that the use of the dominant organisational terminology compromises the proposal itself, or fails to force the organisation to come to terms with an issue of importance. These may well be persuasive considerations. The key point is that the prevailing culture, particularly the official culture, may be open to use by workers. It provides opportunities as well as constraints.

Using the official or dominant culture also involves strategic employment of established organisational processes and procedures. If there is a strong organisational norm that proposals for organisational changes be presented in writing and be directed via certain official channels, compliance with this norm may be a prerequisite to effective action. Clearly, on occasions, and in situations that are viewed as critically important, there may be shock value in acting in a deviant manner. The key point is that if the dominant culture is understood, informed strategic and tactical decisions can be made.

Important opportunities for organisational action also arise from the discrepancies or contradictions that typically exist between an organisation's official culture and the culture in practice. For instance, many human service organisations espouse a strong belief in the importance of staff and consumer participation in decision-making. In reality such participation is often token at best. However, the official commitment to such beliefs can be used as a lever to boost staff and consumer involvement. Management-initiated attempts 'to create an organisational culture' are themselves opportunities for individuals and groups to advance their own perspectives on organisational issues.

Workers are sometimes faced with dominant organisational values, beliefs, ideologies and norms that they find unsatisfactory or unacceptable. In such circumstances they must consider the possibilities of going beyond strategies for survival in and use of the dominant culture. In the first instance, this involves participation in attempts to modify and work towards change of the prevailing organisational culture. Strategies and tactics associated with organisational change are discussed in detail in chapter 9, but some general points can be made here. Several writers have pointed to the considerable difficulties involved in engineering significant cultural change in organisations (Lundberg 1985; Dick 1988). Many of the factors, discussed earlier in this chapter, that create, shape and sustain organisational culture are relatively enduring, and cultural change, therefore, is likely to be incremental in nature. Rapid cultural change in an organisation is probably most likely to occur in circumstances of sudden change in the organisational environment, or displacement of the organisation's senior management or ruling coalition. According to one writer, the achievement of significant cultural change in organisations' 'calls for an outlook and mode of operation more akin to revolutionary war than to group therapy', that is it involves the toppling of an existing regime by political means, including the use of force, and the instigation of a new regime committed to the new cultural values (Paterson 1983, p. 12). Social and welfare workers are rarely in a situation to bring about fundamental changes of this kind. The essential requirements for carrying out such a change in complex, modern organisations are administrative authority, the strong support of key external bodies (for example, funders, sponsors, the minister), and a high level of organisational–political skill. In reality, workers are much more likely to be involved in ongoing 'guerilla tactics' designed to modify particular aspects of organisational culture, in the expectation that accumulated changes, over time, will be substantial.

Attempts by social and welfare workers to modify organisational culture can be of three main kinds. First, there are attempted modifications to organisational symbols. Take the case of the struggle for the use of non-sexist language in human service organisations. The language used in organisations, as we have seen, is important symbolically as it expresses, reflects and reproduces shared meanings. Thus, attempts to remove sexist bias from publications, titles and other nomenclature and the spoken word in organisations has great significance as an indicator of organisational culture. Modifying language symbolises and influences, to some degree, an organisation's commitment to different values and norms. Other examples of important modifications to other kinds of organisational symbols could be given. Making waiting rooms more friendly and accessible symbolises a norm of treating consumers with respect. The way the annual meeting is conducted is symbolic of the organisation's relations to its members. Symbols influence, as well as reflect, cultural meanings, and the manipulation or manoeuvring of symbols provides one approach to modification of organisational culture.

The second level of intervention is attitudinal, that is involving attempts to directly modify the values, beliefs, ideology or norms of organisational members. In a sense, a considerable part of the daily, informal interaction among organisational members could be seen in this light. Tea-room conversations, interactions in staff meetings and private discussions often involve, explicitly or implicitly, attempts to modify the values or norms of others. In addition to these informal exchanges, however, workers can become involved in attempts to modify the shared meanings of organisational members in more formal ways. Often this means participating in management-initiated or endorsed efforts to change aspects of organisational culture. For example, many organisations in the disability field have made conscious efforts, via training programmes, to change staff attitudes to people with disabilities and inculcate values and norms associated with the values of 'normalisation'. Similarly, social workers in the Department of Social Security have been involved in training programmes for counter staff concerned to promote positive and helpful attitudes and behaviours towards consumers. Awareness and sensitivity training relating to issues of equal employment opportunity have become established activities in many public sector organisations (Wilensky 1985, p. 44). Sometimes, although relatively uncommonly in the human services, organisations explicitly and directly attempt to re-appraise their organisational culture via training and workshop activities. All such activities may provide social and welfare workers with significant opportunities for involvement in modification of organisational culture.

The third level of intervention may also involve participation in structural change. The ways in which organisational structures embody and reinforce culture have been discussed earlier in the chapter. Cultural change and structural change often, perhaps always, need to go hand in hand. Thus, attempts to change cultural values in organisations relating to equal opportunity may need to address structural factors such as recruitment of members of minority groups into senior management positions, alongside initiatives designed to change values, beliefs, ideologies and norms (Wilensky 1985, pp. 45-46).

Attempts to modify and change the corporate culture may not, in some circumstances, be considered appropriate or feasible. Workers may decide in some situations that an open, oppositional stance is required. This requires workers to resist and conflict with the corporate culture. Resisting the corporate culture involves refusing to accept values and norms that management require of participants in the organisation. For example, the organisation may be strongly committed to a particular religious ideology that has implications for the kinds of services provided and the treatment of consumers. A group of workers in the organisation may refuse to accept this ideology as incompatible with their professional or secular view of human service provision. They may decide to actively conflict with the dominant culture by refusing to operationalise it. This can be thought of as 'contracultural' activity: it involves overt conflict with the organisation's presumed mission and shared meanings (Van Maanen and Barley 1985, p. 45).

Openly resisting and conflicting with the corporate culture involves high risks, including loss of status, loss of organisational rewards and even dismissal from the organisation. Effective resistance and conflict, therefore, is most likely to be a group activity, involving the development of sub-group culture as discussed earlier in the chapter. Whether or not resistance and conflict with the dominant culture can be sustained will depend on various factors including the political and economic importance of the group to the organisation and the group's links and legitimacy with groups outside of the organisation.

Finally, cultural competence involves recognition of the limits of culture and cultural intervention. An understanding of culture is, we argue, essential to effective work in human service organisations. But the other concepts examined in this section of the book—environment, goals and structure—are equally important. Each of the four concepts draws attention to critical aspects of organisational processes. Social and welfare workers can draw on the various frameworks that we have provided to understand what is happening around them in organisations, and to act in considered and strategic ways. It is particularly important to understand the inter-relatedness of these four aspects of human service organisations. The organisational environment, goals, structure and culture are in reality closely intermeshed, and a particular set of circumstances facing a worker will likely require an understanding of all four elements.

Conclusions

Organisational culture can be thought of as the social or normative glue that holds an organisation together. It is to do with shared meanings, and with the ways that these are created, expressed, reproduced, challenged and changed within organisations. An organisation often has a dominant culture, but may also be characterised by competing sub-cultures. Understanding organisational culture is essential for social and welfare workers as it impacts on all key areas of organisational life: the scope and boundaries of organisational endeavour, the ways in which work is done, relations among organisational members, and the treatment of consumers.

There are essentially three essential areas of knowledge and understanding in relation to organisational culture for social and welfare workers. First, it is necessary to have a clear picture of the elements that collectively comprise organisational culture. These can be thought of as shared meanings, including values, beliefs, ideology and norms, and shared symbols, including myths, stories, rites, language and artefacts. These elements are summarised in Table 7.1. The second requirement is an understanding of the factors that create, sustain, reproduce, challenge and change organisational culture. These include the individuals who participate in the organisation, organisational groups, the management or dominant coalition, organisational structures and technologies, and the history and environment of the organisation. It is as a result of interactions among these complex elements that organisational culture and cultures are developed.

The third and final requirement is an understanding of the practice implications of culture for workers. We portray this as the need for workers to acquire cultural competence, that is the ability to relate to the cultural system of an organisation in a conscious and strategic manner. This involves competencies at a personal, group, consumer relations, and overall organisational level as outlined in Table 7.2. Workers need to understand the inter-relatedness of culture with the other key elements of human service organisations discussed in this section: environment, goals and structure. Collectively, these four concepts provide workers with a detailed framework for understanding and participating in human service organisations.

Chapter review questions

1 What do you understand by the term organisational culture?
2 Why is an understanding of organisational culture important for social and welfare workers?
3 What do you understand by the terms: values, beliefs, ideology, and norms in relation to organisations?
4 What is meant by 'shared symbols' in organisations? What are some of the different kinds of organisational symbols?
5 Define the following terms: overt culture, covert culture, official culture, operative culture, corporate culture, and dominant culture.
6 What are the main factors that impact on the creation, development and change of organisational culture?
7 What is meant by cultural competence?
8 What are the four main areas of cultural competency for social and welfare workers?
9 How can workers make organisations more responsive to the culture of individual consumers?
10 What is the relationship of organisational culture to the other concepts examined in this section: environment, goals and structure?

Further reading

An excellent introductory collection of articles on the concept of organisational culture is Frost et al. (1985). See in particular the contributions by Van Maanen and Barley, Smircich, and Louis. Two comprehensive overviews of the theoretical literature are Allaire and Firsirotu (1984) and Smircich (1983). Managerial approaches to the creation of organisational culture are critiqued in Turner (1986) and Ray (1986). These articles stress the links between the creation of culture and the maintenance of organisational control. An overview of the managerial literature on culture, drawing out the applications for human service organisations is Gummer (1990). For two differing approaches to practice issues in assisting groups and organisations to develop a critical understanding of their culture or cultures see Egan (1985, chapter 16), and Dalmau and Dick (1987). For the ways in which male culture dominates many organisations read Eisenstein (1985), and for the possibilities of a feminist administrative style in human services see Hooyman and Cunningham (1986). The links between structural and cultural change in relation to equal opportunity are drawn out by Wilenski (1985). Edmunds (1990) looks closely at cultural issues in relation to the treatment of Aboriginal people by white organisations, in an important paper for the Royal Commission into Aboriginal Deaths in Custody. Cox (1989, chapter 6), provides a thorough, practice-focused account of organisational responses to issues of multi-culturalism. Sacks (1989) shows the critical importance of cultural issues in the area of disability, specifically in relation to the world of the deaf. The Fitzgerald Inquiry's discussion of 'Police Culture' (1989, chapter 7) is a fascinating account of how a covert culture of inefficiency and dishonesty can come to dominate an organisation with devastating consequences. Paterson's account (1983) of how to bring about 'cultural revolution' in organisations is important reading for those concerned with the politics of cultural change.

Case study

COMING TO TERMS WITH MUNGUMBBA

It is a long, hot drive from the city to Mungumbba, and Claire Anderson's non-air-conditioned, twelve-year old, Toyota Corolla was feeling and acting its age. Three times it had overheated while traversing the 500 kilometres from the state capital, and each time Claire had to wait, not particularly patiently, in the hot sun at the side of the road for 'Sammy' to cool down. It was with a great sense of relief that she read the sign 'Welcome to Mungumbba, pop. 10 476', alongside the hoarding informing all travellers that Mungumbba was served by Apex, Rotary and Lions, and that it had been runner-up in the Tidy Towns competition twice, and 'highly commended' on no less than four occasions. 'Just what I need', Claire said to herself with a mixture of amusement and irritation, 'a town obsessed with cleanliness'. None-the-less, she was pleased to have arrived in Mungumbba, and she looked around with interest at the town that she planned to make her home for at least the next twelve months.

Claire was a 'big city' person, born and bred, and Mungumbba was intended as something different. Actually, the decision to come to Mungumbba had all been a bit sudden. After graduating in social work the previous November, Claire had found it harder than she expected to find a job. Part of the problem was that she was not sure of what she wanted to do. When she saw the Department of Social Security (DSS) advertising a social work position in their Mungumbba Regional Office, she put in an application with the vague thought that it might be nice to work in the country. A week later she was interviewed, and two days later received a phone call asking, 'Can you start next week?' Claire was given a week of orientation in area office, and now here she was, driving down Mungumbba's main street, past the War memorial, looking for the Ace Motel where she was booked to spend her first night as a Mungumbba resident.

Claire's prior knowledge of Mungumbba and district was limited to say the least. Lying on her bed in the motel that first evening she read with interest the brochure in her room entitled 'Magical Mungumbba', put out by the Mungumbba and District Development Board. 'Mungumbba', it read, 'is a thriving district with a total population of some 35 000 people. The township of Mungumbba itself is the main commercial and service centre for the region. It boasts a wide range of public services and amenities including modern shopping, recreational and sporting amenities. Many government departments have their regional headquarters in Mungumbba. The surrounding region includes several small and quite remote townships, engaged primarily in open-cut coal mining. Agriculture is an important mainstay of the area, and a significant proportion of the populace is involved in primary production. Mungumbba is in the process of developing a local tourist industry, capitalising on our region's unique, natural beauty, quiet rural life style, and high quality accommodation and facilities.' Claire rolled over and fell asleep.

The following morning Claire turned up at the DSS Office, dressed neatly, but casually, in jeans and T-shirt. She was surprised to find that she was the only woman dressed this way—blouses and skirts, or cotton dresses seemed to be the norm. She was met by Bill O'Connor, the Regional Manager, who welcomed her warmly, showed her the social worker's office, and introduced her to the other staff. 'We are really pleased to see you,' he said, as the two of them sat down briefly in his office to talk over Claire's work, 'The position's been vacant for nearly two months now. I hope you enjoy the work, and that you get on better than the other young city girls who have come to Mungumbba as social and welfare workers.' Claire was about to ask Bill to elaborate on this rather worrying statement, but one of the Determining

Officers came in with an urgent problem, and Bill asked to be excused. Claire's first impressions of Bill were mixed. His welcome had been warm and apparently sincere. But would she be able to develop a good working relationship with this mid-forties man, a life-long resident of Mungumbba, a member of Lions and, as she soon learnt, a lunchtime regular at the Victory Hotel? 'Time will tell,' she thought to herself, 'and I mustn't make premature judgements just because he's wearing shorts and long socks'. Claire was sensitive about such matters, but, as she soon discovered, Bill's attire was pretty much standard for professional and clerical workers in the Mungumbba central business district.

Back in her office, Claire spent some time looking through the files and materials left behind by her predecessor. She was particularly interested in the file headed 'community profile', which, although incomplete, contained some important information. She was particularly interested in the data showing that a high proportion of the mine workers and their families in the outlying townships were from non-English speaking backgrounds, and that industrial problems and temporary closures of some of the mines had resulted in economic difficulties for many families. There also appeared to be a high level of family break-up in these communities. She was also interested to read of the economic difficulties being experienced by many farming families as a result of poor commodity prices on overseas markets. 'Asset rich but income poor' was a phrase used regularly in the clippings from editorials in the *Mungumbba Independent* that the previous worker had kept. Claire was also interested to find that the region contained a large number of Aboriginal people, many living in remote areas and communities as well as in Mungumbba township. She discovered that there was a local Aboriginal community located a few kilometres out of town, running a large, cattle property, bought with funds provided by the Aboriginal Development Corporation. 'None of this was mentioned in "Magical Mungumbba"' Claire thought, as she gradually pieced together her picture of her new community.

The other file that caught Claire's attention was marked 'regional office structures and procedures'. Flipping through it, Claire found an organisational chart of the Mungumbba DSS Office, showing, at a formal level at least, how the thirty or so staff fitted together. At the apex of the chart was the Regional Manager joined by a dotted line to the Regional Office Management Team (ROMT), comprising the manager, three officers-in-charge, and the social worker. Beneath the officer-in-charge were a number of cells of about four or five workers, headed up in some cases by a determining officer. Each cell had responsibility for a particular area of operations, for example review, new claims, the counter, family payments, pensions, and unemployment. An Aboriginal and Islander Liaison Officer, two field staff and a switchboard officer completed the staff complement. Scribbled in the margin in pencil next to the ROMT was the comment 'all men, except me!'

By now it was 10.00 a.m., the time for the weekly meeting of ROMT. Claire joined the other senior staff and was formally introduced to the meeting. There were three main issues on the agenda. The first, simply headed 'complaints' turned out to be about a number of alleged incidents relating to DSS services for Aboriginal people and people from ethnic minorities. There had been a number of complaints to state headquarters and the local Member of Parliament, as well as to the Regional Manager. The issue had also been widely reported in the local press. Claire gathered from the discussion that a local minister, Rev. Con Demetris, had been a vocal critic of the Department, and that the other members of the ROMT saw him as the main instigator of the complaints. He recently preached a sermon on poverty in Mungumbba in his church, and argued that the Department had a very low take-up of pensions and benefits by Aboriginal people, and by people from non-English speaking backgrounds in the local area. He subsequently was quoted in the local press as saying, 'This low take-up is a result of discriminatory attitudes and practices within the local office.' In the same article, support for the minister and his views was voiced by the local welfare council and the local Aboriginal Legal Service.

Staff at the meeting were eager to give their version of these events. It appeared that the minister was a recent arrival in Mungumbba. His predecessor, according to one staff member was 'a decent bloke who umpired the local footy and would even have an occasional drink with the boys'. However, 'This new bloke is just another blow-in from the big smoke who doesn't know his arse from his ears . . . He won't last long.' The Regional Manager, while apparently not in disagreement with this comment, expressed himself more moderately, saying, 'The Reverend is a bit naive and open to being manipulated. His complaints are exaggerated, not representative of local community opinion and don't show any understanding of the administrative complexity of servicing these client groups. Still, we will have to do something about this—what do you think Claire?' Claire had been hoping not to say anything very much, but some of the discussion had disturbed her. She was also still very much aware of some of the materials that had been discussed at her orientation in Area Office the previous week. Much attention had been paid to the Charter and Corporate Goals of DSS, and Claire felt that this was highly relevant to the discussion. She had it with her in one of her folders. 'In my view', she said, 'we must keep in mind the charter of our organisation which is, and I quote, "To deliver social security entitlements with fairness, courtesy and efficiency". We also need to keep in mind that our written corporate goals include:

Client service: we strive to provide high levels of service to clients, seeking to be fair, courteous and efficient at all times.

Quality: in all aspects of our work we seek to achieve the highest possible standard, prompt delivery, consistent quality and technical competence.

Perhaps we have a duty to take the Minister's complaints very seriously indeed?' There was a pause—a long pause. Then the Regional Manager said, 'Thank you for reminding us about the Charter, Claire. We are all very much aware of it. I'm quite sure we will be able to handle these complaints satisfactorily, and anything you can do as the social worker to help the

Minister understand the complexities of the issues would be much appreciated. Now what is the next item?'

The second item was a letter from Area Office reminding the Regional Manager of the visit to Mungumbba, in two weeks time, of officers from state headquarters to review the progress being made in regional offices in implementation of the Department's 'Access, Equity and Participation' policies. Claire was knowledgeable about this issue, as it too had been covered during her orientation week. These policies had implications both for staff employed by DSS and for clients. The broad aims concerning staff were the development of equal employment practices in recruitment and promotion. For clients there were three main goals: eliminating discrimination in access to services on the grounds of gender, race, or ethnicity; promoting equal access to services for members of racial or ethnic minorities; and promoting services which are culturally sensitive. After reminding staff of these matters, the Regional manager said, 'Claire, it's usually the case that our social worker handles this issue. Would you be willing to write our report on this and organise all the arrangements for this visit?'. Claire replied that she would need to think about it, and could she see him to talk about it later in the week?

The final item concerned the increasing number of requests for unemployment and other benefits being received from members of the farming community, as a result of the economic downturn in that sector. The officer-in-charge of Unemployment Benefits expressed the view that the rules governing payments to 'effectively unemployed' farmers were too severe. 'These guys may own their farms, but they have had virtually no income for a couple of years. Why shouldn't they get benefits like everyone else?' 'I quite agree' replied Bill O'Connor, 'but we are obliged to enforce Department policy. Still, I am sure that everyone can be relied on to be as fair and reasonable as they possibly can be in relation to applications for benefits from our farming friends, as they go through this difficult period'.

During Claire's first two weeks in Mungumbba she picked up some further impressions about local community attitudes towards outsiders, Aboriginal people and ethnic mine-workers. On Friday afternoon it was an office tradition that everybody from the office go to the Victory Hotel for a drink before going home. Claire joined everyone else and took a bit of a flak for sticking to mineral water. She overheard a conversation between two counter staff, concerning an invalid pension claim by a mine worker of Italian origin, who happened to be in the public bar: 'Another classic case of Mediterranean back . . . it doesn't stop him going to the pub every day'.

A few days after Claire's arrival in Mungumbba, the Rev. Con Demetris rang and asked to see her. He suggested meeting at his vestry as he would prefer not to come to the DSS Office. When she arrived he told her that an Aboriginal woman has complained to him about discriminatory treatment by counter staff. Staff allegedly made sexist and racist comments to her, and the office had been inordinately slow in processing her claim for Supporting Parents Benefit. She had been asked to come in personally on three occasions, at which time staff went over exactly the same details with her.

This was one in a long string of complaints he had received concerning the local office from people of non-English speaking backgrounds and Aboriginals. The local Aboriginal Legal Service wants the case to be referred to the Human Rights and Equal Opportunity Commission. Con wants to know if Claire can be of any assistance in resolving these issues.

Key question

Analyse the issues of organisational culture raised in this case. How would you address these cultural issues in both the short and long term? Include in your answer your proposed course of action in relation to the forthcoming visit of the officers from State headquarters, the issues being raised by Rev. Demetris, and any other matter requiring immediate attention. Give reasons for your proposals.

Case discussion points

1 What are the main elements of the culture of the Mungumbba Office of DSS? How are these manifested?
2 Are there any conflicting elements in this culture? In particular, are there differences between the culture of the regional office and that espoused by the broader organisation? What are the implications of any such differences?
3 Describe the overt, covert, official, operative, corporate and dominant culture in this organisation.
4 What factors shape the culture of the Mungumbba Office of DSS? What does the case illustrate about how organisational culture is created, maintained, transmitted and challenged?
5 What cultural competencies does Claire need to deal effectively with the organisational issues facing her and work effectively in the organisation?
6 How could Claire attempt to make the organisation more aware of and responsive to the culture and needs of the client groups of the organisation?
7 How can Claire maximise her chances of surviving in the culture of this organisation? Can she realistically aim to do more than survive? How long will it be before she is driving 'Sammy' back to the city, and leaving Mungumbba behind?

Practice in human service organisations

PART III

Practice in human
service organisations

In part I we explored the relevance of organisation theory for workers in human service organisations and provided a basis for workers to develop a critical perspective on the organisations in which they work. Part II comprised a detailed framework for organisational analysis, focusing on the concepts of organisational environment, goals, structure and culture. This framework provided a set of ideas and concepts to analyse, make sense of and work as a practitioner in human service organisations.

In this third and final part we focus on the nature of social and welfare work practice in organisations. We begin, in chapter 8, by showing that it is useful to think about social and welfare workers as 'front-line workers' or 'street-level bureaucrats'. This conceptualisation of human service work has important practice implications which are explored in the chapter. In chapters 9 to 11 we focus on three critical aspects of front-line work. Firstly, in chapter 9 we examine the relationship between organisations and consumers, and the roles and responsibilities of front-line workers in organisation–consumer relations. Then, in chapter 10, the possibilities of influencing organisational change, or of resisting change, in the front-line are examined. Finally, in chapter 11, we examine the contemporary demands for efficiency, effectiveness, equity, and excellence in human service organisations, and discuss the responses required of front-line workers to these organisational expectations.

8

Front-line work: choices, conflicts and contradictions

> The pyramid-shaped organisation chart depicting at the bottom the front-line worker as passively receiving and carrying out policies and procedures dispensed from above is a gross oversimplification (Weatherley, quoted in Ham and Hill 1984, p. 139).

The ways in which social and welfare workers perceive and define their roles and functions have significant effects on what they do and what they try to do. Workers often describe their own work, or the work of colleagues, in such terms as 'professional', 'change agent' or 'agent of social control'. These terms are indicative of an approach or a stance on the nature of social and welfare work. Each draws attention to important aspects of social and welfare work. However, our central theme is that social and welfare work should be viewed as an activity located within complex organisations. None of these terms encompasses this reality. We are left with the question: how can the role of social and welfare workers be defined and conceptualised to fully take into account the significance of organisational context?

In our view, the concepts that best address this issue are those of front-line worker and street-level bureaucrat. These concepts, drawn from the literature on public policy and organisation theory, provide a means of understanding the organisational complexities of social and welfare work and of describing the practice skills and tasks necessary to effectively perform such roles. In this chapter we will outline the theory of front-line work and street-level bureaucracy, show its applicability to social and welfare workers, and outline practice skills and strategies associated with effective front-line work.

The theory of street-level bureaucracy

The theoretical context

A common assumption of people working in human service organisations is that the power to control organisational activities is located in the upper echelons of the organisational hierarchy. Social and welfare workers involved in direct work with consumers are often perceived to have little control over their day-to-day activities, and to be tightly constrained by control mechanisms such as rules, procedures and sanctions imposed by officials located above them in the organisational hierarchy. This view of organisational life has strong roots in organisation theory. In particular, it stems from Robert Michels' famous 'iron law of oligarchy'. Michels, writing early in the twentieth century, argued that there was a general tendency in all organisations, even those committed to democratic decision-making, for power to become centralised in a small leadership group. He called this an iron law as it stemmed, in his view, from the very nature of organisations. The size and complexity of organisations, the need for quick decisions, expertise and continuity, and the control of information and communication by organisational elites, lead inevitably, according to Michels, to oligarchical control (Etzioni-Halevy 1985, pp. 18-23; Smith 1979, pp. 34-35).

The general applicability of this iron law to all organisations began to be questioned in the mid-1960s in studies of human service organisations such as psychiatric hospitals (Smith 1974). Researchers found that in these organisations critical decisions were often made by those organisational members in direct contact with consumers. Individuals and groups working in hospital wards, for example, tended to operate with a high degree of functional autonomy, and there were major obstacles to direct supervision of their activities. Organisations which shared these characteristics were dubbed 'front-line organisations' (Smith 1974, p. 351). It was subsequently argued that many of the organisations employing social and welfare workers closely resemble the model of a front-line organisation. 'There is a formal hierarchy of authority but operational control is located in peripheral units' (Smith 1979, p. 39).

The concept of front-line organisation led to an increasing interest in the roles and circumstances of workers operating in the front-line. In popular parlance this is often referred to as working at the 'coal-face' or, in the case of teachers, working at the 'chalk-face'. Lipsky coined the term 'street-level bureaucrat' to refer to 'public service workers who interact directly with citizens in the course of their jobs, and who have substantial discretion in the execution of their work' (1980, p. 3). Lipsky and his colleagues explored such issues as the role of street-level bureaucrats in policy-making, their degree of autonomy, their conditions of work, the nature of their relations with consumers, their role in rationing services, the attempts by human service organisations to control them, and the links between the broad social and economic context and street-level work (Lipsky 1980; Weatherley and Lipsky 1977; Prottas 1978).

This literature on street-level bureaucracy and front-line work provides a useful framework for social and welfare workers to understand the complexities of their roles and tasks in organisational terms. Our version of the key elements of the theory of street-level bureaucracy is summarised in Table 8.1 and discussed below.

Location in the front-line

Most social and welfare workers are located at the front-line of human service organisations. Although many human service professionals occupy supervisory, managerial and support positions elsewhere in organisations, most social workers and community welfare workers, together with youth workers, rehabilitation counsellors and so forth are, in Lipsky's terms, street-level bureaucrats. For example, social workers in hospitals operate mainly at the ward level, and are involved in direct patient care. Child protection workers in departments of family and community services are predominantly involved in direct ways in child protection and family support, or in developing local services or support networks. In the Department of Social Security, social workers work with the front-line counter staff in dealing with complex issues faced by consumers related to income security. In organisations providing services to people with disabilities, a range of human service professionals work directly with people with disabilities to improve

Table 8.1 The theory of street-level bureaucracy: key propositions

1   Social and welfare workers are located at the front-line of human service organisations

2   The front-line is strategically important in human service organisations

3   Many front-line workers experience a relatively high level of autonomy in their day-to-day work, because of the limitations of organisational control strategies

4   Thus front-line workers have extensive opportunities for choice and the exercise of discretion

5   This choice and discretion is often used to enable front-line workers to cope with the pressures they face, rather than to provide high quality services to consumers

6   This can be largely explained in terms of the constraints on front-line workers, in particular, heavy workloads and limited resources, organisational requirements and demands, the alienating nature of the work, conflicting interests within the organisation and the organisation's 'constitutional norms'

7   Workers must be aware of these pressures and the paradoxical nature of organisational life, and develop a range of skills and strategies to maximise their effectiveness (these are summarised in Table 8.3)

social and physical functioning. In supported accommodation services, workers are engaged directly with consumers experiencing homelessness and associated loss of social support. All such workers can be thought of as street-level bureaucrats.

The concept of street-level bureaucrat is usually associated with front-line work in large public sector organisations. However, we view the term as equally applicable to workers directly involved with consumers in smaller non-government and community organisations. Workers in youth refuges, community centres, welfare rights centres or migrant resource centres, for example, structurally have a similar location in their organisations to front-line workers in the public sector. We use the terms street-level bureaucrat and front-line worker to refer to all workers directly involved with consumers, irrespective of the size or auspice of their organisation.

Location at the street-level of organisations is highly significant in shaping the nature of social and welfare work. Essentially, the work of street-level bureaucrats is shaped by three sets of relations. Firstly, there are the relations with the managers of the organisation that have responsibility for providing the service and employing the worker. These relations are fundamentally about control. Supervisors, managers, management committees, and regulatory and funding bodies have a strong interest in influencing, and if possible controlling, what happens in the front-line of organisations. They attempt to exercise this control in a variety of direct and indirect ways. Managers are responsible for the quality of services, the efficient use of resources, and organisational effectiveness and survival. They need to establish control of the front-line to achieve these goals.

Street-level bureaucrats have to handle these managerial demands while being cognisant of their second main set of relations those with their co-workers. Front-line workers usually operate as part of a unit, office or department and developing effective relations with other workers is an essential part of the job. Co-workers may all be from the same professional background, such as lawyers in a community legal service. Or, more commonly, the front-line unit may be multi-functional or multi-professional comprising individuals from a range of occupations and professions. Negotiating roles, boundaries and working relations with co-workers and establishing and maintaining sound interpersonal relationships with them are inherent elements of front-line work.

The third set of key relations are with the consumers of the organisation. It is these relations that most sharply distinguish street-level workers from other organisational participants. Street-level work is characterised by the immediacy of the interaction with consumers, and the direct impact of the worker's actions and decisions on people's lives. Street-level workers, unlike managers and other organisational members, have to deal daily, as part of their regular routine, with consumers' personal responses to their actions and to the decisions of the organisation. Because human service organisations are centrally concerned with processing, sustaining, changing or controlling people, these relations are often highly emotionally charged. 'Clients of street-level bureaucracies respond angrily to real or perceived injustices, develop strategies to ingratiate themselves with workers, act grateful and elated or sullen and passive in reaction to street-level bureaucrats' decisions' (Lipsky 1980, p. 9). Front-line work involves dealing with these demands in ways that are fair, sensitive, and manageable.

Social and welfare workers located in the front-line are, therefore, confronted with a highly complex, and typically conflicting, set of relations which they must be able to manage. The demands of management, co-workers and consumers are often conflicting and contradictory. Consumers seek ready access to the organisation's services; management tries to ration resources and control expenditure, co-workers seek to make their work orderly and predictable. Consumers want to be treated as individuals; managers seek productivity increases; co-workers attempt to control their rate of work. Negotiating these diverse pressures is an inherent part of social and welfare work in the front-line.

The strategic importance of the front-line

These pressures are, in large part, a reflection of the strategic importance of the front-line in human service organisations. The front-line is important, firstly, because of its impact on consumers. 'The ways in which street-level bureaucrats deliver benefits and sanctions structure and delimit people's lives and opportunities' (Lipsky 1980, p. 4). Painter points out that 'government for most people is not an experience of democracy in action, but of bureaucracy at work' (1980, p. 265). The ways in which front-line workers operate is of great importance to the relationship of citizens and the state.

It follows that the front-line is often of considerable political significance. The ways in which people are treated in public hospitals, in schools, in prisons and in government departments concerned with human services are regularly, if somewhat haphazardly, subject to public scrutiny. Perceived failings of the front-line to operate appropriately (too generous with social security applicants, too lax on prisoners, too inflexible with public housing tenants, not caring enough about patients, and so on) can lead to political controversy.

The front-line is also of great strategic importance in policy terms. As explained in chapter 1, the actions of street-level bureaucrats collectively constitute the actual policies of governments and organisations. Take the example of child protection. While all state governments have legislation, policy statements, procedures and so forth, setting out their child protection policies, in the final analysis the actual policy is determined by what front-line child protection workers do in their daily work. Similarly in the field of social security, policy in action is determined by counter staffs' interpretations and applications of policy manuals, procedures and legislation. Street-level bureaucrats are policy-makers, whether they are conscious of it or not.

The front-line is also a strategic location organisationally. Street-level bureaucrats are the initiators of organisational activities. By and large, it is they who determine which consumers the organisation will and will not accept, and the nature of the organisation's intervention with that consumer. They also have a high level of control over the information that the organisation obtains about the consumer, and generally on how the consumer is portrayed or constructed within the organisation. The decisions of front-line workers can thus be of great importance in determining the level and pattern of use of organisational resources. Front-line workers play key gate-keeping and rationing roles in human service organisations and systems. They also provide important linkages with organisations in the task environment. The achievement of organisational goals is directly dependent on workers in the front-line.

The autonomy of front-line workers

The strategic importance of the front-line means that there are sustained, ongoing attempts, particularly by management, to control the work of street-level bureaucrats. However, it can be argued that there are considerable obstacles to such attempts. Organisational control of front-line workers is, it can be argued, inherently difficult, and many front-line workers experience a relatively high level of autonomy in their day-to-day work. This statement contradicts the view that social and welfare workers are essentially cogs in a bureaucratic machine with very little autonomy and discretionary freedom. Analysis of the nature of front-line work, and of the control mechanisms available to managers, suggests a more complex picture.

The inherent difficulties in controlling the front-line in human service organisations stem in part from the nature of human service organisations, as discussed in chapter 3. The indeterminate technology of much human service work, including social and welfare work, and the associated lack of clear measures of effectiveness, makes it difficult to specify in unambiguous terms what is expected of front-line workers. Moreover, human service work is often not visible or readily observable. Counselling, for example, usually takes place behind closed doors. Social and welfare workers, together with other human service workers, often stress the confidentiality of their relations with consumers, and of the information they obtain in this relationship.

Furthermore, monitoring human service work can be extremely costly of personnel and time. All this makes managerial control of the front-line problematic (Hasenfeld 1983, pp. 156-157).

Organisational strategies to control front-line workers fall broadly into five categories as shown in Table 8.2 (a different classification of control strategies is provided by Hasenfeld 1983, pp. 166-175). While each of these have considerable potential as control mechanisms for managers, workers need to be aware that they each have significant limitations. The most common form of control is the establishment of standardised operating procedures. This may involve reducing tasks to a series of standard forms, and specifying responsibilities and the order in which tasks are performed. This reduces the decision options of front-line workers, defines the boundaries of their work, minimises discretion, and provides a basis for monitoring worker behaviour. Some degree of standardisation of this kind characterises the front-line of all human service organisations. Virtually all such organisations have standard intake procedures, standard forms for obtaining information from the consumer, and rules and procedures for a range of exigencies. These undoubtedly shape the daily work of the front-line worker. However, as control mechanisms they are imperfect. Procedures are often complied with in token fashion, such as in the nominal filling out of forms. Workers often provide information to justify the decision they wish to make, and the information they provide is difficult for the organisation to verify. Rules proliferate to deal with the great variability of human experience, but the capacity of the organisation to ensure compliance does not necessarily keep pace. As Lipsky points out, 'Rules may actually be an impediment to supervision. They may be so voluminous and contradictory that they can only be invoked or enforced selectively' (1980, p. 14). Competent and experienced workers know that there is usually room to manoeuvre around standardised procedures, rather than being dominated by them.

Another common strategy for controlling the front-line is the monitoring of the more visible or measurable front-line activities. Street-level workers are asked to record the number of consumers they see, the nature of their intervention, the time or money they allocated to each consumer, when they arrived and left work, and so forth. Monitoring exercises of this kind, both spot-checks and ongoing processes, are common in human service organisations, and can serve useful purposes. They are relatively inexpensive for managers, although filling out the forms and data sheets can be extremely time consuming for workers and thus a drain on overall organisational resources. They provide a means of monitoring in general terms the inputs and outputs of front-line workers. As a form of control, however, they are of limited value. The information provided is hard to verify,

Table 8.2 Organisational strategies used by managers to control front-line workers

Control strategy mechanisms	Strengths as control mechanisms	Limitations as control mechanisms
1 Standardising operating procedures e.g. forms, job specialisation and formalisation, scheduling and routing of activities	• reduces decision options • defines limits to work • provides a basis for monitoring worker behaviour • minimises discretion	• procedures can be complied with at a token level only • information provided can be manipulated and is hard to verify • the variability of individual cases
2 Monitoring observable and measurable aspects of activities e.g. caseloads, consumer contacts, use of resources, adherence to work schedules	• relatively inexpensive • defines the limits of activities at a general level	• information is difficult to verify • does not address the content or substance of activities
3 Supervision i.e. influencing and monitoring decisions, attitudes, values and practices	• is viewed as professionally legitimate • deals with content and substance	• expensive of time and personnel • can be manipulated by front-line staff e.g. feigned compliance • supervisors may identify strongly with front-line workers rather than the organisation
4 Performance appraisal linked to rewards and punishments e.g. promotion or dismissal, allocation of pleasant or unpleasant tasks, public approval or disapproval, etc.	• appeals directly to the self-interest of workers • does not require continuous monitoring • often viewed as legitimate by workers	• constrained by organisational personnel practices • effectiveness measures difficult to specify unambiguously • the range of worker motivations
5 Culture control e.g. recruitment, team building, training, etc.	• does not require continuous monitoring - is more subtle, and thus less likely to be resisted, than direct controls	• values and attitudes often change slowly • the official organisational culture has to compete with other sub-cultures

and the more information requested the more likely it is that the data will be of poor quality. This form of monitoring rarely addresses issues of the quality or substance of front-line work. To do so effectively would require extensive investment of organisational resources.

An organisational process familiar to many social and welfare workers is supervision, that is the procedure whereby the actions of front-line workers are carefully and closely scrutinised and reviewed by more senior workers who hold either direct administrative authority or professional authority acknowledged by the organisation. Supervision is often viewed by human service professionals primarily in terms of professional development and personal support. Important though these are, supervisory roles in organisations are typically rather more complex than this. Supervisors, whether or not they hold direct managerial responsibilities, are to some degree viewed by managers as responsible for what occurs in the front-line, that is they are part of the organisational control structure. Supervision should therefore be viewed in large part as a process of influencing and monitoring the decisions, attitudes, values and practices of street-level workers. How effectively it can achieve this purpose depends on a number of factors. Effective supervision is extremely time consuming and many organisations are not able to give it a high priority. Moreover, many supervisors may identify more strongly with their front-line workers than with the organisation, particularly if they share common background experiences or membership of the same professional group. Workers being supervised may or may not carry the precepts learned in supervision sessions into their front-line practice.

Organisations also attempt to control front-line workers via rewards and punishments. Workers are told, and shown, that positive performance appraisal will be rewarded by promotion, allocation of pleasant tasks, and public displays of approval, while those who do not perform satisfactorily will be disciplined or penalised in some ways. This form of organisational control, which has its roots in Taylorism and scientific management, appeals directly to the self-interest of workers. Compliance with organisational expectations is rewarded; non-compliance is not. These forms of control, however, are limited in important ways. The capacity of organisations to reward and punish are limited by factors such as organisational resources, personnel practices, industrial awards and agreements, and so forth. Moreover, the indicators of good performance often contain elements of ambiguity and unpredictability. Most importantly, the rewards and penalties available to the organisation may not be of great significance to front-line workers. The more front-line workers are motivated by factors other than those controlled by the organisation, the greater their opportunities for autonomous practice.

Finally, as discussed in chapter 7, organisations attempt to control front-line workers via the development and use of the dominant organisational culture. Control is exerted indirectly by recruiting workers with the 'right' values, beliefs and ideologies, and by inculcating and reinforcing these values through team building and training activities. This approach has the advantage of being relatively unobtrusive, and not requiring continuing monitoring. However, as we have seen, complex organisations are characterised by competition and conflict among competing cultures, and there are no guarantees that the dominant or official culture will prevail.

In summary, while most organisations go to great lengths to influence and, if possible, control the front-line, they are often thwarted, at least partially, in these efforts. Front-line workers, particularly if they are adept at resisting control, often have the opportunities to function with a significant degree of autonomy. The nature and extent of this autonomy varies considerably from organisation to organisation. However, social and welfare workers, in common with other front-line workers, usually have extensive opportunities for choice and the exercise of discretion in their daily work.

The choices facing front-line workers

The choices that confront street-level bureaucrats fall into six main groups. Street-level bureaucrats must make choices about how they spend their time. While in some organisations the work of street-level bureaucrats is largely predetermined by the organisation, a more typical situation is one where the worker has some discretion over the investment of his or her time or at least can negotiate this issue with the organisation. Workers may have to choose between direct consumer work and developmental or preventive work, between different areas of specialisation, between different ways of doing the job, between different projects, between providing indepth services to a small number of consumers and providing a more superficial service to a larger clientele. These are critical choices. Most human service organisations are labour intensive and staffing costs are the major budget item. What staff actually do in the hours they are employed largely determines the nature of the organisation's work.

Front-line workers are also involved in the exercise of discretionary decision-making. The source of their discretionary authority may be administrative and/or professional. Administrative discretion refers to the process whereby the authority and responsibility to make certain decisions or determinations is delegated to workers at various levels of the organisation, including front-line workers. The exercise of this authority inherently involves critical choices. Rules and regulations, no matter how extensive, never cover all circumstances and situations, and front-line workers are constantly faced with the need to exercise judgement and discretion in relation to specific circumstances and individual situations (Lipsky 1980, pp. 13-16). Professional discretion refs to the claims by a professional group that certain kinds of decisions require the knowledge, skills and judgement possessed only by themselves. Workers who have established such claims are able to resist, to varying degrees, administrative supervision of the decisions they make.

The discretion exercised by social and welfare workers in the front-line is often based on a mixture of administrative and professional authority. The discretionary decisions that they make generally fall into two main categories: regulative and distributive (Schnit 1978). Regulative decisions involve intervention at the level of an individual's freedom or other basic human rights. For example, decisions to recommend removal of a child from a home, or to hospitalise a psychiatrically disturbed person. Distributive decisions involve the allocation of service resources such as nursing home beds, rehabilitation services, social security payments, child-care places, home help, emergency accommodation and so forth. While all such decisions are governed to some degree by rules and procedures, it often falls to social and welfare workers, together with other front-line workers, to interpret and apply the rules to individual cases. Organisational supervision and control of these decisions is quite often limited or ineffective, for the reasons already discussed (Ham and Hill 1984, pp. 148-173).

Choices involving the treatment of consumers are another integral part of street-level work. All workers have to make decisions about their level of respect for consumers: how available they will be? How accommodating, supportive, tolerant and understanding? A fundamental issue is the extent to which consumers are treated as unique individuals with different life experiences, personalities and circumstances, or as 'cases' to be processed by the organisation in certain prescribed ways. This is often a major practice dilemma for workers, whose professional orientation and training strongly emphasises the importance of acknowledging the uniqueness and individuality of consumers, but who experience strong organisational pressures to take part in processes of assessment, classification and categorisation of consumers (Hasenfeld 1983, pp. 191-197). Working through these contradictions is an inherent part of front-line work.

A closely related set of choices for front-line workers concerns the giving or withholding of information. Workers can decide to enhance access for consumers and potential consumers by providing information about services, procedures and 'how the system really works', or they can ration services by minimising the flow of information. Front-line workers also make choices about what information concerning individual consumers to share with the organisation as a whole. This can have a major bearing on a consumer's access to the organisation's services and on the quality of the treatment received.

A further set of choices for front-line workers has been described by Bailey in terms of putting the pressure down or up (1980, pp. 223-227). Putting the pressure down involves regulating consumer demand on behalf of the organisation. Putting the pressure up means persistently and consistently working to improve the responsiveness of the organisation to consumer needs. This may involve advocacy on behalf of individual consumers and engaging in organisational change activities. It may also involve supporting, collaborating with, or directly participating in political activities external to the organisation.

Finally, front-line workers need to make choices about the boundaries of their commitment to and involvement in their work. Tomlinson points out that a high level of commitment to consumers can lead to high levels of family stress, loss of career prospects and employment, and even, in some circumstances, loss of personal freedom (1982, pp. 2-4). Social and welfare workers in the front-line have to make choices between their personal aspirations and their public commitments. Reconciling personal goals, organisational demands and responsibilities towards consumers and co-workers are ongoing complexities for those working in front-line positions.

These choices facing front-line workers are complex, involving a mix of ethical, strategic and personal considerations. From a professional perspective, it could be argued that a worker should always act in the consumer's best interests, should always exercise discretion in the consumer's favour, should always treat the consumer as unique and individual, should always provide full information to the consumer, should always put the pressure up, and should, if need be, sacrifice their own well-being in favour of consumers. However, the evidence suggests that, in reality, social workers and other front-line workers rarely act in this way. Studies of the actual practices of front-line workers show, rather pessimistically, that the ideals that many street-level bureaucrats bring to their work are stifled by the pressures that they face on the job. Most workers tend to develop practices to enable them to cope with the demands of their work. This may involve developing methods of processing people in relatively routine or stereotyped ways, lowering expectations of themselves and their consumers, and developing survival mechanisms (Ham and Hill 1984, pp. 136-142). Lipsky summarises the research as follows:

> Ideally, and by training, street-level bureaucrats respond to the individual needs or characteristics of the people they serve or confront. In practice, they must deal with clients on a mass basis, since work requirements prohibit individualized service . . . At best, street-level bureaucrats invent benign modes of mass processing that more or less permit them to deal with the public fairly, appropriately, and successfully. At worst, they give in to favouritism, stereotyping, and routinizing—all of which serve private or agency purposes (1980, p. xii).

These conclusions, even if only partially applicable, present a major challenge to social and welfare work, and indeed to all occupational groups located in the front-line of human service organisations. They suggest that front-line workers experience pressures to use their considerable autonomy largely in their own interests, rather than in the interests of consumers. If this is the case, what is needed is an understanding of the factors that lead front-line workers to substitute personal survival goals for service goals, despite their ideals and professional training. If these factors are understood it may be possible to develop skills and strategies to deal with them, to maximise the likelihood of service provision that is responsive to consumer needs.

The constraints on front-line work

It has been suggested that the circumstances of front-line workers can be understood in terms of the Marxist dictum, 'Man [sic] makes his own history, even though he does not do so under conditions of his own choosing' (Ham and Hill 1984, p. 139). Social and welfare workers and other human service workers in the front-line have, as we have seen, considerable opportunities for autonomous action, and wide areas of choice on how they approach their work. However, these are certainly not open-ended choices. On the contrary, they are choices that are made under significant constraints. Workers who wish to provide a consumer-oriented service need to be aware of these constraints and to be prepared to deal with them. Four broad types of constraints can be identified.

The first set of constraints are those arising from heavy workloads and limited resources. Social and welfare workers often feel overworked and feel that they have inadequate resources to perform well the tasks confronting them. They complain of lack of time, excessively high caseloads, and inadequate material resources— equipment, facilities and specialised staff—to do a good job. While the extent of under-resourcing varies, there are sound reasons for viewing lack of resources as an intrinsic part of front-line work in publicly provided human services. The lack of clear cut, measurable outcomes, and the public perception that human services are unproductive, makes them vulnerable to cost-cutting in difficult economic circumstances. Moreover, there is almost always a large reservoir of demand for services. Employing more social and welfare workers, or other human service workers, often simply results in more services being provided to more people—caseloads do not necessarily come down. Improvements in the quality or accessibility of services also typically leads to greater public demand for the service. Lipsky suggests that front-line workers are often 'trapped in a cycle of mediocrity' (1980, p. 38). The more resources they have, and the better the service they provide, the greater the demands on them, and the more difficult it becomes to do the job well.

Other constraints arise from the requirements of the organisation. Front-line workers spend considerable amounts of their time recording their decisions, writing casenotes, and generally meeting a wide range of organisational demands for information about their activities. Paperwork is a major part of the daily life of most social and welfare workers in the front-line. Record keeping is important for accountability both to the public and to consumers. However, much of the information demanded of front-line workers may also reflect managers' attempts to monitor and control workers or, not infrequently, may serve no apparent purpose. Other organisational requirements relate to adherence to defined processes and routines. Many workers experience their workplace as a factory engaged in processing people, with little opportunity for the exercise of judgement and creativity (Fabricant 1985).

Constraints on front-line workers also arise from the alienating nature of much front-line work in human service organisations. Many workers in the front-line experience considerable doubt about the value and meaning of their work (Rein and White 1981). This stems partly from the characteristics of human service organisations discussed in chapter 3. Conflicting and ambiguous organisational goals result in unclear and contradictory expectations of front-line workers, which must be dealt with daily on the job. Unclear technologies and lack of definitive measures of effectiveness often mean that social and welfare workers are unclear about their role and their effectiveness. Lack of control over the factors shaping the lives of consumers and inability to deal with the root causes of social and personal problems are further sources of frustration. Relations with consumers, while sometimes meaningful and positive, are often characterised by disagreement, conflict and, on occasions, physical violence. Consumers of street-level bureaucrats are usually, to varying degrees, non-voluntary; they seek the services that the organisation provides because they are required to or because there is no viable alternative.

Finally, constraints arise from the conflicting interests that exist within the organisation, and from what was described in chapter 2 as the organisation's constitutional norms, that is the understood limits of legitimate organisational activity. In structuring their roles and activities, workers have to take into account the values and interests of other organisational actors and groups. They are also limited by the prevailing understandings of what can legitimately be done by or through the organisation. These understandings, interpreted and enforced by managers in the organisation, reflect the structural constraints operating on the organisation as a whole. Their actions as front-line workers take place in the context of the relations between the organisation and its environment, including the broader society.

Actions that are perceived to go beyond, or to threaten, these relations are likely, if detected, to result in censure from the organisation. Front-line workers, it might be argued, are faced not with the daily exercise of control, but with the ever-present threat of control if their actions transgress perceived norms.

The practice of street-level bureaucracy

Social and welfare workers need to develop skills and strategies to enhance their competence as front-line workers. Seven strategies to enhance effective front-line work are listed in Table 8.3 and discussed below.

Table 8.3 Strategies for effective front-line work

1 Carefully assess your level of autonomy and constraint

2 Develop your political base and skills

3 Use your professionalism strategically

4 Use your industrial base strategically

5 Take care of yourself

6 Think organisationally

7 Develop a personal organisational plan

Assessing autonomy and constraint

The fundamental skill needed by social and welfare workers operating in the front-line is that of accurately appraising their organisational location. By this we mean that they must be able to analyse the autonomy and constraint intrinsic to their position, and thus the actual and potential power, authority and influence that they have in the organisation. The theory of front-line work, as well as other material that we have examined, indicates that the opportunities and constraints facing street-level bureaucrats are considerably more complex than is suggested by examination of an organisation chart or a formal job description. A more detailed analysis using the ideas presented in the first part of this chapter is required. This should not be a one-off activity undertaken at one point in time. Rather, it is an ongoing task, involving continuous reappraisal in the light of the worker's organisational experiences. In Table 8.4 we outline a series of questions, based on our discussion of the nature of front-line work, that can be used by workers to examine and review their organisational location.

Table 8.4 A framework for analysing organisational location for front-line workers

---

1　What expectations and/or demands are placed on me in my work by:
　a　managers and supervisors?
　b　co-workers?
　c　consumers?

2　How significant and strategic is my work in the front-line in the context of the organisation as a whole? Specifically:
　a　What is my impact on consumers?
　b　What is the political significance to the organisation of my work?
　c　What is my role in the policy-making process?
　d　What is my role in initiating organisational 1activities?
　e　What is my role in the flow of information within the organisation?
　f　What part do I play in gatekeeping, rationing and, generally, the allocation of organisational resources?
　g　Do I provide important linkages to organisations in the task environment?

3　How much autonomy from the organisation do I actually have in my day-to-day work? How effective are the following forms of organisational control:
　a　standardised operating procedures?
　b　monitoring?
　c　supervision?
　d　rewards and punishments?
　e　the dominant organisational culture?

4　What are the key choices that I can or must make in my day-to-day work?
　a　How to spend my own time?
　b　How to make discretionary decisions?
　c　How to treat consumers?
　d　Whether to give or withhold information?
　e　Whether to put pressure up or down?
　f　What the boundaries of my commitment to my work will be?

5　What are the major constraints on me as a front-line worker?
　a　Heavy workloads and limited resources?
　b　Organisational requirements?
　c　The alienating nature of the work?
　d　Conflicting interests within the organisation?
　e　The organisation's 'constitutional norms' i.e. the understood and enforced limits of legitimate organisational activity?

6　What are the overall implications of this analysis for my actual and potential power, authority and influence as a worker?

Developing a political base and skills

For many workers, the key to effective and personally rewarding practice in the front-line lies in maximising their level of autonomy within the organisation. This does not imply an isolationist stance.

Rather, maximising autonomy means establishing the conditions under which workers, individually or collectively, can have as high a level of control as is possible and desirable over the key choices that they face in their daily work. Pruger refers to this as 'nurturing the scope and consciousness of discretionary behaviour' (1973, p. 28). The social and welfare work literature has paid limited attention to this issue. Workers often attempt to deal with this issue simply by asserting the desirability of professional autonomy. However, this is likely to be an inadequate response due to the strategic importance of front-line work, and the ongoing attempts by management and other groups within the organisation to control and influence workers. If workers in the front-line are to exercise choice in their daily work, they need to know how to enhance their autonomy within the organisation.

Enhancing and protecting autonomy involves developing a strong political base within the organisation. This political base is not only important in developing autonomy, but is also a cornerstone of organisational change activities. The underlying determinants of the political power and influence of groups and individuals in organisations were outlined in chapter 2 in the discussion of the political economy perspective. It was argued that the power and influence of an individual or group within an organisation rests on their structural position or function and on their political skills viewed in the context of the authority and control structure of the organisation. Building on that discussion, and on our analysis of the nature of street-level bureaucracy, we can identify five broad approaches to building a political base in the front-line of human service organisations.

The political power and influence of a worker or group of workers in the front-line is closely related to their legitimacy, that is to the credibility or standing that they have inside and outside the organisation. Legitimacy stems from a number of factors including the prestige of the profession or occupation the workers belong to, their perceived competence and track record, personal prestige, and the clarity of the workers' mandate to perform organisational tasks and responsibilities. Developing legitimacy within the organisation is a key approach to developing a sound political base. Jansson and Simmons (1986, pp. 340-341) outline five broad credibility-enhancing strategies. 'Mission-relevant strategies' involve developing services and activities that are supportive of broader organisational goals and objectives, or presenting existing activities as contributing to such goals and objectives. 'Logistical strategies' involve developing activities that contribute to the solving of organisational problems, or of raising awareness of the significance for the organisation of existing activities. Segal (1970), for example, shows how hospital social work units can gain credibility and autonomy through playing a significant role in hospital planning processes. 'Diplomacy strategies' involve contributing to the organisation's relations with its task environment, by addressing issues or concerns relevant to outside organisations. 'Networking strategies' involve the cultivation of formal and informal linkages with individuals and groups elsewhere in the organisation, thereby gaining greater standing. 'Image strategies' seek to enhance the impression held of workers by significant groups throughout the organisation. In these ways, individuals and groups in the front-line can maximise their credibility, and thereby their political base and autonomy.

Political standing is also closely linked to access to and control of organisational resources. As we have seen, workers in the front-line often play significant roles in the allocation of organisational resources. Workers should be aware of the considerable strategic importance of this role and its potential as a political lever. It is also important for front-line workers to determinedly seek to obtain the resources that they need to do their job well. This may involve seeking extra staff, more travel funds, better facilities, and improved training opportunities. This requires competency in what Jansson and Simmons refer to as 'asking and presenting strategies' (1986, pp. 339-340). They argue that front-line units should be assertive in seeking greater resources, and that such issues as the timing and frequency of the request, the avenues through which the request is made, the amounts sought, and the linking of the request to the unit's mandate are critical. It should be kept in mind that size itself can be an important political resource. A single, isolated worker, or a small work unit, can be more readily ignored in organisational decision-making than a large coalition of workers.

The third political resource needed by front-line workers is organisation. Most political activity in organisations is undertaken in groups or in the name of groups. Social and welfare workers need to be well organised in order to be able to defend and promote issues of concern to them in the organisation. Political organisation involves such matters as leadership, morale, communication, and systems for effective decision-making. Take the case of a group of social and welfare workers operating in isolation in the regional offices of a human service organisation providing rehabilitation services. If they are to be able to take collective action on the organisational issues of concern to them they will need to develop effective means of communicating with one another, and of deciding what their position is on issues. They will need a spokesperson, someone to convene meetings, and, most importantly, a sense of common identity and common purpose. Similarly, multi-disciplinary teams operating in the front-line need to be organised to deal with the demands of the broader organisation (Luntz 1985, p. 20). Professional and industrial associations provide important avenues for political organisation, and are discussed in detail later in the chapter. Establishing a political base also requires sustained attention to network creation and development. This was mentioned earlier as one of the strategies for enhancing legitimacy. However, networks are also important as sources of support, information, co-operation and collaboration. Front-line workers need to take and create opportunities for developing effective relationships with workers from other sections of the organisation, with people in middle and senior management positions, and with people from outside organisations. Conferences, workshops, union and professional meetings, social events, and collaborative work activities all provide valuable opportunities for network development.

Finally, the power and influence of social and welfare workers in the front-line is conditional on their political skills, that is their ability to engage effectively in political relations with other individuals and groups within and outside the organisation. Political skills are acquired gradually, mainly through experience, and an individual's political style and effectiveness are largely shaped by their personality and temperament. However, there is a large body of theoretical and practical material providing instruction in political strategy and technique. For example, the literature on negotiation and bargaining provides workers with valuable guidance on organisational situations involving competition and conflict (Lewicki and Litterer 1985; Scott 1988; Winkler 1984). Some of this material will be examined in chapter 10 when we discuss organisational change.

In summary, if social and welfare workers are to maximise their opportunities to exercise choice in the front-line they need to consciously and strategically develop their political footing in the organisation. This involves paying attention to legitimacy, resources, organisation, networks and political skills. Clearly, there are limits to the political power and influence that any group of front-line workers can acquire. But the challenge for workers is to fully explore, and if possible extend, these boundaries.

Using professionalism strategically

The limits of viewing social and welfare work solely as a professional activity were discussed in chapter 1. The emphasis of this book is on viewing social and welfare work principally as organisational, as well as professional, occupations. However, this is not to discount the importance of professionalism, although the precise nature of professionalism should be debated (Weeks 1988). Professionalism, in so far as it implies commitment to high quality service to consumers, high ethical standards, a concern for accountability, and the development of useful knowledge and skills, represents an important set of aspirations for any occupation. The credibility of social and welfare workers, both generally and in specific organisational settings, is directly linked to their competency and the standard of service they provide.

Our emphasis here, however, is on the strategic use of professionalism in organisations. We argue that the acquisition, maintenance and enhancement of professional status is important politically for workers in their attempts to effectively manage the opportunities and constraints of the front-line. Professional status is a key source of power and influence within organisations. Indeed, Ham and Hill define professionals as 'street-level bureaucrats who have been able to develop special claims to autonomy' (1984, p. 146). Wilding has elaborated the kinds of powers that professions in human services acquire (1982, pp. 19-58). These include power and influence in the policy-making process, the power to define needs and problems, power in resource allocation, power over consumers, and the ability to control their own area of work. Occupations with professional status can counterbalance the demands of administrative authority with their claims for professional authority. For example, workers can claim that certain decisions should be left to them alone on the grounds that they are matters requiring professional judgement. On similar grounds, they can argue for confidentiality in their relations with consumers, for exclusive jurisdiction over certain activities, and for organisational structures to accommodate their professional skills.

The distinctive characteristics of human service organisations makes them especially susceptible to demands by occupations with professional standing. As discussed in chapter 3, organisations rely on professions for legitimacy, and for the skills and knowledge to accomplish organisational tasks. The difficulties of supervision and control of front-line workers, discussed earlier in this chapter, add to dependency on professionals, whom, it is hoped, can be relied on to get the job done without extensive and expensive organisational surveillance. Moreover, many human service organisations have a strong ideology of professionalism, and are dominated by people with a professional background and orientation. In such contexts, professional status is a pathway to organisational power and influence.

The social and welfare work literature sometimes portrays practitioners in organisations as facing a fundamental and dichotomous choice between their professional and organisational allegiances. Green (1966), for example, states that ' . . . when responsible to both a profession and a bureaucracy, the individual finds himself [sic] confronted by two sets of mutually incompatible demands' (p. 71). Probably there are some occasions on which practitioners are faced with clear cut choices of this kind. However, more commonly, workers are called on to make 'continuous and varied adjustments between professional and administrative authority' (Warham 1977, p. 22). What this means in practice is that workers use their professional status to buffer or deflect organisational demands.

Our emphasis on the strategic use of professionalism could be interpreted as running counter to the strong emphasis on deprofessionalisation in some of the Australian social work literature over the last two decades. Professionalism is often associated with elitism, exclusivity, monopoly on skills, and domination of consumers, and it has been argued that there is a need for new forms of professional practice that re-emphasise accountability to consumers (Weeks 1988, pp. 33-36). The issues of accountability to consumers and the power relations between workers and consumers are critically important, and are the central concerns of chapter 9. However, our emphasis here is on viewing the issue of professionalism in a broader context than simply that of worker–client relations. Workers do indeed have more power than consumers in many contexts and this power imbalance must be understood and addressed. But workers may themselves be relatively powerless if they have not developed effective strategies to maximise their autonomy in the front-line. The issue of professional status thus presents social and welfare workers with a paradox. They may need to de-emphasise (or re-interpret) their professionalism in their relations with consumers, while using strategically whatever professional status they have or can muster in their relations with most other organisational participants.

In practical terms, the strategic use of professionalism has a number of elements. Fundamentally, it means supporting and participating in professional associations. It also means creating a professional presence in the workplace through regular meetings, collective action and participation as a professional group in organisational processes. Links and good working relations with other professions are also important, particularly in organisations where much of the work is organised through inter-disciplinary or multi-disciplinary teams.

Use the industrial base strategically

A key resource for street-level workers in negotiating the front-line is their access to membership of industrial associations. Workers employed in the public sector have access to industrial organisations with large memberships, substantial resources, a long history of representing the interests of government employees, and an established and influential role in organisational decision-making. Industrial coverage of workers in the non-government sector is not as well developed. However, the overall trend in the sector appears to be towards increasing unionisation of human service workers.

Membership of industrial organisations is important for front-line workers in a number of ways. Unions, particularly in the public sector of the human services, play a central role in negotiating the working conditions and remuneration of workers. Key issues such as workloads, the physical environment of the workplace, tenure and promotion, and health and safety are primary concerns of trade unions. Many unions have also developed a considerable capacity to research policy issues of concern to their members, and to participate in policy processes and social action. As most unions cover a broad spectrum of workers, union participation also provides significant opportunities for developing links with other groups of workers.

There has been considerable debate over the relative merits of professional and industrial organisation (Galper 1975, pp. 156-189; Lightman 1982). It has been suggested by some that unionisation and professionalisation are incompatible. We support the opposite position, namely that unionisation and professionalisation are complementary forms of organisation, both of which provide workers with resources and opportunities to control and shape the nature of their practice in the front-line.

Take care of yourself

The strategies examined so far have focused on the political relations between front-line workers and the broader organisation. However, it is equally important for workers to consider the personal and psychological aspects of their work. The constraints, demands and ambiguities of front-line work not infrequently lead to low morale, high stress and worker 'burn-out'. Burn-out, a term coined and applied to human service workers since the mid-1970s, refers to the situation in which a worker becomes exhausted and worn out as a consequence of excessive demands on her or his energy, strength and resources. Symptoms of burn-out include anxiety, fatigue, illness, alienation from colleagues and consumers, poor job performance, absenteeism, and problems in the worker's personal life (Zastrow 1984, pp. 141-142). There are no comprehensive studies of the extent of low morale, high stress and burn-out in human service workers in Australia. However, the belief that such circumstances are commonplace is widespread. For example, Crago argues that low morale and high burn-out is endemic and self-perpetuating in many small, non-government, welfare organisations:

> Over and over again, when you talk to [staff]... you will hear the same complaints: . . . the clients are demanding and difficult; the work is exhausting and draining; successes are rare and failures are many; preservice training (if any) was inadequate; funding is insufficient; administrators and management committees fail to understand what it is like 'at the front-line'; the community as a whole does not appreciate the organisation's work. This is how staff explain the fact that workers who started off enthusiastic and dedicated rapidly decline into cynicism, apathy and eventual resignation . . . 'You can only take a year or two of this before you start going crazy', they tell you (1988, p. 32).

The high potential for stress and burn-out for front-line human service workers is undoubted. Workers, individually and collectively, need to develop strategies to deal with the personal demands of the job.

The advice to be found in the literature falls broadly into three categories: general orientations, individual strategies and organisational strategies.

Much of the advice on how to deal with the stresses of the front-line concerns the general orientation that workers have towards their employment. Four main themes can be identified. Firstly, workers are encouraged to have realistic expectations. Zastrow suggests that many people seeking careers in the human services have unrealistic expectations that make them particularly vulnerable to burn-out. These expectations include the beliefs that services will decisively improve the lives of practically all their consumers, that their services will be highly appreciated by their employers and by their consumers, that they will be able to bring about substantial organisational change, and that there will be considerable opportunities for career advancement (1984, p. 146). Crago argues that unrealistic expectations are exacerbated by administrators who lay down unclear and ambiguous goals and expectations: 'Given no realistic goals, (staff) strive for unreachable ones, like the total rehabilitation of their clients' (1988, p. 33).

Relatedly, it is argued that workers need to set limits on their commitment to their work. Front-line staff, it is suggested, 'experience their clients' neediness principally as a challenge to their own capacity to give' (Crago 1988, pp. 33-34). Defining the boundaries of commitment is a difficult issue for all occupations underpinned by a helping or altruistic ethos. Workers need to be able to find a workable balance between their commitments to work, friends, family and themselves.

Front-line workers are also counselled to conserve energy. There are many aspects of organisational life that lead to feelings of frustration, anger, and disappointment. In particular, 'complex organisations are notoriously inefficient distributors of appreciation and recognition' (Pruger 1973, p. 29). Workers often feel that their hard work is unrecognised and unappreciated by colleagues, employers and consumers. While well-managed organisations do provide staff with personal rewards of various kinds, it is helpful to see this as a bonus rather than as a right. 'He [sic] who expects to receive in the bureaucratic milieu the emotional support that is only possible where relationships are intimate is doomed to suffer disappointment' (Pruger 1973, p. 29).

A fourth piece of advice for workers is to develop staying power. The complexity of human service organisations means that things often happen slowly. Moreover, it takes time for a worker, particularly a worker with little or no formal authority, to establish personal credibility and influence. 'Whatever ideas, changes, projects, or other professional aspirations the social worker may have, he [sic] will not be able to realise them unless he stays in the organisation and keeps working for his goals over a sufficient period of time' (Pruger 1973, p. 27). At the same time, it is important to maintain vitality of action and independence of thought, and 'continue to be led by some progressive vision of what the organisation might accomplish' (Pruger 1973, p. 27).

Setting realistic expectations and clear limits, conserving energy and developing staying power are key orientations for workers in the front-line. Individual workers also need to develop personal strategies for handling the tensions and demands of the front-line. Zastrow lists and discusses a range of personal strategies including goal-setting, time management, positive thinking, challenging self-defeating thoughts, relaxation techniques, exercise, outside activities, pleasurable goodies, developing personal support systems and maintaining a sense of humour (1984, pp. 150-154). All workers need to develop a set of activities from such a list as part of their own personal strategy for organisational survival.

While individual workers need to develop their own strategies to deal with stress and burn-out, it must be emphasised that organisations have an underlying responsibility for worker well-being. Burn-out and stress are organisational responsibilities, and it is important for workers to use their industrial and professional associations, and whatever other political resources they can mobilise, to ensure that these responsibilities are taken seriously. While many of the constraints and difficulties of front-line work are inherent in the job (Snook 1984, pp. 19-23), there are many strategies that management can adopt to minimise worker stress. These include reducing case-loads, limiting the hours of highly stressful work, expanding training programmes, improving the work environment, developing social support systems, and promoting variety at work (Zastrow 1984, pp. 148-150). It is also important for management to fully acknowledge the complexities and constraints of front-line work in human service organisations.

Thinking organisationally

Dealing with the pressures of the front-line is aided, we believe, by developing the habit and capacity to think about social and welfare work practice in organisational terms. Partly, this means acknowledging and understanding the perspective on front-line work developed in this chapter, and indeed in the whole book. But, equally importantly, it means re-conceptualising the nature of direct practice to encompass all the work of negotiating the front-line, with service to consumers as the guiding focus. If workers conceptualise the whole set of tasks and responsibilities involved in working in the front-line as direct practice, their capacity to see their work as a whole will be enhanced. The nature and quality of services to consumers are not solely (and often not even primarily) based on social worker–consumer interactions, but rather reflect the operations of the whole front-line and the whole organisation. It therefore makes sense to see everything that social and welfare workers in the front-line do as direct practice.

There are several models in the literature that encompass this view of practice. Weissman, Epstein and Savage in their book *Agency-Based Social Work*, suggest that clinical practice be thought of as comprising ten organisational roles. These are diagnostician, expediter, case manager, colleague, advocate, programme developer, organisational reformer, supervisor, practice researcher, and employee (1983). These roles are essentially those played by front-line workers. A good worker, viewed from this perspective, is a person who practices these skills with a high level of expertise, within a value framework emphasising consumer service.

Another direct practice model with a similar emphasis is provided by Lister (1987, p. 384). He suggests that contemporary direct practice roles can be conceptualised as fourfold:

system development: the worker helps to create organisations and resources to meet the psychosocial needs of consumers;

system maintenance: the worker attempts to maintain and enhance resource systems so that they do not succumb to goal displacement or organisational inertia;

system linkage: the worker links consumers (individuals, families, groups, or community segments) with resources;

direct client intervention: the worker uses clinical skills for intervention with clients.

All models have both weaknesses and strengths, and we do not uncritically endorse the two outlined here. However, we suggest that social and welfare workers who view their front-line activities in terms such as these, are better equipped to address the complexities of practice than those who view direct practice as solely involving direct client intervention.

Developing a personal organisational plan

The pressures and constraints of front-line work can easily divert workers. Workers start off with a particular set of goals and aspirations, but often find that they are shaped by organisational pressures into doing things and being someone not originally intended. The strategies examined in this chapter are intended to assist workers to optimise their level of autonomy over their work, so that they can maximise their achievement of personal and professional goals, and in particular the goal of service to consumers.

If social and welfare workers are to exercise autonomy, control and influence in the front-line, they must have, individually and collectively, a clear sense of purpose and direction in the organisation. Hence, the final strategy that we propose is to develop a personal organisational plan. Workers need to carefully, and regularly, think through what they are trying to do in the organisation, and how they are going to achieve it. Some of the key issues are summarised in Table 8.5. Workers can develop such a plan in a formal way in writing or in a quite informal fashion. The exercise can be conducted individually or collectively, and the frequency with which the issues are examined is a matter of personal choice. However it is done, we strongly suggest that workers attempt to maintain clear purpose in their organisational life. It is easy to lose a sense of direction in human service organisations.

Table 8.5 A framework for developing a personal organisational plan

---

1 What are the broad goals that underpin my work in this organisation? Why am I here?
   a personal (job satisfaction, remuneration, career, etc.)
   b professional (nature and quality of work with consumers, development of skills, experiences, etc.)
   c political and organisational (organisational changes, broader political causes that the work is linked to, etc.)

2 What are the opportunities and constraints associated with my present position in the organisation? What can I do?
   a What level of autonomy do I currently have?
   b What are the major constraints and limitations of the job?
   c How much power, authority and influence do I have?

3 How strong is my political base in the organisation? Can I strengthen it via:
   a legitimation strategies?
   b resource enhancement strategies?
   c political organisation strategies?
   d networking strategies?
   e development of political skills?
   f strategic use of my professionalism and my industrial base?

4 What measures am I taking to ensure that I can cope personally with the demands and stresses of the job?
   a Do I have realistic expectations, have I set limits, do I know how to conserve energy, and have I got staying power?
   b What strategies do I have for looking after myself?
   c What could management do to reduce the stress of my job?

5 Do I conceptualise my work in a way that 'fits' my organisational situation and experiences?

6 In the light of this analysis, what are my specific objectives for the forthcoming period?
   a What are my priorities in terms of these objectives?
   b What activities, tasks or projects need to be initiated or accomplished to achieve these objectives?
   c What implementation difficulties do I foresee and how will I deal with them?
   d When, and how often, will I review my plan, and how will I evaluate progress towards the achievement of my objectives?

Conclusions

Social and welfare workers are typically located in the front-line of human service organisations. They are street-level bureaucrats. This location is highly significant in shaping the nature of their work. It means that the nature of practice is directly shaped by three sets of relations: those with managers, those with colleagues and those with consumers. Managing and negotiating this complex, and often conflicting, set of relations is a central and inherent part of social and welfare work roles.

The front-line in human service organisations is of considerable strategic importance. Front-line workers have a major impact on the nature and quality of services to consumers. Their work is of considerable political and policy significance. Organisationally, front-line workers initiate much organisational activity, play a central role in information flow and dissemination, are important gatekeepers, and provide linkages with other organisations.

Many front-line workers experience a relatively high level of autonomy in their day-to-day work. This is because of the inherent difficulties that organisations have in exercising effective control over them. Organisations make many attempts to control the activities of front-line workers via standard operating procedures, monitoring, supervision, rewards and punishment, and the dominant organisational culture. However, all of these measures have drawbacks and limitations as control mechanisms. Social and welfare workers, like many other front-line workers, often have extensive opportunities for choice in their daily work. Key areas of choices include how to spend their time, what decisions to make within areas of discretion, how to treat consumers, whether to give or withhold information, whether to put pressure up or down, and the boundaries of commitment to work.

Several studies suggest, rather pessimistically, that front-line workers tend to use their considerable autonomy in their own interests, rather than in the interests of consumers. This is largely because of the considerable pressures and constraints on front-line workers: heavy workloads and limited resources, the alienating nature of the work, conflicting interests in the organisation, and the 'understood' and enforced limits of legitimate organisational activity. If front-line workers, and in particular social and welfare workers, are to give high priority to consumer service, while at the same time respecting their own needs, a range of skills and strategies is needed. These include carefully assessing the level of autonomy and constraint, developing a political base, using professionalism and the industrial base strategically, taking care of one's self, thinking organisationally, and developing a personal organisational plan.

Front-line work is fraught with paradox and contradiction. Street-level workers are low in organisational hierarchies, yet often function with high levels of autonomy in their daily work. They need to deal with the conflicting demands of the organisation, of consumers, of colleagues, and of their own personal needs. They have many choices to make, but the circumstances in which these choices are made impose considerable constraints. Workers must attempt to enhance their autonomy within the organisation, through strategies designed to increase their power, authority and influence. They must then use their political resources, not simply in their own interests, but rather to enhance organisational responsiveness to consumers. Awareness of these paradoxes and tensions, acknowledgement of their complexity, and the development of the necessary skills and strategies to handle them, are the foundations for effective front-line work.

Chapter review questions

1 What is meant by a 'front-line organisation'?
2 What is a 'street-level bureaucrat'?
3 In what ways does location in the front-line of human service organisations influence the nature of social and welfare work?
4 Why is the front-line a strategically important location in human service organisations?
5 Why is it often difficult for organisations to control what happens in their front-line?
6 What strategies do organisations use to impose control over front-line workers, and what are the strengths and weaknesses of these strategies?
7 What are the key choices that front-line workers make in their day-to-day work?
8 To what extent do front-line workers, including social and welfare workers, put personal survival goals above service to consumers?
9 What are the major constraints on front-line workers?
10 What are the major strategies that front-line workers can adopt to enhance their competence as front-line workers?
11 What are the major approaches to building a political base in the front-line of human service organisations?
12 Is the strategic use of professionalism consistent with social and welfare work values?
13 Are industrial and professional modes of organisation complementary or in conflict with one another?
14 What do you consider to be the most important strategies for workers and employers in reducing the stress of front-line workers, and avoiding 'burn-out'?
15 How do you conceptualise the nature of 'direct practice'?
16 What are the key elements of a personal organisational plan?

Further reading

The major elaboration of street-level bureaucracy is Lipsky (1980). Ham and Hill (1984, pp. 136-142) provide a useful, brief summary and critique of the concept; and Smith (1979, pp. 34-39) briefly outlines the concept of a front-line organisation. Hasenfeld (1983, pp. 166-175) provides an excellent account of the strategies that organisations use in their attempts to control the front-line. Pruger (1973) is a source of good advice on how to survive and work effectively in the front-line. Jansson and Simmons (1986) suggest a range of political strategies for social work units in host organisations. Much of their material is directly relevant to front-line workers. Wilding (1982) provides a critical account of the place of professions in human services. His material on the nature of professional power (pp. 19-58) is especially pertinent. The issues raised by the 'deprofessionalisation' debate in Australia are well covered in Weeks (1988). Lightman (1982) presents interesting material on the attitudes of social workers to unions and professional associations. Zastrow (1984) is a good overview of strategies to prevent burn-out. Crago (1988) outlines graphically the problems of burn-out and stress in non-government human service organisations. Snook (1984) argues for a structural, as well as a social psychological, understanding of burn-out. Weissman, Epstein and Savage (1983) and Lister (1987) provide conceptualisations of 'direct practice' that encompass the range of roles, tasks and skills required to practice effectively in the front-line.

Case study

'ONCE MORE INTO THE BREACH': A DAY IN THE LIFE OF A FRONT-LINE WORKER[1]

You are a child protection officer (CPO) located at the Fernbrook office of the Department of Family and Community Services. Fernbrook is a provincial city and the office services the city and surrounding rural hinterland. The Department has statutory responsibilities for child protection involving both control and care functions, and, as a CPO, you have been delegated responsibilities for these matters. You report to a senior CPO who acts as supervisor to members of your team. CPOs have a background in social work, community welfare and psychology.

---

1 This case differs from the others in this book in that it presents a series of tasks and demands experienced by a worker in the course of a 'typical' day, and asks how the worker can best organise his or her work in response to these pressures. The case can be analysed, answered and discussed

Under the leadership of its current Minister, the Department has also expanded its functions to include a community services development role. The Minister has stressed the partnership between the Department and community being forged by his new policy initiative. The responsibility for undertaking community services development and for liaison with non-government organisations has been passed onto CPOs. The Department makes significant financial allocations to community organisations for such services as neighbourhood centres, homemaker programmes, parent effectiveness training, supported and crisis accommodation and emergency relief. CPOs often represent the Department on the management committees of community organisations, as well as providing advice on departmental policies and programmes, assisting with submission writing, and similar tasks. These community service development functions have been added to the statutory child protection work without increases in staff or funding. This has created a great deal of organisational tension.

A recent delegation to the Minister by the staff representatives from the Professional Officer's Association complained of 'enormous case loads', 'worker burn-out' and the 'inordinate stress that staff are experiencing in carrying out these wide ranging functions'. The association also pointed out that CPOs were recruited on the basis of their interpersonal helping skills, and that community services development was a specialised area demanding special skills and training. One outcome of the meeting was that the Director of the Department issued a directive that 'Officers of the Department are to attend to their statutory responsibilities (that is, child protection matters) as a priority in all departmental operations'. Some of your colleagues have taken this directive literally, and have withdrawn from all involvement with local community organisations. This has led to a great deal of anger and resentment from many community organisations who took seriously the Department's publicly stated policy of 'constructing a partnership with the non-government sector to respond to community needs'.

Your own experience as a CPO has confirmed for you that in an area like Fernbrook, community-based programmes are of great importance. Without them many people simply would not obtain many essential services and supports. Without the co-operation and assistance of these community organisations, many of the children and families that the Department works with in its statutory role would require far more intensive support from front-line workers like yourself.

---

in the same way as the other cases. However, to add to the real-life nature of the case, we have also provided, at the end of the case, a section entitled 'information not known by the worker'. This material can be used selectively by the convenor of the group discussing the case to add to its 'dynamic' nature, that is the convenor can indicate, in response to various suggestions made by the class, that if a certain choice was made, certain consequences follow. Convenors may like to construct alternative or additional scenarios of their own. This would be particularly useful if they suspect that those analysing the case fail to heed our instruction that the section on 'information not known by the worker' should not be read by those analysing the case prior to answering the key question.

You have just arrived at work on a Monday morning at 9.00 a.m. Outlined below are a number of tasks and circumstances that face you at different times in the course of the morning.

9.00 a.m.
This is your first day in the office since last Wednesday. On Thursday and Friday of last week you were out on a country visiting programme in rural areas of the region. You have brought some of your reports on your visit up-to-date during the weekend, but you still need to write a report regarding Fred Smith, aged fourteen. There have been concerns in the past that Fred is neglected and abused by his parents, with whom he lives. The local school is concerned that Fred's family, who are farmers, are treating Fred like an unpaid worker on the farm, and that his schooling is being neglected. You visited his teacher on this trip, and told that Fred is out mustering cattle at dawn and begins work again as soon as school is finished. He is frequently absent from school, and when he attends he is often so tired that he falls asleep at his desk.

On your visit to the family Fred seemed to be a relatively happy child, if somewhat apprehensive. He seems uninterested in school. Fred's father is very angry and obviously resents your visit, calling you 'a bloody snooper from the welfare, sitting pretty with a government car on fat wages, while ordinary people have to struggle just to keep themselves together'. You must write this case report as soon as possible, and decide what action to take (Task 1).

9.05 a.m.
On your desk are a number of telephone messages and notes:
• 'Friday 10.00 a.m.—Please ring me before 9.30 a.m. Monday—urgent—Father Flynn, St Mary's Church' (Task 2).
• 'Friday 4.35 p.m.—I need to see you first thing Monday morning—please come straight to my office—Mary (Supervising CPO)' (Task 3).
• 'Don't forget Monday's meeting at 9.30 a.m.—Kathleen' (This refers to your membership of a group set up by yourself and Kathleen, one of your less experienced co-workers. The group are attempting to set up a local community centre. A submission has been written. It must go to the Department this week. You have missed the last two meetings of the group) (Task 4).

You open your diary. In addition to the 9.30 a.m. meeting, you have an appointment at 11.30 a.m. to appear in the Children's Court to provide a pre-sentence report on Fiorenza Bugatti, aged fifteen. 'Fio' has been before the Court on previous occasions for a range of offences and is currently living with her mother under the supervision of the Department. You have been her CPO for the last six months. Recently, she has been convicted of shoplifting and under-age drinking. The last time she appeared in Court, the magistrate warned her that if she appeared again she might be removed from home and placed in an institution. You spoke to Fio and her mother early last week and have prepared the draft of a pre-sentence report recommending probation.

You feel strongly that she should not be committed to an institution. However, you need to do some final work on the report prior to the Court hearing. Ideally, you would spend one to two hours on this task. The Court hearing itself may take between half an hour and two hours, and because of the pressure of other Court business it does not always start at the designated time (Task 5).

2.00 p.m.
You are due to attend a meeting of the Management Committee of the Fernbrook Family Support Group at 2.00 p.m. Because of your morning commitments you are running late. On your way to the meeting, you grabbed a sandwich and a milkshake and consumed them while driving, spilling crumbs all over the seat of the government car and chocolate milk down the front of your clothes.

The meeting fails to get down to business. You want them to put a submission into the Department under the 'Community Welfare Subsidy Scheme' which would allow the group to get a full-time worker. The tasks undertaken by the group are now so numerous and complex that a full-time worker is urgently needed. You have raised this idea on a number of occasions. It has been firmly resisted by the Chairperson, Mrs Warmington, and about half of the other members of the committee, on the grounds that the group should remain voluntary. Mrs Warmington is a key figure, and her energy and commitment have been vital to the group. You know from your Regional Manager that funding is available, and that the Minister is supportive. But the submission must be in by the end of the month. Unfortunately, at the last minute, Mrs Warmington is not able to attend the meeting, and sends her apologies. A committee member who supports applying for funds suggests that the meeting proceed without her, due to the urgency of the issue. It appears that a majority of people at the meeting support putting in an application. A minority feel that the meeting should be postponed to another time, when Mrs Warmington can attend. People look to you to provide some leadership (Task 6).

4.50 p.m.
You are back at the office. On your desk is a message from an ex-client asking you to ring him urgently, before you go home. Ross is a young man who had lots of problems but seemed to be able to sort them out recently. Last time you saw him he had a girlfriend, a job, and an old station wagon full of rust. You were his CPO, but as he turned eighteen three months ago, he is no longer in the care of the Department (Task 7).

It is also your wedding anniversary and you have planned to stop by the shops on your way home to buy a present for your spouse. A celebratory dinner party has been planned by your family for that evening. The shops close at 5.15 p.m. (Task 8).

The phone rings. It is Sheila, the union representative. She says, ' I'm just ringing to remind you about the branch meeting tonight. It's really important that as many CPOs as possible attend. We have arranged a meeting with the Director and the Minister for next week. We need you all to endorse the claim for more staff. If we can demonstrate solidarity we think we can get at least two new CPO positions for the Fernbrook Office.' The meeting had completely slipped your mind (Task 9).

Key question

Outline your schedule and priority of work for the day, including the choices you would make in relation to each tasks needing to be done. Provide a rationale for your overall plans and for each of the choices you make. What does analysis of this case illustrate about the nature of front-line work in human services organisations, and the practice strategies needed for effective functioning in the front-line?

Case discussion points

1 What does the case suggest about the strategic importance of front-line work?
2 What level of power, authority and influence does the front-line worker in the case have?
3 How effectively can the organisation control the activities of the worker? How much autonomy does the worker have?
4 What is the nature of the choices that the worker in the case has to make?
5 What are the major constraints on the worker in the case?
6 What could the worker do to strengthen his or her political base in the organisation?
7 What strategic use could the worker make of his or her professionalism and industrial base?
8 What measures should the worker take to cope with the demands and stresses of the job?
9 Given the opportunities and constraints on the front line worker in this case, whose interests is he or she likely to put first, those of the organisation, the consumer, or herself/himself? Whose interest should the worker put first?

Information not known by the worker in the case
The following information can be used in discussion of the case, at the discretion of the convenor. *It is essential that people working on the case study do not read this section prior to analysing the case.*

Task 1
If you go ahead and write up your case notes straightaway, you fail to find out any of the information stemming from the messages waiting for you. But if you do not do it straightaway, when will it be done? Can you fit it in later in the day, or will it wait until a 'quieter day'?

Task 2

If you ring Father Flynn straightaway the message is either Father Flynn has heard you are a qualified umpire in volleyball, and he is wondering whether you would be available to umpire the inter-school final tonight at 7.00 p.m.? (What will you say?) Or Father Flynn has heard of Fio's forthcoming Court appearance. He is ringing to offer a personal character reference and to provide some important insights into the problems Fio has been having recently. This information could be central to your Court report (What will you do with this information?)

Task 3

If you decide to see Mary straightaway she tells you one or both of the following messages: she is concerned about the amount of time that CPOs are spending on community service work given the recent directive. She suggests that you, 'Don't waste your time on all this community activity, as your first priority must be the children and families in your case load. If you still have time left after doing that, then by all means do some community work.' And/or Mr Smith (Fred's father) has rung his local member of parliament and complained that the Department is harassing his family. The Minister has been contacted and the Director wants to know what happened. 'Where is your written report and what is your recommendation regarding Fred? The Director has asked for a report to be on her desk by noon today. She may wish to see you personally later in the day.'

Task 4

Will you go to the meeting or send your apologies? What you do not know, because you missed the last two meetings, is that a delegation has been set up to meet with your Minister on Thursday to discuss the submission for the community centre. Kathleen's inexperience means that the draft submission has a number of important mistakes. If you do not go to the meeting you will lose the opportunity to work with the group to improve the submission. Kathleen will also be annoyed at your lack of personal support for her. But have you the time to attend the meeting?

Task 5

Either you spend most of the morning working on your report for the Court. But despite this the magistrate has absolutely no sympathy for Fio (he comes from a family of shopkeepers). He listens to your pre-sentence report and says, 'It amazes me that some of you welfare workers are not much older than the people you claim to report on. What are your professional qualifications exactly, and what experience do you have in this field to make such sweeping assertions regarding the child before the Court?' Or you decided not to spend much time on the report. Fortunately you had rung Father Flynn, and his testimony made all the difference and Fio was able to remain living with her mother.

Task 6

Do you go ahead with the meeting or not? Do you try to use Mrs Warmington's absence to achieve your goal? If you don't go ahead, there may not be time to convene another meeting and get the submission in on time. How many activities have you postponed today already? If you do go ahead you will be accused of attempting to 'railroad' the meeting simply because Mrs Warmington is unwell and unable to be present. If the meeting finishes early there may be opportunities to deal with the other tasks waiting for you.

Task 7

If you phone Ross, he tells you that his girlfriend has left him. He says to you, 'Life just isn't worth living any more. You are the only person who has ever really cared for me. I just don't know what to do. I have got to see you now. I feel confused. Tomorrow won't do. It must be now.' If you don't phone Ross, you find out tomorrow that he is in hospital following an attempted overdose. Alternatively, you might meet him on the street next morning and he will say, 'Yeah, I was a bit pissed and just needed someone to lean on. I'm all right now'.

Task 8

Whether or not you meet Ross makes no difference to your anniversary, because you have forgotten that the local shops close early today. It will have to be chocolates from the local shops. You know you are in trouble.

Task 9

If you go to a union meeting on your wedding anniversary the consequences are unpredictable. If you go home, the meeting is in danger of collapsing because they need one more person for a quorum. In the middle of your dinner party, the phone rings. Sheila asks, 'We desperately need one more for a quorum. Can you come just for a few minutes so that we can get the meeting started?' When you return from the phone your spouse begins to talk about the need for you both to have a serious talk about your relationship.

9

Responding to consumer needs in organisations

The aim is not merely to please the recipients of public services (difficult and worthy though that may be) but to empower them (Pollitt 1988, p. 86).

All human service organisations lay claim to being primarily concerned with the needs of their consumers. Human services managers routinely make declarations such as 'our clients are the reason we exist' and 'the bottom line of management improvement . . . is to provide the best possible services to our clients as quickly and directly as possible' (Volker 1987, p. 192). Many human service workers also assert their commitment to consumers. For social and welfare workers in particular, the centrality of consumer interests is a key principle.

For these reasons, analysis of the relations between consumers and human service organisations, and of the ways in which these relations can be improved from the consumer's perspective, are vital concerns. Consumer issues have been addressed throughout the earlier chapters of this book. We have examined the pivotal role of organisation–consumer relations in human service organisations (chapter 3), the significance of consumer organisations in the task environment (chapter 4), ways of involving consumers in goal processes (chapter 5), ways of using structures to promote consumer interests (chapter 6), relating to consumer cultures (chapter 7) and the dilemmas faced by front-line workers in providing services to consumers (chapter 8). However, these themes need to be drawn together. It is important to examine what it means to be a consumer of a human service organisation, the politics of consumer–organisation relations, the processes involved in organisation–consumer relations and the range of strategies available to enhance responsiveness to consumer needs. These are the issues dealt with in this chapter.

The relations between human service organisations and consumers are often contradictory. On the one hand, there are the claims by managers, professionals and other workers that the needs of consumers are paramount. But on the other hand, there are the experiences of workers and consumers alike that organisations rarely work like this, and that consumers have to compete and conflict with other interest groups, with other policy goals, and often with one another, to get what they want. Levels of consumer satisfaction, while variable, are often reported as quite low. For example, the much quoted Report of the Commission of Inquiry into Poverty, published in 1975, reported the following findings on user experiences of welfare services:

- often people did not know about or understand the services;
- the services were often unavailable, inaccessible, or could not meet all the demands made on them;
- people often avoided using the services because it was too difficult or degrading to do so;
- when people did use services they often did not find them helpful or effective in dealing promptly with their needs (Australia, Commission of Inquiry into Poverty 1975, p. 93).

Not all studies of consumer attitudes to community welfare services present such a dismal picture (Martin 1986). Undoubtedly, considerable numbers of consumers are satisfied to some degree with what they get. Nevertheless, the gap between rhetoric and performance in service provision to consumers is a feature of most human service organisations and a common source of frustration and disappointment for human service workers.

If social and welfare workers are to participate effectively in attempts to bridge this gap and make services more responsive to consumers, an organisational analysis and perspective is essential. This, firstly, means acknowledging that the issue of responsiveness to consumers cannot be viewed solely in terms of the worker–client relationship. Social and welfare work has stressed the principle of 'client self-determination' as a means of upholding and protecting the preferences and needs of the consumer. However, self-determination is limited by many factors, particularly the constraints on both worker and consumer arising from the organisational context (Rothman 1989). Organisations structure relations between consumers and workers by imposing boundaries on the range of issues covered by the interaction, the kinds of information that can be processed, the range of alternatives available to workers and consumers, and the ways in which decisions are to be made (Hasenfeld 1987, p. 471). While these boundaries are not fixed, their influence on both workers and consumers is pervasive. Workers need to conceptualise their relations with consumers in organisational terms and not simply in terms of a professional relationship.

An organisational analysis means seeking organisational explanations for lack of responsiveness to consumers and developing organisational strategies to address the issue. The perspectives on organisational analysis discussed in chapter 2 provide a number of different ways of attempting to understand organisation–consumer relations. From the standpoint of scientific management, the problems of lack of responsiveness to consumers stem primarily from inefficiencies of the organisational machine. Solutions lie in designing better systems for processing the organisation's human raw materials. From a human relations standpoint, the issues are essentially interpersonal and measures need to be found to promote better understanding, tolerance and respect between members of the organisation and the public who uses their services. Systems perspectives stress the interdependency of consumers and organisations. Organisations need a steady supply of consumers that can be successfully 'treated', while consumers need the services the organisation offers. The satisfaction of these mutual needs, within the broader context of the organisation's role in the broader social system, define and shape organisation–consumer relations. Market perspectives treat organisation–consumer relations essentially as transactions between buyers and sellers. Neo-Marxian perspectives suggest that relations with consumers can only be understood in terms of the role of human service organisations in a capitalist society and economy. Responding to consumer needs, from this perspective, is an entirely secondary consideration, as so-called human service organisations are essentially concerned with political and economic functions such as the legitimation of the existing order, the maintenance of order and control, and the reinforcement of dominant values. Feminist perspectives call for a recognition of the role of gender in organisation–consumer relations. Some feminist writers also propose a re-conceptualisation of organisation–consumer relations, involving a dismantling of the distinctions between 'worker' and 'consumer', and a restructuring of organisational participation based on the concepts of mutuality and equality. Aboriginal perspectives point to the exploitative relations that have existed between mainstream human service organisations and Aboriginal people, and propose that Aboriginal people should have control of their own organisations rather than being treated as consumers.

Our analysis in this chapter draws, to some degree, on all of the above perspectives. However, it is fundamentally based on a political economy analysis. This perspective emphasises both the structural constraints on human service organisations, and the importance of the political relations within, and immediately surrounding, organisations. Organisation–consumer relations are thus examined in political terms, that is, through analysis of the political resources that consumers can mobilise and bring to bear in their relations with individuals and groups in the organisation, and with organisational structures. Strategies to improve responsiveness to consumers must, from this point of view, address the issue of the power, influence and authority of consumers, relative to other participants in the organisation.

What is a consumer?

Every individual in a modern, industrialised society is a consumer of human service organisations. In Australian society, almost every individual at some stage of his or her life uses the services of schools, hospitals, the police, Medicare and the Department of Social Security. Many individuals use child-care centres, nursing homes, domiciliary care agencies, child and family support services, public housing authorities, counselling agencies, community centres, and many other human services organisations. Being a consumer is inherent to life in contemporary society. We all rely on electricity supply authorities, retailers, garbage disposal companies, banks, restaurants, and myriad other organisations for the goods and services we need in daily living. Consumers are not, and should not be viewed as, a separate and distinct group within the community.

The words used to describe people on 'the receiving end' (Timms 1973) of human service organisations are many. Some of these words are specific to a particular type of organisation, for example: patient, student, taxpayer or prisoner. Others denote or suggest a particular type of relationship, for example: member, target, recipient, claimant, user, client, customer or consumer. The terms used can carry positive, neutral or negative connotations. Thus, people living in a residential setting may be called guests, residents or inmates, depending on the status and standing that the members of the organisation wish to ascribe to them. In addition, there is often a difference between formal and informal terminology, as when clients of the Department of Social Security are called 'welfare bludgers'.

Human service organisations are often highly sensitive to these issues of terminology and may go to considerable lengths to ensure that particular words or phrases are used. In the Department of Social Security, the term 'client' is officially fostered in preference to words such as 'beneficiary', 'pensioner' and 'recipient'. The Family Planning Association uses the term 'client' in preference to 'patient' to emphasise the social as well as medical elements of its services. In the disability field, the term 'people with disabilities' is increasingly used rather than the terms 'the disabled' or 'the handicapped' to emphasise that consumers with disabilities are people whose fundamental needs are those of all human beings, and that they should not be viewed and treated as a separate social category. The importance placed by organisations on terminology is graphically illustrated by the following quotation from a memorandum from a senior manager circulated to all staff in a large health-care organisation:

> Please note the preference of this office for official use of the term 'long term seriously psychiatrically ill patients' or 'intermittently seriously psychiatrically ill patients' rather than 'chronically mentally ill' or 'chronically mentally disabled', 'chronically psychiatrically disabled' etc. . . . The favoured terminology is more strongly scientifically based, less stigmatising, and less pejorative. It is also less likely to cause administrative underestimates or misconceptions of the service requirements of many of our patients.

There are several reasons for this organisational regard for language. The words used to describe consumers are an expression of, and are intended to reproduce, the official ideology of the dominant or ruling group within the organisation. They contribute to the construction of the 'reality' of the organisation, and in this sense, they are a part of the organisational culture. For example, the use of the term 'patient' in hospitals reflects and reinforces the dominance of medical and nursing professions in that setting. Choice of the word 'client' by a social service organisation may reflect the professional aspirations of some occupational groups, or an official commitment to treat users with a certain level of respect. Words are also used to mask realities, sometimes in a quite blatant fashion. For example, the 'hostages' taken by Iraq in the Gulf War of 1990–91 were called 'guests' by their captors. Similarly, prisoners are sometimes facetiously referred to as 'guests of Her Majesty'. At other times, euphemisms are employed with more subtlety. For example, we can question the meaning of the word 'client' when it is used in human service organisations which have a monopoly on services, where users are non-voluntary, or which offer little opportunity to users to control their relations with the organisation.

The terminology used to describe users is often contested within organisations. Different organisational groupings view relations with users in disparate ways, and seek the adoption of language to reflect their own perspective. 'Patients', for example, are increasingly viewed as 'health consumers', reflecting the growing strength of non-medical groups in the health field. When occupational groups such as social workers and therapists became more influential than doctors in the Commonwealth Rehabilitation Service, 'client' replaced 'patient' in official usage.

Social and welfare work has historically used the term 'client' to refer to the users of its services. This reflects in part the occupation's aspirations to professional status, and its ideological commitment to a non-directive stance. However, it has been argued that the term 'client' should, strictly speaking, be restricted to those relations in which the user and worker have jointly and equally arrived at a working agreement as to the nature of the relationship:

> This agreement . . . includes some exchange of mutual understandings about what the applicant wants and expects of the helper and what the helper can or cannot, will or will not do about the problem-to-be-worked. It includes agreements as to 'who does what' and 'where do we go from here'—of joint and separate tasks, and of next steps (Perlman, in Alcabes and Jones 1985, p. 50).

Many of the relations between social and welfare workers and consumers do not meet this demanding criterion. They are either too brief, involve the application of authority by the worker, or are so structured by the organisational context that they cannot usefully be viewed as a private exchange between two parties. If the term 'client' is used in connection with relations that do not involve 'exchange of mutual understandings' in any meaningful way, it may conceal rather than accurately depict the true situation.

Throughout this book, we prefer the term 'consumer' to the more customary 'client'. Partly, this reflects contemporary usage, and our organisational rather than professional, focus. It also reflects our own ideological concerns with quality service and consumer rights. The term 'consumer' refers to a person who acquires and uses goods and services to satisfy needs (Perlman 1975, p. xi), and we find it desirable to view users and their relations with human service organisations from this perspective. However, we recognise that the term 'consumer' is, itself, misleading in some contexts. For example, to talk about prisoners as 'consumers' of correctional services would be a crude disguising of the basic reality of being in jail, namely, the loss of personal freedom. As discussed in chapter 3, the activities of human service organisations encompass processing, sustaining, changing and controlling people, and the term 'consumer' does not fully capture all of these elements. It could also be argued that the term 'citizen' is more appropriate, as users of human service organisations make claims primarily on the basis of their citizenship status rather than as consumers in a private market.

Some of the inevitable shortcomings of terminology are lessened by recognising that the role of consumer (or client, patient, prisoner, and so on) contains a number of dimensions. Recognition of these dimensions is a necessary prerequisite to devising strategies to make organisations more responsive to consumer needs. Five dimensions can be identified: consumers as people, recipients, targets, members, and resources.

Most importantly, consumers are people. This self-evident statement raises difficult and important issues for human service organisations, and more particularly for social and welfare workers. Social and welfare work traditionally emphasises the importance of dealing with 'the whole person', that is, of viewing people and their needs from a holistic perspective. However, modern organisations rarely, if ever, treat people in this way. Bureaucratic organisations tend to deal with people in fragmented, impersonal and segmented ways, reflecting the nature of social relations in contemporary society. They are concerned with a person's specific needs such as for health care, accommodation, or income. Organisations are also concerned to fit consumers to their own categories and classifications, and are often only interested in those elements of a consumer's biography that relate to this fit. Organisations are also frequently prone to neglect or ignore consumers' perceptions of the organisation and its services. Much of the antipathy that social and welfare workers feel about working in organisations may be inspired by the belief that they are unable to be responsive to the needs and wants of individuals. The emergence of alternative organisations, discussed in chapter 6, is underpinned by this concern.

Social and welfare work's emphasis on the uniqueness of every person, and the need to view consumers from a holistic perspective, can make an important contribution to human service organisations. Organisations need to be continually reminded that they are dealing with complex human beings, not inert raw materials. Nevertheless, in the circumstances of modern society it is inevitable that organisations will to a considerable degree relate to people in segmented ways. This is a reflection of the nature of social relations in modern society, which are characterised by segmented roles and relationships (Plant 1974, pp. 16-22). All organisations process and categorise people, and deal only partially with their needs. An important task for social and welfare workers is to leaven these processes by promoting an awareness of the consumer as a whole person, while recognising the inherent limitations to this in our society.

Consumers are also the recipients of the services offered by organisations. Viewed as recipients, they are entitled to good quality treatment by the organisation, and respect for their needs and wants. In the private marketplace, these expectations are enforced, at least in theory, via the cash nexus between the consumer and the service provider. The slogan, 'the customer is always right', is based on the belief that if customers are not satisfied, they will not pay for the service or will take their custom elsewhere. In human service organisations, particularly those in the public sector, this incentive to provide a high standard of service is often absent. Other ways need to be found to promote excellence in service provision, and respect for consumer preferences.

Part of the complexity of organisation–consumer relations in human service organisations is that consumers are often the targets as well as the recipients of the organisation's activities. Satisfying the consumer is not the only goal, and may not even be the primary goal. For example, the Department of Social Security stresses the desirability of delivering entitlements with 'fairness, courtesy and efficiency' (Australia, House of Representatives 1989). This is a highly desirable goal, but it clearly tells only part of the story. The Department is also concerned to implement government policy of promoting the workforce participation of its consumers, and to minimise dependency on the public purse. Its relations with consumers are shaped by these goals. Similarly, a state government department with responsibilities for the protection of children from abuse and neglect is not primarily concerned with the preferences of its consumers. A family in which abuse or neglect of children is taking place are the 'targets' of the organisation's interventions, and their preferences as 'recipients' are a subordinate consideration.

Consumers may also be members, or have quasi-membership, of human service organisations. Membership implies a sense of belonging to and identification with an organisation. Some organisations, including many describing themselves as community-based, are explicitly membership-based. In a community centre or a sporting club, for example, the members of the centre are likely to be the same people who are receiving its services and taking part in its activities. Similarly, the members of self-help organisations are simultaneously recipients and targets. Sometimes, however, membership is less formally acknowledged or defined. For example, in long-term residential or institutional services, residents are often perceived, or perceive themselves to be, members of the organisation. Therapeutic communities treat patients as members of the community. Whenever consumers have a long-term, intensive involvement with an organisation, they are likely to demand or acquire some of the trappings of membership.

Membership of an organisation implies rights and responsibilities. Formal or informal acknowledgment of the membership status of consumers in a particular organisation may mean that consumers are seen to have the right to participate in certain decisions, to have access to certain entitlements, and to be treated in a certain manner. They may also have responsibilities to assist with certain activities, behave in certain ways, attend certain functions and pay membership fees. Consumers who have, formally or informally, acquired the status of member, can use this status to shape their relations with the organisation.

Consumers are also an organisational resource. Organisations need consumers, particularly consumers with whom they believe they can work successfully, or whom they are required by some external directive to serve. When human service organisations face an over-supply of potential consumers, they have significant problems of selection and ensuring access by priority groups. When there is an under-supply, the viability of the organisation is potentially threatened. These vulnerabilities can have a considerable impact on organisational treatment of consumers.

Recognition of the various roles of consumers alerts workers to the complexities of organisation–consumer relations, and helps in understanding why organisations treat their consumers as they do. It is often the case that organisations, implicitly or explicitly, make assumptions about consumer roles that influence the way consumers are treated. For example, organisational resistance to consumer participation in decision-making may reflect some people's inability to move from a view of the consumer as recipient and target to a view which encompasses the consumer as member. The ongoing debates in human service organisations about relations with consumers are often, implicitly, about the roles that consumers play, and the roles that should be acknowledged.

A further complexity concerns the issue of identifying the consumer. Human service organisations are often involved in complex social and personal problems in which there are many competing interests. In the investigation of a child abuse allegation, for example, who is the consumer? Is it the person providing the information, the mother of the child, the father of the child, the child, the child's brothers and sisters, or the society as a whole? Even though the primacy of the interests of one party, such as the child, may be stressed, the reality may be that all of the competing or conflicting interests of the individuals involved need to be acknowledged and dealt with to some degree. Take the case of an organisation working with a person suffering with AIDS. Who is the consumer? The person with AIDS, past or potential sexual partners, the person's family and friends, the person's employer, or society? Undoubtedly, it is possible in some settings, for example individual psychotherapy, to focus exclusively on the interests of the consumer, to the virtual exclusion of all other considerations. But these situations are the exception rather than the rule.

Finally, the dangers of stereotyping consumers needs to be stressed. Consumers, like workers, are not all good or all bad. They can be co-operative, honest, helpful, insightful, polite, grateful and responsible, and also obstructionist, deceitful, violent, ignorant, demanding, manipulative, and rude. Often consumers contact human service organisations when their own resources are depleted, or when they are facing a crisis of some kind requiring or demanding outside assistance. Most of us are not at our best under such stressful circumstances. Workers should avoid tendencies either to romanticise or to vilify consumers, either as individuals or as a group.

The politics of being a consumer

The relations between consumers and human service organisations are shaped by the complexities of consumer roles that we have described. Further understanding of these relations can be gained through an analysis of the politics of being a consumer. A political analysis of organisation–consumer relations starts from the assumption that the interests of consumers are distinct from the interests of workers, and of other groups in the organisation. In general, consumers can be thought of as trying to get the best service that they can at minimum personal cost. Cost, in this context, is broadly defined to mean such things as personal inconvenience, loss of privacy and dignity, and challenge to personal values and identity, as well as financial cost. While consumers may not always make a calculated, dispassionate appraisal of benefits and costs each time they approach a human service organisation, some such calculus underlies their approach to and dealings with the organisation. Similarly, workers can be thought of as trying to provide a service that meets their own personal and professional expectations, while not imposing unacceptably high personal costs. These costs may include the worker's relations with colleagues or superiors, the worker's career, personal stress, and personal values. The interests of managers, on the other hand, are in rationing the use of resources, in ensuring that organisational goals are being achieved, and in making sure that what takes place between worker and consumer does not jeopardise intra or inter-organisational relations. The personal and professional interests of managers are bound up in these purposes. While these various interests may overlap to a greater or lesser degree, no assumption of harmony should be made.

It follows that relations between consumers and organisations involve attempts by all parties to mobilise their political resources in order to achieve successful outcomes within the context and constraints of existing structures and policies. Much of this political activity occurs in the interactions between individual consumers and workers. Workers and consumers may not consciously act politically in these interactions, and individuals vary in the extent to which they are prepared to push or resist claims. Nevertheless, the political nature of all these interactions should be acknowledged.

The politics of the front-line has been examined in overseas and Australian studies. Satyamurti provides a detailed account of the politics of social worker–consumer relations in British Social Service Departments. Individual consumers employed a range of strategies to influence the outcomes of decisions. Some attempted to obtain resources from the Department by dressing shabbily and showing deep distress as a means of convincing workers of their plight. Others took the view that in order to get effective help you had to make your presence felt and make trouble. They adopted strategies such as repeatedly making inquiries about their concerns, and enlisting the support of councillors, Members of Parliament and newspapers. Some were skilled in using workers in this advocacy role in relation to other services. Consumers also used other tactics such as withholding information, threatening to abandon children or to commit suicide, attempting to engage the sympathy of the worker and expressing gratitude (1981, pp. 113-124 and pp. 145-152).

Social and welfare workers, for their part, also had a repertoire of strategies to exert control of their relations with consumers. Satyamurti found that they often stereotyped their clients as people who were unable to use information, unable to act rationally, incompetent, and unwilling to plan ahead. The use of councillors or Members of Parliament by consumers was called manipulative, and there were also many accusations against consumers of playing off one worker against another. Consumers were classified into difficult or routine cases, and there was a tendency for workers to avoid those viewed as difficult. Distance between worker and consumer was maintained by such devices as containing consumers in particular parts of the building, discouraging the use of workers' first names, refusing to accept favours or meals from consumers, and the arrangement of furniture in interviewing rooms (1981, pp. 124-158). These practices, and those of consumers discussed in the previous paragraph, arose, Satyamurti suggests:

> ... out of the differing needs and interests of each party. Just as the client's need for help led him/her to view the social worker in a particular way, so social workers' need to survive in a stressful situation led to their resisting the client's definition of the situation ... and generating and defending their own perspective (1981, p. 112).

The politics of consumer–worker relations is also described by Sanders in his study of the front-line in Australian income security administration. The rules governing the income security categories that comprise the Australian social security system are, inevitably, somewhat indeterminate, and there is significant room for manoeuvre and negotiation. Sanders shows through a number of case studies how consumers vary in their assertiveness, their knowledge of the system, and their understanding of how to present a claim to maximise its likelihood of success. Workers also vary with some being sympathetic, active facilitators of consumer access, and others suspicious or passive service inhibitors. 'When clients and officials who span these ranges of behaviour encounter each other in service delivery there is considerable potential for these encounters to vary' (Sanders 1985, p. 40).

These accounts focus on politics in the front-line. Other processes where political struggle between consumers and organisations occurs include the activities of consumer lobby groups, consumer participation in decision-making within organisations, and broader political processes in which consumers have a stake. A number of writers have argued that in all these processes, organisations and workers are likely to have the upper hand: 'the power advantage of human service organisations enables them to exercise considerable control over the lives of the recipients of their services' (Hasenfeld 1983, p. 180). This is a key point as it suggests an explanation for the lack of responsiveness by human service organisations to consumer needs, namely, consumers' limited power, influence and authority. In earlier chapters, particularly chapters 2 and 8, we have examined the sources of power, authority and influence for workers and other participants in human service organisations. We will now analyse, in a similar way, the political position of consumers.

The power, influence and authority of consumers varies from organisation to organisation, and between different consumers. Six criteria can be identified as crucial influencing factors. The most fundamental of these is the extent of consumer authority and control. In most human service organisations there is a separation of consumption and control (Etzioni 1964, pp. 94-97). Consumers typically have no authority, as authority rests either with management committees, ministers and senior managers, or workers and professionals who are delegated authority. Consumers sometimes have representation on authoritative bodies, such as management committees, but this is often of a token nature. Organisations run by management committees of consumers (or a majority of consumers), and elected by consumers, are relatively unusual in the human services. In any case, while such organisations increase opportunities for consumer power and influence, they do not guarantee accountability and responsiveness to consumers. Management committees comprising former or current consumers often experience tensions between their managerial responsibilities and consumer demands and expectations. Even in alternative organisations in which formal distinctions between consumer, worker and decision-making roles are abandoned, there may be tensions and inequalities of power between different consumer/ members.

Consumer choice is also a critical factor. Consumers of organisations that have a monopoly on the provision of a needed service are in a weaker political position than those who have a choice of organisations. Similarly, consumers who lack the financial resources to shop around for services are in a weaker position than consumers who can purchase services in the marketplace. High levels of consumer demand for limited service places also restricts choice. Consumers who are required by law to use a particular service, such as prisoners, persons on probation, and residents of psychiatric institutions, have the least choice of all. If consumers cannot exit, or even threaten to exit, from an organisation, their capacity for influence is weakened.

The power of consumers is also linked to their knowledge and information about the organisation. To make effective demands on an organisation it is necessary to understand such matters as how claims are processed, what are the boundaries of the possible, how rules are interpreted, what decision-making processes are used, and so forth. Much of this information can be difficult to access from outside.

Consumers are usually temporary, part-time members of organisations. They may lack the expertise to understand technical or specialised materials. Moreover, many organisations become adept at concealing information from consumers, particularly if they feel that information dissemination will result in excessive demands on the organisation.

The social status of consumers also has a major bearing on their power position in organisations. Human service organisations are not insulated from the norms and values prevailing in the overall society, and play a significant role in reproducing them. Hence, the class, ethnicity, age, Aboriginality, gender, occupation and income of consumers influence their ability to deal successfully with the organisation. There is extensive evidence that low status consumers have considerable difficulties in accessing services and receiving good treatment by service providers (Hasenfeld 1983, p. 201). Being a consumer of some organisations itself carries stigma and predisposes inferior or discriminatory treatment. Groups such as prisoners, patients of public psychiatric hospitals, residents of emergency hostels and income security applicants are typically accorded low status, simply by virtue of their association with the organisation. Other organisations carry high status. For example, there appears to be a certain cachet for America's rich and famous in attending high profile drug and alcohol rehabilitation centres such as the Betty Ford Clinic. High status consumers in high status organisations are most likely to be able to make effective claims for good quality service.

The power of consumers also reflects their level of political organisation. Consumer groups that are organised politically have much greater potential to voice collective concerns, and support the claims of individual consumers. There is wide variation in the extent to which consumer groups are organised, and in the political effectiveness of consumer organisations. These differences reflect a variety of factors. Some groups, such as income security recipients, are inherently difficult to organise due to their ever-changing composition, vulnerability, and scattered location. Consumers who are highly dependent on organisations, such as public housing tenants or people with disabilities, may be reluctant to bite the hand that feeds (Brown and Ringma 1989). Consumer organisations vary in expertise, leadership, access to financial resources, status, size and access to decision-making structures. All of these factors affect their capacity for influence.

Finally, the position of consumers is influenced by the extent to which their legal and moral rights to services are established and acknowledged. If consumers have a legal right to a service by virtue of citizenship, their political position is much stronger than if the organisation has no legal obligations towards them. Compare, for example, the position of a consumer approaching the Department of Social Security with one approaching an emergency relief organisation. In the former case, the key issue is whether the consumer has a legal right to income support. If that right is established, the Department is obliged to make the payment. However, in an emergency relief situation, there is no such obligation, and consumers are dependent on the assessments made by the organisation. Often consumers are forced to make claims on the basis of the moral obligations of organisations to provide assistance, but the effectiveness of such claims is limited by the organisation's ideology and capacity to respond.

The ideas presented in this section provide a framework for analysing the power position of consumers in any specific human service organisation. This framework is summarised in Table 9.1. Workers concerned to improve the responsiveness of their organisation to its consumers should undertake such an analysis prior to formulating action strategies. Firstly, this will provide a realistic basis for assessing the potential for improving the political position of consumers. Secondly, it will indicate the specific factors that need to be addressed, and assist in the formulation of action strategies.

Table 9.1 A framework for analysing the actual and potential power, authority and influence of consumers in an organisation

1 Do the consumers of this organisation have any authoritative role in decision-making?
  a Do they have a dominant role on authoritative bodies such as the management committee?
  b Are they represented on authoritative bodies? What is the form of this representation?
  c Is there a requirement or expectation for consultation with consumers? What form does this take?
  d What mechanisms exist to ensure accountability to consumers?

2 Do consumers have real choices about the service they receive?
  a Does the organisation have a monopoly or quasi-monopoly on the service?
  b Do consumers have the financial resources and opportunity to purchase an alternative service?
  c Are consumers involuntary users of the service?
  d Is exiting from the service a realistic possibility for most consumers?

3 What knowledge and information do consumers have?
  a To what extent do consumers understand organisational structures and processes?
  b Does the organisation facilitate access to information or seek to conceal information?
  c How technical or specialised is the information needed by consumers if they are to have a voice in the organisation?

4 What is the social status of consumers of the organisation?
  a From which socio-economic status groups in the society as a whole are they drawn?

  b What is the impact of consumers' class, gender, ethnicity, Aboriginality,
    age, disability and geographic location?
  c Is there any status, positive or negative, associated with being a consumer
    of the organisation?

5 How well-organised politically are consumers?
  a Are they represented by consumer organisations?
  b What is the political capability of these organisations?
  c What factors facilitate or impede political organisation of the consumer
    group?
  d What level of political skill do consumers have?

6 Do consumers have a right to the services of the organisation?
  a Is there a legal right to service?
  b Is there acknowledgment of a moral right to service?

Strategies to improve responsiveness to consumers

Social and welfare workers wishing to initiate, participate in or respond
to attempts to improve the responsiveness of human service
organisations have a wide repertoire of strategies to consider. The
twelve major approaches to improving organisation–consumer relations
in the human services are listed in Table 9.2. Workers need to
understand the assumptions, strengths, limitations and applications of
each of these approaches, and the roles that they can play in relation to
them. Each of them is briefly analysed below.

Improving consumer relations

Excellence in service delivery is an issue that until recently has received
limited consideration in the literature on organisation–consumer
relations in the human services. This contrasts with the central
importance given to these issues in some parts of the private sector.
Retail organisations, for example, are often actively concerned about
such matters as time spent at check-out counters, the characteristics of
physical surroundings, and the ways that staff treat consumers. Interest
in these matters has not been part of the dominant ethos in many parts
of the human services. Much of the attention that has been paid to these
issues has been with regard to large, public sector organisations such
as the Department of Social Security and the Commonwealth
Employment Service (e.g. Australia, Royal Commission on Australian

Table 9.2 A repertoire of strategies for improving responsiveness to consumers

Strategy	*Example*
1 Improving consumer relations	• staff training • improved administrative procedures • better information dissemination • enhanced physical surroundings
2 Restructuring the organisation	• corporate management techniques • multi-disciplinary teams • decentralisation
3 Enhancing service quality	• increasing professionalism • developing empathy and trust between workers and consumers
4 Facilitating access to information	• provision of information as part of outreach strategies • consumer access to their files • ensuring ethical design and use of computerised information systems
5 Increasing consumer choice	• anti-monopoly strategies • strengthening consumer demand via vouchers and insurance arrangements
6 Addressing issues of access and equity	• developing access services and processes • clarifying and monitoring access policies • monitoring the equity of treatment practices • developing programmes to enhance equity in treatment and service • supporting anti-discrimination laws

Strategy	Example
7 Promoting consumer participation	• consumer membership of committees, boards and task groups • consumer evaluation of services • consumer involvement in service provision
8 Establishing consumer rights	• endorsing declarations of rights • incorporating rights into standards, procedures and routines • linking with external rights organisations
9 Creating opportunities for redress	• providing information and access to redress processes • supporting consumers' rights to appeal or make complaints • contributing to the development of redress mechanisms
10 Undertaking consumer advocacy	• performing internal consumer advocacy • accessing external, independent advocacy • encouraging self-advocacy
11 Pressuring the organisation	• promote the policies of consumer groups in the organisation • provide support to consumer organisations
12 Transforming authority structures	• assist in the formation and operation of consumer-directed organisations • work to develop alternative organisations

Government Administration 1976, pp. 128-133; Australia, House of Representatives 1989). These and other studies suggest a number of common problems.

A major concern of consumers is with the amount of time taken to receive attention, to sort things out when they go wrong, and to actually receive the service that they have applied for. People do not like queuing for long periods, being transferred from one officer to another, and dealing with staff who do not have the authority to actually make the decision required. They find the complexities of decision-making processes, and the number of forms to be filled out, confusing. Inadequate and misleading information is another issue. Consumers find that staff often cannot provide the information that they need, and that written materials are difficult to understand.

Other concerns relate to the attitudes and behaviour of human service staff. Allegations against staff include: rudeness, intolerance, sexist and racist attitudes, intimidation, and lack of explanation of and information about their actions. Social and welfare workers are sometimes seen as being excessively intrusive (Hill 1976, pp.131-133), and a major concern in residential settings such as nursing homes is lack of respect for the individuality and rights of consumers (MacKenzie-Thurley 1986). Staff are sometimes viewed as too helpful to some consumers, bowing to the demands of trouble-makers or treating socially acceptable consumers with undue favour, and thus acting in an inequitable manner (Painter 1980, p. 268). The physical surrounds and settings of human service delivery are also matters that give rise to consumer complaints. Overcrowding, lack of privacy, inadequate provision for children, lack of access for people with disabilities and shabby, poorly maintained premises are some of the issues raised.

Social and welfare workers should concern themselves with these matters, which pertain to both community and public sector organisations. Workers need to be aware of the range of interventions available to improve consumer relations. These include staff training, reform of administrative procedures, better information dissemination, and attention to physical surroundings.

At the same time, workers need to be aware of the limits of consumer relations strategies. There are structural, resource and political impediments to improving consumer relations in human service organisations. Many of the matters that consumers find irritating—routinisation, the filling out of forms, standard procedures, queuing and being treated as cases—are, as we have seen, inherent to bureaucratic organisation and are linked, albeit sometimes tenuously, to equitable and efficient administration. Poor physical facilities and ill-trained staff may reflect resource constraints rather than lack of commitment to excellence in consumer relations. Politically, front-line workers, as we saw in the last chapter, are often placed in a double-bind. The official ideology of the organisation may emphasise consumer service, but the informal organisational expectation of front-line workers may be to ration resources and deflect consumer demand. Most importantly, the inherent limitations of consumer relations strategies must be understood. Winkler calls consumer relations the 'harmless version of consumerism' (1987, p. 1), as it does not directly address questions of consumer power, participation and rights.

Consumer relations is primarily about treating consumers with respect, not about structural change in the position of consumers in human service organisations.

Restructuring the organisation

Changes to organisational structures are often justified in terms of improved responsiveness to consumer needs. The introduction of corporate management methods, programme budgeting, flatter structures, upgraded management information systems and performance evaluation are sometimes described as expressions of an organisation's desire to 'care for clients' (Volker 1987). Undoubtedly, there are links between such corporate planning techniques and the efficiency and effectiveness of services to consumers, but these need to be demonstrated in each particular instance rather than simply being asserted. For example, it cannot be assumed that the introduction of systems to evaluate the performance of programmes will benefit consumers. It depends on the nature of the evaluation, its purpose and the use that is made of the data gathered. Similarly, as discussed later in the chapter, management information systems may be a mixed blessing from the consumer's perspective.

A number of structural reforms directly related to the role of consumers are examined separately below. These include consumer participation in organisational decision-making, opportunities for redress, and transforming authority structures. Two others need special mention. The creation of multi-disciplinary teams is often portrayed as a means of improving service in professionalised organisations (Luntz 1985). Teams are viewed as a response to the problem of fragmented and discontinuous consumer service stemming from professional specialisation. Rather than dealing separately with segments of the consumer's problems, teams aspire to a sharing of knowledge and perspectives in order to provide an integrated, holistic service to consumers. However, difficulties with teams include inter-professional rivalries, leadership issues, and the time and resources expended in joint planning and decision-making. Teams may also be intimidating for consumers, and may weaken their negotiating position. Like the corporate management techniques discussed above, the benefits of teams for consumers need to be carefully appraised in each instance, rather than assumed.

Decentralisation of organisational structures is another structural change frequently assumed to benefit consumers. The underlying reasoning is that by localising decision-making and/or service provision, services will be more open to consumer influence and more responsive to consumer need. These claims have considerable validity in some circumstances, but need careful examination. One celebrated example of an experiment in decentralisation was the establishment, under the auspice of the Royal Commission on Australian Government Administration, of the North-West One-stop Welfare (NOW) Centre in inner-suburban Melbourne in the mid-1970s (Hawkins 1977). The idea was 'to provide as nearly as possible a complete service (including if possible the power to make decisions) in one place, at one visit, and with members of the public having to deal with not more than one or two different officers' (Australia, Royal Commission on Australian Government Administration 1976, p. 161). The NOW Centre embodied many of the themes commonly associated with decentralisation strategies: co-location of state, local and Commonwealth services, a more personal style of dealing with consumers, localisation of decision-making within organisations, better information about services, closer community contact, and the development of community participation (Painter 1980, p. 269). The experiences of the NOW Centre illustrated the difficulties of achieving these goals, via decentralisation strategies. One lesson was that there are tensions between some of these goals and the delivery of reliable, predicable, efficient services. Decentralisation, whatever its merits, is no panacea for unresponsiveness to consumers.

Enhancing service quality

Closely related to the two strategies we have examined are those that focus on enhancing service quality. The issue of quality in human service provision is somewhat problematic. Quality is often a concern of service providers with a strong professional orientation, who define it in terms of professionally derived standards. It is not uncommon for professional workers to equate quality with the employment of professionally trained and accredited personnel, and to emphasise techniques such as peer review as the main means of sustaining high practice and service provision standards. The difficulty is that quality may be perceived quite differently by consumers, and that consumers themselves may have a variety of perspectives on quality. A consumer's perspective on the quality of a service is based on many factors including the level of trust in workers and the organisation, the compatibility between the consumer's goals and the goals of the worker, the reputation of the organisation, the adequacy of the organisation's resources, the level of worker commitment, and the extent to which staff treat consumers as people rather than as objects or cases (Hasenfeld 1983, pp. 197-200). Enhancing service quality can, therefore, take two broad directions. It can take the professional route by emphasising the importance of professional education and accreditation, peer review, improvement of practice theory and method and so forth. Or it can emphasise the development of empathy and trust between organisation, worker and consumer.

Facilitating access to information

The old adage that information is power is as applicable to the place of consumers in human service organisations as to any other political relationship. Accurate, reliable, understandable and accessible information is a key element of good consumer relations, as we have already seen. However, broader issues are also involved. Firstly, information is an important aspect of accessibility. Human service organisations need to take a proactive stance towards making their services available and accessible to those consumer groups for whom they are designed. Information strategies can play a key role in these outreach processes. Consumer access to human service organisations depends on the availability of timely, understandable, acceptable information, in the language and terminology of the groups for whom the service is intended.

Access to information is also critical to the political relations between the consumer and the organisation. In complex organisations, considerable reliance is placed on 'the files' to construct the biography and character of consumers. If a consumer's record is controlled by the organisation, without any consumer access, the balance of power is weighed heavily in favour of the organisation and its workers. Recognition of this issue has led to considerable attention to consumer access to records (Abel and Johnson 1978). Little information is available on consumer access policies and practices in the non-government sector. However, in the public sector, the Commonwealth's Freedom of Information Act, passed in 1982, gives individuals the right to access to information about them held on government files. Individuals have the opportunity to know the stated reasons for decisions affecting their lives, and may have the opportunity of correcting information which is untrue or misleading (Bell and Watchirs 1988, p. 298).

Freedom of information provisions have a number of consequences for consumers, over and above the right to inspect their file. Access to files assists consumers in challenging and seeking review of administrative decisions affecting them. It is also claimed that it results in the keeping of more accurate and careful records by workers. The knowledge that files are potentially available to consumers makes workers more judicious in their written comments. Freedom of information legislation also makes available information on a variety of matters other than personal files. These include documents such as manuals outlining the criteria for governmental decisions, and documents relating to policy-making processes (Bell and Watchirs 1988). These rights are potentially of great significance for consumer organisations seeking to influence policy. Freedom of information legislation is gradually extending to state government jurisdictions, where its impact on social and welfare work practice in fields such as child welfare, mental health and corrections will hopefully be considerable. Achieving similar rights for consumers of non-government organisations is a matter requiring the attention of human service workers.

The issue of information access has become particularly critical with the advent of computer-based consumer information systems. These systems are often assumed by managers and technicians to have mainly positive consequences for consumers, by improving the quality of decision-making. However, this assumption is open to question. The costs and benefits of the new information technology are rarely carefully assessed. Moreover, these systems may increase managerial control over front-line workers, endanger privacy and confidentiality, lead to the omission of important but difficult to standardise information, and create further barriers between workers and consumers (McCulloch 1989). Sharing of information about consumers among different organisations will be facilitated by the new technology, increasing the need for safeguards against inaccurate or misleading information. At the same time, computer technology opens up new possibilities for consumer access to their own personal records and to organisational information (Australia, House of Representatives 1989, pp. 56-59). Consumer access and use of terminals to examine their files and obtain other information about the organisation is likely to become a significant issue.

Increasing consumer choice

Earlier in the chapter we saw that choice was one of the factors affecting the power of consumers in organisations. One set of strategies for improving responsiveness to consumer needs focuses on expanding consumer choice. The main impediments to consumer choice, excluding situations such as imprisonment in which the individual's choices are deliberately restricted, are monopolies and the limited availability of services. Breaking up monopolies has been a goal of public policy in some human service fields. For example, in the area of disability, the growth of large organisations dealing with the range of needs of individuals with a particular type of disability has been discouraged by the Commonwealth government. Instead, people with disabilities are encouraged to relate to a variety of organisations in relation to different aspects of their lives. Provision of services via the non-government sector is also sometimes justified in terms of consumer choice, the alternative of direct provision of services solely by government being seen as monolithic and monopolistic.

These anti-monopoly strategies are limited, however, by the overall limits on the supply of services. For example, provision by the non-government sector does not present consumers with real choice, if this is the only service available to them. Other limits relate to consumers themselves. To exercise real choice, consumers need good information about the alternatives available to them and the capacity to exercise the choice they make. Often, lack of information, money, transport and other factors limit the real choices available.

One influential tradition in analysis of the human services, sometimes labelled 'the new right', seeks to increase consumer choice via market mechanisms. Underlying this approach is a belief in the desirability of reconnecting consumption and control via the cash nexus between consumers and providers. Unresponsiveness to consumers stems, it is argued, from the lack of direct accountability of providers to consumers in publicly provided and funded human services. True accountability requires that providers be dependent on consumer satisfaction for their livelihood. Hence, it is argued, the organisation of human services should resemble, as far as possible, a free market in which providers compete with one another for the consumer's custom.

Specific proposals to increase consumer choice via market mechanisms encompass both the supply of and the demand for human services. On the supply side, it is argued that private sector organisations should play an even more central role in the provision of services. The current pattern of dominant or substantial private sector provision in such areas as medical services, housing, nursing homes, hostels and child care should be expanded to encompass counselling, adoption, rehabilitation, community-care services, prisons and so on. On the demand side, consumers should be given vouchers to purchase services from private sector providers, or insurance coverage similar to that currently operating in health and medical services.

The extent to which proposals such as these can actually deliver responsive consumer services in all fields of human service provision is debateable. There is no substantial evidence that privately owned services are more responsive to their consumers than public sector services, or that private monopolies behave substantially differently from public monopolies. Vouchers and insurance arrangements do not necessarily enable consumers to make effective claims; in conditions of high demand for services they may simply increase price. Nevertheless, limited choice is a significant problem for consumers in some fields of human service provision, and market mechanisms, used selectively and in conjunction with other strategies, may have a place.

Addressing issues of access and equity

Fundamental to the whole question of responsiveness to consumers is the issue of accessibility, that is, the capacity of consumers to obtain the services being provided. Patterns of entry to human service organisations vary in terms of the amount of control that consumers have over their choice, and that the organisation has over its admissions

(Hasenfeld 1983, pp. 185-191). However, in general, it is useful to think about accessibility in terms of a series of obstacles that consumers must overcome in order to gain entry to the service (Gates 1980, pp. 148-160; Jones 1984, pp. M37-M42). These obstacles include lack of availability of the service, lack of information, inability to overcome geographic or psychological barriers, inability to meet eligibility or priority criteria, and lack of money to meet user charges. Potential consumers must overcome all of these hurdles to gain access.

The issue of accessibility is one that should be of great concern to social and welfare workers. Individuals vary in their capacity to access services. If organisations do not have explicit access policies, services will tend to be used by the most 'capable' consumers, that is, those most able to obtain and understand information, who have ready access to transport, who are near to the service, who can articulate their requirements and present themselves positively, and who have the greatest economic capacity. Workers need to understand the barriers to access that confront consumers from socially and economically disadvantaged groups, and initiate and participate in programmes to enhance their access. These include outreach campaigns, information and referral services, transportation schemes, visiting services, case channelling procedures and the development of specialised services (Gates 1980, pp. 160-169).

Workers also need to be aware of a number of common organisational practices that significantly influence access and intake processes. 'Creaming' is the process whereby organisations select the more amenable, promising and socially desirable consumers, while turning away those that are viewed as difficult, unco-operative and unappealing (Gates 1980, pp. 169-170). This practice is widespread in situations where organisations are under strong pressures to demonstrate effectiveness, or where a high value is placed on the successful exercise of professional skills. Scott's study of organisations serving the visually impaired found that they consistently favoured young blind children and 'employable' blind adults over elderly blind people and the multi-handicapped. This was due, in large part, to the organisations' need to raise funds and gain public support in a society where cultural stereotypes linked 'blindness, youth, work and hope' (Scott 1974). The converse process to creaming is the concentration of disadvantaged, socially devalued people in under-resourced, low status services and organisations, which perpetuate their exclusion from the mainstream society.

Arbitrary rationing is the process whereby organisations restrict access on grounds and through mechanisms other than those intended and formally stated. Almost all organisations have to ration their services as need and demand typically exceed available resources. However, organisations often choose or drift into rationing methods that bear little relationship to stated access policies. Parker (1967) distinguishes four types of arbitrary rationing. Deterrence involves making the service uninviting or unattractive to discourage use. Deflection involves referral to other organisations. Delay involves the establishment of a waiting list or queue. Dilution means spreading resources thinly by lowering the standard or amount of service provided to each individual consumer. Each of these rationing practices may disadvantage or discriminate against certain groups of consumers in unintended and undesired ways. Workers need to monitor access and intake policies of their organisation and work with others to secure equitable access policies and processes.

The inequities and discriminatory practices associated with access to human service organisations may also characterise the actual provision of services. For example, studies of hospital emergency wards have found that the quality of a patient's treatment is linked to staff judgements of their 'moral worth', gauged by such attributes as ethnicity, age, mode of dress, language, employment status, marital status and income (Roth 1974). Teachers' expectations of kindergarten and primary school students, and hence the way they are taught and encouraged, have been found to be based on criteria associated with the child's social class (Rist 1974). Overt and deliberate discriminatory practices are now illegal in most jurisdictions, but much discrimination on the basis of ethnicity, Aboriginality, gender, class and so forth is covert and intrinsic to existing structures and ways of working.

Many such inequities arise as part of the processes of what has been termed 'typification' (Hasenfeld 1983, pp. 192-197). This refers to the processes of diagnosing consumers as belonging to a certain types of 'case', and developing a corresponding treatment or service plan. While assessment, diagnosis and planning are often portrayed as professional, even scientific processes, there is no doubt that these processes are also influenced by workers' personal perceptions of the character of a consumer. For example, a decision that a resident of a nursing home is a frail elderly person whose condition will steadily deteriorate, and who should be treated accordingly, may reflect dominant community attitudes about old age as well as the actual physical condition of the person. Dominant societal stereotypes about age, gender, race, ethnicity, disability, class and place are likely to be applied to consumers, unless the organisation's own culture challenges such evaluations.

Social and welfare workers have a number of roles to play with respect to such inequities. Firstly, they need to be aware of these potential inequities, monitor organisational practices, and bring issues to the attention of the organisation. They can also initiate or participate in programmes and activities designed to address the issues, such as training programmes for staff and changes to organisational practices and structures. An analysis of what this means in practice with regard to ethnic residents in nursing homes is provided by Westbrook and Legge (1990). They can also support the implementation of reforms designed to increase the presence and influence of disadvantaged groups in human service organisations, such as equal employment opportunity and anti-discrimination legislation (Wilensky 1985).

Promoting consumer participation

Consumer participation has been a central theme in discussion of human services reform since the early 1970s. However, the gap between rhetoric and reality remains wide. For example, a study of organisations providing services to people with disabilities, a field where the goal of consumer participation has been actively promoted by the Commonwealth government, professionals and consumers alike, found that 'consumers do not participate in any significant way in planning and decision-making processes' (Brown and Ringma 1989, p. 36). Part of the difficulty is that the nature and purpose of consumer participation is not always clear. It has been suggested that 'the idea of participation is a little like eating spinach: no-one is against it in principle because it is good for you' (Arnstein, in Council of Social Service of New South Wales 1984). Social and welfare workers' broad commitment to consumer participation needs to be linked with a strategic understanding of what participation means, why it is important, and how it can be put into practice.

Participation is essentially a straightforward concept. In the context of human service organisations, it means the introduction of a new set of actors into the various processes of the organisation (Richardson 1983, p. 23). These processes may be about decision-making, planning, service development, evaluation, service delivery, or any other organisational function or activity. Consumer participation is about service users being involved in these processes. On the surface, this may sound quite unremarkable. However, the introduction of a new set of actors into organisational processes is not a simple matter. It provides the new actors with opportunities for political influence, and may impinge on existing alliances and agreements. Participation by consumers can be particularly disturbing for other groups in the organisation, as their interests and perspectives may sharply vary from those of workers, managers and community representatives. The difficulties of implementing consumer participation are often attributed to the shortcomings of consumers themselves (Council of Social Service of New South Wales 1984, pp. 9-16). However, a more convincing explanation, from our theoretical perspective, is the potential impact of consumer participation on the existing power distribution in human service organisations.

Consumer participation in human service organisations can take many forms. Workers need to be clear and explicit about the particular form of participation they are promoting. Some of the most common and important mechanisms for consumer participation are:

- representation on management committees;
- representation on advisory boards;
- input and involvement in planning processes;
- membership of committees and task groups examining particular issues;
- evaluation of the organisation and its services;
- involvement in the actual provision of services;
- involvement in management tasks such as information dissemination, recruitment of members and fund-raising;
- attendance at consultative meetings, forums and conferences;
- involvement in decision-making processes relating to the individual consumer.

A consumer participation strategy for a particular organisation is likely to include a combination of these elements.

Just as there are many different mechanisms for community participation, so there are many different purposes that community participation can serve. Clarifying the purposes of consumer participation is essential, as these are commonly misunderstood. Consumers, workers and managers all need to have clear and realistic expectations of participative processes. Some of the purposes commonly pursued through consumer participation are:

- to provide a consumer perspective on organisational issues;
- to provide consumers with an opportunity for protest or veto on particular decisions;
- to facilitate the generation of innovate or creative solutions to problems;
- to encourage greater understanding between managers, workers and consumers;
- to give consumers greater organisational influence;
- to give consumers opportunities to acquire new skills and knowledge.

Consumer participation strategies have considerable potential for improving organisational responsiveness to consumers. However, the theoretical and practical difficulties associated with participative strategies need to be appreciated. In particular, the distinction between participation, on the one hand, and power, influence and authority (as defined in chapter 2) on the other, is critical. Consumer participation strategies often give consumers the potential to increase their influence over organisational decisions. But whether or not this potential is realised depends on many factors including the information and other resources given to consumers, and their political skills. It is relatively uncommon for consumers to be given organisational authority, although later in the chapter we discuss the possibilities for transforming authority structures. As for consumer power, this is rarely attained via participative strategies initiated by managers and workers, other than in such rare cases as the granting of a veto to consumer representatives over particular decisions.

The relations between consumer, worker and community participation also needs consideration. As we have seen, consumers are only one of the groups with a legitimate interest in organisational decisions, and their claims to participate in important processes compete with those of workers and outside community members. It has been argued that worker and consumer participation are fundamentally in tension, and that prospects for co-participation are limited (Katan and Prager 1986). Another issue is that of representation. Direct participation by all consumers in all decisions is neither possible nor desirable in most situations, hence some form of representation is required. But organising fair and effective representation is difficult. Participation is often costly of time and money, and these costs have to be weighed up against the anticipated benefits. Moreover, finding mechanisms that enable consumers to participate in ways that are meaningful to them requires skill and imagination (McGrath 1989).

Finally, it needs to be stressed that participative processes are, themselves, inherently political. That is, they will be used by all participants to further their own interests. Underlying the official rhetoric surrounding participative processes are a multitude of partially hidden purposes. Managers and workers may be interested in legitimating decisions, co-opting dissent, creating a forum for negotiation and persuasion, postponing decisions, deflecting opposition, getting tasks accomplished on the cheap, and building their own image. Consumer representatives may be interested in the personal rewards of participation, in acquiring personal influence, in acquiring status and leadership, or in sabotaging organisational processes. Their involvement may be reluctant, based on a judgement that the costs of not participating are greater than those of taking part. Workers must acknowledge these realities of participative processes, and develop strategies that take them into account.

Establishing consumer rights

We have already noted that one of the factors influencing the power of consumers in human service organisations is the extent to which their rights to services have been established. It follows that establishing rights is an important strategy for enhancing responsiveness to consumer needs. Rights issues have become a central part of the debate about the role of consumers in human services. Australia is a party to several international conventions with direct implications for the rights of consumers (Bailey 1990). These include the International Covenant on Civil and Political Rights, the International Covenant on Economic, Social and Cultural Rights, the Declaration of the Rights of the Child, the Declaration on the Rights of Mentally Retarded Persons, and the Declaration on the Rights of Disabled Persons. These conventions are administered by the Human Rights and Equal Opportunity Commission, which has become an important participant in social policy processes. For example, the issue of youth homelessness became prominent on the political agenda during the late 1980s, largely through the efforts of the Human Rights Commission (Australia, Human Rights and Equal Opportunity Commission 1989). The rights of prisoners (Hawkins 1986), residents of nursing homes (Ronalds 1989), people with disabilities, income security recipients and Aboriginal people have all been significant public issues in recent years.

In considering rights-based strategies, it is important, firstly, to distinguish between moral and legal rights. A moral right is one based on an individual's beliefs and values. A legal right is one that is established by the constitution, legislation, regulations or case law, and is enforceable in the courts. The statement 'everyone has a right to a reasonable basic income' is a statement of a moral right, whereas 'persons over sixty-five have a right to an aged pension' is a statement about a legal right (albeit one hedged with various qualifications). Another important distinction is between the right to a service and procedural or treatment rights. Rights to services include such things as the right to a pension, to shelter, to an education, and so forth. Procedural or treatment rights are such things as the right of access to documents, the right to be consulted on decisions, and the right to be treated with dignity and respect.

The practice issues for workers are about using rights issues strategically in human service organisations to improve responsiveness to consumers. There are primarily three aspects to this task. Firstly, workers can participate in attempts to have their organisation endorse statements of consumer rights as official organisational policy. For example, organisations working in the field of children's services could endorse the Declaration of the Rights of the Child as a guide and standard for organisational activities. Increasingly, organisations are under external pressure to embrace such guidelines. For example, nursing homes and hostels are being encouraged by the Commonwealth government to adopt and implement a Charter of Residents' Rights and Responsibilities (Ronalds 1989, pp. 103-104).

Secondly, workers can take part in the implementation and execution of existing legal rights. Rights need to be incorporated into service standards and procedures, contracts, and the daily routines of organisations. Broad statements need to be interpreted, and there needs to be monitoring of compliance with legal provisions. Where rights do not have a legal basis, workers can attempt to persuade fellow workers that consumers have a moral right to certain services and kinds of treatment. Finally, workers need to be aware of the range of external organisations that can take up rights issues on behalf of consumers, both individually and collectively. These include welfare rights centres, legal services, information services and consumer organisations. Developing close working relationships with such organisations is essential for workers in many settings.

Creating and using opportunities for redress

In all organisations it sometimes happens that consumers feel that the treatment they have received is unfair, that a decision is incorrect, that they wish to make a complaint, or that they would like a second opinion. An organisation's willingness and ability to respond to these situations is an important aspect of its overall responsiveness to consumers. Redress procedures begin within the organisation itself. In organisations which accept a consumer's right to voice concerns and complaints, there will be well publicised procedures for internal, relatively independent, review of decisions. Consumers will feel that they have a right to a second opinion, and to express reservations about the service. A key element of internal redress procedures is consumer access to supervisors and management. If consumers cannot get past the front-line worker, their position is substantially weakened.

External review and redress procedures, which can be activated if attempts to change decisions internallly are unsatisfactory, provide consumers with a significant counterweight to organisational power. A key development in the public sector in Australia during the last two decades has been the emergence of a wide range of mechanisms designed to provide consumers with remedies for unfair treatment (McMillan 1981). Consumers of Commonwealth government services, and to a lesser extent state services, now have a number of options if they feel badly treated. Firstly, a complaint to a Member of Parliament or Minister may result in a ministerial request for an explanation of a decision taken by a departmental officer, and possibly a review of the decision. Secondly, complaints about unsatisfactory decisions may be referred to an independent or quasi-independent tribunal such as the Social Security Appeals Tribunal (SSAT) or the Administrative Appeals Tribunal (AAT). The SSAT is an independent body which can review social security matters, and change decisions made by the Department of Social Security. The AAT is a totally independent tribunal, spanning most areas of Commonwealth government activity, which has the powers to inquire into the merits of an administrative decision and change it if it sees fit (Sassella 1989). Similar tribunals, dealing with quite specific matters such as adoption applications, operate at State government level.

The ombudsman is another redress mechanism, now firmly established in Australian public administration at Commonwealth and state levels. An ombudsman is a full-time commissioner appointed by the government to receive and investigate individual complaints about administrative decisions and actions, and to make representations to the government agency concerned if the action is considered wrong (Spann 1979, p. 162). The ombudsman has quite extensive powers of investigation, and a high level of independence. The activities of ombudsmen on behalf of consumers have been described as 'a strange mixture of counselling, mediation, investigation, analysis and administrative recommendation' (Selby 1989, p. 174).

Complaints units are a further type of redress mechanism that have emerged, particularly in the areas of health and police services. In New South Wales a complaints unit exists as an independent investigate body within the Department of Health. In Victoria, a health services commissioner is available to investigate consumer complaints. The emphasis of the Victorian scheme is on conciliation of complaints in an informal and non-intimidating manner, and, through monitoring of complaints, to identify problems in the provision of health services (Darvall 1990). The office was established partially in response to perceived inadequacies of professional registration boards as mechanisms for dealing with consumer complaints (Victoria, Health Services Complaints Office 1986). State Consumer Affairs Departments are another avenue of complaint sometimes used by consumers of human services.

If this array of tribunals, commissioners and complaints units prove unsatisfactory, consumers of public services have the possibility of seeking redress through the Courts, although the slowness and expense of Court proceedings were principal considerations leading to the establishment of the tribunals and other mechanisms described above. In the United States, but not at this time in Australia, significant opportunities for consumers of human service organisations are provided by class-action suits, that is, actions brought by a number of people on behalf of others who share common characteristics, such as all residents of a nursing home or all persons receiving a particular benefit (Stein 1987). Class actions can be brought to change organisational policies and practices that allegedly violate consumers' rights. This provides consumers with opportunities to use the Courts to pressure organisations, without incurring large personal expense.

The array of redress mechanisms now available in the public sector provides consumers with significant opportunities for appeal and review of administrative decisions. Many individual consumers undoubtedly have benefited from these arrangements. However, judgements about the overall effectiveness of review processes for consumers are mixed. One perspective is that appeal mechanisms have led to much greater care in decision-making about consumer entitlements, changes to ambiguous rules and regulations, and better practices in the maintenance of files (Sassella 1989; Volker 1989). Others suggest that these effects are grossly exaggerated, and that there is widespread non-compliance with administrative review rulings. One commentator has suggested that the whole strategy of trying to create crystal clear legal entitlements through administrative review is mistaken: 'Discretionary processes may be superior to rules, especially if there is adequate accountability and some attempt to "structure" their exercise by way of guidelines, presumptions and so on' (Carney 1989, p. 130).

Social and welfare workers need to be aware of the redress opportunities available to the consumers of their organisations. Workers can play a significant role in making information about these opportunities available, and advising consumers on appropriate use of them. Workers can also contribute to an organisational culture that is supportive of consumers' rights to make complaints or appeal decisions. In contexts where review and appeal processes are rudimentary or non-existent, such as in many parts of the non-government sector, workers can contribute to their development.

Undertaking consumer advocacy

Advocacy, as a technique or method, has long held a central place in social and welfare work practice (Sosin and Caulum 1983). Workers often portray themselves as the champions or representatives of their clients in relation to the Courts, the police, and other professionals and organisations. Much social and welfare work in many organisational contexts resembles this model. Workers engage in finding resources for consumers, sorting out administrative hassles, obtaining information, and speaking for consumers in their dealings with the organisation. In this broad sense, consumer advocacy is part and parcel of the worker's role.

Viewed in organisational terms, however, workers' claims to being consumer advocates can be questioned. As we saw in the previous chapter, front-line workers need to negotiate the competing demands of the organisation, co-workers and consumers. They also have their own personal and organisational agenda. Their formal accountability is to the organisation. Their relationship to consumers is not that of an independent advocate, with no interests but those of the consumer. Take the example of workers in the Department of Social Security. They will often 'advocate' on behalf of a consumer to obtain a benefit, or to sort out an administrative tangle. But in so doing, they will necessarily take into account their relations with co-workers, office policies, their own sense of what is fair in the light of other cases that they have dealt with, and their own organisational workload. Similarly, a worker in a State Family Services Department may 'advocate' in the Courts and the Department on behalf of a child for whom he or she is responsible. But this advocacy will take place in a context of legitimate concern about other matters: the management of departmental resources, the need to maintain good relations with the Courts and other agencies, the expectations of co-workers, and so forth.

This begs the question of the definition of advocacy. From the standpoint of organisational analysis, our view is that the term is best applied to situations where a consumer is provided with an independent person or organisation, whose sole function is to further the interests and well-being of that consumer. The advocate has a relationship to the consumer analogous to that of a barrister to a client. This is structurally distinct from situations where a member of an organisation, such as a social or welfare worker, upholds or promotes the cause of a consumer. This latter activity is important, and it is often convenient to call it advocacy. But it is conceptually distinguishable from 'independent advocacy'.

There has been a considerable expansion in recent years in the availability of independent advocacy for consumers. Much of this has occurred in the field of disability. Advocacy can take a number of forms. Most states now have guardianship provisions for intellectually disadvantaged people. Guardianship allows for the legal transactions of an intellectually disadvantaged adult to be made for them by another person, called their guardian (Carney 1990). Another approach is to set up a statutory body with general responsibilities to advocate on behalf of consumers. An example is the Office of the Public Advocate in Victoria. Its charter states that it ' . . . is unashamedly on the side of people with disabilities. It encourages, supports or actively takes their part to ensure that their voice is heard—to develop, present and sustain their case where their choices, interests or rights are prejudiced' (Nicholls and Andrew 1990, p. 8). Independent, non-statutory bodies can also be given responsibilities of this kind. Advocacy can be undertaken on behalf of individuals, or individuals can be assisted in 'self-advocacy', that is, in developing or maintaining the skills and self-confidence needed to represent their own interests.

Advocacy is a particularly important strategy in situations where consumers are unable to speak for themselves or need assistance in doing so. It can be viewed as a means of altering the power balance between the consumer and the organisation by giving consumers access to skills and knowledge they would not otherwise possess. Workers need to both continue their traditional advocacy activities and recognise situations where independent advocacy is called for. Workers should be knowledgeable of existing advocacy agencies and aware of the potential role of advocacy arrangements in their field of human service provision.

Pressuring the organisation

Many of the approaches discussed above involve enhancing consumers' capacity to exert political pressure on human service organisations. This can also be achieved through consumer pressure groups which have the explicit purpose of promoting the interests of consumers in their dealings with organisations. Examples of consumer pressure groups are tenants' unions, health consumers' organisations, organisations of parents of disabled children, and parents' and citizens' councils. Just as workers gain political strength through industrial and professional association, so consumers can gain from organisations that promote their interests. Consumer pressure groups can represent consumers in consultative processes, advocate on behalf of individual consumers, conduct research and investigation of consumer issues, and keep a watching brief on organisational policies and practices that impinge on consumers. They can also conduct campaigns designed to persuade or force human service organisations to change their actions.

The level of political organisation of consumer groups, and their political influence and effectiveness, varies for the reasons outlined earlier in this chapter. A major issue for all consumer groups is co-option by the organisation. It is common for human service organisations to provide funding for consumer organisations, and for senior managers to attempt to forge close relations with the leaders of these organisations. This gives managers access to information about consumers, and a way of structuring discussion and contact with consumers at a policy level. Consumer organisations can themselves gain from close links with management. But the dangers of being incorporated into the decision-making processes of the organisation, and of losing contact with consumer needs and aspirations are real. Because of these dangers, some consumer groups decide to accept the consequences of remaining as outsiders, and adopting an adversarial stance towards the organisation. Alinsky's well-known writings and experiences of organising people's movements provide a model for consumer groups contemplating engaging in oppositional politics (Alinsky 1969). The issues associated with the use of consensus, contest and conflict tactics are examined in chapter 10.

Social and welfare workers should endeavour to develop close relations with consumer organisations, while recognising the distinct and separate nature of their own interests and position. They should give all due weight to the positions and policies of consumer groups, and contribute to the dissemination of these perspectives within the organisation. They can assist consumer organisations by providing information about organisational policies and processes by assisting groups to access the organisation and by giving other forms of support as requested.

Transforming authority structures

The strategies we have examined involve modifying the power balance between consumers and human service organisations in the consumer's favour. It needs to be acknowledged that, while each strategy may have a contribution to make to organisational responsiveness to consumers, they all leave existing authority structures intact. They assume the continuing existence of an organisation in which authority is vested in a management structure that is separate to consumers. Earlier in the chapter, the extent of consumer authority was identified as one of the basic factors shaping the power of consumers. The final options to be considered involve the transfer of organisational authority from the existing managers to consumers.

Two distinct approaches to transforming authority structures in this way can be distinguished. The first involves the creation of consumer-directed organisations, that is, non-government orga–nisations whose managing board comprises a majority or a totality of consumers elected by consumers. Consumer representatives would, in this way, acquire decision-making power over key organisational processes such as the appointment and direction of staff, the allocation and use of resources, and the formation of organisational goals and policy. Clearly, this would quite significantly shift the balance of power in the organisation. It would involve moving beyond consumer participation in decision-making into consumer authority over decision-making. Whether or not this would result automatically in consumer control, as assumed by some writers (e.g. Arnstein 1969, p. 217), is debatable. A consumer-directed organisation has to respond, like all other organisations, to pressures and influences arising in the organisational environment. Moreover, a consumer board, like other management bodies, is likely to have difficulties controlling the front-line workers in the organisation. Consumer boards have to take decisions that balance the needs and preferences of consumers with available resources, the preferences of staff, and other organisational constraints. In short, they have to grapple with the same issues of ensuring responsiveness to consumers as any other human service organisation.

The second approach to transforming authority structures involves the development of alternative organisations as discussed in chapter 6. In the alternative model of organisational structure, the distinctions between the roles of manager, worker and consumer are minimised or abandoned, with all persons involved in the organisation being viewed as equal, participating members of the collectivity. Such structures represent a radically different way of thinking about the issue of responsiveness to consumer needs. However, they present difficulties for consumers unable to give a wholehearted commitment to the collective and its processes. Given the segmented and fragmented nature of social relations in contemporary society, the full repertoire of strategies that we have outlined are needed to foster organisational responsiveness to consumer needs.

Conclusions

In many human service organisations there is a wide gap between the rhetoric of consumer service and the realities of service provision. If social and welfare workers are to contribute to a narrowing of this gap, they need an organisational analysis and perspective. Firstly, it is important to be aware of what it means to be a consumer of a human service organisation. Consumers are people, recipients, targets, members and resources in relation to organisations. Recognising these various roles helps us to understand why organisations treat their consumers as they do. Secondly, organisation–consumer relations need to be conceptualised in power terms. Attempts to improve responsiveness to consumers must begin by analysing the power, influence and authority of consumers, relative to the organisation and its participant groups. Factors influencing the power of consumers include the extent of their formal authority, their degree of choice, their knowledge and information, their social status, the extent to which they are politically organised, and the extent to which they have rights that are legally and morally recognised by the organisation. These factors are summarised in Table 9.1. Workers should be particularly aware of the influence of gender, ethnicity and race in organisation–consumer relations, and should be conscious of the ways in which women, non-English speaking people, Aboriginal people and other disadvantaged, marginalised or excluded groups are treated by the organisation.

There is a wide repertoire of strategies available to human service organisations and workers to improve organisational responsiveness to consumers. These are summarised in Table 9.2. All of them entail, directly or indirectly, increasing the power, authority or influence of consumers. Workers need to understand these different strategies, and be able to apply them selectively in differing organisational contexts and situations. It is of paramount importance that workers use all opportunities to keep in touch with consumers, and not assume a knowledge and understanding of consumer needs and aspirations. Equally importantly, workers need to continually acknowledge and accept that consumers have interests that are distinct from, and may be in conflict with, those of workers and the organisation.

Chapter review questions

1 What does an organisational perspective on organisation–consumer relations entail?
2 What is distinctive about a political economy perspective on organisation–consumer relations? What do other perspectives on organisational analysis suggest about organisation–consumer relations?
3 What are some of the terms used to refer to those 'on the receiving end' of human service organisations? What term or terms do you prefer to use, and why?
4 What are the dimensions or elements associated with being a consumer in human service organisations? What are the implications of each of these elements?
5 What is meant by the phrase 'the politics of consumer–worker–organisation relations'?
6 What are the six factors impinging on the power, influence and authority of consumers in relation to human service organisations?
7 What are the twelve strategies that comprise the repertoire for improving service responsiveness to consumers? Which of these do you see as applicable to specific human service organisations that you are familiar with?
8 What particular problems and issues are faced by disadvantaged, marginalised or excluded consumer groups, such as Aboriginal people, non-English speaking people, women, people with disabilities, people living in remote and isolated locations, and elderly people?

Further reading

Theoretical discussions of organisation–consumer relations are provided by Hasenfeld (1983, pp. 177-203) Forder (1974, pp. 140-150) and Etzioni (1964, pp. 94-104). Interesting descriptions of the politics of the front-line can be found in Sanders (1985), Painter (1980), and Satyamurti (1981). Case studies of inequitable practices in organisations relating to class, status, age and gender can be found in Scott (1974), Roth (1974) and Rist (1974). A useful framework for analysing access issues is provided by Gates (1980, pp. 48-60). Brown and Ringma (1989) analyse the difficulties of expanding consumer participation in the field of disability. Rights-based strategies in the field of nursing homes are illustrated by Ronalds (1989), and, in the field of youth homelessness, by the Report of the Human Rights and Equal Opportunity Commission (1989). Recent developments in administrative law relating to redress opportunities for consumers are critiqued in Carney (1989). McCulloch (1989) critically assesses the implications of new information technology for consumers.

Case study

RESIDENTS' RIGHTS IN THE BANKSIA NURSING HOME

The Banksia Nursing Home operates under the auspices of a Protestant church with subsidies provided by the Commonwealth government. It includes a nursing home and hostel-style accommodation. Seventy of the 100 residents are women. The home is under the overall control of a Director of Nursing who is responsible for day-to-day management. The Director of Nursing reports to a management committee appointed by the Social Care and Services Division of the church. The committee mainly comprises church members with a professional or personal interest in aged care. The staff includes registered nurses, enrolled nurses and personal-care assistants, together with kitchen, domestic and gardening staff. The nature and extent of illness and disability varies considerably from resident to resident. About half of them receive various support services, but are able to look after many of their own needs. Others need extensive nursing care, and there are a number who are considered to be suffering from dementia-related disorders. A range of professional staff visit the home to provide services. These include a chiropodist, a physiotherapist and a recreation officer. Local clergy also regularly visit the home. Medical services are provided on a daily visiting basis by a local medical partnership.

Recently, a number of new members have been appointed by the church to the Board of Management. One of these is a well-known member of the State Council on the Ageing. This appointment reflected a view that closer links should be developed with other organisations in the aged-care area. One of the matters raised by the new members is the need to respond to anticipated changes in Commonwealth government policy on residential-care facilities for elderly people. A recent review sponsored by the Commonwealth government has been highly critical of existing standards of care in many services. It has proposed a series of measures to make the management of residential care facilities more accountable and responsive to consumers, and to protect resident's rights. Some of the proposals emanating from the review are:

- the adoption of a Charter of Residents Rights to be endorsed by all funded services;
- a requirement that there be explicit contracts between residents and the service providing organisation;
- a requirement for resident participation in the management of residential institutions;
- a requirement for adequate internal complaints mechanisms and for access to external complaints and redress procedures;
- better information to be made available to elderly people about their rights as residents of nursing home or hostels;

- the development of advocacy mechanisms in nursing homes and hostels including the appointment of community visitors, available to residents to assist them to raise issues of concern with management.

All of these would require considerable changes to the management structures and practices of the Banksia Nursing Home.

In response to the concerns of the new committee members, the Board of Management decided that there was a need to consider the implications of these proposals for the Banksia Nursing Home, and in particular to ensure that the organisation was ready to meet any future requirements or revised guidelines for funding. The Board decided to do this by appointing a qualified social worker/community welfare worker for a six month period to look at organisation–resident relations in the light of the report. The appointment would be evaluated and reviewed at the end of the six months. Employment of a social or welfare worker had been considered from time to time previously by the Board, as it had been felt by some Board members that such a worker could assist residents with many of their personal tasks and difficulties. In particular, some Board members felt a worker could assist residents to have more contact with their families and with the local community. As a result of these different concerns, a job description was developed stating that:

The worker will provide a welfare service to residents, and, drawing on the knowledge that he/she acquires of residents' needs, will recommend to the Board ways in which the Banksia Nursing Home might most appropriately respond to the consumer issues raised in the recent Commonwealth government report. In her/his day-to-day work, the worker will report to the Director of Nursing.

At her interview for the job, the worker was told by the Chairperson of the Board that, 'Our basic concern is for the overall well-being of the patients, and we want you to use all your professional skills to make them happy and comfortable'.

On her first day, the worker met with the Director of Nursing to discuss her role. The Director was friendly, but did not disguise her misgivings about the appointment. She expressed her view that, 'There is a greater need for the appointment of an experienced occupational therapist than for a welfare worker. However, the Board has made its decision'. She added that she 'Felt sure that you will be able to contribute to the smooth running of the Home, once you understand our routines and the needs of the patients'. The Matron stressed the need for the worker to focus on the 'welfare needs of the patients', and to leave matters concerning their nursing care to the nursing staff. It was agreed that for the first six weeks, the worker would become involved in working with residents to get a feel of the place, and that at the end of that time the worker's activities would be reviewed.

During the first six weeks the worker became extremely busy dealing with the many financial, personal and family problems of residents. She also observed the practices and routines of the organisation, and attempted to familiarise herself with its policies and regulations. A number of incidents and events caused her considerable concern. These included:

- There seemed to be very few written guidelines or manuals. When problems arose they were referred to the Director. Some of the her decisions seemed quite arbitrary.
- Many of the domestic staff came from non-English speaking backgrounds. It was obvious that on many occasions they simply did not understand what the residents were saying to them.
- One non-English speaking resident seemed to have no family, friends, and no visitors. She seemed to be losing her very limited ability to communicate in English, often responding to questions in her own language or not at all.
- There was a routine practice of referring to residents as 'dear', 'love' and 'gran' and referring to elderly women in conversations among staff as 'old biddies'.
- A birthday party was held where everyone wore child-size, shiny party hats and had their own basket of lollies.
- A 'diversion therapy session' involved residents cutting out pictures of flowers and taping them to the walls. An elderly woman who had walked a few paces away from this activity was firmly returned and reseated by an attendant.
- The worker had a discussion with a resident who said that, 'Before I came here, I always used to have a flutter at the TAB on Saturdays, but I can't do that any more. They don't approve of gambling'.
- All staff were required to wear uniforms. Nursing staff wear white, domestic staff blue. Everyone wears a name tag. The residents often address the Director as 'mother'.
- In dealing with a number of problems concerning the operation of the home, bought to her by residents, a common response has been, 'It doesn't help to complain, and besides, I was brought up not to complain, dear'.
- On one occasion a female staff member expressed shock at a female resident's burst of anger and use of a mild expletive over a medical problem, 'Mrs Jones, I thought you were a lady!'
- The staff commonly refer to one section of the home where the most dependent residents live as the 'Babies' wing'.
- A woman resident said to the worker, 'It's the men here that I feel sorry for. We women are used to being tied up, we've had it all our lives'.
- The worker overheard a nurse responsible for allocating rooms say, 'Mrs Smith will have the best room. I've never heard her complain once'.
- A proposal from a small group of residents that they would like to play cards rather than carpet bowls during the recreational period was over-ridden by the residents helping to organise the recreational programme.
- A man who wanted to smoke his pipe while watching television was told by a nurse that it was a 'filthy, smelly habit, that offends the other residents'. He was asked to smoke outside.

After the worker had been in the organisation for about four weeks she was told by the Director that there would be a visit the following week from a 'standards monitoring team' from the Commonwealth government. The role of the standards monitoring teams was to periodically visit homes to investigate service standards and the quality of care. The worker was surprised by the intense preparations made for the visit of the monitoring team. At the beginning of the week all staff received a pep talk from the Matron on the importance of presenting a good image to the team. Two extra casual nursing staff were hired, and several rooms were given a spring clean. One room was repainted and a problem with smells from a defective drain was remedied. There seemed to be a greater variety of food on the menu during the visit, and the food was better presented. One resident told the worker, 'Oh, you always know when they're going to inspect us because they fix everything up. Don't worry, we will soon be back to normal'. Following the visit, which seemed to go well, the worker asked the Director of Nursing if she might see the report of the monitoring team. The Director replied, 'That's no concern of yours. Dealing with the monitoring team is my responsibility. Your function relates to the residents' welfare, not the running of the home'.

Six weeks have now passed by, and it is time for the worker to discuss her work, role and future plans with the Director.

Key question

What factors are shaping organisation–consumer relations in the Banksia Nursing Home? Analyse the factors that may have led to the present circumstances and treatment of the residents. What would you say in your discussions with the Director of Nursing, and how would you approach the task of making the organisation more responsive to the needs of residents? Give reasons for your answers.

Case discussion points

1 How are the residents perceived by the staff of the Home?
2 Discuss the different roles that the residents have or potentially have in the organisation. Are they treated as people, recipients, targets, members, resources or in some other ways?
3 Are the interests of the residents, the staff, and the organisation in conflict? Explain your answer.
4 Do the residents have any significant sources of power, authority or influence in the Banksia Nursing Home? If so, what are they?
5 What factors should influence the approach that the worker will take in this situation? What should be her strategies to deal with the issues she sees as problematic? How successful is she likely to be?
6 How does an analysis of the organisational environment, goals, structure and culture impinge on your analysis?
7 What reforms are necessary and possible to make the organisation more responsive to the needs of the residents?

10

Change and resistance in organisations

... organisations change continually but they rarely do what everyone, or even some people, intend (Dawson 1986, pp. 211-212).

Social and welfare work and organisational change

Change is a central theme in social and welfare work and in the study of organisations. Social and welfare work portrays itself as a change-oriented occupation, concerned with change at many levels: individual, group, community, organisation and society. Workers often view themselves as change agents in these various contexts. Many of the recurrent theoretical and practice issues in the profession concern the nature of change, the possibilities of achieving real change, and strategies for bringing about change. Throughout this book, change has been a recurrent theme. We have examined the impact of the environment on stability and change in organisations, and the ways that organisations can bring about changes in their task environment. We have looked at the dynamic nature of organisational goals, including the processes of goal displacement, succession and adaptation. Organisational structure has been presented as a set of social relations that are continually re-created. Culture, too, has been portrayed as being continuously disseminated, reproduced, challenged and changed. It is impossible to understand organisations, or any significant aspect of social and welfare work, without addressing questions of change.

Our perspective on the relations between social and welfare work, organisations and change has three main emphases. Firstly, we stress the centrality of organisational change for social and welfare work. Clearly, all the other levels of change listed above are critically important. However, workers need to be aware of the centrality of organisations in most change processes. Organisations are the context, the vehicle and the target for many change-oriented activities. They are the context in that workers typically undertake change-oriented activities as members of organisations, and this membership creates opportunities and constraints that cannot be disregarded. They are the vehicle in that the resources to take part in change processes are mobilised through and largely controlled by organisations. They are the targets of change processes because of the impact that their policies, practices and structures have on consumers and society. Workers cannot understand change without understanding organisations.

Our second emphasis is the importance of seeing change from a political perspective. There are, of course, many different ways of viewing change, and specifically organisational change. The perspectives on organisational analysis introduced in chapter 2 suggest a number of approaches. Scientific management approaches organisational change as essentially a structural issue linked to efficient production. Organisational change, from this point of view, is essentially about alterations to structures, production processes and technologies to bring about a better product at lower cost. Much management-initiated change in human service organisations is couched in these terms. The human relations perspective, by contrast, focuses on personal and inter-personal change processes in organisations. Change occurs, it is argued, largely through social psychological factors. Those wishing to bring about change must focus on issues such as motivation, leadership, group process and culture. Systems theory sees change arising from an organisation's need for survival and growth. In particular, the need to adapt to the ever-changing environment provides much of the impetus for organisational change. Decision theories view change as driven by the attempts by organisational participants to cope, as best they can, with uncertainty. Market theorists view change as the outcome of transactions among individuals and groups with a stake in the organisation, all pursuing their self-interest. Neo-Marxian analysts stress the importance of understanding the relations between processes occurring in modern capitalist societies and changes in organisations. Change and continuity in human service organisations can best be explained, they suggest, in terms of the structural constraints and needs of the capitalist economy and political system. Feminist perspectives seek fundamental changes to gender relations in modern organisations and societies. Aboriginal perspectives similarly see the need for fundamental change in the treatment of Aboriginal people by non-Aboriginal organisations.

All of these frameworks contribute to our understanding of organisational change. However, it is the political economy perspective that most directly underpins the analysis of this chapter. Organisational change, from this point of view, occurs as an outcome of ongoing political struggle among the stakeholders in a human service organisation, which itself is located in broader social, political and economic structures. Hence, change and continuity are understood in terms of the power, authority and influence of the various organisational participants. Workers wishing to bring about organisational change must, therefore, seek ways to acquire authority, exercise influence, and maximise their political power. Change processes must include an assessment of the political resources of the individual or group initiating the change, and of all other parties to the process.

Thirdly, we stress the need to maintain a critical perspective on change and change processes. Change is not desirable for its own sake. In times of challenge and cut back to human services, workers may more often find themselves defending the status quo, and resisting the change initiatives of others. Moreover, the risks and difficulties associated with initiating organisational change should be recognised. Change objectives may have unintended and undesired consequences. Change processes, once initiated, may veer off in directions not anticipated by their sponsors. The costs of change, in terms both of personal and physical resources, are often considerable, and must be taken into consideration. Change may also be ephemeral, failing to meet the test of time. For these, and other reasons, workers need an understanding of the nature of organisational change, the factors influencing organisational change, and strategic and tactical issues in change processes. These are the key topics covered in this chapter.

The nature of organisational change

The proverb 'the more things change the more they stay the same', captures the ambiguity and paradox of the issue of organisational change. On the one hand, change is part of the ongoing experience of workers in organisations. People come and go, job definitions change, new technologies modify and sometimes transform work practices, structures are reorganised, and goals and programmes are introduced or abandoned in response to changes in the organisational environment. The rapid pace of such changes in some organisations presents major difficulties for workers. The key issue facing many workers in practice is not 'how can I bring about change?' so much as 'how can I cope with, or resist, the rapid changes taking place around me?'

On the other hand, workers are faced with the awesome persistence of many features of organisational life. Sometimes, it seems that no matter what happens and no matter what attempts are made to bring about change, things stay the same. Dominant attitudes and values, no matter how dysfunctional in new circumstances, often prove impervious to all attempts to change. Large scale re-organisations, heralded as major reforms, end up reproducing the characteristics of the structures they were intended to replace. The position of consumers remains unaltered, despite repeated initiatives designed to increase organisational responsiveness to their needs. Inherited goals, structure and culture sometimes seem to have an enduring quality that resists all known change methodologies.

The key to this paradox lies in acknowledging the co-existence and complementary of change and continuity. It is unhelpful to think of continuity or stability as somehow a natural state of affairs, and change as something that has to be engineered. The converse position is equally unhelpful. Rather, we need to recognise that all organisations, and social phenomena generally, are concurrently persisting and changing. Workers need to understand the factors impinging on continuity and change, and need to be adept in strategies and techniques both to preserve valued elements of their organisation and to modify or transform its undesirable features (Watzlawick, Weakland and Fisch 1974, pp. 1-2).

Attempts to define organisational change typically focus either on the elements of change or on the significance of change. Brager and Holloway's major work on change processes in human service organisations takes the first of these approaches. They distinguish three main elements of organisational change: people-focused change, technological change and structural change. Each of these, they suggest, can bring about significant changes in the actions and interactions of organisational participants, although the impact of structural change is likely to be the most lasting and profound, and that of changes in people the least significant (1978, pp. 18-21). The theoretical framework for organisational analysis developed in part II suggests a somewhat different classification of the elements of organisational change to that suggested by Brager and Holloway. From this perspective, organisational change can be viewed as entailing modification to the environment, goals, structure or culture of an organisation, as well as to its technology. Identifying the elements of change is helpful in formulating change strategies. A key issue for those involved in initiating and participating in change processes is analysis of the nature of the problem at hand, and hence the nature of the required change.

Attempts to define change in terms of its significance have to grapple with the issue of what constitutes real change as opposed to mere modification or alteration of organisational processes. A number of useful distinctions have been made. Hasenfeld distinguishes change from both adjustment and innovation (1983, pp. 219-220). An innovation is the adoption of a practice, service, idea or method perceived as new within the organisation. For example, the adoption of a computerised management information system in place of conventional files would be an organisational innovation. Innovations often entail importing practices and techniques developed elsewhere. An organisational adjustment involves processes designed to maintain stability by responding to pressures arising inside and outside the organisation. For example, an organisation faced with increased workloads but no extra resources may decide to close its doors for one afternoon per week in order to catch up on report writing and record keeping. Organisational change, by contrast, involves 'transformation of both the internal polity and the economy of the organisation' (Hasenfeld 1983, p. 220). Change, from this perspective, is a term that should be applied only to situations involving re-allocation of organisational resources, or alterations in the patterns of organisational power, authority and influence. Thus, a decision to replace a casework service with a preventative programme would be a change, insofar as it involves a significantly different use of resources. Similarly, the introduction of a redress system for consumers would represent a change if it significantly altered the power balance between consumers and workers. Whether or not a particular set of events amount to a change, an innovation or an adjustment is clearly a matter of judgement and interpretation, and may well be disputed.

A closely related distinction is that between symbolic and real change (Hasenfeld 1983, p. 220). A symbolic change involves alterations to structure, goals, culture or technology that purport to bring about, but do not in fact produce, re-allocation of resources or alterations in patterns of power, authority or influence. For example, giving a consumer a place on the managing board of an organisation may be portrayed as a means of increasing the power of consumers, but may actually result in the co-option of consumer interests. The distinction between formal and informal change is also relevant here. Changes in the formal structure of organisations may appear to alter political relations among organisational participants, while informal processes may maintain and sustain existing power relations. The opposite may also occur.

It is also useful to consider the distinction sometimes drawn between major and minor organisational changes. In theory this is a relatively clear distinction, at least at the extremes. A major change is one having an extensive impact on the problem or concern in question. A minor change represents but a small step towards dealing with the problem. However, in practice the distinction is rather more ambiguous. Firstly, the significance of a change will not be viewed in the same way by all participants. For example, a major re-organisation of a government department may have great significance for senior managers for whom it represents a restructuring of the pattern of power, authority and influence in the organisation. But for a front-line worker struggling with a massive caseload it may seem almost totally irrelevant. Secondly, minor changes may well trigger major changes at some future time (Brager and Holloway 1978, p. 21). For example, a decision to introduce a modest pilot programme may lead eventually to a re-vamping of an organisation's whole service repertoire. Thirdly, the distinction between major and minor change can be viewed in political terms, rather than in terms of impact on a perceived problem. From this perspective, a change is major or minor to the extent that it impacts on the interests of many or few organisational participants, and to the extent that it challenges or modifies existing patterns of power, influence and authority.

Another distinction often drawn is between first-order and second-order organisational change (Watzlawick, Weakland and Fisch 1974; Levy 1987). This distinction suggests that many changes, those called first-order changes, occur within the established framework of 'what is acceptable and possible'. However, there are other changes, second-order changes, that involve challenge to the existing ways of viewing problems and organisational responses to them. First-order change ' . . . involves a variation that occurs within a given system which itself remains unchanged'. Second-order change ' . . . involves a variation whose occurrence changes the system itself . . . it is a change of change . . . it is always in the nature of a discontinuity or logical jump' (Watzlawick, Weakland and Fisch 1974, pp. 10-12). Other writers have used other sets of terms to make this distinction, including transition and transformation, normal and paradigm change, branch and root change, superficial and real change, and momentum change and revolutionary change (Levy 1987, pp. 8-9).

To illustrate this kind of distinction, take the case of an organisation providing services to people with an intellectual disability. First-order changes might include such things as developing new services, improving the standard of buildings and accommodation, and employing more professional staff. However, all of these changes might be based on an organisational understanding that the potential for growth and development of people with intellectual disabilities is extremely limited. If the organisation and its members fundamentally changed this perspective to acknowledge the untapped potential for growth and development in all persons, including those with intellectual disabilities, a whole new set of possibilities for the organisation would be opened up. This would be second-order change. Many alternative organisations, such as those discussed in chapter 6, can be viewed as experiments in second-order organisational change.

A further, important distinction is between planned and unplanned organisational change. Organisational change is planned when 'the organisational variables to be modified have been identified in advance, and the objectives of the desired change have been explicitly stated' (Hasenfeld and English 1974, p. 680). Unplanned change involves response to external and internal exigencies that are largely unanticipated or uncontrollable. The distinction is sometimes one of perspective and position. The planned change of one organisational group may be experienced as an unexpected difficulty by another. On other occasions all groups within an organisation face unanticipated changes induced by factors arising in the organisational environment.

Another distinction sometimes drawn is between changes that are radical and fundamental in nature and those that are not. It is sometimes suggested, for example, that many of the kinds of organisational changes discussed in this chapter are mere 'band-aid solutions' that do not address the root causes of consumers' problems. Undoubtedly, the root causes of many of the problems that human service organisations attempt to address are embedded in the economic, political and social structures of Australian society. Indeed, it can be plausibly argued that their origins lie in the global political and economic order. However, in our view, it does not follow that solutions that fall short of some supposed total solution should be dismissed as mere alleviation or amelioration. There are no simple panaceas for broad-scale social reform. Any conceivable future society will have to address the same kinds of organisational and policy issues that currently confront the human services and other social institutions. Furthermore, it can be argued that significant social change and social progress often occurs incrementally via piecemeal reforms. Indeed, all solutions to problems are, at some level, partial and incomplete. It is undoubtedly important for workers to give consideration to the relations between their work and their understanding of broad-scale social change processes. But the immediate, tangible challenges of participating in the ongoing changes occurring in human service organisations are not of secondary or lesser significance.

Finally, it must be kept in mind that change in human service organisations is inherently problematic because of their distinctive characteristics. Because human service organisations work with people they often have indeterminate technologies, unclear and contentious goals and disputed and imprecise measures of effectiveness. This means that the issue of whether real change has been achieved is often perplexing and debateable. There is no litmus test to definitively prove, for example, that an organisation has become more responsive to consumers as a result of increased consumer representation on decision-making bodies. In the final analysis, the issue of whether a set of events amounts to change or to continuity is a matter of judgement, analysis and interpretation.

What makes organisations change?

Organisational change occurs via the actions of individuals and groups seeking to alter aspects of organisational life, specifically organisational goals, structure, environment, culture and technology. In this sense, all organisational change is political: it involves the exercise of power, authority and influence by some organisational participants over others. However, this political activity does not take place in a vacuum. All participants in organisational change processes, even those viewed as extremely powerful, act in circumstances that are largely not of their own making. Their actions are shaped by factors only partially under their control. It is these factors promoting change or maintaining continuity in organisations that we are attempting to identify.

Social and welfare workers participating in change processes in organisations need an understanding of these factors. Without such a theoretical framework, attempts to bring about or to resist change will be random and haphazard. In the literature on organisational change, the factors involved are often presented as forces for stability and forces for change (e.g. Hasenfeld 1983, pp. 221-239). Our approach is somewhat different. Following the framework developed in part II, we suggest that the factors resulting in change and stability in organisations can be examined through the four key concepts of environment, goals, structure and culture. Each of these fundamental elements contribute in complex ways to change and continuity in human service organisations. Many of the links between these elements and organisational change and continuity have been discussed in earlier chapters. The most important of these are briefly examined below.

The environment, change and continuity

The organisational environment is arguably the most significant force for change and continuity in human service organisations. This is because of the high level of environmental dependency of many organisations providing human services. If organisations are dependent on external bodies for key requirements such as resources and legitimation, it follows that external factors will be pivotal influences on change and continuity processes.

The environment's potentially stabilising influence can be grasped via the concept of domain consensus introduced in chapter 4. Often organisations establish relatively stable exchange relations with the range of organisations in their task environment. This domain consensus, that is agreement in the task environment about what the organisation is and what it will do, is often difficult to build and maintain. Proposed organisational changes that threaten this balance are likely to be resisted by groups within the organisation committed to the existing domain consensus.

Take the case of a non-government organisation providing a parent-aide service via volunteers for families in which child abuse has occurred. The organisation operates on a shoestring budget with funds from service clubs, the state government department responsible for child welfare, and a local hospital. It is widely perceived as doing good work in a highly cost-efficient manner, and receives many referrals from the department, the hospital and other social agencies. However, this domain consensus has been hard won, and, in the view of the underpaid co-ordinator of the organisation is extremely fragile. In her view, the support that the organisation has managed to obtain from the task environment is based on the cost-efficiency of the service stemming from the exclusive use of volunteers, and its ideological acceptability to major external groups. She is, therefore, highly resistant to proposals to change the organisation in ways that appear to threaten this domain consensus. Suggestions that the organisation employ qualified staff, change its service technology, or engage in public criticism of state government policy on the funding of child abuse services are likely to be opposed on the grounds of their perceived impact on the organisation's delicate domain consensus. Of course, there are many strategies and tactics open to the organisation to deal with these environmental issues (these are described in chapter 4). The point being made is that perceived environmental exigencies often restrain organisational change.

Change in the environment can, however, be a potent source of organisational change. To continue with the above example, there are many external factors that could prompt or force the parent-aide service to change. Its funding, albeit meagre, might be cut. An incident involving service to a consumer might lead to questioning of the appropriateness of volunteer work in such a sensitive area. Changes in industrial awards might result in a legal requirement that the co-ordinator be paid a better salary, with consequences for the financial viability of the service. A change of policy or personnel in the hospital or the establishment of a similar service by some other organisation may lead to a decline in referrals. All of these circumstances would require or call for changes of some kind in the operation of the organisation.

Several writers have listed the main environmental factors that provide impetus for change in human service organisations. Hasenfeld lists shifts in political sentiments in the political environment, shifts in legislative and governmental policies, changing funding patterns, transformations in consumer characteristics and needs, and new developments in service technologies (1983, pp. 225-231). Similarly, Brager and Holloway emphasise the shifting availability of funds, technological developments including programme fads and fashions, changing societal norms, values and beliefs, and changes in the viewpoints and political resources of significant actors. This last category comprises groups and individuals representing the interests of the public, consumers, and providers (1978, pp. 39-56).

The impact of the passage of the Commonwealth Government's Disability Services Act of 1986 on organisations providing services to people with disabilities illustrates the role, and inter-relatedness, of all these environmental factors (Morrison 1990). This legislation and subsequent government policies were a response to changing societal norms and shifts in political sentiments concerning the place of people with disabilities in the society. The new norms stressed the importance of providing opportunities for people with disabilities to fully participate in society, and the protection of their rights. The legislation sought to bring about major changes in the goals, structures, culture and services of funded organisations. It went about this by detailing the new service philosophy, specifying new programme types such as advocacy and competitive employment that reflected this philosophy, and tying the availability of funds to compliance with the new policy direction. Underlying and accompanying these developments were significant changes in consumer characteristics and needs. People with disabilities had developed different expectations of services which were articulated by organisations representing consumer interests. Other significant actors included professional groups committed to the new service philosophy and individuals such as the Commonwealth Minister of the time. This combination of environmental pressures created an impetus for change in service organisations in the disability field that lasted into the 1990s.

While environmental factors such as these are of great significance to organisational change and continuity, they are clearly not the whole story. In the field of disability, some organisations changed far quicker than others in response to the new environmental demands posed by the 1986 legislation. These variations in response reflect the major internal factors impacting on change and continuity: goals, structure and culture.

Goals, change and continuity

An organisation's predisposition towards change or towards continuity is influenced by the characteristics of its goals. The different kinds of organisational goals, the nature of goals in human service organisations, and the dynamic nature of goals were examined in chapter 5. Clearly, the content of goals can predispose an organisation towards change or towards continuity. An organisation committed, officially or informally, to 'experiment with new methods of working with young offenders' is more prone to change, at least in the area of service technology, than one that has a goal of 'continuing the approach to youth work set in train by our revered founder'. Organisations with goals concerning research, experimentation, policy development, demonstration and innovation, and political action are likely to be more oriented to change than those that frame their goals exclusively in terms of service delivery and policy implementation. For example, the goal of 'finding new means of increasing societal responsiveness to poverty and disadvantage' suggests a far greater openness to change than the goal of 'providing emergency relief payments to families in distress'.

Several other characteristics of organisational goals can be linked to a propensity for change or continuity. Goals that give expression to broad social values in vague and imprecise terms provide opportunities for organisational participants to validate change proposals by linking them to these statements. Conflict among organisational goals can provide tension that creates an impetus for change. Organisations with multiple goals that are reinforcing of one another tend to produce stability: 'only those changes that refine or elaborate the unified set of goals can be considered' (Brager and Holloway 1978, p. 65). However, goals that are difficult to co-ordinate may lead to change-inducing competition among organisational participants with differing priorities. The intensity with which goals are held and pursued by people in the organisation is another key factor. When goals are held and pursued with vigour and passion the outcome may be either rapid change or deep entrenchment of the status quo. Low levels of goal commitment leave the organisation wide open to externally induced pressures.

Finally, organisations that engage in regular, formal re-examination and re-appraisal of goals and objectives are more likely to be open to change than those that do not. Processes of goal analysis and strategic planning, and similar exercises, provide participants with opportunities to influence the direction the organisation will take. Regular undertaking of such activities may indicate an organisational willingness to innovate, although it must be borne in mind that planning processes can also be used to bolster managerial control.

Structure, change and continuity

The relationship between organisational structure and an inclination towards change or continuity has been extensively researched and discussed (Brager and Holloway 1978, pp. 66-75). Much of this has been in terms of the three basic characteristics of organisations distinguished in chapter 6: complexity, centralisation and formalisation. The major conclusions, which are somewhat equivocal, can be readily summarised. Firstly, it is argued that organisations that are more complex in terms of diversity of tasks and thus the 'number of specialisms' tend to generate more new ideas and ways of doing things. An organisation providing a single service type through workers with the same occupational background is less likely to generate new ideas than one with a diversity of tasks and a range of professional workers, each competing for organisational acceptance of their perspective. On the other hand, complexity may make it difficult for new ideas to be accepted and implemented. Professionals tend to resist being told what to do by members of other professional groups, and complexity may thus impede change unless there is one group able to impose its will because of its higher status and authority.

Organisations with highly centralised authority have traditionally been assumed to inhibit change. Hierarchical structures, it is argued, make organisations sluggish in their decision-making, and discourage lateral communication and localised initiative. If everything has to be approved by head office, the pace of change is slowed and innovation stifled. While there is undoubtedly some validity in this view, the scale of change envisaged is a key factor. Small-scale changes may well do best in decentralised organisations that permit and encourage localised initiative. But major changes may require concentration of power to succeed (Hasenfeld 1983, pp. 233-4). For example, the major changes required of organisations in the disability field, discussed earlier in this chapter, may only be possible through the vigorous exercise of power and authority by the central management of those organisations. Decentralisation may facilitate innovation, but centralisation may be needed to effect organisational transformation, particularly in circumstances in which change is resisted.

A high degree of formalisation, that is, the codification and standardisation of rules, roles and relations, is usually viewed as a factor inhibiting organisational change. Changes that have to go through elaborate processes of formulation and ratification may be more difficult to achieve than those that can be put into effect through informal agreements. Conversely, however, formalisation may be important in sustaining change. Changes that are institutionalised in the form of written rules and statements are more difficult to alter than informal arrangements and understandings.

Finally, the impact of the nature and availability of resources on continuity and change needs consideration. In general, resource rich organisations find change easier than those struggling with inadequate funds, facilities and personnel. Changes involving significant expenditure are likely to be resisted in resource poor organisations as they involve re-allocation from existing programmes or units. Major organisational change often requires specific allocation of resources to experimentation, development, research and planning. A key factor is the extent to which an organisation's resources are tied up in sunk costs, that is 'investments of resources that cannot readily be recovered and converted to other purposes' (Hasenfeld 1983, p. 223). For example, many organisations in the disability field find it difficult to convert from activities-based in large residential settings to community-based programmes due to their heavy investment in the buildings and staff needed to run institutional services. The greater the investment in sunk costs, the greater the inducement to organisational stability and continuity.

Culture, change and continuity

Organisational culture, as described in chapter 7, comprises the shared meanings, values, beliefs, ideology and norms of an organisation, and their expression in symbols, myths, stories, rites, language and artefacts. If an organisation has a dominant culture internalised by most or all organisational members, this can be a powerful force for organisational continuity. An intensely held ideology justifies existing practices, structures and service methods, and provides a screen through which incidents and information that challenge the organisation can be interpreted. Organisations characterised by competing cultures, on the other hand, provide fertile ground for change induced by competition among differing perspectives of the organisation's nature and purpose.

Culture, like goals, can be harnessed in change processes. 'An organisation with a dominant ideology is vulnerable to any innovation . . . that can be defined in terms of the prevailing belief and sentiment system . . . ' (Brager and Holloway 1978, p. 60). Thus, for example, in an organisational culture that stresses the values of efficiency and economy, a change proposal couched in these terms is more likely to be positively perceived. Conversely, culture can be used to stifle innovation. Proposals for new initiatives are met with the response that they are inconsistent with the organisation's traditions, norms and beliefs. This happens particularly in organisations with 'venerational' ideologies or cultures, that is, 'belief systems that have as their reference point some unique feature of the agency—its tradition, quality, leadership, or the like' (Brager and Holloway 1978, p. 59). In such organisations, change proposals confront arguments that they are inconsistent with the organisation's historic mission or 'the spirit of our founders'.

This raises the issue of the importance of the organisation's values and beliefs regarding change itself. Some organisations are change oriented, in the sense that workers and managers at all levels are oriented towards innovation in service methods and programmes. Others are oriented towards continuity and stability, with new ideas being evaluated in terms of their degree of conformity with the historical values of the organisation. All organisations are conscious to some degree of their past, present and future. But they vary in the extent to which they are shaped by past experiences or by anticipated challenges.

A framework for action and response

Social and welfare workers are interested in organisational change primarily from a practice perspective. They want to know how to participate as effectively as possible in change processes. To this end, we present in Table 10.1 a framework to guide workers as they endeavour to be significant actors in organisational change. It is constructed around the key elements of change processes detailed in this section, and indicates the key questions that workers must consider. Other writers have developed similar frameworks (e.g. Hasenfeld 1983, pp. 234-245; Brager and Holloway 1978, parts II-III; Dawson 1986, pp. 213-219) and we draw on their work. However, our framework has a number of distinctive features.

Firstly, it conceptualises the involvement of workers in organisational change as involving both initiation of and support for change and resistance to the change activities of others. Change is a ubiquitous feature of human service organisations, and is initiated by many different participants and in many different places. Certainly, social and welfare workers should view the initiation of change as part of their professional responsibility. However, the reality of organisational life is that workers are involved in many change processes that they themselves do not sponsor or control. Change processes are initiated by senior management, by other professionals and specialists, by funders and regulators in the organisational environment, and by consumers. Sometimes workers want to support such changes, and sometimes they want to resist them. The volume of change processes and issues coming from the organisation typically far exceeds those emanating from an individual worker or a single work unit. Indeed, one of the most difficult issues in change is that of getting one's own issue onto an already crowded organisational agenda. It is important to have a model of change that acknowledges that the worker is not necessarily, or even usually, at the centre of the action.

Our framework for change is also distinctive in that it is applicable to workers located at any point in the organisation. Some frameworks for change take a managerial stance: they are essentially concerned with showing how managers can bring about change in those areas of the organisation for which they are responsible (e.g. Stoner, Collins and Yetton 1985, pp. 446-485). Others are essentially concerned with change initiated by workers in the front-line (e.g. Brager and Holloway 1978). Our framework makes no such assumptions. It is undoubtedly true that the organisational location of a worker is a major consideration when considering participation in change processes. The location of workers affects their power, influence and authority, and their access to resources, information and key decision-making processes. However, whether workers are located at the front-line or in senior management positions, the basic elements of change and resistance operations are the same.

We conceptualise these elements as threefold: awareness, analysis and action. Awareness refers to the perception of the existence of a problem or difficulty requiring participation in change processes. Analysis involves examination of the nature of the problem, possible

Table 10.1 Participating in organisational change and resistance: key questions

---

Awareness

1   What issues are of concern to me in this organisation?
    a   What is my orientation to organisational change?
    b   What is my critical perspective on the organisation?
    c   What are my sources of information about the organisation and the issues it faces?
    d   How can I define and present these issues in organisational terms?

2   Which issues shall I choose to participate in?
    a   Which issues impinge on my personal and professional values and beliefs?
    b   Which issues impinge on my interests or stake in the organisation?
    c   Which issues do I have a significant chance of influencing, given my political resources?

Analysis

3   What is my change or resistance agenda?
    a   What specific outcomes am I trying to achieve?
    b   What are the elements of my change/resistance agenda, and in what ways are they inter-dependent?
    c   What are the stages of my change/resistance process?
    d   What elements of flexibility should I build into the process?
    e   What is the nature of the changes I am initiating, supporting or resisting?
    f   What is the scope of my change/resistance agenda?

4   What is my overall strategy?
    a   What strategic opportunities and constraints am I faced with, and how can I respond to them?
        i   Are existing organisational circumstances (environment, goals, structure, culture) supportive of or hostile to my change/resistance agenda?
        ii   How can my change agenda be shaped so as to take advantage of existing circumstances?
        iii What level of political resources do I have, or potentially have, in relation to the change agenda?
        iv   What is the level of support and resistance to my agenda from significant actors in the organisation?
    b   What is my broad approach to intervention?
        i   What mode of intervention will I use?
             • Should I use rational/empirical interventions?
             • Should I use normative/re-educative interventions?
             • Should I use power/coercive interventions?
             • Is some combination of interventions needed?

Analysis

      ii What is my overall stance towards the other participants in the change process?
- Will I take a collaborative approach?
- Will I take a campaign or contest approach?
- Will I take a conflict approach?
- Will I take a mixed approach, dealing with different participants and situations in different ways?

Action

5 How will I incline the organisation towards the impending change/resistance process?
  a Will I introduce new information into the organisation?
  b Will I bring new participants into the process?
  c How can I reframe currently 'accepted problems' to support the perceptions I am trying to create?

6 How will I initiate the change/resistance process?
  a Who should initiate the change?
  b To whom should the change initiative be addressed?
  c Which venue or mechanism should be used?
  d How should the change be presented?
    i What medium should be used?
    ii What image should be created?
  e If I am resisting an initiative, what potential is there for tactics of delay, diversion, deflection and dilution?

7 How will I implement the change/resistance process?
  a How will I plan the implementation process?
  b How will I maintain the commitment of my supporters?
  c How will I deal with ongoing resistance?
  d How will I deal with conflicts with other policies and procedures?
  e What will my role be throughout this process?

8 How will I institutionalise the process, and evaluate its outcomes?
  a How can the change be formalised?
  b How can the change be bonded to the organisation?
  c How should the change be evaluated?

---

responses to and resolutions of the problem, and the ways of working towards and achieving these resolutions. Action is the actual activity engaged in by the worker to bring about or to resist the change in question. These elements are mutually reinforcing and do not necessarily, or even typically, occur sequentially. Rather, the entry and exit points in change processes may involve any of these processes, and typically there is a continuous and dynamic process of feedback and re-appraisal of awareness, analysis and action as events unfold. Workers need to recognise this interactional, incremental nature of change processes. They also need awareness of the skills and issues involved in each of the three areas.

The final point that we emphasise is the element of chance, accident, hunch and unpredictability in organisational change processes. Participation in change processes is a risky and uncertain business. Usually, most of the factors affecting the process are outside the control of the individual worker. Often the best he or she can hope for is to influence events. A planned intervention can be stymied by one entirely unpredictable happening, such as the unexpected resignation of a key player or a trivial circumstance such as the inability of a person to attend a key meeting due to illness. Action, analysis and awareness of issues all need to be flexible enough to adapt to ongoing events.

Our approach to planned organisational change is, we suspect, somewhat counter-intuitive for some workers. Unlike many intervention models, it does not assume a central role for the worker. Workers may play a central role, but a more realistic assumption is that they are but one of the participants in complex organisational processes. Furthermore, we do not assume that workers are necessarily committed to change for its own sake; often they may be resisting the change initiatives of others. Moreover, the change process is not necessarily sequential, moving neatly from awareness, through to analysis and finally action, although it invariably includes all three elements. Nor is it typically a rational and predictable process. Examining their assumptions about change is, we suggest, a prerequisite for workers who hope to participate effectively in organisational change processes. The next step is to develop an appreciation of what is involved in the three elements of awareness, analysis and action.

Awareness of the need for change and resistance

A worker's involvement in planned organisational change or resistance begins with an awareness of an organisational change or resistance issue. A change or resistance issue can be any aspect of the organisation that the worker considers problematic. Any aspect of current or anticipated organisational goals, structure or culture, or any facet of service delivery methods and processes can become such an issue for a worker. Awareness is about both identification and choice of issues. A worker in a human service organisation needs to be attuned to identifying actual or potential difficulties or problems, and to have a capacity for making sound judgements as to which issues to address and which to leave alone.

Identification of change and resistance issues is itself a complex and demanding process. Firstly, it requires workers to have an orientation to organisational change. Social and welfare workers, no less than other individuals in organisations, can often be attracted by the advantages of organisational stability and of going with the flow. Involvement in change and resistance processes can be personally costly, and while there may also be personal benefits, these are rarely assured. Indeed, the benefits are often vicarious in that they are experienced by consumers, rather than by workers themselves. Involvement in change and resistance almost certainly involves at a minimum some extra effort, inconvenience, or uncertainty. It also involves the exercise of imagination. It is not uncommon for workers, particularly after they have been in an organisation for a considerable time, to arrive at the conclusion that the organisation, for all its undoubted shortcomings, represents about the best that is possible given all the circumstances. Workers also sometimes conclude that the organisation is completely beyond redemption. Neither of these positions facilitates awareness of change possibilities. Workers who lose, or who never acquire, a faculty for vision and imagination in relation to the organisation cannot be active identifiers of change and resistance issues.

Identification of change and resistance issues is also dependent on workers having a critical perspective on the organisation. This derives from workers' own values and beliefs and their theoretical perspective on organisations. Workers carry with them a view about the purposes of the organisation, how it should operate, and what their individual role in and relations with the organisation should be. Workers who lack a strong personal commitment about these issues are likely to simply adopt the dominant organisational view, and to accept received organisational wisdom about what is an issue and what is not. Organisations tend to recognise two kinds of issues as problematic, and thus requiring organisational action. Firstly, there are issues relating to the maintenance of the organisation itself, such as difficulties in the areas of funding, legitimation or production. Secondly, there are issues that appear to jeopardise the interests of dominant groups within the organisation. Workers wishing to promote other issues, such as responsiveness to consumer needs, need determination and strong personal conviction.

To effectively identify change and resistance issues, social and welfare workers need good information about the organisation and the issues it faces. For many workers a key source of information is their interaction with the consumers of the service and their observation of the front-line. Talking with consumers, and observing the effects of the organisation on them, generates awareness of issues from a consumer perspective. Workers need to be able to identify the organisational implications of the individual problems of consumers that they encounter in their daily work. There are also other important sources of information that can be used to identify issues. Workers should keep abreast of intra-organisational information available to them, both through official and unofficial channels. They should use their networks to find out what is happening around the organisation. Meetings are important as sources of information about current developments and clues as to likely developments. Issues can also be generated from sources outside the organisation. One reason for reading the professional literature, attending conferences and seminars, and developing links with workers and organisations in cognate fields is to obtain new ideas and outlooks on organisational issues.

Finally, issue identification involves being able to define and present issues in organisational terms. A worker may, for example, feel that the organisation is not reaching the consumers that most need the service. But this needs to be framed in ways that can be dealt with in an organisational context. Depending on the particular organisation, this might involve designating the issue as one of intake procedures, or referral patterns, or accessibility, or information and access, or inter-organisational linkages. The concepts, language and frameworks used throughout this book provide the basis for definition of change and resistance issues in organisational terms.

Workers with a change and resistance orientation, a critical perspective, good information, and a facility with organisational concepts will have no difficulty identifying issues that could be addressed within their organisation. Indeed, the problem is likely to be a surfeit of possible issues. Workers with a broad understanding of their organisation are able to generate an almost limitless number of desirable change possibilities. Workers also face an unending stream of change initiatives emanating from elsewhere in the organisation. Some of these they will want to support, others they will want resist, and many they will want to ignore. Workers may also be organisationally responsible for bringing about certain changes. Time, energy and commitment are limited. Hence, the issue of choice is critical. Workers need ways of deciding which issues to take up and which to leave well alone.

The choice of issues will be guided by considerations of the worker's values, strategic interests and political resources. Clearly, the worker's values and beliefs are central factors. Issues that impinge directly on matters affecting personal or professional values will be high on a worker's agenda. For social and welfare workers, these will often be matters relating to organisational responsiveness to consumers and to professional practice. Issues relating more generally to disadvantage, injustice and inequality, be they related to class, gender, ethnicity, Aboriginality, disability, age or place, are also likely to be key concerns. Issues impinging on the worker's interests or stake in the organisation will also be of concern. Attempts to impose greater control on professional practice, to decrease the resources or increase the workload of workers, or to adversely change working conditions are matters that workers will often want to resist. Programmes and services in which the worker has invested time and energy, and to which the worker is committed, are also likely to be a focus.

The impact of workers' political resources on choice of issue is somewhat less obvious, but equally significant. In essence, the organisational issues workers choose to address should not only be important in value and interest terms, but also be potentially achievable. Workers should take care not to squander their limited resources of time, energy and commitment on impossible or improbable political enterprises. While issues can sometimes be chosen for their symbolic significance, workers should be careful to avoid participation in change or resistance activities that amount to no more than symbolic gestures. For example, if a progamme of great concern to a worker is cut back, but there is no conceivable chance of the decision being reversed, the worker must ask what purpose is served by protesting or campaigning against the decision? One purpose might be to try to dissuade management from repeating the decision in relation to another programme. Another might be to enhance one's legitimacy with supporters of the programme. But if there is no particular purpose in mind, the worker must consider the costs and ultimate futility of merely flailing at windmills.

Finally, we stress that awareness of change and resistance issues is an active, changing process, that develops as a worker gains experience in analysing and taking action in an organisation. A worker's identification of issues changes as he or she gains more information or a different perspective through organisational analysis and action. Similarly, choice of issues can be influenced by ongoing analysis of the organisational response to the worker's actions. Awareness, like the other key elements of analysis and action, is never complete and should never stand still.

Analysis of the change and resistance process

Prior to initiating action on a change or resistance issue, a worker needs to carefully analyse what he or she is proposing to do. There are two basic analytical questions: 'what is the change or resistance agenda?' and 'what overall strategy is most likely to achieve this agenda?'.

Formulating the change agenda involves moving from awareness of a change issue to a delineation of the nature of the change or changes that the process is intended to achieve. This can be a surprisingly complex task. Take the example of a worker in a community centre who is concerned about the under-representation of people from non-English speaking backgrounds among users of the centre. While her broad aim may be to increase usage from this group, her change agenda needs to be formulated in more detail. Firstly, it would be helpful for her to be specific about the number or percentage of non-English speaking persons that would constitute equitable or reasonable usage. It might also be important to indicate the time by which it is hoped this figure should be achieved. The change agenda should also indicate what changes will need to occur to bring this about. Will it require a change to the formal goals of the centre? Is there a need to develop a new outreach project, to alter centre activities, to hire workers from ethnic minority groups, or to re-locate the centre? If more than one of these tasks is envisaged, issues relating to their inter-dependence are important. In what order should these processes occur? Can they be pursued separately or do they comprise an integrated package, all elements of which are needed?

A change agenda comprises a listing of the intended elements of change. Several rules of thumb, some of which are illustrated by the above example, can be spelled out. The change or changes should usually be specified as precisely as possible. Almost all change is difficult to accomplish; change described in woolly terms is harder still. The elements of the change package, and their inter-dependency need to be identified. It is also helpful in some situations to specify the stages of the change process, that is, in what order should the various elements be addressed.

The change agenda also needs to be flexible. The requirement for precision does not imply that the change agenda should not be reviewed and revised in response to changing circumstances. Indeed, it is rarely the case, other than for quite straightforward and unambitious change agendas, that the process ends up exactly where it was initially intended. Because change involves some degree of uncertainty, workers often have to settle for something less or different to their original change agenda. There is no clear calculus for these decisions. Determining when and in what ways to amend the agenda, without losing sight of and awareness of the change issue, requires careful assessment of political possibilities and the desirability of various change prospects.

It can also be helpful to have a clear understanding of the nature of the changes being proposed. Most changes involve alterations to the organisational environment, goals, structure or culture, or some combination of these. Identifying a change in these terms enables the worker to relate the change to the theoretical materials presented in chapters 4 to 7. Other key types of change are those involving organisational technology, for example, the introduction of a new service type. Finally, the scope of the change agenda is a significant consideration. Agendas that are highly complex, that involve extensive changes in many aspects of organisational life, that are difficult to reverse, and that challenge entrenched interests, will present far greater challenges to their initiators and supporters than more modest plans (Brager and Holloway 1978, pp. 114-115).

Resisting change involves a similar process of analysis. It is important to try to understand precisely what it is that others in the organisation are attempting to achieve, and which aspects of this agenda you wish to resist. Often, change agendas are not presented fully and frankly, and it is necessary to analyse the implications of what is formally announced. 'What are they really trying to achieve?' can often be a key question. Sometimes, a worker may wish to support some aspects of a change agenda, while opposing others. Or a worker may be happy enough to provide support, provided it is clear that the changes proposed are limited in certain ways. Resistance to change also needs to be flexible. While it is important to know your bottom line, it is equally necessary to be able to recognise the circumstances in which change is inevitable and further resistance futile.

As well as examining what should change or be resisted, analysis must address the question of how change will be brought about or impeded. Together these comprise a change or resistance strategy. The issue of 'how' essentially involves a political analysis of the organisation. There are two broad sets of questions. The first focus on matters of political feasibility, that is, what are the strategic opportunities and constraints present in this situation, and how can the opportunities be maximised and the constraints minimised? The second set revolve around issues of strategic choice, that is, what broad approach to intervention will be employed?

Opportunities and constraints arise in the first instance from current organisational circumstances. Workers need to analyse whether the current goals, structures, cultures and environment of the organisation are supportive of or hostile to their change agenda. Often this involves considering ways in which the change agenda can be shaped and presented so as to take advantage of existing conditions. Key questions for workers to ask are: 'how can the change agenda be framed to appear to be supportive of current goals?', 'how can the proposed change be seen as responsive to significant changes in the organisational environment?', 'how can the implications of the change agenda on organisational structures be presented in a positive manner?' and 'how can it be demonstrated that the change agenda is compatible with the dominant culture or significant sub-cultures?' These questions do not imply that change agendas should never challenge entrenched and established organisational arrangements. Rather, they signify the importance of a thorough analysis of all of the opportunities and constraints inherent in existing circumstances, whatever the change agenda may be.

Assessing feasibility also involves an analysis of one's own political resources. The strategic opportunities available to workers are dependent on their underlying political position in the organisation (discussed in chapter 2) and on the extent to which they have developed their political base and skills (discussed in chapter 8). Of particular importance is the fit between the political resources of an individual or group and a change issue. Workers will be perceived as having greater legitimacy on some issues than others. Similarly, their organisational location, networks and political skills will be of greater use for some change processes than for others. Workers need to thoroughly examine their political strengths and weaknesses in relation to the change issue, and take any necessary action. For example, a group of workers may, after careful analysis, decide that they are well placed to initiate a certain change process, except that their network of contacts in the organisation in relation to the issue is limited. They may therefore decide to delay the initiation of the change process until they have developed a more extensive network. Similarly, an attempt may be made to define an issue in such a way that it matches the established or perceived legitimacy of the individual or group.

One of the reasons that analysis of this kind is vitally important is that an individual or group's reputation for effective participation in change and resistance is itself an important political resource. Those whose political activity in the organisation is marked by careful analysis, consistency, persistence and, above all, success, are likely to be taken seriously by other organisational participants. Those who gain a reputation for ineffective or unsustained action, and who rarely get their way, will suffer declining influence. Thus, a key strategic consideration is the likely impact of participation in a particular change process on the overall political standing of the individual worker and the group with which she or he is associated.

Analysis of strategic opportunities and constraints also requires consideration of the likely stance of other significant organisational participants. Significant participants include all those who have, or potentially have, power, authority or influence over the issue in question. Analysis involves listing all significant participants, determining their likely stance for or against, and considering ways of increasing their support or minimising their opposition. One way of listing all significant participants is to chart the steps that need to be taken for the change agenda to be fully accepted and implemented, and list every individual or group that will be involved along the way. Particular note should be taken of critical actors (Brager and Holloway 1978, p. 115), that is, individuals or groups whose support is essential in order for the change to become a reality. This may include people in management positions who have authority in the issue area in question, or the front-line workers who would be involved in putting the change into effect. It is also essential for all change proposals in human service organisations to consider the stance or likely stance of consumers. Consumers are the supposed beneficiaries of all organisational change, and their views on the issue in question should be considered on that basis alone. However, their stance may also be of considerable strategic consequence. Consumer support or opposition influences the legitimacy of an issue, particularly if matters directly related to consumer service are in question.

Determining the likely stance of individuals and groups on an issue is far from straightforward. Directly asking people about their position is possible in some, but not all circumstances, and in any case the information provided needs to be treated with caution. Support and opposition is typically conditional, that is, it depends on how the proposal is presented, prevailing circumstances, the stance of other actors, and so forth. Private expressions of support are not always sustained when public declarations are required. Hence, it is also necessary to analyse the structural relationship of individuals and groups to the change agenda. This includes consideration of how their interests are affected by the change proposal, how it impinges on their values and beliefs, and how they have responded to similar issues in the past. These may provide a clearer picture of likely support or opposition than private affirmations. It is also important not to treat support or opposition as 'given'. The key question is not 'who is for us and who is against us?', but rather, 'what can be done to maximise support and minimise or nullify opposition?'

In considering the building of support for a proposal it is helpful to distinguish between willingness and ability to provide support. Some individuals and groups are both willing and able: the task in their case is to maintain support. Some are willing, but not able: the task here is one of facilitation, that is, finding ways of overcoming the impediments to active support. Some groups are unwilling to support, but would have the ability to do so if they wished to: the task here is one of considering ways of converting them to the cause. Those who lack both willingness and ability need to be isolated as much as possible from the process. Maintaining, facilitating, converting and isolating are all important elements of strategic planning for change and resistance.

In summary, strategic opportunities and constraints arise out of organisational circumstances, the political resources of workers, and the potential support and resistance of significant actors. Analysis involves judgements about political feasibility based on these factors. It follows that there is never one right answer concerning the action that workers should take in relation to an issue of concern. It all depends on careful analysis of the political circumstances. Similarly, the question of strategic choice, considered below, is not susceptible to definitive answers.

The issue of strategic choice concerns the overall approach to intervention to be adopted by participants in change and resistance processes. In short, it concerns the questions 'how will we bring about change?' and 'how will we resist change?' The first issue concerns the mode of intervention. Chin and Benne suggest that general strategies for affecting changes in human systems can be classified into three modes: rational–empirical, normative–re-educative and power–coercive (1976). Rational–empirical strategies involve the use of research, reasoning and argument to promote or resist a change proposal. Typical instruments are policy papers, planning documents, evaluations and detailed assessments of issues and proposals. Most change processes in formal organisations involve some use of rational–empirical tools. A change proposal has at least to have the appearance of rationality, irrespective of the actual nature of the decision-making processes. Normative–re-educative approaches focus on changes in the attitudes, values, skills and relationships of organisational members. Change instruments include education and training, and a myriad of organisational development techniques focused on improving relationships among workers and organisational culture (Huczynski 1987). Power–coercive approaches involve the use of power, influence and authority to bring about change. This includes the direct use of authority as in the issuing of directives, the use of powers to reward and punish, and interventions such as strikes, sit-ins, non-compliance and other disruptive tactics. This classification is useful in helping workers to consider what the main focus of their intervention will be, although often interventions involve elements of all three modes. It is important to recognise that all three approaches are political, in that they each involve the exercise of power, influence or authority.

The final analytical question concerns the general attitude to be adopted towards other participants in change and resistance processes. It is common to distinguish between collaborative (or co-operative), campaign (or contest) and conflict approaches (Brager and Holloway 1978, pp. 130-134). A collaborative approach involves working together to find solutions to problems and issues in an atmosphere of openness and trust. While the approach may encompass mild forms of disagreement and persuasion, the underlying expectation is that resolution can be achieved by teamwork and co-operation. In a campaign, the predominant style is one of bargaining, negotiation, and political manoeuvre. There is clear acknowledgment of differing interests and perspectives. There is less openness than in a collaborative process, but continuing commitment to the rules of the game and an expectation that resolution can be arrived at within established frameworks. Conflict strategies involve open clashes of position, political struggle and polarisation of participants in the process. Established norms of behaviour may be broken and illegal activities may be threatened or undertaken. Activities typically associated with conflict strategies include petitions, open confrontation, sanctions, public criticism, deliberate non-compliance, strikes, picketing, litigation and, in the extreme, forms of violent action (Warren 1977, p. 188).

Choice of approach is influenced by a number of factors, not least of which is the worker's own personal style. The degree of agreement that exists within the organisation on the issue in question is also important. Conflict strategies are hardly necessary in situations of widespread or fundamental agreement. The political resources of an actor are also a significant consideration. Campaign and, more especially, conflict strategies require the mobilisation of considerable forces to be effective, and the costs of defeat can be considerable. The prevailing organisational culture is another factor to be considered. Some organisations are tolerant of high levels of intra-organisational conflict. But most seek to contain political activity within fairly narrow boundaries, and actions that go beyond the prevailing limits need especially careful planning and analysis.

Workers need to be sensitive to the personal impacts of the strategies they choose. Bringing about organisational change may be likened in some ways to a game of chess, but unlike chess the workers cannot put the pieces back in the box halfway through the process. Conflict strategies may not only generate resistance, but counter strategies directed at the initiator or initiating group. These strategies sometimes target the worker, not the issues. Character assassination, rumour, innuendo and verbal harassment can become a commonplace part of organisational life.

For these reasons, workers need to be aware of their own personal style and their preferred approach to change strategies. They need know the limits to their personal capacity to deal with the criticism that participation in change processes can bring. A worker who is predisposed to consensus and collaboration needs to be aware that others may use this knowledge by adopting conflict strategies to gain the advantage. A worker predisposed towards conflict and campaign needs to be aware how intimidating this can be to co-workers and other organisational participants.

Workers need to be sensitive to the gender and cultural issues related to the use of different strategies. As noted in chapter 2, feminist writers have pointed to the masculine culture permeating much organisational life. 'Boy's games' is one description applied by feminists to the manner in which organisational processes become a venue for displays of personal power and domination. For many people coming from non-European cultures such behaviour is inexplicable and inexcusable. For Aboriginal people such processes may be seen to reflect the historical reality of their relations with non-Aboriginal Australia.

Action for change and resistance

The action elements of participation in organisational change and resistance can be thought of as fourfold: inclination, initiation, implementation and institutionalisation (Brager and Holloway 1978, pp. 154-236). Issues involved in each of these aspects are discussed below.

Inclining the organisation towards change is an often neglected aspect of change processes. Having become aware of an organisational issue, and formulated a change agenda and strategy, the temptation is to move directly into the initiation process. Frequently, however, preliminary work undertaken prior to the actual presentation of the change idea is critically important. This can be thought of as preparing the ground or creating a receptive climate for the change process. This process is described in the organisational change literature in a number of different ways. Weinbach, drawing on the work of Kurt Lewin, suggests that the process is one of 'unfreezing' (1984, p. 282). This means that key organisational participants must become sufficiently uncomfortable with existing ways of doing things that they are receptive to new ideas. Brager and Holloway describe the process as 'the inducement and management of stress' (1978, pp. 162-171). Essentially, this involves heightening awareness and a sense of urgency concerning the issue under consideration. Unless this exists, the change proposal, when it is eventually presented to the organisation, is likely to be ignored or dismissed as unnecessary.

There are many different ways in which workers can attempt to heighten perception of a problem prior to launching their change agenda. A common method is to introduce new information into the organisation that indicates a problematic situation. For example, a worker wanting to extend the organisation's services to a particular ethnic minority might introduce information about current under-representation of the group among the organisation's consumers, or data showing the increasing numbers of people from the minority group in the local population. This might be supplemented with information showing extensive concerns about under-servicing in government or the local community. Information about problems can be introduced informally through discussion with colleagues in the coffee-room or over lunch, or more formally at committee and staff meetings. Sometimes issues raised by managers or other staff can be reframed to highlight the problem of primary concern to the worker. Another common way of heightening awareness of issues, and challenging or disturbing existing assumptions and beliefs, is to bring in outsiders known to be sympathetic to the cause. Interventions by outsiders can range from one-off lectures and discussions with staff to ongoing involvement through consultancy arrangements or secondment. It is important to keep in mind that heightening awareness of a problem may take sustained activity over a considerable time, and that it may require a range of activities.

While most writers stress the need to induce a degree of stress prior to initiating a change process, this must not be approached in an uncritical manner. Too much stress can result in a feeling that a problem is so large and intractable that nothing can be done about it. Exaggeration of problems can also dent a worker's credibility. Workers must also be aware of the dangers of being perceived as negative, unsupportive and fault-finding during this process, and will often want to induce stress in ways that do not bring their loyalty to colleagues and commitment to organisational goals into question.

Workers engaged in processes of resistance clearly must direct their efforts towards disinclining the organisation to change. Essentially, this involves processes contrary to those described above.

Resisting change might involve questioning the veracity or interpretation of information presented about the alleged problem, calling the credibility of outside experts into question or submitting alternative experts, and generally suggesting that concerns are exaggerated. Resistance strategies often rely heavily on the inertia that is characteristic of many organisations. 'What is so wrong about the way we do things now?' is the central resistance theme.

When a worker decides that the time has come to actually initiate the change process there are four key considerations (Brager and Holloway 1978, pp. 177-205). Firstly, who will initiate the change process has to be decided. Often there is a strong case for this being someone other than the worker most involved in promoting the change. The basic rule of thumb is that it ought to be the person or persons most likely to be able to persuade the audience of the value of the proposal. This will usually be someone who has a substantial commitment to the contemplated change, combined with other qualities or attributes. These may include their credibility based on acknowledged expertise, integrity or membership of a particular group, their skills in raising and discussing issues, and their commonality with the audience, that is, whether the individual is perceived as one of the group. A key attribute is the individual's power, authority and influence. Changes proposed by an individual with authority in the area of change, or by someone perceived as influential, are more likely to be taken seriously than changes emanating from someone perceived as powerless. Often it is useful for a change to be presented as the initiative of a group rather than an individual. Collectively, the group may have the credibility, skills, commonality and power that are needed, and that no one individual possesses.

The individual or group to whom the change proposal is presented is equally significant. The basic issue is whether to go directly to the person or group with the power to bring about the desired change (if any one such person or group exists) or whether to first raise the issue with potential supporters with the aim of forming an influential alliance. If analysis suggests that those with power are likely to be in favour of the change agenda then the direct approach may be recommended. However, if this support is unlikely, uncertain or unpredictable, initiating the change among likely supporters may be the wisest option. Sometimes this choice is portrayed as a choice between 'top down' and 'bottom up' approaches to change. Top down involves harnessing the authority of managers to endorse and operationalise a change proposal. Bottom up involves mobilising support among workers, particularly those in the front-line, and using this to exert pressure on those with the authority to make decisions.

A further issue is the forum, or mechanism, through which the change agenda is presented. Sometimes there are defined procedures for initiating change proposals, and a key issue is whether or not to use these right channels. Awareness of the importance of informal organisational processes is critical. In some organisations the main role of formal meetings is to ratify decisions arrived through negotiations conducted in ad hoc or informal 'pre-meeting meetings'. In these circumstances, formal meetings only become significant when differences cannot be resolved through these informal processes. Choices also have to be made among different formal forums. Workers have to decide whether to introduce their change proposal at staff meetings, at executive meetings, at planning meetings, at consultative meetings, at committee meetings, at annual general meetings, through the newsletter, via the staff suggestion box, and so on. The key considerations are the composition of the group (supporters and opponents), and the authority and legitimacy of the forum for the issue of concern. Brager and Holloway refer to this issue as 'structural positioning', that is, the use of organisational structures to maximise the chance of a receptive hearing (1978, p. 171).

Finally, workers have to consider how their change agenda should initially be presented in the organisation. One issue is whether it should be presented verbally or in writing. Verbal presentations provide greater opportunity for immediate feedback, exchange of ideas, conveying of emotional messages, and gauging of the receiver's reaction. A verbal presentation may be seen as more negotiable, less prescriptive than one put in writing. On the other hand, written presentations provide a permanent record, can be more deliberate and considered, can more readily convey detail and complexity, and can be easily circulated to all relevant parties. A combination of verbal and written presentation in the form of 'speaking to a paper' is commonly used to gain the advantages of both media. Choice of method is also influenced by prevailing organisational expectations. Often there are protocols, formal or informal, for the presentation of proposals, and departure from these may create needless difficulties.

Presentation also involves the way an issue is portrayed to the organisation. Often, the same change proposal can be presented, with equal candour, as 'an urgently needed innovation' or as 'a logical next step in our development'. It can be characterised as a 'significant policy initiative' or as 'an essentially procedural matter'. A report can make a clear recommendation, or, alternatively, it can present a series of options biased towards the preferred outcome. These are matters relating to the image of the change proposal. Those initiating a change proposal need to decide whether it will be presented as innovative, necessary, major, logical, exciting, technical, routine or whatever impression is felt will be most facilitative.

Resistance, at the initiation stage, can involve a wide array of tactics. Questions can be raised about the credibility of the individual or group initiating the proposal. This can often be done in relatively unobtrusive ways, without wholesale character assassination. For example, it might be suggested that 'Peter's proposal is interesting, but as a newcomer to the organisation he is probably not aware of a number of historical factors that need to be taken into account . . . ' Or, 'Jill's idea is a good one, but as a non-medical person she is probably underestimating the significance of . . . ' Another resistance tactic is to question the format of the proposal. It can be suggested that a verbal proposal needs to be put in writing, or that established protocols and procedures have not been followed. Resisting change may also involve fostering and spreading negative images of the proposal.

Resistance tactics at this stage may also entail delay, deflection, diversion and dilution. An example of delay is to ask that a proposal be sent back for further examination or elaboration. Deflection might involve channelling the proposal for consideration by a committee or individual known to be hostile or powerless. Another form of deflection is to argue that the proposal is the responsibility of some other body. Diversion involves effecting changes to the proposal that undermine or subvert its main purpose. Dilution is the tactic of watering down the proposal, by readily accepting some minor elements while rejecting the broader package as unrealistic, too difficult or not appropriate in current circumstances.

The change initiation process involves the presentation of a policy or proposal to the organisation. The initiation phase can be thought of as involving this presentation, consideration of it by the organisation, and the decision to accept, modify or reject the change. Formal acceptance of the change proposal must, however, be clearly distinguished from realisation of the change itself. What happens in between can be conceptualised as the change implementation process.

Workers need, firstly, to be aware of the importance of planning the implementation phase of a change process. It is important to anticipate the issues that are likely to arise, and to have considered the means of dealing with them. The literature on policy implementation emphasises the many ways in which change initiatives can be deflected or sabotaged, so that outcomes only vaguely resemble the original objectives (Pressman and Wildavsky 1973). Workers need a clear picture of what is to be achieved, the resources that will be needed, the timing and sequencing of actions and events, the roles of individuals and groups in the process, and key decision-points. Often, but by no means always, these details are required to gain support during the initiation process. The more they can be anticipated, and provision made at the outset, the greater the likelihood of successful implementation.

It is important for workers to conceptualise change implementation processes in political, as well as technical, terms. Often opponents of a change proposal, having been unable or unwilling to stop it at initiation, use the implementation process to block or frustrate change efforts. Certainly, the implementation phase provides many opportunities for resistance. Successful change implementation involves maintaining or securing the support of organisational participants whose co-operation and backing is required, and nullifying or side-stepping opposition. It is often the case that the implementation process requires the support of different individuals and groups from those that were central during initiation. For example, the front-line workers involved in setting up a new service may replace managers as the group with the most influence. Good communication, provision of opportunities for participation in decision-making, and maximising benefits and minimising costs for participants are key considerations. Close attention must be paid to any negative impacts of implementation on other organisational policies and procedures, which may provoke resistance.

A key consideration for workers is the role that they should play in change implementation processes. This will depend on the nature and scale of the change, the worker's organisational responsibilities, and the worker's style and skills. Brager and Holloway distinguish a number of possible, alternative roles (1978, pp. 212-217). Workers can maintain a central involvement as managers of the change process, that is, they acquire the formal, organisational responsibility for bringing the change about. Alternatively, they can be change advocates or interpreters, that is, involved in a facilitative way without taking on prime responsibility. The role of troubleshooter is more intermittent; the worker only becomes involved when the implementation process runs into difficulties. Finally, workers can decide not to be involved at all. The implementation process is left in the hands of others or in the lap of the gods.

The final action element is the institutionalisation of change. Put simply, this means finding ways to make the change last. Often this involves some degree of formalisation of the change, that is, the embodiment of the change into the rules, records, prescribed roles and other written documents of the organisation. It usually also involves finding ways to bond the change to the organisation, that is, maximising the interdependency of the change and the organisation. For example, if the change has involved the establishment of a new programme, all efforts should be made to ensure that the programme becomes central to the organisation's reputation in the community, that it has close operational links with other organisational programmes, and that it contributes to key organisational processes such as the acquiring of funds, staff and consumers. The more the organisation, and groups within the organisation, have a stake in the new programme, the greater its capacity for endurance. It is axiomatic that resistance involves countering all such tendencies towards institutionalisation.

Evaluation of change processes can be used by workers either as a means of further institutionalisation or as a means of re-opening issues and drawing attention to the need for further change. Evaluation, like all elements of change and resistance processes, should be viewed as a political as well as a technical activity that is finely shaped by the purposes of the individual or group sponsoring or conducting the evaluation. Issues associated with appraisal and evaluation in human service organisations are considered in detail in the next chapter.

Conclusions

Workers need a critical, political perspective on change and resistance in human service organisations. Firstly, this must be based on an understanding of the nature of organisational change. Workers need an understanding of the paradox of change and continuity in organisations, and of the definitions of change based on the elements and significance of particular changes. Important distinctions are those between innovation, adjustment and change, symbolic and real change, formal and informal change, major and minor change, first-order and second-order change, planned and unplanned change, and radical and non-radical change. It is also important to have a theoretical understanding of why and how organisations change. This can be approached through the four key concepts of environment, goals, structure and culture.

Workers also need to be able to apply their understanding of change to their actions as organisational members. In the second part of this chapter we outlined an analytical framework to guide organisational change and resistance activities. The framework portrays change activities as involving three elements: awareness, analysis and action. The key issues to be considered under each of these headings are listed in Table 10.1 and elaborated in the text.

Chapter review questions

1 What is the importance of organisational change for social and welfare work?
2 Describe the power perspective on organisational change, and indicate how this perspective differs from other approaches?
3 Is organisational change desirable for its own sake? Why or why not?
4 What is the relationship between change and continuity in organisations?
5 What are the main elements of organisational change?
6 What are the meanings of the following sets of terms as applied to organisations: innovation, adjustment and change; symbolic and real change; formal and informal change; major and minor change; first-order and second-order change; planned and unplanned change; and radical change?

7 What makes organisations change? In particular, what is the influence of the environment, goals, structure and culture on change and continuity in organisations?

8 How central are social and welfare workers in change and resistance processes in organisations?

9 What is involved in awareness of change and resistance issues?

10 What are the key elements of analysis of a change or resistance issue?

11 What are the main stages of a change or resistance process, and what is involved in each stage?

12 Why do workers need to be sensitive to issues of gender and culture in relation to change and resistance processes?

Further reading

An excellent theoretical introduction to change in human service organisations is provided by Hasenfeld (1983, pp. 218-247). Brager and Holloway (1978) analyse the political and practice issues involved in change processes in depth from a front-line worker perspective. More managerially oriented treatments of organisational change can be found in Dawson (1986, pp. 211-220) and Stoner, Collins and Yetton (1985, pp. 446-485). A useful perspective on organisational resistance and change is provided by Patti (1978). Bennis et al. (1976) provide a wide-ranging overview of approaches to planned change in societies, communities and organisations. The nature and possibilities of second-order change are explored in Watzlawick, Weakland and Fisch (1974).

Case study

INITIATING CHANGE IN THE FRASER-MCMAHON DAY THERAPY CENTRE

Sue Makim sat back in her chair and looked around the room. It was her first day in her new job. Her attention was immediately drawn to the sound of a dripping tap in the sink located in one corner. The high ceiling and walls, with their cracked and peeling green gloss paint provided a perfect resonance. Outside someone hurried down the corridor past her door, the click-clack of high heels providing a staccato counterpart to the amplified and echoing sound of the tap. A tall rusty metal filing cabinet sat across from the sink blocking the little light which had managed to fight its way through the opaque glass window. Two low vinyl armchairs which had long since seen better days, sat facing the desk. The room looked, felt and smelled like a small hospital side ward, which was in fact, exactly what it had been, before being converted to the new social worker and community welfare worker's office.

It was not until the old black phone on her desk rang that Sue noticed the small vase of flowers on her desk. The bright flash of yellow looking incongruous among the sombre faded green. She wondered who had left this welcoming sign. She answered the phone: 'Ah, Miss Makim, Sister Smeaton here. I am ringing to tell you that Dr Forthright, our Consultant Psychiatrist, will see you this morning at nine-thirty, in his office on the first floor. Please be on time'. Before Sue could respond the Sister had hung up. 'Thank you for such a warm welcome,' Sue muttered to herself as she replaced the receiver.

To prepare for the meeting with Dr Forthright, Sue decided to go over the copy of the recently published *Annual Report of the Princess Diana Hospital* which had come with her letter of appointment. The organisation chart, spread over two pages, was a complex mass of lines and boxes. She discovered that Dr Forthright was a private consultant on contract to the Day Centre. She turned to the pages concerned with the Fraser-McMahon Day Therapy Centre and read:

> The Centre is located in the grounds of the psychiatric hospital, which is in turn part of the Princess Diana Hospital, a public hospital situated on the south side of the city. The Day Centre services approximately seventy-five people who live in the community. Most of these people have at some time been residents of the psychiatric hospital. All have disabilities resulting from psychiatric illness. Their ages range from eighteen to eighty. The clients of the Day Centre have a wide range of diagnoses. For many, their illness results in recurring hospitalisation. The majority of referrals, which number two to three per week, come about as a result of the discharge planning procedures used in the psychiatric hospital.
>
> The goals of the Centre are:
> 1   to provide rehabilitation to optimal functioning within the community;
> 2   to maintain the optimal functioning of patients within the community by providing social support, rehabilitative activities and medical services.
>
> The Day Centre has four full-time staff: a receptionist–secretary, a psychiatric social worker, an occupational therapist and a psychiatric nurse. There are also four part-time staff: a doctor (a psychiatric registrar undertaking post-graduate training employed for twenty hours per week), a consultant psychiatrist (ten hours per week), and two psychologists (eight hours per week each). In addition, it is proposed to appoint a full-time, qualified social worker or community welfare worker in the near future.
>
> Patients may attend the Day Centre four days per week, for approximately four hours a day. However, most choose to attend only two days per week. The majority of these patients attend the Day Centre for a period of at least one year. Indeed, over half of those currently in contact with the Day Centre have been in contact for over five years.

At half-past-nine precisely Sue met Dr Forthright. After welcoming her to the staff, he got straight down to business:

I will not beat around the bush, Miss Makim. If you are to work effectively, it is important that you know the full background. As you know, the hospital's decision to appoint a social worker/community welfare worker was prompted by the recent inquiry into the Day Centre. This inquiry was undertaken because of public concern over the suicide of one of our patients, whom the media dubbed 'Miss X'. You may recall that the patient's family made her suicide note public, and extracts were included in a highly critical article published by a certain tabloid newspaper, renowned for sensationalism. In the note, which I want to quote from, she wrote of her feelings of hopelessness and despair and how, ' . . . nothing seems to help. I've been going to the centre for two years, but it is a waste of time. No one has time to talk to you and when they do they just talk jargon. All we do is sit and talk or play stupid games. There has got to be more to life than this'.

As a consequence of this unfortunate and unnecessary publicity, there was a ministerial inquiry into the Day Centre. The inquiry found that there was no evidence to suggest any negligence on the part of staff or the hospital in relation to the standard of patient care provided. The patient had a long history of suicide attempts. However, during the investigation a number of procedures relating to case management were found to be need of tighter supervision. Action has now been taken to ensure those procedural problems will not recur.

In addition, the inquiry, whose report is confidential, made three recommendations that are directly related to your appointment. These are:
1 that the existing goals of rehabilitation and maintenance of patients within the community should be endorsed;
2 that the Centre should orient its therapeutic programmes towards maximising the integration of patients into the community;
3 that a social worker or community welfare worker be appointed for the purposes of developing and implementing a community integration programme and to work towards the above objectives.

Dr Forthright stood and came round the desk. Sue stood up and found herself being steered towards the door:

Well, that is the full picture. I suggest that you spend a bit of time getting to know us and finding your way around. Hospitals are funny places if you have never worked in one before. I am here three mornings a week. If you wish to see me just make an appointment with Sister Smeaton. Other than that I will see you again at the staff meeting on Friday. Good luck.

Back in her office, Sue considered the interview. She thought about all of the questions that she wished she had asked, and, not for the first time, promised herself to try to become more assertive. She decided that she should spend the next few days finding out more about what went on in the

Day Centre. She took every opportunity to talk to other members of staff about how they saw the Centre and her role. She discovered that the situation was far more complex than she had been told. It became immediately apparent to her that there was a high level of dissatisfaction among many staff over current policies and processes of the Centre. One of the part-time psychologists had written a report to Dr Forthright, prior to the suicide of Miss X, questioning the 'maintenance focused goals' of the Centre and drawing attention to 'the need for a more developmentally oriented programme based in the community, that would link patients to their families and the community, and provide a more natural setting for the rehabilitation process'.

She also discovered that an increasing number of referrals to the Centre from the Psychiatric Hospital during the past eighteen months had led to increasing patient numbers and higher individual caseloads. These pressures were in turn resulting in a tendency in the Day Centre to discharge patients from the programme prematurely, without clear discharge criteria or processes. This whole situation was made worse as a result of a recent Health Department review of staffing within the entire Princess Diana Hospital system, in the context of state government budget cuts. One consequence of the review was that the Day Centre lost its full-time Registrar position, which was converted to the current half-time arrangement. Staff protests about this change were ignored.

Sue also became aware of significant patient dissatisfaction. Some of the patients openly expressed concern to her and others about the lack of clarity in the operations of the Centre. At a group therapy session she attended during her first week, there were complaints by patients about the unpredictability of discharge planning procedures and the lack of personal rehabilitative planning and counselling. Patients also complained about the manner in which professional staff spoke to them and about them, and lack of patient involvement in plans for their own rehabilitation. There was a high level of emotion at the session, and one patient threatened staff with personal violence if something was not done about these issues.

It was also becoming apparent to Sue that Sister Smeaton was in reality the co-ordinator of all activities in the Centre, even though this was not part of her formal duties. Her office was next to the receptionist's, whose work she supervised. All phone and written communications were processed through the receptionist and Sister Smeaton unless personally directed to other members of the staff. The office contained all patient files, and appointments were made through Sister Smeaton. She sat in on all case management team meetings. At morning tea, Sue overheard Sister telling the receptionist:

What we need here is a full-time Registrar, another psychiatric nurse and more sessions for the psychologists. What we do not need is a useless social worker or community welfare worker or whatever they are called, running around in the community like a chook with its head chopped off!

The two part-time psychologists seemed to be supportive of Sue and her task, although she had a sneaking feeling that they would have preferred a member of their profession to be doing her job. They both warned her to 'watch out' for Sister Smeaton, because of her close links with Dr Forthright. They told Sue that the Sister uses these links to monitor the work of other staff. Sister Smeaton has been known to use her influence to get Dr Forthright to intervene in particular cases where she has disagreed with proposed actions. Sue was told similar stories by the occupational therapist and the psychiatric social worker.

Sue's impression of the psychiatric social worker was that he did not seem to have much energy for his work. He seemed to spend a great deal of his time working in groups, seeing individuals and keeping his case records up-to-date. He was supportive and welcoming, and invited Sue to Friday afternoon drinks with other social work and welfare staff from the hospital. But he warned Sue that:

> The task in front of you is going to be difficult. Most of our patients are chronic, they go out, they come back in, they cannot hold down a job for any period of time and they have trouble getting and keeping a roof over their heads. Many of them come from socially disadvantaged backgrounds, and their disability has made almost all of them highly marginal in the broader society. It does not help that many of the discharge referrals we get from the psychiatric hospital are just not ready for what we are trying to do. But what can you do? The hospital policy is to empty the beds as soon as possible and the medical staff oblige.

Sue also discovered that it was he who was responsible for the flowers that appeared on her desk on her first day of work.

At the end of her first week in the job, Sue attended her first staff meeting. She was introduced and welcomed by Dr Forthright, who did much of the talking at the meeting. He described her role to other staff as:

> To get out there in the community and organise support groups of patients and their families, as well as raising community awareness concerning the needs of patients, identifying community resources and linking patients and their families to them. I would stress that Sue does not have any therapeutic role as such, so she will not need to attend case management meetings on a regular basis. She will, of course, be supervised by me, and in my absence will report to Dr Smith, our part-time Registrar. But in any case, her job is to work out there in the community, and I am sure she will be pleased to leave the responsibility for ongoing therapeutic work to the rest of us. Now Sue, is there anything you would like to add?

Key questions

Critically analyse the situation facing Sue in her tasks of bringing about and resisting change in the organisation, using the concepts introduced in this chapter. What should be her plan of action in the immediate, medium and long term? Provide a rationale for your answer.

Case discussion points

1   What does the political economy perspective on change contribute to an understanding of this case? Do other perspectives on organisational analysis contribute to an understanding of the situation?

2   Does the case illustrate the co-existence and complementarity of change and continuity in organisations?

3   How would you describe the main elements of organisational change and continuity that are central to this case, and that the worker will need to address?

4   How would you describe the changes that the worker should try to bring about in this organisation? Are they adjustments, innovations, or changes? Are they symbolic or real, major or minor, first-order or second-order, planned or unplanned, formal or informal, radical or not?

5   What are the factors that are prompting change in this organisation, and what are the factors inclining the organisation towards continuity?

6   To what extent is the worker in this case involved in promoting change or in resisting the change initiatives of others?

7   What is involved in becoming 'aware' of the change situation for the worker in this case? Consider what is involved for her in identifying the issue and choosing which issues to address.

8   How should the worker define the objectives of her change efforts in this case?

9   What are her sources and potential sources of power, authority and influence in this case?

10   What factors internal and external to the organisation should the worker take into account in developing her analysis and plans for change? In particular, what are the forces for change and the forces for resistance?

11   What strategic issues should be taken into account?

12   What are the stages of action involved in bringing about lasting change in this organisation?

13   How do you rate the chances that the worker can achieve worthwhile change? How predictable is the situation?

14   What is the relevance of factors relating to gender and to disability in this case?

11

Beyond the managerialist agenda

The notion of 'effectiveness' in a market-oriented society . . . is, in great part, a rhetorical one used to justify rather than to describe or analyse something (Gummer 1988c, p. 257).

The demands for efficiency and effectiveness

Among the issues facing social and welfare workers in the final decade of the twentieth century, the need to deal with demands from their critics for greater efficiency and effectiveness is perhaps the most challenging. Many workers in both government and non-government organisations are increasingly being told to 'do more with less'. A prevailing view among politicians and policy-makers in Australia and many other nations is that expenditure on human services is essentially a drain on the economy, and should be restrained and reduced. At the same time, major structural changes in social institutions such as the labour market and the family, demographic shifts, increasing social dependency, continuing urbanisation, changing technologies, rising political consciousness among disadvantaged minorities, increasing professionalisation and rising expectations are generating increasing demands on these services. In this context, social and welfare workers are being told that they, and the organisations they work in, must become more efficient and that they must demonstrate that the services they provide 'really work'. The purpose of this chapter is to assist workers to understand the nature of these demands, deal strategically with them, challenge them where necessary, and maintain and advance a broader perspective on the role, nature and purposes of human service organisations in our society.

The managerialist agenda and social and welfare workers

Contemporary demands for efficiency and effectiveness in human services stem from the dominance of an approach to management labelled by supporters and critics alike as 'corporate management' or 'managerialism'. Managerialism needs to be understood as a management ideology and as a set of management techniques. But it also needs to be viewed as an element of a political programme and campaign to curtail the role of the state in society. As a management ideology its central concern is with managing for results. The management of human services is viewed essentially as a process of production. The basic tenets are that human service organisations should be as clear as possible about what they are trying to achieve, should try to find the most cost-effective programmes to achieve these objectives, and should attempt to monitor and evaluate performance and progress (Keating 1990). The two central concepts of effectiveness and efficiency are viewed as essentially straightforward. Effectiveness means meeting the objectives that have been set. Efficiency means doing so while keeping costs to an irreducible minimum (McCallum 1984, p. 207).

This approach to management is not original or unique to human services in the late-twentieth century. The concept of efficiency, normally used in association with economy, has been central in government administration in Australia since the nineteenth century (Spann 1979, p. 497). The focus on effectiveness, the main distinguishing feature of corporate management, has its roots in scientific management (Yeatman 1987), as discussed in chapter 2, and, more generally, in private sector management. Underpinning managerialism is the view that the approach and techniques of business management are applicable to the management of human services, whether public, non-profit or private. This is often stated explicitly. For example, a handbook on evaluating government programmes produced by the Commonwealth Department of Finance stated in its introduction that:

> Just as business managers consider new investment proposals . . . in relation to their impact on business goals, new expenditure proposals and current programmes of Commonwealth agencies should be evaluated in the light of their impact on Government goals (1987, p. v).

Managerialists tend to view management as 'a generic, purely instrumental activity, embodying a set of principles that can be applied to the public business, as well as in private business' (Painter 1988, p. 1). It can be labelled 'content-free management', in that it views management as a higher order set of skills and perspectives that can be universally applied to organisations, irrespective of their auspice, technology or purposes. In this view, the management skills required to run a vehicle assembly plant are seen as essentially the same as those needed to direct a child guidance clinic.

This approach to management is embodied in a set of management techniques, that is the vehicle for the implementation of the managerialist agenda. One of the consequences of managerialism has been the addition of many new terms to the lexicon of organisations, including human service organisations. Words and phrases such as mission statements, corporate and strategic planning, efficiency and effectiveness auditing, targeting, programme budgeting, performance indicators, quality assurance and programme evaluation are now part of the language of human service workers and managers. Managerialism is often equated with, and defined in terms of, these techniques (Weller and Lewis 1989, p. 1). They are listed and defined in Table 11.1. These techniques are based on the management tenets outlined above.

Managerialism is often presented by its adherents as an approach and a set of techniques whose virtues are self-evident (Baker 1989, p. 54); critics are often portrayed as 'tilting at windmills' (Paterson 1988, p. 287). However, it is vital that social and welfare workers understand that managerialism is not a set of unquestionable techniques, but rather a political programme and campaign to bring about far-reaching changes in human service organisations. Managerialism has to be understood in relation to the political and economic context of the state in the late twentieth century. The dominance of managerialism is closely linked to prevailing views that a great deal of social expenditure is wasteful, unproductive or unnecessary, that there is a need to reduce expenditure for reasons relating to macro-economic policy, and that many state functions can be better performed by the private sector, communities and families. The rise of managerialism has coincided with what some have termed the 'fiscal crisis' and the 'crisis of legitimacy' facing modern 'welfare states' (these terms are discussed in Mishra 1984 and Hasenfeld 1984). Managerialism, far from being self-evident, often reflects a broader perspective that the role of the state should be limited, and that social goals and individual needs should be met in other ways (e.g. Keating 1990, p. 393; Department of Finance 1987, p. v). Michael Pusey's study of the Commonwealth government's senior executive service entitled *Economic Rationalism in Canberra: A Nation-Building State Changes its Mind* found this ideology to be dominant in the national government in the late-1980s (Pusey 1988 and

Table 11.1 The techniques of managerialism

Technique	Definition
Mission statements	Written statements of the purposes of the organisation, that may include the mission, the goals and the objectives (see chapter 5)
Corporate (strategic) plans	A written document and an ongoing process involving the development and operationalisation of mission statements, strategies to meet goals taking into account the environment and capabilities of the organisation, detailed plans and programme to implement the strategy, and monitoring and evaluation mechanisms
Efficiency auditing or review	Formal scrutiny of the relationships between inputs (costs) and outputs of a programme or activity
Effectiveness auditing or review	Formal scrutiny of the extent to which a programme is meeting stated objectives
Programme budgeting	Linking of budget processes to corporate planning processes to ensure that resource allocation and usage reflects stated priorities and purposes
Performance indicators	Quantitative or qualitative measures of the outcomes of programmes or activities, to assist in decision-making
Programme evaluation	Assessment of the outputs and outcomes of programmes, including the extent to which stated goals have been achieved
Management review	An overall examination of the efficiency and effectiveness of a unit, system, activity, programme or function
Performance payment	Rewarding managers on the basis of results achieved
Risk management	Devolution of broad responsibility to programme managers for the success or failure of programmes: let the managers manage
Targeting	Directing resources to the intended beneficiaries, and to no others
Quality assurance	A planned and systematic approach to assessing and evaluating the quality of service

1991). Managerialist concerns with efficiency and effectiveness are rarely linked to proposals for increased public expenditure and social intervention. As Considine concludes: 'Its overwhelming concern is to spend effort on systems to limit goals, focus effort on key programmes, cut slack and tie all activities to narrowly prescribed outputs' (1990, p. 177). The implicit, and sometimes explicit, agenda is about cutting back on human services.

Managerialism also legitimises the status, influence, identity, ideology and technology of managers in human service organisations. The advocacy and introduction of managerialist techniques have been accompanied by the creation of senior executive services in most public services with an emphasis on management skills. There is an emphasis in the public service on giving programme managers at all levels greater responsibility and accountability for the efficiency and effectiveness of their services—this is sometimes referred to as 'risk management' or 'letting the managers manage' (Keating 1989, pp. 124-125). New units, branches and agencies have been created to undertake tasks such as corporate planning, efficiency auditing, programme evaluation and so forth. The skills required to manage human services are viewed as those of 'content-free management': a record of involvement in, knowledge of and commitment to a field of service is viewed as of secondary importance, or even as a liability. These developments serve to increase the influence of managers and managerialism in human service organisations in both the government and non-government sectors. Workers need to recognise and equip themselves to meet this political challenge, as well as the ideological and technical challenges posed by the managerialist agenda.

Social and welfare workers experience managerialism, and the issues raised by managerialism, in many direct and indirect ways. Workers in both the government and non-government sectors are now frequently asked to analyse their programmes and activities in managerialist terms. This may involve requests or requirements to take part in developing mission statements, strategic plans, performance indicators or evaluations, or to specify the outputs and outcomes of programmes. More generally they may find their organisations or programmes being appraised, and decisions being made, according to effectiveness and efficiency criteria. Workers are often asked to provide information to be used to monitor or evaluate their performance or effectiveness. Those involved in management of programmes or organisations are often required to demonstrate the efficiency and effectiveness of their activities, in formal and informal ways, to funding bodies and other significant groups in the task environment. Increasingly, the dominant cultural values in many human service organisations, particularly those in the public sector, are those of efficiency and effectiveness, as defined by managerialists. The organisational agendas of social and welfare workers, emphasising responsibilities to consumers and social justice aims are often portrayed as subservient to or conflicting with this view of efficiency and effectiveness.

For all of these reasons, the managerialist agenda cannot, and should not, be ignored. Workers need to respond to managerialism in two ways. Firstly, they need to understand the managerialist agenda, challenge and re-define it, and expropriate it for their own purposes. Secondly, they need to transcend managerialist concerns and frames of reference, and develop and implement a broader perspective on the roles and purposes of human service organisations.

Understanding, challenging and expropriating managerialism

Social and welfare workers often find themselves in direct conflict with managers and managerialism. There are several reasons for this. Managerial techniques are often perceived, often correctly, by workers as attempts to monitor and control their activities, and to limit or ration their services. The ideology of managerialism is seen as contrary to that held by many workers, and not in the interests of consumers. The managerialist agenda of cutting services back is unacceptable to workers who are aware, through their work experience, of the extent and diversity of unmet human needs and the paucity of existing service responses. For these reasons, social and welfare workers often reject managerialism outright, and view effectiveness and efficiency as concepts largely irrelevant to human service organisations and their own agendas.

In our view, this outright rejection is understandable, but mistaken. The terms effectiveness and efficiency need not and should not carry inherent, pejorative overtones. On the contrary, efficiency and effectiveness should be accepted as core values for social and welfare workers. Consumers are entitled to service which are efficient and effective. Workers should seek to critically understand and expropriate the concepts of effectiveness and efficiency. We will first discuss the significance of the concepts of effectiveness and efficiency for workers, and show how a critical understanding of these concepts can be incorporated into social and welfare work. This will be followed by consideration of strategies and skills that follow from this analysis.

Expropriating effectiveness

There are two main reasons for social and welfare workers to incorporate the concept of effectiveness into their work in human service organisations. Firstly, considerations of effectiveness are inherent in the politics of human service work and human service organisations. All organisations are continually, albeit often sporadically, being assessed by groups both in the task environment and inside the organisation. The backdrop to the daily activities of an organisation is ongoing scrutiny of its effectiveness, and of the contribution of individuals and groups within the organisation. These assessments of effectiveness are politically significant. They determine the flow of resources and legitimation to the organisation, and the influence and position of groups within the organisation (Hasenfeld 1983, p. 204). Organisations that are considered to be effective are well positioned to attract resources and responsibilities, and the positions of those that work in them are likely to be relatively secure. If effectiveness is questioned, resources, legitimacy and relations within the organisation are likely to be challenged. Workers cannot afford to ignore or neglect the perceptions that are held of the effectiveness of themselves as workers, and of their programmes and organisations. This is particularly so in times when human services are under attack and when difficult economic conditions result in strong competition for resources.

The significance of the concept of effectiveness also stems from workers' commitment to the value and importance of their work, and the need for ongoing, critical analysis of what they do. All workers should regularly address such questions as 'Does what I am doing really make a difference?' and 'Does my programme really work?' Workers should be concerned about the impact of their service on consumers and the society, and not assume that their activities and programmes have beneficial consequences. Consumers of human services, and citizens who pay for them directly or indirectly, have a right to services that do what they claim to do. For workers, concern with effectiveness is an ethical responsibility as well as a political necessity.

Central though the concept of effectiveness is, there is not universal agreement about what it means. For this reason, workers need a critical understanding of the concept that goes beyond the rather narrow definitions of the managerialists. In organisation theory, there are essentially three approaches to the meaning of effectiveness (Hasenfeld 1983, pp. 206-208). From a scientific management perspective, organisational effectiveness is defined in terms of the achievement of stated objectives. For example, a competitive employment programme may have the stated objective of assisting people with a disability to obtain open employment. From the standpoint of scientific management, its effectiveness will be judged on the number and proportion of consumers who obtain jobs. If it achieves a sufficiently high placement rate it will be judged effective and will continue to receive funding and support. But if the placement rate is too low, it will be seen to have failed to meet the test of effectiveness and its support would be discontinued.

Managerialism is essentially based on this 'rational' view of effectiveness. However, this perspective has many limitations deriving from the nature of human service organisations, as discussed in chapter 3, and the nature of organisational goals, as discussed in chapter 5. The criteria of success are not clear cut in human service organisations. How many people with disabilities would need to get jobs for the competitive employment programme to be considered successful? How long would they have to hold the jobs? Would it matter what kinds of jobs they obtained? Would they have to like the jobs? Would success be related to the severity or the nature of a person's disability? It is often unclear what factors influence the level of effectiveness. Low success rates may be related to the resources made available to the service, the quality of the work, the characteristics of the consumers, the prevailing levels of unemployment, the degree of support received from the task environment, and many other factors. There is also likely to be a difference between official and operative goals. For example, the main original purpose of the service, from the perspective of the funding body, may have been to give the appearance of concern for people with disabilities, rather than to actually achieve employment outcomes. The service may serve symbolic as well as substantive goals. Additionally, there may be multiple objectives, with different groups in the organisation pursuing different ends. For many consumers a major outcome of the service may be that they acquire valued employment-related skills, irrespective of whether this results in suitable paid employment in the short term. When such factors are taken into account, as they should be, effectiveness becomes a blurred and disputed concept, rather than the crisp and decisive measure implied by the rhetoric of managing by results.

Furthermore, reliance on and adherence to narrowly defined notions of effectiveness can have detrimental consequences for human services. If competitive employment programmes were told that they would be held accountable for their success in terms of proportion of people with disabilities placed in paid employment, there would be strong pressures on workers in the service to only work with people with relatively good employment prospects (the practice of 'creaming'), to encourage them to take any work available irrespective of their personal preferences, and to focus on short-term employment outcomes rather than long-term employment potential. Such practices marginalise and exclude those consumers most in need. Supposedly 'objective' measures of effectiveness are by no means neutral in their consequences for consumers.

The second approach to effectiveness found in organisation theory stems from systems perspectives on organisations (see chapter 2). From this perspective, effectiveness is equated with organisational survival and growth. For example, a competitive employment programme would be considered effective if it managed to obtain funding from a variety of sources, to develop a high level of legitimacy from other organisations, and to achieve a high level of staff and consumer satisfaction. The difficulties with this approach to effectiveness are clear. Essentially, it confuses the well-being of the organisation with its outcomes. A distinction must be made between organisational success and organisational effectiveness. Human service organisations can be highly successful in the terms listed above without necessarily producing effective outcomes for consumers or the society as a whole.

The third approach to effectiveness, found in the political economy perspective, views the concept as essentially political in nature. This is the approach we consider to be most useful to social and welfare workers. The definition and measurement of effectiveness is viewed as a political contest among individuals and groups who have an interest in the organisation. This does not imply that consideration of effectiveness is meaningless, and that attempts to assess it are 'merely political'. On the contrary, it essential that workers take effectiveness seriously. The key point is that there cannot be a final, unambiguous, definitive, scientific statement about the effectiveness of a human service organisation or programme. All assessments of effectiveness reflect the values and interests of those undertaking the assessment and are open to varying interpretations. 'All evaluations can be contested' (Davis et al. 1988, p. 139). Workers should take assessments of effectiveness seriously because of their ethical and political responsibilities. But the search for a definitive answer to the question, 'Are we effective?' will always prove elusive, due the political nature of the assessment and the diverse and conflicting expectations held of human service organisations.

The practical implications of this perspective can be illustrated once again by the example of the competitive employment service. Imagine that the service is under threat as a result of a finding of an external evaluation by a consultant employed by the funding body that 'only 30 per cent of consumers are in full-time paid employment twelve months after registering with the service'. What should be the response of workers in the service? If they are of the view that the service is in major need of reform, they can use these findings to pursue their change agenda (see chapter 10). But what if they are of the view that the service is doing valuable work, but is constrained by limited resources or environmental factors? In that case they need to dispute the findings of the evaluation by contesting its definition and measures of effectiveness (Hasenfeld 1983, pp. 212-217). Firstly, they can question the assessment criteria—why should the standard of full-time paid employment after twelve months be applied, given what we know about the discrimination and difficulties experienced by people with disabilities in our society? Secondly, they can question the selection of the client population used to make this assessment—it may be that the figure for people with a 'mild disability' is much better than 30 per cent. Thirdly, they can question the measurement instruments and procedures used in the study—what is meant by 'full-time paid employment'? Has the measuring instrument taken into account intermittent work, near full-time work, full-time unpaid work or other productive activities? Finally, they can question the interpretation of the findings—surely 30 per cent is an excellent outcome, given the resources available to the service, the problems faced by consumers, and the nature of the labour market? Is there not a justification for increased rather than decreased resources to be made available? More fundamentally, the workers in the organisation could act more pro-actively by undertaking their own evaluation, or by endeavouring to shape the nature of the external evaluation. These strategies are discussed further below. The key point is that the assessment of effectiveness, while often involving research and other technical processes, is inherently a matter of political contest.

Expropriating efficiency

For many social and welfare workers, the idea of incorporating the concept of efficiency into their work in human service organisations is particularly difficult to accept. As we have already discussed, demands for efficiency are often made in a context of cutting back on human services, and workers, stretched to the limit in poorly resourced organisations, are right to treat such demands with scepticism. Demands for greater efficiency are invariably applied unequally across organisations or sections of organisations, and often it is the groups with the most limited resources from whom the greatest economy is demanded. The concept of efficiency is often used to justify funding levels that have a detrimental impact on effectiveness or service quality: efficiency can simply be a euphemism for cheap, second-rate service provision.

Nevertheless, workers should not fall into the trap of viewing efficiency as a concept with only pejorative connotations (Wilenski 1988, p. 216). Efficiency is an important and legitimate goal for human services, and workers should not allow themselves to be type-cast as indifferent or opposed to the efficient use of resources. Rather, social and welfare workers need to be aware of the ways in which they can use the concept of efficiency to defend and improve human services. They require, firstly, an awareness of the different meanings of the term efficiency. Three different uses of the term in relation to human services can be distinguished: administrative efficiency, economic efficiency and target efficiency (Podger 1990, p. 55).

Administrative efficiency (also called cost efficiency) refers to the ratio of costs to the units of output of the organisation. For example, the efficiency of an organisation providing a parent-aide service to families in which children have been abused could be measured in terms of numbers of families served divided by the total costs of providing the service. This example illustrates the clear conceptual difference between cost efficiency and effectiveness. The parent-aide service could achieve efficiency gains by reducing the level of contact with consumers, thereby serving more families for the same cost. Whether or not this impacted on the effectiveness of the service (for example, in reducing child abuse) is a separate question.

The demand for administrative efficiency can be approached by workers in several ways. Firstly, there is no reason why workers should not readily agree in principle with the desirability of administrative efficiency in the human services. 'Greater efficiency means satisfying more wants at the same cost, or the same number of wants at lesser cost and thus freeing resources for other . . . purposes' (Wilensky 1988, p. 217). Social and welfare workers have no brief to defend administrative inefficiency, wherever it occurs. Indeed, workers should press for efficiency criteria to be applied fairly across all industries, and across all types and levels of organisations, rather than selectively to human service organisations that are poorly resourced.

Workers also need an understanding of the organisational factors that impinge on cost effectiveness. An assertion that social and welfare workers often need to confront is that public and non-profit provision of human services is inherently less cost-efficient than provision in the private or commercial sector. This view underpins much of the contemporary interest in the privatisation of human services (Evatt Research Centre 1989, pp. 9-11). While there are some writers who argue that the private sector has an innate ability to achieve greater efficiencies than the public sector, a more convincing position is that there are many factors that impinge on the unit cost of human services. These include the employment conditions of staff, the quality of facilities and equipment, the characteristics of consumers, the abilities of staff, management practices, incentives structures, the scale of operations, and the standard of service provided. Levels of efficiency are linked to this complex array of factors, rather than to public or private provision as such. Workers need an awareness of the impact of these factors on the cost-efficiency of their own organisations.

Another important point is the nature of the relationship between administrative efficiency and effectiveness. It is often assumed that the two are complementary: managerialists exhort human service organisations to be simultaneously more efficient and more effective. However, reducing unit costs can often have a negative impact on outcomes. For example, the parent-aide service described above might increase its efficiency by cutting back on its training programmes for volunteers, reducing the level of contact with families, minimising supervision and refusing to take 'difficult cases'. But these practices may result in reduced effectiveness in preventing child abuse, and displacement of costs to other organisations and sectors. The proclaimed managerialist aim is to find efficiencies that do not lead to reduced effectiveness, that is, cost-effectiveness, the achievement of maximum outcomes for minimum cost. However, the labour intensive nature of many human services means that the scope for efficiency improvements that do not impinge on quality or effectiveness is often severely limited. Bryson suggests that efficiency should always be considered a second order goal: 'The question must always be asked, efficiency for the achievement of what goal?' (1987, p. 262).

Workers should also be aware that efficiency, as defined by managerialists, often has a narrow definition of 'costs' that overlooks costs borne by workers and consumers. Many non-government human service organisations are highly efficient in managerialist terms. Because they rely heavily on volunteers, employ staff at relatively low rates of pay and are undercapitalised in terms of facilities and equipment, they are able to provide services at highly competitive unit costs, compared to public and private alternatives. However, these practices often impact negatively on service quality and effectiveness, and are unfair to workers and consumers. The real costs of the service are borne by underpaid and overworked employees and volunteers, and poorly serviced consumers. Workers should draw attention to these hidden costs when organisational and service efficiency is under consideration (May 1991, p. 197).

Economic efficiency, the second type of efficiency pertinent to the human services, refers to the impact of a service on the overall economy. Managerialists often portray expenditure on human services as a drain on the nation's resources. However, many human service programmes including those in education, health, employment and community services make a major contribution to the functioning of the economy. For example, public expenditure on child-day care enables many parents to participate in the labour market and in educational and training programmes, reduces public expenditure on sole parent payments and dependant spouse rebate, and generates taxation revenue from child-care workers and parents able to take paid work. Many human services assist in the prevention and amelioration of costly social problems, and contribute to social stability. For example, the economic costs of domestic violence to the society have been calculated at $6707 per victim per year (Queensland Domestic Violence Task Force 1988, p. 460). Expenditure on services that prevent or minimise the impact of domestic violence result in considerable savings to the society as a whole. Workers need to be aware of the ways in which their organisations contribute to economic and social efficiency, and the importance of such efficiency to a social justice agenda (Podger 1990, pp. 54-60).

The third type of efficiency is target efficiency, which can be defined as the extent to which human services are directed to those groups for which they are intended. Focusing human service programmes on the so-called 'truly needy' to contain or reduce public expenditure is a principle associated with managerialism, and target effectiveness is often viewed as part of the managerialist agenda (Keating 1989, p. 129). However, the concept of target efficiency does not necessarily reflect this stance, and can be used in other ways. Many human service organisations are officially committed to serving disadvantaged groups such as Aboriginal people, people from ethnic minorities, people with disabilities, and people from remote areas. To the extent that they fail to do so they can be considered target inefficient. Social and welfare workers can seek in this sense to increase the target efficiency of their organisations. Similarly, many human service organisations only have the resources to serve a relatively small proportion of those who are in theory eligible for the service: those who use the service are a much smaller group than the target or need population. This is another form of 'target inefficiency' (Gates 1980, pp. 144-147). Workers should be using the concept in arguments to gain a greater allocation of resources for those excluded from services.

In summary, efficiency, like effectiveness, is a concept that workers can expropriate for their own purposes. These two concepts have been constructed and used by managerialists as part of an agenda requiring human service workers to do more with less. However, workers need to adopt a less defensive stance when confronted with demands for efficiency and effectiveness. A more strategic approach is to re-define these concepts and to incorporate them into the vocabulary, philosophy and practice of social and welfare work. The challenge is to harness the concepts to the agendas of workers, and to expropriate and re-define the terms in order to argue for improved services for consumers and the promotion of social justice.

Strategies and tactics

Expropriating the managerialist agenda requires a critical understanding of the concepts of efficiency and effectiveness and of the ways in which they can be used. However, workers also need to know how to participate in the ongoing organisational contest around the defining and assessing of efficiency and effectiveness. To be successful in this workers need:

- to adopt a proactive approach to effectiveness and efficiency;
- to strategically and selectively use the language of managerialism;
- to develop a capacity to use, or strategically participate in the use of, managerialist techniques;
- to develop an organisational culture that emphasises effectiveness and efficiency;
- to involve consumers and workers in processes of assessing effectiveness and efficiency.

Each of these are briefly discussed below.

A key strategy for workers in the current political and economic climate is to adopt a pro-active approach to effectiveness and efficiency in their organisations. Workers should not wait for outside pressure to force them to take effectiveness and efficiency seriously. By the time such pressure comes it is too late to seize the initiative. Workers should take the initiative in developing and implementing ways of monitoring and assessing organisational effectiveness and efficiency in the interests of consumers. This is an integral part of good service provision. It is also good organisational politics. Organisations that can demonstrate an active concern with the assessment of their own performance are less vulnerable than those which ignore this issue. They are also able to set the parameters of the assessment process. Processes of evaluation and assessment, necessary as they are if organisations are to serve consumers well, always carry risks for organisations as they can expose deficiencies and vulnerabilities. But these risks are lessened if workers committed to the organisation and to its consumers take a central role in these processes.

A pro-active approach to assessment requires workers to become adept at strategically and selectively using the language of managerialism. Concepts and techniques such as effectiveness, efficiency, cost effectiveness, target efficiency, strategic planning, evaluation and performance indicators can become part of the conceptual armoury of workers, to be used as the occasion requires. It is not suggested that workers adopt this vocabulary in its entirety or in an uncritical manner. In many organisations this language may be unacceptable or unhelpful as it breaches cultural values of the organisation, other workers or consumers. Rather, workers should acquire the capacity to use managerialist language in circumstances where this will further their own organisational agendas and consumers' interests. These circumstances might include negotiations with funding and regulatory bodies, defending the organisation, development of the public image of the organisation, and the initiation of organisational change and resistance processes.

A pro-active approach also requires workers to develop a capacity to use, or strategically participate in the use of, managerialist techniques. Strategic planning and programme evaluation methods and procedures can be helpful tools for organisations wishing to monitor and assess their effectiveness and efficiency. These techniques are sometimes given a mystique by their proponents that makes them inaccessible to workers and consumers: they are seen and portrayed as highly technical processes in the province of specialised planners and researchers. This is a misleading view. While there are some highly technical approaches to planning and evaluation, many useful skills that can be applied in typical organisational situations can be readily acquired by workers and consumers. Workers who have gained these skills are well placed to assist their organisations to improve services and meet political challenges. It should be noted, however, that the utility and track record of many managerialist techniques has been sharply questioned (Considine 1990). Workers should adopt a critical and careful approach to the use of the techniques listed in Table 11.1. They need to carefully monitor the actions of managers who make grandiose claims about their benefits, and demand that such claims be demonstrated.

In some human service organisations there is a lack of interest in effective and efficient service provision, and lack of awareness of the importance and usefulness of these concepts. Workers in such organisations will need to facilitate the development of an organisational culture that emphasises the strategic use of efficiency and effectiveness. Issues associated with the creation and change of organisational culture were examined in depth in chapter 7. Workers may need to demonstrate to other members of the organisation the value of monitoring and assessing effectiveness and efficiency for improving consumer service and dealing with political demands in the task environment.

Finally, workers need to involve consumers and front-line workers in processes of assessing effectiveness and efficiency. Managerialism tends to view these processes as essentially top-down: effectiveness and efficiency are to be appraised by those with managerial responsibilities for organisations and programmes. Workers should be trying to ensure that a bottom-up view is also considered, and that consumer and worker perspectives are taken into account. What do consumers and front-line workers consider to be the significant criteria of effective and efficient service? How effective and efficient do consumers and workers consider the service to be? Because assessment of effectiveness and efficiency is a political process, workers need to address such questions and promote the active involvement of those likely to be excluded from these crucial organisational processes.

Transcending managerialism

We have outlined how workers can challenge the managerialist agenda by re-defining and expropriating the concepts of effectiveness and efficiency. However, these two concepts, taken alone, provide an inadequate and incomplete basis for evaluation of human service organisations. Social and welfare workers need a broader perspective that reflects a concern with social justice and responsiveness to the needs of consumers. We propose that workers go beyond the relatively narrow criteria offered by the managerialists, and argue for the assessment of the activities of human service organisations according to five, rather than two, principles. These five are: effectiveness, efficiency, equity, excellence and expansion. We have already examined the first two of these concepts, which were expropriated from the managerialist agenda. We will now examine the meanings, inter-relations and implications of the remaining principles.

Towards equity

Like effectiveness and efficiency, equity is a contested concept with many differing meanings (Pateman 1981). It is closely related to fairness, and to the concepts of equality, justice, rights, participation and access. Equity can be applied to both processes and outcomes. Equitable processes can be viewed as those that deal with people in a fair, impartial and consistent manner, or that positively discriminate in favour of certain groups or classes of people to compensate for unequal opportunities. Equitable outcomes are those that are considered fair and reasonable according to certain specified criteria. Considerations of equity always involve value judgements. While almost everyone claims a belief in the importance of equity in societal arrangements, there is widespread debate and disagreement about what this means. For example, what is an equitable distribution of income and wealth in a society? Some would answer this question solely in terms of process: provided there is a 'level playing field' for economic activity the resulting distribution of wealth and income is equitable, irrespective of its shape. Others would argue that any distribution of wealth and income that departs significantly from complete equality of outcome is inequitable. The latter group may argue for re-distribution of income and wealth in the name of equity. Or they may propose changes to economic and other processes to give greater opportunities or advantages to those less well off. The political reality is that there is often a close relationship between the stake that an individual or group have in an issue, and their views on what constitutes an equitable process or outcome.

Proponents of managerialism claim a concern with equity, and contend that improvements in equity flow directly from their approach to efficiency and effectiveness (Keating 1989, pp. 128-129; 1990, pp. 392-394). They make several arguments. Equity is seen as being enhanced through tighter targeting of human service programmes. Equity objectives are seen as having a better chance of being achieved and evaluated if managerial techniques are employed. Equity and efficiency are viewed as complementary goals, that reinforce one another rather than being in conflict (Podger 1990). However, managerialists do not provide a detailed or critical analysis of what they mean by equity in an organisational context, or of how to monitor and achieve equity. Thus, they propose efficiency and effectiveness auditing and review, but present no techniques for 'equity auditing' of human services. It is sometimes suggested by managerialists that because equity issues involve value judgements, they should be confined to the political rather than the organisational arena (Keating 1989, p. 129).

In contrast to this last position, we argue that workers should give the concept of equity a central place in the assessment of human service organisations. As discussed in the chapter on street-level bureaucracy (chapter 8), all the activities of human service organisations involve policy-making and the exercise of value judgements. Human service organisations and workers are not merely instruments of policy: everything they do involves equity considerations (Wilensky 1988, p. 217). Workers need to be aware of the equity implications of organisational activities and decisions, and should attempt to ensure that equity is a central criterion in organisational practices and the assessment and evaluation of human service organisations.

In order to do this, workers need a framework for identifying and analysing equity issues in organisations. The concept of equity raises key questions about an organisation's relations with its environment, its goals, its structures and its culture. Each of these will now be briefly examined.

The assessment of human service organisations must begin with an awareness that the social, economic and political environment in which they operate is itself inequitable in many fundamental ways (Troy 1981). The needs and problems that consumers bring to a human service organisation are constructed and shaped by political, economic and social processes largely beyond the control either of the consumers themselves or of the organisation. The resources and mandate that the organisation is given often fall far short of what is required to seriously address the problems that the society faces. The work of human service organisations is constantly undermined and challenged by the activities of other institutions and organisations in the society. Human service organisations themselves are part of these broader inequities: they reproduce and reinforce, as well as ameliorate and challenge, social inequalities. These features of the environment cannot be ignored when organisations are being evaluated. Much criticism of the ineffectiveness of human services stems from a lack of recognition of these underlying structural inequities.

The implications of this position can be illustrated by the example of an organisation providing emergency relief payments to individuals and families in financial crisis. A managerialist perspective on the assessment of this organisation may look at its 'effectiveness' in terms of the numbers of families it has assisted, its 'efficiency' in terms of the administrative costs per payment made, and its 'equity' in terms of whether families in similar circumstances received similar treatment, or whether resources were directed towards those in 'greatest need'. These are important considerations, but they miss, and divert attention from, larger equity issues. These are that the demand for emergency relief reflects the failure of the economy to provide full employment and adequate pay, that the income security system fails to provide an adequate safety net for all families, that the amounts allocated for emergency relief are trifling compared to the level of demand, and that the organisations involved in providing relief are grossly underresourced for the task they have to perform (VCOSS 1990; QCOSS 1990). Social and welfare workers must attempt to ensure that a critical analysis of the impact of broad societal inequities is integral to the assessment of human service organisations. If this is not done, human service organisations, and those that work in them, will be held accountable for social conditions that they neither cause nor control, and narrow analysis of the effectiveness of human services will be seen as a substitute for critical analysis of social processes and institutions which produce these conditions (Miller 1978).

Relatedly, the assessment of human service organisations must involve a critical analysis of the equity of organisational goals. A managerial perspective takes the official goals at face value, and is concerned mainly with attempting to state goals and objectives in measurable ways. However, as we saw in chapter 5, this is a blinkered view. Official goals serve many purposes including the legitimation of the organisation and its ruling coalition. It is necessary to distinguish between official and operative goals, and to understand that human service organisations serve many purposes, and have many effects, other than those that are publicly stated. Analysis of these hidden goals may lead to quite different conclusions about the equity of an organisation. From a managerialist perspective, an emergency relief organisation with the goal of 'assisting those in financial crisis' may be highly equitable in so far as it targets its limited resources on 'the most needy'. But from a broader, critical perspective, the operative goals of the organisation may be interpreted as 'reinforcing traditional notions of the family, keeping the work ethic in good shape, maintaining notions of deservingness, and enforcing a spectrum of economic, status and power distinctions . . . ' (Bryson 1981, pp. 111-112). A concern with equity leads human service workers to question official goals, and to examine the wider constellation of interests served by the organisation.

Workers should also be concerned with the equity of organisational structures. Structural equity applies to the position of both workers and consumers. For workers, key equity issues include working conditions and pay, opportunity structures within the organisation and chances to participate in decision-making. A central concern is ensuring fair treatment of all workers irrespective of gender, class, race, Aboriginality, disability or age. Much of the discussion of equity in human service organisations has focused on the position of women, and the implementation of equal employment opportunity policies (Bryson 1987, pp. 265-268; Sawer 1989, pp. 139-148). Equal opportunity structures can be valued not only for workers themselves but also for their contribution to more equitable organisational outcomes. The concept of 'representative bureaucracy' suggests that key positions in organisations should be held by people who are representative of the broader society in terms of gender, race, class, and so forth, as this will result in organisational decisions and processes that more accurately reflect the diversity of values in the society (Wilensky 1988, p. 215). A major challenge facing human service organisations is to restructure themselves in more equitable ways, to ensure that they are representative of the consumers they seek to serve.

From a consumer perspective, structural equity involves issues of the availability and distribution of services, access, rights and participation. These concepts, and strategies to address them, were examined in chapter 9. Workers should be concerned with the equity of the processes whereby services are allocated to consumers. They should be concerned with the accessibility of services to consumers, and potential barriers such as non-availability of suitable services, inadequate information, discriminatory eligibility requirements, prohibitive costs, and geographic and psychological inaccessibility. They should be concerned with the ways in which a person's gender, class, ethnicity, race, disability or age makes access to services difficult or impossible. They should be concerned with the rights of consumers to receive quality services, to be treated respectfully, to be assured of confidentiality, and to be able to appeal against decisions. Opportunities for consumers to participate in decision-making processes are also important. Workers should be aware of the equity implications for consumers of even seemingly commonplace decisions about structural matters:

> Administrative decisions, even of a minor nature, such as the amount to be allocated to advertising for a benefit programme, the siting of an employment office, the office opening hours, the design of an application form for benefits, the choice of qualifications required of interviewing officers for welfare beneficiaries, the financial report required of groups in receipt of community development grants, all alter the outcome of programmes [and] . . . the distribution of publicly provided goods and services (Wilensky 1988, p. 217).

Finally, workers need to consider the extent to which the organisation's culture promotes or impedes equitable processes and outcomes. For example, do the prevailing values emphasise fair treatment of workers and consumers? Is there an ethos that is supportive of participation by consumer groups in decision-making? Do dominant values lead the organisation to favour some social groups and discriminate among others? Are there sub-cultures which work against the needs and interests of consumers? It has been argued that organisations dominated by the managerialist culture tend to be unsympathetic to values such as collectivism, consultation and participation and state intervention (Sawer 1989, pp. 149-150), and blind to issues such as the relationship between the family and work (Bryson

1987, pp. 267-268). A key cultural variable is the extent to which equity, effectiveness, efficiency, excellence and expansion are valued in the organisation.

Towards excellence

The concept of excellence provides workers with a fourth criteria by which to assess their own work and the work of their organisations. The term was first popularised by Peters and Waterman in their much-quoted private sector management text entitled *In Search of Excellence* (1982). Their key themes are that the most profitable companies are those that treat their workers as valued organisational resources, that convey to them a sense of the meaningful nature of their work, and that emphasise the paramount importance of high quality service to consumers and of responding to consumers' needs. The ideological emphasis in the excellence literature on profitability raises questions for many workers about its applicability to human services. As with the previous concepts of efficiency and effectiveness, it is necessary to consider ways in which it can be re-defined and expropriated.

Managerialists in the public sector have assimilated the main themes of the excellence literature in a selective fashion. They emphasise the importance of obtaining the commitment and loyalty of staff, and investing in human resources, in order to realise 'the full benefits of managerialism' (Baker 1989, p. 54). However, there has been relatively little attention from managerialists on the theme of responsiveness to consumers.

From the perspective of social and welfare workers this is a major omission. The possibilities of expropriating the excellence concept lie in its emphasis on commitment to consumers. Managers and workers in human service organisations should be strongly committed to high quality consumer service. Workers should strive to ensure that the provision of high quality service becomes a central part of the ethos and culture of the human services. Key elements of quality include accessibility, timeliness, consistency, humaneness, and technical proficiency (Patti 1988, p. 8). Consumers should be seen punctually, be consulted and listened to, be informed of their rights and entitlements, be given full and accurate information, be assured of confidentiality, be treated with dignity and respect, and have available a range of effective grievance procedures. Human service organisations should be encouraged to develop service standards around these issues.

Excellence, like the other key concepts discussed in this chapter, is a disputed concept involving value judgements about what constitutes a good service. It is therefore important that the development of standards involves all relevant groups, and particularly consumers and front-line workers. Factors that have been found to be associated with perceptions of quality service by consumers include: compatibility between the consumer's personal goals and the aims and interests of workers and the organisation; the reputation of an organisation; the level of availability of resources; worker commitment to, or alienation from, their work; and the way in which the consumer's 'moral identity' is constructed and perceived by the organisation (Hasenfeld 1983, pp. 197–200).

Many, but not all, of these factors can be influenced by social and welfare workers. However, it should be stressed that there are structural and historical reasons that impede the pursuit of excellence in human service organisations. Many human services are deliberately designed to be degrading to recipients. The history of income security since the Poor Laws has emphasised the importance of deterring potential recipients, and this has been reflected in organisational practices (Gummer 1988b, p. 261). The treatment of prisoners in correctional systems is similarly based to a considerable degree on ideas of shame, punishment and deterrence. The perceived low status of many consumers of human services also obstructs a commitment to excellence in consumer service. The professionalisation of human services, while supportive in important ways of quality service, can also result in a devaluing of consumer perceptions on quality standards. Professionalisation can also result in a sharpening of class and status differences between workers and consumers that inhibit trust and good communication. Many consumers, who are excluded from the mainstream economic and social structures of our society, most notably Aboriginal people, rightly recognise that their interests and those of workers and human service organisations do not match. The limited resources of many human service organisations also impose real constraints on service quality. The indeterminate nature of human service technologies can result in some organisations placing little value on technical proficiency.

The search for excellence in human service organisations is, therefore, a difficult one. It has to confront structural as well as cultural barriers. It must be based on a commitment to the rights of all consumers to receive good quality human services, and to participate in processes of defining what excellence means for them. In this sense, the demand for control and self-determination explicit in the Aboriginal perspective on organisations, has implications for all consumers who are rarely given the opportunities of defining in their own terms what it is that human service organisations should provide for them.

Towards expansion

The idea that social and welfare workers should value and work towards the expansion of human services challenges the prevailing political and economic orthodoxy and the managerialist view that in hard times human services should tighten their belts and accept greater levels of control over their activities. Considine describes corporate management as 'essentially a framework to "circle the wagons" and ration supplies' (1990, p. 177). That is, in the face of the major economic and social challenges facing Australian society, managerialism adopts an essentially defensive posture characterised by limiting expenditure, restraining or reducing the size and scope of the state, and increasing central control. This perspective can be challenged at a number of points. Firstly, the view that the state is too big, and should be reduced for reasons of economic efficiency, can be contested. Expenditure on human services in Australia does not rank among the highest in the Western, industrialised world, and there are countries with much higher levels of expenditure whose economic performance is superior (Graycar and Jamrozik 1989, p. 286; May 1991, pp. 200-204). There are undoubtedly strong political pressures to reduce expenditure, and the appropriate size of the human services sector is an important and complex economic question. However, it is by no means self-evident that the state in Australia is too big or that it does too much, or that expenditure on human services is excessive.

Indeed, it can be argued that in the uncertain and demanding social, economic, political and environmental circumstances of the late twentieth century, human service organisations should be meeting new challenges and opportunities (Butler et al. 1988). As Considine argues, 'Public organisations faced with increased pressure and greater uncertainty must do more, not less. They must look for opportunities to do new things, not simply the old ones at cheaper unit costs' (1990, p. 177). The demands and challenges facing human service organisations, now and in the future, are many and varied. Demographic changes, including the ageing of the Australian population, mean that there is a growing need for greater provision of health and community services. Human service organisations also need to respond to needs arising from the changing structure, roles and composition of the Australian family. They will have to find ways to respond to the changing expectations of citizens, particularly those from disadvantaged and marginalised groups and demands for greater participation in all areas of society. They urgently need to find ways of responding to the demands of Aboriginal people for self-determination. The structural changes occurring in the international and Australian economies will probably result in human service organisations finding themselves confronting demands that they address the consequences of rapid and unpredictable changes in the labour market, and respond to the lowering of living standards and quality of life. The increasing size and suburbanisation of our cities will require the development of innovative land use, housing and transport services and policies. At the same time, human service organisations will have to meet the challenge of providing quality services to people living in remote and rural areas.

There is an urgent need for human service organisations to find ways to reduce and respond to growing levels of violence in our society, particularly against women, children and marginalised groups. Underlying all of these issues is the persistence of structural poverty and inequality as central characteristics of Australian society.

These demands and challenges require social and welfare workers, together with all other human service workers, to become more innovative, creative and pro-active in their approach to working in human service organisations. A major criticism of managerialism is that its drive for greater control and standardisation of programmes may stifle the kinds of initiative and experimentation needed to address pressing social issues (Considine 1988, pp. 16-17; 1990, pp. 176-177; Wilensky 1988, pp. 218-222). More fundamentally, the managerialist agenda of reducing the size and role of the state leads to key issues being ignored, contained and suppressed. Workers, because of their strategic location in the front-line of organisations, often have a close knowledge of the needs of consumers, and the issues facing society. They should view it as a central part of their responsibilities to identify and analyse these needs and issues, raise them in the society, and mobilise human service organisations to address them.

The question of how human service organisations, and the social and economic structures of which they are a part, will meet these challenges and demands remains to be seen. What can be stated with certainty is that we will continue to live in an organisationally based society. Organisations, including human service organisations, will continue to be central to key social processes including the exercise of power and authority, and the distribution of resources, including the provision of human services. Existing organisations, and prevailing social and economic structures, are monuments to our past. They reflect responses to issues that have passed or are passing. The challenge for social and welfare workers is to engage in the struggle to transform our organisations and social institutions so that they become pathways towards a better future. This book presents no grand solution and no quick fix to the bewildering array of problems and issues facing our society. It has indicated the ways that workers can engage more effectively in the organisational processes that have a significant bearing on the lives of all citizens.

Chapter review questions

1 What is managerialism? What are its implications for human service organisations and workers?
2 What should be the response of workers to the managerialist agenda?

3 What are the main perspectives on organisational effectiveness? Which approach do you consider most useful, both analytically and from a practice perspective?
4 What are the different meanings of the term 'efficiency' in relation to human service organisations? How can the concept be approached and used by social and welfare workers?
5 What strategies and tactics can workers use to expropriate the managerialist agenda?
6 What do you understand by the term 'equity' in relation to human service organisations? Critique the managerialist formulation of equity?
7 What are the origins of the concept of excellence in relation to organisations? In what ways, if any, is it applicable to human service organisations?
8 Should social and welfare workers actively work towards the expansion of human services? Why or why not? What are the implications of expansion?

Further reading

The academic debate on managerialism in Australia has been mainly waged in the pages of the *Australian Journal of Public Administration*, and the *Canberra Bulletin of Public Administration*. The major critiques of managerialism are Yeatman (1987), Bryson (1987), Painter (1988), Considine (1988), Sinclair (1989) and Considine (1990). Clear statements of the managerialist position are provided by Paterson (1988), Keating (1989) and Keating (1990). Overviews of the issues are provided by Wilenski (1988) and Weller and Lewis (1989). Three issues of the *Canberra Bulletin of Public Administration* have been devoted to the kinds of issues discussed in this chapter: no. 54 (May 1988) looked at efficiency and effectiveness issues, no. 60 (February 1990) focused on equity and social justice issues, and no. 63 (December 1990) examined issues in evaluation. Michael Pusey's *Economic Rationalism in Canberra* (1991) is a major analysis and critique, and Jamrozik's *Class, Inequality and the State* (1991) links management of the state and the emergence of the new middle class. Critical perspectives on the assessment of human service organisations can be found in Hasenfeld (1983, chapter 8), Bryson (1981), Miller (1978) and Gummer (1988b).

Case study

THE YOUTH INDEPENDENCE ASSOCIATION

The Youth Independence Association is a non-government organisation that aims to provide community living skills for young people (seventeen to twenty-five years) with an intellectual disability. The organisation is located in a large Australian city. Its aim is to assist the young people to live independently in the community. The underlying philosophy of the organisation is that the consumers should be enabled to define and develop their own independent living goals.

The organisation was formed two years ago by a group of human service workers with a strong commitment to this philosophy. The group applied successfully for a demonstration grant from the Commonwealth government, and did all the initial organising work including having the organisation incorporated as an association. The organisation has a management committee of nine people elected by the members of the association. Currently the committee comprises three of the workers who were involved in forming the organisation, one ex-worker, four parents of past and present consumers, and one young person who went through the programme during its first year and who is now living independently. The ex-worker is currently the chairperson of the organisation.

The organisation currently employs six workers. There are two case workers who have the primary responsibility for assessing young people for the programme, working with them, and supporting them as necessary after they leave the programme. These positions are filled by a female occupational therapist and a male community welfare worker. There is a family worker/co-ordinator position which is filled by an experienced, female social worker. She combines working with the families of the young people, and managing the day-to-day running of the project. The co-ordinator attends all meetings of the management committee, and is responsible for implementing its decisions and providing the main link between the committee and the workers. There are also two residential programme workers, a man and a woman with residential care qualifications, who supervise and run the activities in the two houses operated by the association. Finally, there is a half-time secretary, a woman, who maintains the organisation's office—a large room located in and rented from a community centre near to the houses. All of the staff are in their early twenties, excepting the family worker who is twenty-eight. They were selected on the basis of their skills in working and communicating with young people, and their commitment to the philosophy of the organisation. All staff have a strong belief in the goals and approach of the Association.

Young people are accepted into the programme through a process of discussion between workers, the young person and her or his family. Usually, prior to coming into the programme, the young people are living at home with their parents, or in an institutional setting. They have little or no experience of independent living, and are often considered by other service providers, and sometimes by their own families and friends, to have little potential for living without extensive support. The organisation rents two houses in the inner suburbs of the city. Young people accepted into the programme live in these houses in groups of three or four at any one time. The organisation's last annual report described what occurs in the houses as follows:

> There the young people learn a lot about themselves as individuals, they learn to cope with the separation from their parents, and they learn how to manage a household with all its ups and downs. In short, they experience the things that most other people in the community experience. Staff can discuss the responsibilities of the young people for household management and personal decisions, but do not intervene in a protective way. Staff encourage the young people to experience and learn from the consequences of their behaviour. Staff endeavour to teach the young people how to make informed decisions; they also support the young people in the decisions that they take. One key to the success of the programme is the close and intensive relationship between the young people and the workers, and the commitment to letting young people develop at their own pace.

Workers are available in a supportive role for the young people living in the houses. Workers are also involved in assisting the young people to move out of the houses into fully independent living in the community, once they have developed sufficient skills and confidence. The time that the young people stay on the programme varies, but is usually between six and twelve months.

The Association is currently funded as a three-year demonstration project under the Commonwealth Government's Disability Services Act. This legislation provides funds to non-government organisations to provide services to people with disabilities. Certain principles and requirements of funded services are specified in the Act. These include:
- that funded services emphasise the achievement of 'positive consumer outcomes';
- that services for people with disabilities be provided, wherever and whenever possible, in 'normal' living situations;
- that services promote positive images of people with disabilities;
- that services provide an environment of 'high expectancy' for people with disabilities;
- that consumer involvement in organisational decision-making be maximised;
- that funded organisations can demonstrate financial and administrative viability.

Because the Association is a demonstration project there is an additional requirement, 'that the organisation's activities be evaluated at the end of the three year funded period'. The nature, scope and form of this evaluation have not been clarified with the funding body during the first two years.

The Commonwealth government currently provides approximately 90 per cent of the organisation's funding. The remainder comes from the young people who pay a standard contribution in the form of a rental payment of $50.00 per week. Most of the young people receive financial support from the Department of Social Security, and pay a proportion of this to the Association. Some, who come from financially secure families, receive financial assistance from their parents. It would be possible for the Association to require a higher charge, but it is seen as important to the goals of the programme to leave the young people with a significant amount of discretionary income and to encourage them to be financially independent.

Funding of the organisation as a demonstration project was guaranteed for three years, but the Association is keen to receive ongoing funding after this time. The project will soon be entering its third year of operation. During the first year of operation the Association operated with a small deficit, which has increased somewhat during the second year. The Association has just been told that their grant for the third year will held at the same real level, with a 5 per cent increase to allow for inflation. This falls far short of the amount requested by the Association. The Association is anticipating a 20 per cent increase in expenditures on salaries as a result of a new award that has been handed down for workers in the community services industry. The Commonwealth has refused to undertake to meet these additional costs, but the Association has a policy of paying award rates. There is no likelihood of a change in the Commonwealth's position. The funding climate is difficult and all governments are seeking ways of cutting back on social expenditures. In a recent speech by a senior member of the Department responsible for disability funding the view was expressed that funded organisations should seek to be more cost-effective via 'more efficient administration and service delivery, more extensive use of volunteers, the application of appropriate user charges and more vigorous private fund raising'. Some of the Association's other expenses are also due to increase. This combination of factors means that the organisation anticipates a significant rise in its budget deficit during the coming year. Unless there are significant changes in policy by the funding body or the Association, this deficit is likely to increase even more in future years.

The Association's treasurer, one of the parents on the management committee, has outlined this situation for the management committee in a financial statement. The statement assumes a 5 per cent increase in the Commonwealth grant, no changes to resident's contributions and fund raising, salary increases in accordance with the new award, and a 5 per cent increase in most recurrent expenses. The treasurer has expressed grave concern about the financial situation, and the issue is to be discussed at the next meeting of the management committee.

YIA - Income and expenditure for years two and three (anticipated)

Item	Current year two	Next year three
Income		
Commonwealth grant	195 000	204 750
Residents' contribution	21 000	21 000
Donations	1 200	1 200
Total income	217 200	226 950
Expenditure		
Salaries		
Family worker/co-ordinator	35 000	42 000
Two case-workers	60 000	72 000
Two residential-care workers	50 000	60 000
Secretary half-time	15 000	18 000
Housing		
Rental per annum house 1	12 000	12 600
Rental per annum house 2	13 000	13 650
Miscellaneous expenses	5 000	5 250
Office		
Rental from wattle Neighbourhood Centre	5 000	5 000
Office expenses	15 000	15 750
Transport	10 000	10 500
Total expenditure	220 000	254 750
Deficit carried forward from previous year	(2 500)	(5 300)
Final deficit	(5 300)	(33 100)
Brackets indicate deficit		

The organisation has worked with a total of thirty-two young people during its first two years. Fourteen of them are now living independently, eight are back living with their parents or in residential care having been unable to make the transition to independent living at this time, and ten are still with the programme. There is a waiting list of twenty-three families with a young person wishing to join the programme. Most of those who did not complete the programme successfully were admitted despite doubts held by workers about the likelihood of a successful outcome, given such factors as their level of disability, previous experiences and family situation. Their admittance reflected the views of the two case workers that the organisation should take a proportion of young people whose chances of success are marginal at best. As one of the case workers explained to a staff meeting:

If we only take young people with a high chance of success, we are not being fair to some highly disadvantaged young people. They deserve a chance as much as the others do. And anyway, what is success? We can't assume that because they go back home, or whatever, that they haven't had a valuable and worthwhile experience.

A contrary view was expressed by the treasurer at a recent meeting of the Management Committee. He argued that because the programme had achieved such good results with fourteen young people, the best strategy would be to carefully examine their characteristics, and select young people with similar backgrounds and qualities for the programme. He put it this way at the Management Committee:

We should be aiming for a 100 per cent success rate, and because of our highly professional staff I believe that we can achieve this. If we carefully select those most likely to benefit from the programme it will have many benefits. We will not only have a high success rate, but we will also have a faster turnover of young people in the programme. This will mean that we will be more efficient, and that we will be able to serve a greater number of young people. This means that we will be able to reduce the length of our waiting list. There are advantages for everyone.

Most of the workers in the organisation have a strong belief in the effectiveness of what they do, and point to the number of young people who have been through the programme and who are now living in the community. There has been a great deal of impatience expressed by some workers with the expectations of the funding body that 'specific outcome measures' be developed and monitored for each individual young person. The caseworkers in particular feel that developing such measures and collecting the information on the young people is obtrusive and artificial, and takes time and attention away from the real work with the young people: 'Why should we waste our time collecting useless statistics. Nobody ever takes any notice of them anyway. We know we are doing useful work'. A system for monitoring outcomes was instituted during the first year of the Association, but during the last year it has not been rigorously followed. Workers keep in touch with young people who have left the programme on an informal basis, but there is no formal monitoring of progress other than in the first three months after leaving.

Recently, the Association has received a letter from the funding body indicating that an evaluation of the programme is required during the third year of operation. The letter indicates that the funder's preference is that this be undertaken by an external consultant and that it address the following issues:

- the short and long-term effectiveness of the programme;
- the cost-effectiveness of the programme;
- the administrative and financial efficiency and viability of the programme;
- specific issues, including the scope for increasing the number of young people using the programme, the scope for reducing the current 'high' staff–consumer ratio, the possibility of raising a higher proportion of programme costs from the young people and their families, the scope for increased private fund-raising, and the need to target the programme on those most likely to benefit from it.

The letter concludes, 'We are sure that you will agree that thorough evaluation of important demonstration programmes such as yours is vital if people with disabilities are to receive the services they need. We are sure that you will give the consultant, who is to be appointed within the next month, your full co-operation'.

One of the difficulties facing the Association is an emerging conflict between the workers and certain members of the management committee. Some of the parent members of the committee feel that, while much good work is done with the young people, the management of the organisation leaves much to be desired. One of the parents on the management committee, Mrs Hewson, is a woman with extensive experience in running a small business. In a recent letter to the management committee she wrote:

This organisation is engaging in practices that no private enterprise organisation could afford to tolerate. We must institute better management practices. Too much time is spent by staff in so-called 'collective' decision-making. Duplication of roles among the staff results in considerable inefficiency. The current staff–consumer ratio has led to 'mollycoddling' of some residents. This encourages them to stay too long in the programme, and interferes with the goal of facilitating independence.

We should look at the possibility of a complete restructuring of our organisation. I propose that one caseworker position and one residential programme officer position be abolished, and that the family worker do family work and case work full-time. It is an inappropriate use of her skills for her to be engaged in administration. The resultant savings (estimated at $66 000 for next year) could be used to employ a professional manager and to reduce our anticipated deficit. Ideally, we should be looking for a person with a track-record of success in small business or industry. The Manager could have special responsibility for fund-raising. I am convinced we could raise considerable funds from the corporate sector and the community if we conducted a properly run and managed campaign. We should also consider the possibility of raising the financial contribution made by the young people to at least $80.00 per week. In my experience, they only waste their spare money on video-games, Mars bars and the like. It would be better for the money to be used productively in the running of the programme.

Mrs Hewson has also expressed some concern about the presence of a former consumer on the committee. She says that having her on the committee slows down decision-making, and that some parents feel that the election of a former consumer was 'a token gesture, made without consideration of the practicalities of running the organisation'. The organisation is also facing a complaint from one of the parents of the young people in the programme. Their daughter, aged twenty-one and living in one of the houses, has begun a sexual relationship with a young man who left the programme three months ago, and is now living independently. The parents are immigrants to Australia and come from a culture which traditionally emphasises the need for a protective attitude towards young women. They have asked that the organisation not permit the relationship to take place. There is some concern that they might take their complaint to the Commonwealth Minister or their local member of parliament.

The chairperson of the organisation has convened a special all-day planning meeting for the management committee and staff to discuss 'the challenges now facing the organisation and the direction that we should take in the forthcoming year'. You hold the position either of the community welfare worker or the 'family worker/co-ordinator' and will be attending the meeting.

Key questions

Critically analyse the issues of efficiency, effectiveness, equity, excellence and expansion facing this organisation. In the light of this analysis, and bearing in mind your position in the organisation, what recommendations would you bring to the meeting? Provide reasons for your recommendations.

Case discussion points

1 How should efficiency and effectiveness be defined in this organisation?
2 What are the issues of equity, excellence and expansion raised in this case?
3 What does this case illustrate about the political nature of the evaluation process?
4 How influential can and should you be in relation to the issues facing the organisation?
5 Has the organisation been sufficiently pro-active in its approach to efficiency, effectiveness, equity, excellence and expansion? Could it be more pro-active in the future? How?
6 In what ways is the managerialist agenda impinging on this organisation? What should be the response of the human service workers in the organisation?

Bibliography

Abel, Charles and Johnson, Wayne (1978), 'Clients' access to records: policy and attitudes', *Social Work*, vol. 23, no. 1, pp. 42-46.

Abels, P. and Murphy, M. J. (1981), *Administration in the Human Services: A Normative Systems Approach*, Englewood Cliffs, NJ, Prentice-Hall.

Abrahamson, Mark (1967), *The Professional in the Organisation*, Chicago, Rand McNally.

Abrahamsson, Bengt (1977), *Bureaucracy or Participation: The Logic of Organization*, Beverly Hills, Sage.

Adams, Paul and Freeman, Gary (1980), 'On the political character of social service work' in N. Gilbert and H. Specht (eds), *The Emergence of Social Welfare and Social Work*, 2nd edn, Itasca, Ill., Peacock, pp. 445-456.

Albrow, Martin (1970), *Bureaucracy*, London, Macmillan.

Alcabes, A. and Jones, J. A. (1985), 'Structural determinants of "clienthood"', *Social Work*, vol. 30, no. 1, pp. 49-53.

Alinsky, Saul D. (1969), *Reveille for Radicals*, New York, Vintage.

Allaire, Yvan and Firsirotu, Mihaela, E. (1984), 'Theories of organizational culture', *Organization Studies*, vol. 5, no. 3, pp. 193-226.

Argyris, C. (1971) 'The impact of the formal organisation upon the individual', in D. S. Pugh (ed.), *Organization Theory: Selected Readings*, Harmondsworth, Penguin, pp. 261-278.

Arnstein, Sherry R. (1969) 'A ladder of citizen participation', *American Institute of Planners Journal*, vol. 35, no. 4, pp. 216-224.

Austin, D. M. (1981) 'The political economy of social benefit organisations: redistributive services and merit goods', in H. D. Stein (ed.), *Organisation and the Human Services*, Philadelphia, Temple University Press, pp. 37-88.

Australia. Department of Social Security (1984), *Structure and Functions Handbook*, Brisbane, Department of Social Security.

Australia. Royal Commission on Australian Government Administration (1976), *Report*, Canberra, Australian Government Publishing Service.

Australia. Department of Community Services (1986), *Nursing Homes and Hostels Review*, Canberra, Australian Government Publishing Service.

Australia. Royal Commission into Aboriginal Deaths in Custody (1991) *National Report*, vols 1 and 2, Canberra, Australian Government Publishing Service.

Australia. Human Rights and Equal Opportunity Commission (1989), *Our Homeless Children: Report of the National Inquiry into Homeless Children*, Canberra, Australian Government Publishing Service.

Australia. Commission of Inquiry into Poverty (1975) *Poverty in Australia*, vol. 1, Canberra, Australian Government Publishing Service.

Australia. Department of Finance (1987), *Evaluating Government Programs*, Canberra, Australian Government Publishing Service.

Australia. House of Representatives, Standing Committee on Community Affairs (1989), *Fairness, Courtesy and Efficiency? A Report on the Quality of Service Provided by the Department of Social Security*, Canberra, Australian Government Publishing Service.

Australia. Senate Standing Committee on Social Welfare (1979) *Through a Glass, Darkly*, Canberra, Australian Government Publishing Service, vols 1 and 2.

Australia. Department of Social Security (1989) *Achieving Access and Equity in Social Security*, the Report and Proceedings of the Brisbane Outreach Community Workshops, Brisbane, Department of Social Security.

Australian Association of Social Workers (1988), *Code of Ethics*, Canberra, AASW.

Bachrach, Peter and Baratz, Morton S. (1980), 'Nondecision-making: the other face of power', in Andrew Parkin, John Summers and Dennis Woodward (eds), *Government, Politics and Power in Australia: An Introductory Reader*, 2nd edn, Melbourne, Longman Cheshire, pp. 368-373.

Bacharach, Samuel B. (1983), 'Bargaining within organizations', in M. H. Bazerman and Roy J. Lewicki (eds), *Negotiating in Organizations*, Beverly Hills, Sage, pp. 360-374.

Bailey, Ron (1980), 'Social workers: pawns, police or agitators?', in M. Brake and R. Bailey (eds), *Radical Social Work and Practice*, London, Edward Arnold, pp. 215-227.

Bailey, Peter (1990), *Human Rights: Australia in an International Context*, Sydney, Butterworth.

Baker, John R. (1989), 'Management improvement: the human dimension', *Canberra Bulletin of Public Administration*, no. 59, pp. 54-61.

Bell, Robin and Watchirs, Helen (1988), 'Freedom of information: the Commonwealth experience', *Australian Journal of Public Administration*, vol. 47, no. 4, pp. 296-311.

Bennett, Scott (1989), *Aborigines and Political Power*, Sydney, Allen & Unwin.

Bennis, Warren G., Benne, Kenneth D., Chin, Robert and Corey, Kenneth E. (1976), *The Planning of Change*, 3rd edn, New York, Holt, Rinehart & Winston.

Benson, J. Kenneth (1981) 'Organisations: A dialectical view', in Mary Zey-Ferrell and Michael Aiken (eds), *Complex Organizations: Critical Perspectives*, Glenview, Ill., Scott, Foresman, pp. 263-282.

Berg, William E. and Wright, Roosevelt (1980), 'Program funding as an organisational dilemma: Goal displacement in social work programs', *Administration in Social Work*, vol. 4, no. 4, pp. 29-39.

Beyer, Janice M. and Trice, Harrison M. (1987), 'How an organization's rites reveal its culture', *Organizational Dynamics*, vol. 16, pp. 5-24.

Billingsley, Andrew (1964), 'Bureaucratic and professional orientation patterns in social casework', *Social Service Review*, vol. 38, no. 4, pp. 400-407.

Blau, Peter M. and W. R. Scott (1962), *Formal Organization: A Comparative Approach*, Novato, Cal., Chandler Publishing.

Blau, Peter M. and Scott, W. Richard (1980), 'Who benefits?' in Etzioni, Amitai and Lehman, Edward W. (eds), *A Sociological Reader on Complex Organizations*, 3rd edn, New York, Holt, Rinehart & Winston, pp. 116-117.

Blunt, Peter (1986), *Human Resource Management*, Melbourne, Longman Cheshire.

Brager, George and Specht, Harry (1973), *Community Organizing*, New York, Columbia University Press.

Brager, George and Holloway, Stephen (1978), *Changing Human Service Organizations: Politics and Practice*, New York, Free Press.

Brager, George and Holloway, Stephen (1983), 'A process model for changing organisations from within', in R. Kramer and H. Specht (eds), *Readings in Community Organization Practice*, 3rd edn, Englewood Cliffs, NJ, Prentice-Hall, pp. 198-208.

Brake, Mike and Bailey Roy (eds) (1980), *Radical Social Work and Practice*, London, Edward Arnold.

Brennan, Frank, Egan, John and Honnor, John (1985), *Finding Common Ground*, Blackburn, Dove Communications.

Bresnick, David A. (1983), *Managing the Human Services in Hard Times*, New York, Human Service Press.

Briar, Scott and Miller, Henry (1971), *Problems and Issues in Social Casework*, New York, Columbia University Press.

Brotherhood of St Laurence (1979), *Client and Staff Participation in a Government Welfare Agency*, Melbourne, Department of Community Welfare Services.

Brown, Christopher and Ringma, Charles (1989), 'The myth of consumer participation in disability services: Some issues for social workers', *Australian Social Work*, vol. 42, no. 4, pp. 35-40.

Bryson, L. (1981), 'Abuses and uses of evaluation', *Australian Journal of Social Issues*, vol. 16, no. 2, pp. 103-113.

Bryson, Lois (1987), 'Women and management in the public sector', *Australian Journal of Public Administration*, vol. 46, no. 3, pp. 259-272.

Burns, T. (1971), 'Mechanistic and organismic structures', in D. S. Pugh (ed.), *Organization Theory*, Harmondsworth, Penguin, pp. 43-55.

Butler, A. et al. (1988), *Opportunities and Challenges Facing the Community Sector*, Melbourne, Equasearch.

Caplow, Theodore (1976), *How to Run Any Organization: A Manual of Practical Sociology*, Hinsdale, Ill., Dryden Press.

Carney, Terry (1989), 'Cloaking the bureaucratic dagger? Administrative law in the welfare state', *Canberra Bulletin of Public Administration*, no. 58, pp. 123-132.

Carney, Terry (1990), 'Rights of intellectually disadvantaged people', in J. Wallace and T. Pagone (eds), *Rights and Freedoms in Australia*, Sydney, Federation Press, pp. 54-62.

Chin, R. and Benne, K. D. (1976), 'General strategies for effecting changes in human systems', in Bennis, W. G. et al. (eds), *The Planning of Change*, 3rd edn, New York, Holt, Rinehart & Winston, pp. 22-45.

Clegg, S. and Dunkerley, D. (1980), *Organization, Class and Control*, London, Routledge & Kegan Paul.

Collman, Jeff (1988), *Fringe-dwellers and Welfare: The Aboriginal Response to Bureaucracy*, St Lucia, University of Queensland Press.

Compton, Beulah Roberts and Galaway, Burt (1989), *Social Work Processes*, 4th edn, Belmont, California, Wadsworth.

Considine, Mark (1988), 'The corporate management framework as administrative science: A critique', *Australian Journal of Public Administration*, vol. 47, no. 1, pp. 4-18.

Considine, Mark (1990), 'Managerialism strikes out', *Australian Journal of Public Administration*, vol. 49, no. 2, pp. 166-178.

Cook, Karen S. (1977), 'Exchange and power in networks of interorganizational relations', in J. Kenneth Benson (ed.), *Organizational Analysis: Critique and Innovation*, Beverly Hills, Sage, pp. 64-84.

Cook, Peter (1990), 'The role of evaluation in the government decision-making process', *Canberra Bulletin of Public Administration*, no. 63, pp. 21-23.

Coombs, H. C. (1978), *Australia's Policies Towards Aborigines 1967-1977*, London, Minority Rights Group.

Corrigan, Paul and Leonard, Peter (1978), *Social Work Practice Under Capitalism: A Marxist Approach*, London, Macmillan.

Council of Social Service of New South Wales (1984), *'Like Eating Spinach': Participating in Welfare Decisions*, Sydney, NSWCOSS.

Cox, David R. (1989), *Welfare Practice in a Multicultural Society*, Sydney, Prentice-Hall.

Cox, F. M. et al. (eds), (1977), *Tactics and Techniques of Community Practice*, Itasca, Ill., Peacock Publishers.

Crago, Hugh (1988) 'Programmed for despair? The dynamics of low morale/ high burn-out welfare organisations', *Australian Social Work*, vol. 41, no. 2, pp. 31-34.

Dalmau, Tim and Dick, Bob (1987), *Politics, Conflict and Culture*, Chapel Hill, Queensland, Interchange.

Darvall, Leanna (1990), 'Medical complaints', in J. Wallace and T. Pagone (eds), *Rights and Freedoms in Australia*, Sydney, Federation Press, pp. 46-53.

Davis, G. et al. (1988), *Public Policy in Australia*, Sydney, Allen & Unwin

Dawson, Sandra (1986), *Analysing Organisations*, London, Macmillan.

Day, Phyllis J. (1981), 'Social welfare: Context for social control', *Journal of Sociology and Social Welfare*, vol. 8, no. 1, pp. 29-44.

Dick, Bob (1988), *Cultural Interventions: A Brief Overview*, Chapel Hill, Queensland, Interchange.

Dolgoff, Ralph and Loewenberg, Frank (1985), *Ethical Decisions for Social Work Practice*, 2nd edn, Itasca, Ill., Peacock.

Dominelli, Lena and McLeod, Eileen (1989), *Feminist Social Work* ,London, Macmillan.

Donald, Owen (1986), *Social Security Reform* (Social Security Review Background/Discussion Paper no. 2), Woden, ACT, Department of Social Security.

Donovan, Frances and Jackson, Alun C. (1991), *Managing Human Service Organisations*, Sydney, Prentice-Hall.

Edmunds, Mary (1990), 'Doing business: Socialisation, social relations, and social control in Aboriginal society', *Discussion paper for the Royal Commission into Aboriginal Deaths in Custody*.

Egan, Gerard (1985), *Change Agent Skills in Helping and Human Service Settings*, Monterey, Cal., Brooks, Cole.

Eisenstein, Hester (1985), 'The gender of bureaucracy: Reflections on feminism and the state', in J. Goodman and C. Pateman (eds), *Women, Social Science and Public Policy*, Allen & Unwin, Sydney, pp. 104-115.

Etzioni, A. (ed) (1961), *Complex Organization: A Sociological Reader*, New York, Holt, Rinehart & Winston.

Etzioni, Amitai (1964), *Modern Organizations*, Englewood Cliffs, NJ, Prentice-Hall.

Etzioni, Amitai (ed) (1969), *The Semi-professions and their Organization*, New York, Free Press.

Etzioni, Amitai and Lehman Edward W. (eds) (1980), *A Sociological Reader on Complex Organizations*, 3rd edn, New York, Holt, Rinehart & Winston.

Etzioni, Amitai (1980), 'Compliance structures', in Etzioni, Amitai and Lehman, Edward W. (eds), *A Sociological Reader on Complex Organizations*, 3rd edn, New York, Holt, Rinehart & Winston, pp. 87-100.

Etzioni-Halevy, Eva (1985), *Bureaucracy and Democracy: A Political Dilemma*, rev. edn, London, Routledge & Kegan Paul.

Evatt Research Centre (1989), *State of Siege: Renewal or Privatisation for Australian State Public Services?*, Sydney, Pluto Press.

Fabricant, Michael (1985), 'The industrialization of social work', *Social Work*, vol. 30, no. 5, pp. 389-395.

Fallon, Kenneth P. (1985), 'Participatory management: An alternative in human service delivery systems', in S. Slavin (ed.), *An Introduction to Human Services Management*, 2nd edn, New York, Haworth, pp. 251-260.

Ferguson, Kathy E. (1984), *The Feminist Case Against Bureaucracy*, Philadelphia, Temple University Press.

Finch, W.A. (1976), 'Social workers versus bureaucracy', *Social Work*, vol. 21, no. 5, pp. 370-375.

Fincher, Cameron (1986), 'What is organisational culture?', *Research in Higher Education*, vol. 24, no. 3, pp. 325-328.

Forder, Anthony (1974), *Concepts in Social Administration: A Framework for Analysis*, London, Routledge & Kegan Paul.

Foren, Robert and Bailey, Royston (1968), *Authority in Social Casework*, Oxford, Permagon.

Freeman, J. (1972), 'The tyranny of structurelessness', *Berkeley Journal of Sociology*, vol. 17, pp. 151-164.

Frost, Peter J. et al. (1985), *Organizational Culture*, Beverly Hills, Sage.

Furlong, Mark (1987), 'A rationale for the use of empowerment as a goal in casework', *Australian Social Work*, vol. 40, no. 3, pp. 25-30.

Gagliardi, Pasquale (1986), 'The creation and change of organizational cultures: A conceptual framework', *Organisational Studies*, vol. 7, no. 2, pp. 117-134.

Galper, Jeffry H. (1975), *The Politics of Social Services*, Englewood Cliffs, NJ, Prentice-Hall.

Gates, Bruce L. (1980), *Social Program Administration: the Implementation of Social Policy*, Englewood Cliffs, NJ, Prentice-Hall.

George, Janet (1982), 'Professional expectations and practice realities', *Australian Social Work*, vol. 35, no. 1, pp. 9-16.

Georgiou, Petro (1981), 'The goal paradigm and notes towards a counter paradigm', in Mary Zey-Ferrell and Michael Aiken (eds), *Complex Organizations: Critical Perspectives*, Glenview, Ill., Scott, Foresman, pp. 69-88.

Gilbert, Neil (1980), 'The search for professional identity', in N. Gilbert and H. Specht (eds), *The Emergence of Social Welfare and Social Work*, 2nd edn, Itasca, Ill., Peacock, pp. 457 - 466.

Gilbert, Neil and Specht, Harry (eds) (1980), *The Emergence of Social Welfare and Social Work*, 2nd edn, Itasca, Ill., Peacock.

Gilbert, Neil and Specht, Harry (1976), 'The incomplete profession', in N. Gilbert and H. Specht (eds), *The Emergence of Social Welfare and Social Work*, Itasca, Ill., Peacock, pp. 318-335.

Glasson, Ian and Goode, Margaret (1988), 'Corporate planning in the Australian Commonwealth public sector', *Canberra Bulletin of Public Administration*, no. 54, pp. 102-113.

Gouldner, A. W. (1963), 'The secrets of organisations', *Social Welfare Forum*, New York, Columbia University Press, pp. 161-177.

Graycar, Adam (1982), *Government Officer's Expectations of Non-Government Welfare Organisations: A Discussion Paper*, SWRC Reports and Proceedings no. 28 Kensington, NSW, Social Welfare Research Centre, University of New South Wales.

Graycar, Adam and Jamrozik, Adam (1989), *How Australians Live: Social Policy in Theory and Practice*, Melbourne, Macmillan.

Green, A. D. (1966), 'The professional worker in the bureaucracy', *Social Service Review*, vol. 40, no. 1, pp. 71-83.

Green, Bob (1985), 'Something to aspire to: Social work in a seemingly futile setting', *Australian Social Work*, vol. 38, no. 4, pp. 31-33.

Green, David (1976), 'Social control and public welfare practice', in P. J. Boas and J. Crawley (eds), *Social Work in Australia: Responses to a Changing Context*, Melbourne, Australia International Press, pp. 62-70.

Greenwood, Ernest (1957), 'The attributes of a profession', *Social Work*, vol. 2, no. 3, pp. 45-55.

Gregory, G. N. F. (1977), *Rural People, Support Services and Counselling*, Armidale, NSW, Kellogg Rural Adjustment Unit.

Gummer, Burton (1978), 'A power-politics approach to social welfare organizations', *Social Service Review*, vol. 52, no. 2, pp. 349-361.

Gummer, Burton (1985a), '"Committing the truth": Whistle blowing, organizational dissent, and the honourable bureaucrat', *Administration in Social Work*, vol. 9, no. 4, pp. 89-102.

Gummer, Burton (1985b), 'Power, power — who's got the power?', *Administration in Social Work*, vol. 9, no. 2, pp. 99-111.

Gummer, Burton (1988a), 'Post-industrial management: Teams, self-management, and the new interdependence', *Administration in Social Work*, vol. 12, no. 3, pp. 117-132.

Gummer, Burton (1988b), 'Equality of opportunity 1980s style: Opportunity structures within organisations', *Administration in Social Work*, vol. 12, no. 1, pp. 107-123.

Gummer, Burton (1988c), 'Competing perspectives on the concept of "effectiveness" in the analysis of social services', *Administration in Social Work*, vol. 11, nos. 3/4, pp. 257-270.

Gummer, Burton (1990a), 'The organisation woman: poor copy or catalyst for change?', *Administration in Social Work*, vol. 14, no. 3, pp. 111-129.

Gummer, Burton (1990b), 'Managing organisational cultures: Management science or management ideology?', *Administration in Social Work*, vol. 14, no. 1, pp. 135-153.

Gumprecht, Nancy (1986), 'Strategies for change: women employees in social service agencies', in H. Marchant and B. Wearing, (eds), *Gender Reclaimed: Women in Social Work*, Sydney, Hale and Iremonger, pp. 212-222.

Hadley, Roger and Hatch, Stephen (1981), *Social Welfare and the Failure of the State: Centralised Social Services and Participatory Alternatives*, London, George Allen & Unwin.

Hall, Richard H. (1987), *Organizations: Structures, Processes, and Outcomes*, 4th edn, Englewood Cliffs, NJ, Prentice-Hall.

Halladay, Allan and Peile, Colin (1989), *The Future of Worker Co-operatives in Hostile Environments: Some Reflections from Down Under*, Saskatoon, Centre for the Study of Co-operatives.

Ham, Christopher and Hill, Michael (1984), *The Policy Process in the Modern Capitalist State*, Brighton, Wheatsheaf.

Handy, Charles B. (1985), *Understanding Organisations*, 3rd edn, London, Penguin.

Harris, Paul (1983), 'Individuals in organisations: The limits to obedience', in Kouzmin, A. (ed.), *Public Sector Administration: New Perspectives*, Melbourne, Longman Cheshire, pp. 101-124.

Harshbarger, Dwight (1974), 'The human service organization', in H. W. Demone Jr, and Dwight Harshbarger (eds), *A Handbook of Human Service Organisations*, New York, Behavioral Publications

Hasenfeld, Yeheskel, and Richard A. English (eds) (1974), *Human Service Organizations: A Book of Readings* Ann Arbor, University of Michigan Press.

Hasenfeld, Yeheskel (1983), *Human Service Organizations* Englewood Cliffs, NJ, Prentice-Hall.

Hasenfield, Yeheskel (1984), 'The changing context of human service organisations', *Social Work*, vol. 29, no. 6, pp. 522–529.

Hasenfeld, Yeheskel (1987), 'Power in social work practice', *Social Service Review*, vol. 61, no. 3, pp. 469-483.

Hatch, Elvin (1985), 'Culture', in A. Kuper and J. Kuper (eds), *The Social Science Encyclopedia*, London, Routledge & Kegan Paul, pp. 178-179.

Hawkins, Gordon (1986), *Prisoner's Rights: A Study of Human Rights and Commonwealth Prisoners*, Human Rights Commission Occasional Paper no. 12, Canberra, Australian Government Publishing Service.

Hawkins, L. (1977), 'NOW centre—successful or surviving?' *Social Security Quarterly*, vol. 1, Winter/Spring, pp. 18-25.

Healy, Bill (1988), 'Confronting disadvantage through social justice: The case of public welfare practice', in E. Chamberlain (ed.), *Change and Continuity in Australian Social Work*, Melbourne, Longman Cheshire, pp. 187-196.

Healy, J. (1988), 'Packaging the human services', *Australian Journal of Public Administration*, vol. 67, no. 4, pp. 321-331.

Healy, Judith and Martin, Elaine (1989) ,'Social workers in the census', *Australian Social Work*, vol. 42, no. 2, pp. 5-12.

Henderson, Paul and Thomas, David N. (1980), *Skills in Neighbourhood Work*, London, George Allen & Unwin.

Herrick, James et al. (1983), 'Social workers who left the profession: An exploratory study', *Journal of Sociology and Social Welfare*, vol. 10, no. 1, pp. 78-94.

Heydebrand, Wolf (1980), 'Organizational contradictions in public bureaucracies: Towards a Marxian theory of organizations', in Amatai Etzioni and Edward W. Lehman (eds), *A Sociological Reader on Complex Organizations*, 3rd edn, New York, Holt, Rinehart & Winston, pp. 56-73.

Hill, Michael (1976), *The State, Administration and the Individual*, London, Fontana.

Hill, Michael and Bramley, Glen (1986), *Analysing Social Policy*, Oxford, Basil Blackwell.

Hofstede, Geert (1986), 'Editorial: The usefulness of the "organizational culture" concept', *Journal of Management Studies*, vol. 23, no. 3, pp. 253-257.

Holland, T. P. and Petchers, M. K. (1987), 'Organizations: context for social service delivery', in *Encyclopedia of Social Work*, vol. 2, 18th edn, Silver Spring, Md, NASW, pp. 204-217.

Holmes, J. and Riecken, G. (1980), 'Using business marketing concepts to view the private, non-profit, social service agency', *Administration in Social Work*, vol. 4, no. 3, pp. 43-51.

Hooyman, N. R. and Cunningham, R. (1986) 'An alternative administrative style', in N. Van Den Bergh and L. B. Cooper (eds), *Feminist Visions for Social Work*, Maryland, NASW, pp. 163-186.

Hooyman, Nancy R., Fredriksen, Karen, I. and Perlmutter, Barbara (1988), 'Shanti: An alternative response to the AIDS crisis', *Administration in Social Work*, pp. 17-30.

Horsburgh, Michael (1980), 'Relations between government and voluntary organisations in social welfare', in F. Pavlin, J. Crawley and P. J. Boas (eds), *Perspectives in Australian Social Work*, Melbourne, PIT Publishing, pp. 17-34.

Howe, David (1986), *Social Workers and their Practice in Welfare Bureaucracies*, Aldershot, Gower.

Huczynski, A. (1987), *Encyclopedia of Organisational Change Methods*, Aldershot, Gower.

Hugman, Richard (1987), 'The private and the public in personal models of social work: A response to O'Connor and Dalgleish', *British Journal of Social Work*, vol. 17, pp. 71-76.

Hutchison, Elizabeth D. (1987), 'Use of authority in direct social work practice with mandated clients', *Social Service Review*, vol. 61, no. 4, pp. 581-598.

Hyde, C. (1989), 'A feminist model for macro-practice: Promises and problems', *Administration in Social Work*, vol. 13, nos. 3-4, pp. 145-181.

Jackson, John J. and Morgan, Cyril P. (1978), *Organization Theory: A Macro Perspective for Management*, Englewood Cliffs, NJ, Prentice-Hall.

James, Catherine and Jones, Julie (1988), 'The social work role in the Victorian Coroner's Court: Progress notes of a study group', *Australian Social Work*, vol. 41, no. 3, pp. 31–34.

Jamrozik, Adam (1991), *Class, Inequality and the State*, Melbourne, Macmillan.

Jansson, Bruce S. and Simmons, June (1986), 'The survival of social work units in host organisations,' *Social Work*, vol. 31, pp. 339-343.

Johnston, Mark (1990), 'A strategic approach to evaluation', *Canberra Bulletin of Public Administration*, no. 63, pp. 74-78.

Jones, Andrew (1984), 'Access as a management issue', in *Handbook for Day Care*, Canberra, Australian Early Childhood Association, pp. M37-M42.

Jones, Andrew and Nailon, Diane (1984), 'Community management', in Australian Early Childhood Association, *Handbook for Day Care*, Canberra, AECA, pp. M13-M18.

Jordan, Bill (1984), *Invitation to Social Work*, Oxford, Basil Blackwell.

Jordan, Bill and Parton, Nigel (eds) (1983), *The Political Dimensions of Social Work*, Oxford, Basil Blackwell

Kahle, Joseph H. (1969), 'Structuring and administering a modern voluntary agency', *Social Work*, vol. 14, no. 2, pp. 21-28.

Kakabadse, Andrew (1982), *Culture of the Social Services*, Aldershot, Gower.

Katan, Joseph and Prager, Edward (1986), 'Consumer and worker participation in agency-level decision-making: Some considerations of their linkages', *Administration in Social Work*, vol. 10, no. 1, pp. 79-88.

Katz, Catherine and Rotem, Wendy (1989), *Quality Assurance in Community Health*, Sydney, The Australian Council on Health Care Standards.

Katz, Daniel and Robert L. Kahn (1966), *The Social Psychology of Organisations*, New York, Wiley.

Keating, Michael (1989), 'Quo Vadis? Challenges of public administration', *Australian Journal of Public Administration*, vol. 48, no. 2, pp. 123-131.

Keating, Michael (1990), 'Managing for results in the public interest', *Australian Journal of Public Administration*, vol. 49, no. 4, pp. 387-398.

Kramer, Ralph and Specht, Harry (eds) (1983), *Readings in Community Organization Practice*, 3rd edn, Englewood Cliffs, NJ, Prentice-Hall.

Lauffer, Armand (1977), *Understanding Your Social Agency*, Beverly Hills, Sage.

Lauffer, Armand (1978), *Social Planning at the Community Level*, Englewood Cliffs, NJ, Prentice-Hall.

Lawler, Edward and Mohrman, Susan (1987), 'Quality circles: After the honeymoon', *Organizational Dynamics*, Spring, pp. 42-54.

Lawrence, R. John (1976), 'Australian social work: In historical, international and social welfare context', In P. J. Boas and J. Crawley (eds), *Social Work in Australia: Responses to a Changing Context*, Melbourne, Australia International Press, pp. 1-42.

Levy, Amir (1987), 'Second-order planned change: Definition and conceptualization', pp. 5-20.

Lewicki, R. J. and Litterer, J.A. (1985), *Negotiation*, Homewood, Ill., Irwin.

Liffman, Michael (1978), *Power for the Poor*, Sydney, George Allen & Unwin.

Lightman, E. S. (1982), 'Professionalization, bureaucratization, and unionization in social work', *Social Service Review*, vol. 56, no. 1, pp. 130-143.

Lipsky, Michael (1980), *Street-level Bureaucracy*, New York, Russell Sage.

Lister, Larry (1987), 'Contemporary direct practice roles', *Social Work*, vol. 32, no. 5, pp. 384-391.

Louis, Meryl Reis (1985), 'An investigator's guide to workplace culture', in P. J. Frost et al. (eds), *Organisational Culture*, Beverly Hills, Sage, pp. 73-94.

Loewenberg, Frank and Dolgoff, Ralph (1985), *Ethical Decisions For Social Work Practice*, 2nd edn, Itasca, Ill., Peacock Publishers.

Lundberg, Craig C. in P. J. Frost et al. (eds), *Organisational Culture*, Beverly Hills, Sage, pp. 169–185.

Luntz, Jennifer (1985), 'Some problems of being a professional on a team', *Australian Social Work*, vol. 38, no. 4, pp. 13-22.

MacKenzie-Thurley, S. (1986), 'Intimidation of the elderly in institutions', in *Proceedings of the 21st Annual Conference of the Australian Association of Gerontology*, pp. 60-62.

Macleod, Roderick K. (1978), 'Program budgeting works in nonprofit institutions', in Simon Slavin (ed), *Social Administration: The Management of the Social Services*, New York, Haworth Press, pp. 247-263.

Mager, Robert F. (1972), *Goal Analysis* Belmont, Cal., Fearon Publishers.

Martin, Elaine (1982), 'A framework for exploring different judgements of social need', *Australian Journal of Social Issues*, vol. 17, no. 3, pp. 190-201.

Martin, Elaine (1985), 'Human service organizations: useful category or useless jargon?', *Australian Journal of Social Issues*, vol. 20, no. 2, pp. 124-135.

Martin, Elaine (1986), 'Consumer evaluation of human services', *Social Policy and Administration*, vol. 20, no. 3, pp. 185-200.

Martin, P. Y. (1980), 'Multiple constituencies, dominant social values, and the human services administrator: Implications for service delivery', *Administration in Social Work*, vol. 4, no. 2, pp. 15-28.

May, John (1991), 'Social welfare', in J. Henningham (ed.), *Institutions in Australian Society*, St Lucia, Department of Journalism, University of Queensland, pp. 183-209.

McCallum, B. (1984), *The Public Sector Manager*, Melbourne, Longman Cheshire.

McCulloch, Arthur (1989), 'Clients, computers and welfare work', *Australian Social Work*, vol. 42, no. 2, pp. 21-26.

McGrath, Morag (1989), 'Consumer participation in service planning—The AWS experience', *Journal of Social Policy*, vol. 18, no. 1, pp. 67-89.

McGregor, D. (1971), 'Theory X and theory Y', in D. S. Pugh (ed.), *Organization Theory: Selected Readings*, Harmondsworth, Penguin, pp. 305-323.

McGuinness, Padraic P. (1990), 'The deaf can see voices when given the sign', *The Australian*, 19 April.

McGuire, Linda (1989), 'Models of public and private sector strategic management', in Davis, G., Weller, P. and Lewis, C. (eds), *Corporate Management in Australian Government*, Brisbane, Centre for Australian Public Sector Management, pp. 17-28.

McMillan, John (1981), 'Suing the bureaucrats: New federal remedies', *Legal Services Bulletin*, vol. 6, August, pp. 192-195.

Meenaghan, Thomas (1987), 'Macro practice: Current issues and trends', in *Encyclopedia of Social Work*, vol. 2, 18th edn, Silver Spring, Md, NASW, pp. 82-89.

Melville, Roselyn (1985), 'Workshop: Women's Health Centre Collective' Brisbane, (unpublished).

Miller, S. M. (1978), 'Productivity and the paradox of service in a profit economy', *Social Policy*, vol. 9, no. 2, pp. 4-6.

Mishra, Rameth (1984), *The Welfare State in Crisis*, Brighton, Wheatsheaf.

Mitchell, Terence R. and Larson, James R. (1987), *People in Organisations: An Introduction to Organisational Behaviour*, 3rd edn, New York, McGraw-Hill.

Morrison, J. (1988) *Non-Government Welfare Organisations and the Implementation of the Disability Services Act 1988*, Master of Social Work Thesis, University of Queensland.

Mouzelis, N. (1975), *Organization and Bureaucracy*, 2nd edn, London, Routledge & Kegan Paul.

Mulvaney, D.J. and White, P. (eds) (1987), *Australians to 1788*, Sydney, Fairfax, Syme & Weldon.

National Institute for Social Work (1982), *Social Workers: Their Role and Tasks*, London, Bedford Square Press.

Near, Janet P. and Miceli, Marcia P. (1987), 'Whistle-blowers in organizations: Dissidents or reformers?', *Research in Organizational Behaviour*, vol. 9, pp. 321-368.

Nethercote, J. R. (1989), 'The rhetorical tactics of managerialism: Reflections on Micheal Keating's apologia, quo vadis?', *Australian Journal of Public Administration*, vol. 48, no. 4, pp. 363-368.

Neugeboren, Bernard (1985), *Organisation, Policy and Practice in the Human Services*, New York, Longman.

Nicholls, Rob and Andrew, Ruth (1990), *A Stands for Advocacy: The Report of the Advocacy Project*, Melbourne, Office of the Public Advocate.

O'Brien, John (1990), 'Privatising state workers: The case of academics', *Australian Universities' Review*, nos 1 and 2, pp. 30-37.

O'Connor, David Ian (1984), *The Impact of Social Work Education: A Personal Construct Reconceptualisation*, PhD thesis, University of Queensland.

O'Connor, Ian and Dalgleish, Len (1986), 'Cautionary tales from beginning practitioners: The fate of personal models of social work in beginning practice', *British Journal of Social Work*, vol. 16, pp. 431-447.

O'Connor, Ian, Wilson, Jill and Thomas, Kay (1991), *Social Work and Welfare Practice*, Melbourne, Longman Cheshire

O'Faircheallaigh, Ciaran (1990), 'Policy evaluation for efficiency and effectiveness: Some fundamental Issues', Paper presented to the Centre for Australian Public Sector Management Conference, Griffith University, Brisbane, July 1990.

Painter, Martin (1980), 'Bureaucracy and the politics of access', in H. Mayer and H. Nelson (eds), *Australian Politics: A Fifth Reader*, Melbourne, Longman Cheshire, pp. 265-273.

Painter, Martin (1988), 'Public management: Fad or fallacy?', *Australian Journal of Public Administration*, vol. 47, no. 1, pp. 1-3.

Parker, Roy (1967) 'Social administration and scarcity: The problem of rationing' *Social Work*, vol. 24, no. 2, pp. 9-14.

Parkin, Andrew (1980) 'Power in Australia: An introduction', in Andrew Parkin, John Summers and Dennis Woodward (eds), *Government, Politics and Power in Australia: An Introductory Reader*, 2nd edn, Melbourne, Longman Cheshire, pp. 263-284.

Parry, Noel and Parry, Jose (1979), 'Social work, professionalism and the state', in N. Parry, M. Rustin and C. Satyamurti (eds), *Social Work, Welfare and the State*, London, Edward Arnold, pp. 21-47.

Parsons, Talcott (1980), 'Goals or functions', in Etzioni, Amitai and Lehman, Edward W. (eds), *A Sociological Reader on Complex Organizations*, 3rd edn, New York, Holt, Rinehart and Winston, pp. 116-117.

Pascall, Gillian (1986), *Social Policy: a Feminist Analysis*, London, Tavistock.

Pateman, Carole (1981), 'The concept of equity', in P. N. Troy (ed.), *A Just Society? Essays on Equity in Australia*, Sydney, George Allen & Unwin, pp. 21-36.

Pateman, Carole and Gross, Elizabeth (eds) (1986), *Feminist Challenges: Social and Political Theory*, Sydney, Allen & Unwin.

Paterson, John (1983), 'Bureaucratic reform by cultural revolution', *Canberra Bulletin of Public Administration*, vol. 10, no. 4, pp. 6-13.

Paterson, John (1988), 'A managerialist strikes back', *Australian Journal of Public Administration*, vol. 47, no. 4, pp. 287-295.

Patti, Rino (1978), 'Organizational resistance and change: The view from below', in S. Slavin (ed.), *The Management of the Social Services*, New York, Haworth Press, pp. 540-556.

Patti, Rino (1978), 'The new scientific management: Systems management for social welfare', in S. Slavin (ed.), *The Management of the Social Services*, New York, Haworth Press, pp. 345-358.

Patti, Rino J. (1987), 'Managing for service effectiveness in social welfare: Towards a performance model', *Administration in Social Work*, vol. 11, nos 3-4, pp. 7-22.

Pawlak, Edward J. (1976), 'Organizational tinkering', *Social Work*, vol. 21, pp. 376-380.

Pearson, Geoffrey (1975), 'Making social workers: Bad promises and good omens', in Bailey, R. and Brake, M. (eds), *Radical Social Work*, London, Edward Arnold, pp. 13-45.

Perkins, Charles (1986), *The Administration of Aboriginal Development*, Canberra, Royal Australian Institute of Public Administration.

Perlman, Helen Harris (1957), *Social Casework: A Problem-solving Process*, Chicago, University of Chicago Press.

Perlman, Robert (1975), *Consumers and Social Services*, New York, Wiley.

Perlmutter, F. D. (1988), 'Administering alternative social agencies: Educational implications', *Administration in Social Work*, vol. 12, pp. 109-128.

Perrow, Charles (1970), *Organizational Analysis: A Sociological View*, London, Tavistock.

Perrow, Charles (1974), 'The analysis of goals in complex organizations', in Yeheskel Hasenfeld and Richard A. English (eds), *Human Service Organizations: A Book of Readings*, Ann Arbor, University of Michigan Press, pp. 214-229.

Perrow, Charles (1976), 'The short and glorious history of organisational theory', in J. L. Gibson, J. M. Ivancevich and J. H. Donnelly (eds), *Readings in Organisations: Behaviour, Structure, Processes*, rev. edn, Dallas, Business Publications, pp. 3-16.

Perrow, Charles (1980), 'Technology', in A. Etzioni and E. W. Lehman (eds), *A Sociological Reader on Complex Organizations*, 3rd edn, New York, Holt, Rinehart & Winston,

Perrow, Charles (1986), *Complex Organizations: A Critical Essay*, 3rd edn, New York, Random House

Perrow, Charles and Guillen, Mauro F. (1990), *The AIDS Disaster: The Failure of Organisations in New York and the Nation*, New Haven, Yale University Press.

Peters, Thomas J. and Waterman, Robert H. (1982), *In Search of Excellence*, New York, Harper & Row.

Petruchenia, Jude and Thorpe, Ros (eds) (1990), *Social Change and Social Welfare Practice*, Sydney, Hale and Iremonger.

Pettman, J. (1986), 'Rationale' in B. Chambers and J. Pettman (eds), *Anti-Racism: A Handbook for Adult Educators*, Canberra, Australian Government Publishing Service.

Pfeffer, Jeffrey (1981), *Power in Organizations*, Boston, Pitman.

Pincus, Allen and Minahan, Anne (1973), *Social Work Practice: Model and Method*, Itasca, Ill., Peacock.

Plant, Raymond (1974), *Community and Ideology*, London, Routledge & Kegan Paul.

Podger, Andrew (1990), 'Managing as if equity mattered', *Canberra Bulletin of Public Administration*, no. 60, pp. 54-60.

Pollitt, Christopher (1988), 'Bringing consumers into performance measurement: Concepts, consequences and constraints', *Policy and Politics*, vol. 16, no. 2, pp. 77-87.

Powell, D. M. (1986), 'Managing organizational problems in alternative service organizations', *Administration in Social Work*, vol. 10, no. 3, pp. 57-69.

Pressman, J. and Wildavsky, A. (1973), *Implementation*, Berkeley, University of California Press.

Presthus, Robert (1978), *The Organizational Society*, rev. edn, New York, St Martin's Press.

Prottas, J. M. (1978), 'The power of the street-level bureaucrat in public service bureaucracies', *Urban Affairs Quarterly*, vol. 13, no. 3, pp. 285-312.

Pruger, Robert (1973), 'The good bureaucrat', *Social Work*, vol. 18, no. 4, pp. 26-32.

Pruger, Robert (1979), 'On resigning in protest', *Administration in Social Work*, vol. 3, no. 4, pp. 453-463.

Pugh, Cedric (1987), 'Efficiency auditing and the australian audit office', *Australian Journal of Public Administration*, vol. 46, no. 1, pp. 55-65.

Pugh, D.S. and Hickson, D.J. (1989), *Writers on Organisations*, 4th edn, London, Penguin.

Pusey, M. (1988), 'Our top Canberra public servants under Hawke', *Australian Quarterly*, vol. 60, no. 1, pp. 109-122.

Pusey, M. (1991), *Economic Rationalism in Canberra: A Nation-Building State Changes its Mind*, Sydney, Cambridge University Press.

Queensland Council of Social Service (1990), *Begging Behind Closed Doors: A Five Year Report of Emergency Relief in Queensland*, Brisbane, QCOSS.

Queensland. Domestic Violence Task Force (1988), *Beyond These Walls*, Brisbane, Queensland Government Printer.

Queensland. Commission of Inquiry into Possible Illegal Activities and Associated Police Misconduct (1989), *Report*, Brisbane, Queensland Government Printer.

Radin, Beryl A. (1988), 'Why do we care about organisation structure? Reorganisation as a management tool', *Canberra Bulletin of Public Administration*, no. 57, December, pp. 66-70.

Raider, Melvyn C. (1978), 'Installing management by objectives in social agencies', in Simon Slavin (ed.), *Social Administration: The Management of the Social Services*, New York, Haworth Press, pp. 283-292.

Ray, Carol Axtell (1986), 'Corporate culture: The last frontier of control', *Journal of Management Studies*, vol. 23, no. 3, pp. 287-297.

Reid, William J. (1987), 'Service effectiveness and the social agency', *Administration in Social Work*, vol. 11, nos 3–4, pp. 41-58.

Rein, Martin (1976), 'Social work in search of a radical profession', in N. Gilbert and H. Specht (eds), *The Emergence of Social Welfare and Social Work*, Itasca, Ill., Peacock, pp. 459-483.

Rein, Martin and White, Sheldon H. (1981), 'Knowledge for practice,' *Social Service Review*, vol. 55.

Reynolds, H. (1987), *Frontier*, Sydney, Allen & Unwin.

Richardson, Ann (1983), *Participation*, London, Routledge & Kegan Paul.

Rist, Ray C. (1974), 'Student social class and teacher expectations: The self-fulfilling prophesy in ghetto education', in Yeheskel Hasenfeld and Richard A. English (eds), *Human Service Organizations: A Book of Readings*, Ann Arbor, University of Michigan Press, pp. 517-539.

Ronalds, Chris (1989), *Residents' Rights in Nursing Homes and Hostels Final Report*, Canberra, Australian Government Publishing Service.

Ross, J. E. and Murdick, R. G. (1979), 'People, productivity, and organizational structure', in S. Altman and R. M. Hodgetts (eds), *Readings in Organizational Behaviour*, Philadelphia, Saunders, pp. 204-212.

Roth, Julius A. (1974), 'Some contingencies of the moral evaluation and control of clientele: The case of the hospital emergency service', in Yeheskel Hasenfeld and Richard A. English (eds), *Human Service Organizations: A Book of Readings*, Ann Arbor, University of Michigan Press, pp. 485-498.

Rothman, Jack (1989), 'Client self-determination: Untangling the knot', *Social Service Review*, vol. 63, no. 4, pp. 598-612.

Rothschild, J. and Whitt, J. A. (1986), *The Cooperative Workplace: Potentials and Dilemmas of Organisational Democracy and Participation*, New York, Cambridge University Press.

Sacks, Oliver (1990), *Seeing Voices: a Journey into the World of the Deaf*, London, Picador.

Sanders, W. (1984), 'Ethnicity in Australian government administration', *Australian Journal of Public Administration*, vol. 43, no. 3, pp. 275-286.

Sanders, Will (1985), 'The politics of daily life in Australian income security administration', *Politics*, vol. 20, no. 1, pp. 36-47.

Sanders, W. (1987), 'The Department of Social Security's treatment of Aboriginal polygyny and tribal marriage: A saga of administrative debate', *Australian Journal of Public Administration*, vol. 46, no. 4, pp. 402-420.

Sarri, Rosemary (1971), 'Administration in social welfare', *Encyclopedia of Social Work*, vol. 16.

Sarri, Rosemary and Yeheskel Hasenfeld (eds) (1978), *The Management of Human Services*, New York, Columbia University Press

Sassella, Michael (1989), 'Administrative law in the welfare state: Impact on the Department of Social Security', *Canberra Bulletin of Public Administration*, no. 58, pp. 116-122.

Satyamurti, Carole (1981), *Occupational Survival: The Case of the Local Authority Social Worker*, Oxford, Basil Blackwell.

Sawer, Marian (1989), 'Efficiency, effectiveness . . . and equity?', in Davis, G., Weller, P. and Lewis, C. (eds), *Corporate Management in Australian Government*, Brisbane, Centre for Australian Public Sector Management, pp. 138-153.

Sawer, Marian (1990), 'Beyond access and equity', *Canberra Bulletin of Public Administration*, no. 60, pp. 49-51.

Schnit, D. (1978), 'Professional discretion in social welfare administration', *Administration in Social Work*, vol. 2, no. 4, pp. 439-450.

Schorr, Alvin L. (1985), 'Professional practice as policy', *Social Service Review*, vol. 59, no. 2, pp. 178-196.

Schwartz, Allyson Young, Gottesman, Eve Weiss, and Perlmutter, Felice Davidson (1988), 'Blackwell: A case study in feminist administration', *Administration in Social Work*, pp. 5-15.

Schwartz, William (1974), 'Private troubles and public issues: One job or two?', in P. Weinberger (ed.), *Perspectives on Social Welfare: An Introductory Anthology*, 2nd edn, New York, Macmillan, pp. 346 - 362.

Scott, Robert A. (1974), 'The factory as a social service organisation', in Yeheskel Hasenfeld and Richard A. English (eds), *Human Service Organizations: A Book of Readings*, Ann Arbor, University of Michigan Press, pp. 234-253.

Scott, Bill (1988), *Negotiating: Constructive and Competitive Negotiation*, London, Paradigm.

Scott, Richard W. (1965), 'Reaction to supervision in a heteronomous professional organisation', *Administrative Science Quarterly*, vol. , pp. 65-81.

Scott, W. Richard (1969), 'Professional employees in a bureaucratic structure: Social work', in A. Etzioni (ed.), *The Semi-professions and their Organisation*, New York, Free Press, pp. 82-140.

Scott, Robert A. (1974), 'The selection of clients by social welfare agencies: The case of the blind', in Yeheskel Hasenfeld and Richard A. English (eds), *Human Service Organizations: A Book of Readings*, Ann Arbor, University of Michigan Press, pp. 485-498.

Segal, Brian (1970), 'Planning and power in hospital social service', *Social Casework*, vol. 51, July, pp. 399-405.

Selby, Hugh (1989), 'Ombudsman inc.: A bullish stock with a bear performance', *Canberra Bulletin of Public Administration*, no. 58, pp. 174-178.

Senate, Standing Committee on Social Welfare (1979), *Through a Glass, Darkly*, Canberra, Australian Government Publishing Service.

Setterlund, Deborah (1987), 'Age care policy: Can the non-government sector deliver the goods?', in Saunders, P. and Jamrozik, A. (eds), *Community Services in a Changing Economic and Social Environment*, SWRC Reports & Proceedings No. 70, Kensington, NSW, Social Welfare Research Centre, pp. 149-165.

Sharp, Gene (1977), 'Methods of inducing change', in F. M. Cox et al. (eds), *Tactics and Techniques of Community Practice*, Itasca, Ill., Peacock Publishers, pp. 186-194.

Silverman, David (1970), *The Theory of Organisations*, London, Heinemann.

Sinclair, Amanda (1989), 'Public sector culture: Managerialism or multiculturalism?' *Australian Journal of Public Administration*, vol. 48, no. 4, pp. 382-397.

Smircich, Linda (1983), 'Concepts of culture and organizational analysis', *Administrative Science Quarterly*, Sept., pp. 339-358.

Smircich, Linda (1985), 'Is the concept of culture a paradigm for understanding organisations and ourselves?', in P. J. Frost et al. (eds), *Organisational Culture*, Beverly Hills, Sage, pp. 55-72.

Smith, N. J. and Sanford, R. (1980), *A Study of Newly Qualified Social Workers in Australia*, part 1, Melbourne, Monash University.

Smith, D. E. (1974), 'Front-line organisation of the state mental hospital', in Y. Hasenfeld and R. A. English (eds), *Human Service Organizations: A Book of Readings*, Ann Arbor, University of Michigan Press, pp. 347-362.

Smith, Gilbert (1979), *Social Work and the Sociology of Organizations*, rev. edn, London, Routledge & Kegan Paul.

Snook, Veronica (1984), 'Burnout—Whose responsibility?', *Australian Social Work*, vol. 37, no. 2, pp. 19-23.

Social Research and Evaluation Association (1980), *'One Step Forward - Two Steps Back': The Hidden Problems in Community Management of Children's Services*, Sydney, Social Research and Evaluation Association.

Sosin, Michael (1980), 'Social welfare and organizational society', in N. Gilbert and H. Specht (eds), *The Emergence of Social Welfare and Social Work*, 2nd edn, Itasca, Ill., Peacock, pp. 309 - 321.

Sosin, Michael and Caulum, Sharon (1983), 'Advocacy: A conceptualization for social work practice', *Social Work*, vol. 28, no. 1, pp. 12-17.

Spann, R. N. (1979), *Government Administration in Australia*, Sydney, George Allen & Unwin.

Specht, Harry (1975), 'Disruptive tactics', in Kramer, R. M. and Specht, H. (eds), *Readings in Community Organisation Practice*, 2nd. edn Englewood Cliffs, Prentice-Hall, pp. 336-348.

Specht, Harry (1976), 'The deprofessionalization of social work', in N. Gilbert and H. Specht (eds), *The Emergence of Social Welfare and Social Work*, Itasca, Ill., Peacock, pp. 484-503.

Stein, Herman D. (1981), 'The concept of human service organization: A critique', in Stein, H. D. (ed.), *Organization and the Human Services: Cross-Disciplinary Reflections*, Philadelphia, Temple University Press

Stein, Theodore J. (1987), 'The vulnerability of child welfare agencies to class-action suits', *Social Service Review*, vol. 61, no. 4, pp. 636-654.

Steiner, R. (1977), *Managing the Human Service Organisation*, Beverly Hills, Sage.

Stoner, James A., Collins, Roger R., and Yetton, Philip, W. (1985), *Management in Australia*, Sydney, Prentice-Hall.

Stoner, Madelaine R. (1986), 'Marketing of social service gains prominence in practice', *Administration in Social Work*, vol. 10, no. 4, pp. 41-52.

Sykes, Roberta B. (1989), *Black Majority*, Hawthorn, Hudson.

Taylor, I. and Walton, P. (1971), 'Industrial sabotage: Motives and meanings', in Cohen, S. (ed.), *Images of Deviance*, Harmondsworth, Penguin, pp. 219-245.

Thompson, James D. and McEwen, William J. (1980), 'Organisational goals and environment', in Amitai Etzioni and Edward W. Lehman (eds), *A Sociological Reader on Complex Organizations*, 3rd edn, New York, Holt, Rinehart & Winston, pp. 136-143.

Thynne, Ian and Goldring, John (1987), *Accountability and Control: Government Officials and the Exercise of Power*, Sydney, Law Book Company.

Timms, Noel (1973), *The Receiving End: Consumer Accounts of Social Help for Children*, London, Routledge & Kegan Paul.

Tomlinson, J. (1982), *Social Work: Community Work*, Darwin, Wobbly Press.

Toren, Nina (1972), *Social Work: the Case of a Semi-profession*, Beverly Hills, Sage.

Tropman, John E. (1989), 'The organizational circle: A new approach to drawing an organizational chart', *Administration in Social Work*, vol. 13, no. 1, pp. 35-44.

Troy, P. N. (ed.) (1981), *A Just Society? Essays on Equity in Australia*, Sydney, George Allen & Unwin.

Tucker, David J. (1981), 'Voluntary auspices and the behaviour of social service organisations', *Social Service Review*, vol. 55, no. 4, pp. 603-627.

Turner, Barry A. (1986), 'Sociological aspects of organizational symbolism', *Organizational Studies*, vol. 7, no. 2, pp. 101-115.

Van Maanen, John and Barley, Stephen, R. (1985), 'Cultural organisations: Fragments of a theory', in P. J. Frost et al. (eds), *Organisational Culture*, Beverly Hills, Sage, pp. 31-54.

Victoria. Social Justice Consultative Council (1991), *Improving Services for People*, Melbourne, Social Justice Consultative Council.

Victoria. Health Services Complaints Office (1986), *Health Services Complaints Office - Discussion Paper*, Melbourne, Government Printer.

Victorian Council of Social Service (1990), *Off the Street Begging and the Australian Social Security System*, VCOSS Papers no. 1. Melbourne, VCOSS.

Victorian Council of Social Service (VCOSS) (1981), *Consultation and Government*, Melbourne, VCOSS.

Vintner, Robert D. (1974), 'The social structure of service', in P. E. Weinberger (ed.), *Perspectives on Social Welfare*, 2nd edn, New York, Macmillan, pp. 453-471.

Vintner, Robert (1974), 'Analysis of treatment organisations', in Hasenfeld, Y. and English, R. A. (eds), *Human Service Organizations: A Book of Readings*, Ann Arbor, University of Michigan Press, pp. 33-50.

Volker, Derek (1987), 'Caring for clients in a changing environment: The Department of Veterans' Affairs', *Australian Journal of Public Administration*, vol. 46, no. 2, pp. 192-203.

Volker, Derek (1989,) 'The effect of administrative law reforms: Primary level decision-making', *Canberra Bulletin of Public Administration*, no. 58, pp. 112-115.

Volker, Derek (1990), 'Making evaluation work', *Canberra Bulletin of Public Administration*, no. 63, pp. 29-33.

Warham, Joyce (1977), *An Open Case: The Organisational Context of Social Work*, London, Routledge & Kegan Paul

Warren, Roland L. (1965), *Studying Your Community*, New York, Free Press.

Warren, Roland L. (1977), *Social Change and Human Purpose: Toward Understanding and Action*, Chicago, Rand McNally.

Wasserman, H. (1970), 'Early careers of professional social workers in a public child welfare agency', *Social Work*, vol. 15, no. 3, pp. 93-101.

Watts, Rob (1987), *The Foundations of the National Welfare State*, Sydney, Allen & Unwin.

Watzlawick, P, Weakland, J. and Fisch, R. (1974), *Change: principles of Problem Formation and Problem Resolution*, New York, Norton.

Weatherley, Richard A. (1985), 'Participatory management in public welfare: What are the prospects?', in S. Slavin (ed.), *An Introduction to Human Services Management*, 2nd edn, New York, Haworth, pp. 270-284.

Weatherley, R. and Lipsky, M. (1977), 'Street-level bureaucrats and institutional innovation: Implementing special-education reform', *Harvard Educational Review*, vol. 47, no. 2, pp. 171-197.

Weeks, Wendy (1988), 'De-professionalisation or a new approach to professionalism?', *Australian Social Work*, vol. 41, no. 1, pp. 29-37.

Weihe, Vernon R. (1978), 'Management by objectives in a family service agency', in Simon Slavin, (ed.), *Social Administration: The Management of the Social Services*, New York, Haworth Press, pp. 276-282.

Weinbach, Robert W. (1984), 'Implementing change: Insights and strategies for the supervisor', *Social Work*, vol. 29, no. 2, pp. 282-286.

Weinbach, Robert W. (1990), *The Social Worker as Manager: Theory and Practice*, New York, Longman.

Weiss, Carol H. (1972), *Evaluation Research*, Englewood Cliffs, NJ, Prentice-Hall.

Weissman, Harold, Epstein, Irwin and Savage, Andrea (1983), *Agency-Based Social Work: Neglected Aspects of Clinical Practice*, Philadelphia, Temple University Press.

Weller, Patrick and Lewis, Colleen (1989), 'Corporate management: Background and dilemmas', in Davis, G., Weller, P. and Lewis, C. (eds), *Corporate Management in Australian Government*, Brisbane, Centre for Australian Public Sector Management, pp. 1-16.

Westbrook, Mary T. and Legge, Varoe (1990), 'Ethnic residents in nursing homes: A staff perspective', *Australian Social Work*, vol. 43, no. 3, pp. 15-26.

Western, John S. (1983), *Social Inequality in Australian Society*, Melbourne, Macmillan.

Wilding, Paul (1982), *Professional Power and Social Welfare*, London, Routledge and Kegan Paul.

Wilenski, P. (1985), 'Equal employment opportunity—Widening the agenda', *Canberra Bulletin of Public Administration*, vol. 12, no. 1, pp. 42-45.

Wilenski, Peter (1988), 'Social change as a source of competing values in public administration', *Australian Journal of Public Administration*, vol. 47, no. 3, pp. 213-222.

Wilkerson, Albert E. (1988), 'Alternative social agencies: Epilogue', *Administration in Social Work*, vol. 12, pp. 119-128.

Winkler, Fedelma (1987), 'Consumerism in health care: Beyond the supermarket model', *Policy and Politics*, vol. 15, no. 1, pp. 1-8.

Winkler, J. (1984), *Bargaining for Results*, New York, Facts on File.

Withorn, Ann (1984), *Serving the People: Social Services and Social Change*, New York, Columbia University Press.

Women's Liberation Halfway House Collective (1976), *Herstory of the Halfway House*, Melbourne.

Yeatman, Anna (1987), 'The concept of public management and the Australian state in the 1990s', *Australian Journal of Public Administration*, vol. 46, no. 4, pp. 339-353.

Yeatman, Anna (1990), *Bureaucrats, Technocrats, Femocrats; Essays on the Contemporary Australian State*, Sydney, Allen & Unwin.

Zald, Mayer N. (1970), 'Political economy: A framework for comparative analysis', in Mayer N. Zald (ed.) *Power in Organizations*, Nashville, Vanderbilt University Press, pp. 221-261.

Zastrow, Charles (1984), 'Understanding and preventing burn-out', *British Journal of Social Work*, vol. 14, pp. 141-155.

Zastrow, Charles (1985), *The Practice of Social Work*, 2nd edn, Chicago, Dorsey Press.

Zey-Ferrell, Mary and Aiken, Michael (eds) (1981), *Complex Organizations: Critical Perspectives*, Glenview, Ill., Scott, Foresman.

Index